Cognitive
Psychology

Cognitive Psychology

Michael G. Wessells

Randolph-Macon College

HARPER & ROW, PUBLISHERS, New York
Cambridge, Philadelphia, San Francisco,
London, Mexico City, São Paulo, Sydney

1817

This book is dedicated affectionately to my mother, Virginia G. Wessells, and to my father, Neil E. Wessells, a budding octogenarian.

Sponsoring Editor: George A. Middendorf
Project Editor: Holly Detgen
Senior Production Manager: Kewal K. Sharma
Compositor: American Book-Stratford Press, Inc.
Printer and Binder: Halliday Lithograph
Art Studio: J & R Services
Cover Design: Betty Sokol

Cognitive Psychology

Library of Congress Cataloging in Publication Data

Wessells, Michael G., 1948–
 Cognitive psychology.
 Includes bibliographical references and index.
 1. Cognition. I. Title.
BF311.W437   153   81-6689
ISBN 0-06-047009-7   AACR2

Contents

Preface

The field of cognitive psychology is increasing in complexity, diversity, and sheer size at a dizzying rate. In first confronting the welter of contemporary theories and experimental paradigms, many students experience difficulty in discerning the central principles, problems, and assumptions that organize the field and that make it intelligible. This book attempts to reduce these difficulties through several devices.

In order to highlight the principles and to facilitate comprehension and retention of the material, each chapter begins with a statement of the main themes, relates the principles to what the student already knows, and concludes with a comprehensive summary. In order to highlight the problems and the assumptions that guide contemporary research and theory, the historical antecedents of the information-processing approach and of particular theories are examined. Further, the book encourages active analysis of the seminal experiments and theories by presenting them as pieces of ongoing research, by raising unanswered questions, and by showing how scientific investigation proceeds. For this reason, the book provides a relatively detailed examination of a small number of experiments rather than a fleeting glimpse of many. Nevertheless, the book provides a relatively comprehensive introduction to cognitive psychology.

The content of the book is divided nearly equally between topics pertaining to episodic and semantic memory. Chapters 2 through 5 discuss the processes of pattern recognition, attention, and memory and reflect a shift in research away from rigid structural and stage models toward flexible processing models. The approach taken does not dispute that cognitive psychology must determine the constraints on human information processing; rather, it assumes that the search for constraints proceeds best in full recognition of the remarkable flexibility of cognition. In recent years, the importance of understanding semantic knowledge and its use in everyday activities has become apparent, and this view is reflected in Chapters 6 through 9. Chapter 6 discusses concepts, the building blocks of our world knowledge. Chapter 7 examines the representation of knowledge in the context of activities such as imagery and sentence processing. Chapter 8 inquires into sentence and prose comprehension, a pivotal topic that bridges traditional research in psycholinguistics and contemporary research in cognitive science. Finally, Chapter 9 examines the processes involved in reasoning and in problem solving.

I wish to thank Chuck Clifton, Judith Goggin, Richard Mayer, Phil Merikle, Arthur Wingfield, and Dan Yarmey for their careful, helpful reviews of the entire manuscript. Of course, the responsibility for any errors in the book is mine. I also thank Sylvia Farnham-Diggory and Ed Smith, who commented upon an initial outline of the book. I am indebted to John Donahoe, whose suggestions initiated this project, and to Vassar College, whose generous support enabled me to write this book. Special thanks go to my spouse, Sheila, who endured my absence in her presence and who kept four paper-loving cats away from the manuscript.

Michael G. Wessells

Cognitive Psychology

Chapter 1
The Study of Cognition

Each day, we take in and act on information in countless ways. In driving
down a new highway, we acquire information about direction by attending to road signs while ignoring billboards and people standing on side-
walks. In listening to an instructor or to a boss, we try to comprehend
and remember the information that we plan to use at a later time. And in
solving problems such as that of balancing a checkbook, we manipulate
or process numerical information by using our knowledge of how to add
and subtract.

   Traditionally, these everyday activities—attending, remembering,
comprehending, and problem solving—were discussed under the head-
ing of thinking. But today they are seen as aspects of information processing, the subject matter of cognitive psychology.

WHAT IS COGNITIVE PSYCHOLOGY?

Cognitive psychology is the science of human information processing. Its
subject matter, often called *cognition*, concerns the kinds of information
we have in our memories and the processes involved in acquiring, re-

taining, and using that information. Collectively, these processes are called *cognitive processes*. By studying cognition, psychologists hope to achieve a deeper understanding of how we perform everyday activities ranging from perceiving to remembering to problem solving. Equally important, they wish to use that understanding to improve education, to help remedy impairments in thinking and, in general, to enable us to make optimum use of our cognitive resources.

Of course, no simple definition can convey fully what cognitive psychology is, for any branch of inquiry is defined not only by its subject but also by its assumptions, by its methods, and above all, by the activities of its researchers. These aspects of cognitive psychology are best illustrated by a concrete example. Accordingly, we shall examine a case study in which a researcher investigated the hypothesis that imagery aids memory. Then we shall inquire into the historical factors that shaped the present assumptions of cognitive psychology. This inquiry leads into an overview of information processing and of the topics discussed in the chapters ahead.

Imagining and Remembering: A Case Study

The idea that forming mental pictures or visual images can aid memory dates back at least to the times of the ancient Greek orators (Yates, 1966). Ancient orators were charged with delivering important speeches without the aid of written cues, for writing materials were scarce. Accordingly, they used *mnemonic devices*, which are systems designed to aid memory. One such device was called the *method of loci* (loci are places), and it can be illustrated by an example. Assume you have a list of 20 items to remember, three of which are *tree, swim,* and *muffin.* Using the method of loci, you would first imagine in vivid detail the rooms of your home. Next, take a mental walk through the house and picture one or two of the items in each room. For example, if your family room contains a potted plant, you might imagine a large tree growing in the pot. In order to remember *swim,* you might picture your bathtub as a large swimming pool. In order to remember *muffin,* you could imagine your stove shaped like an oversized muffin. You would recall the items by taking another imaginary walk through the house, this time looking into each room and recalling the appropriate items. If you practice using this method, you will probably agree with the ancients that it works well. And once you have mastered the method, you can use the same loci repeatedly with no decrement in recall.

The view that imagery aids memory gains added support from the performance of some mnemonists, experts in the art of remembering. One mnemonist, called S., had the unusual capacity for synesthesia, in which the stimuli presented in one sensory modality are experienced in other modalities as well. S. stated that spoken words automatically generated vibrant colors and even tastes! By remembering his mental images and by using the method of loci in a highly skilled manner, S. was able to perform some truly exceptional feats of memory. On one occasion, the first four stanzas of Dante's *Divine Comedy* were read to him in Italian, which he did not speak. He not only recalled the stanzas correctly on an immediate memory test, but he also did so in a surprise test given years later (Luria, 1968).

Personal experiences also attest to the connection between imagining and remembering. To illustrate, try for a moment to remember how many windows your home has. Many people report that they perform this memory task by forming an image of their home and then counting the windows.

These observations may seem to prove that imagery facilitates memory. On closer inspection, however, these observations turn out to be suggestive but uncompelling. Consider the example of S. Imagery probably did contribute to his amazing memory skills. But his capacity for imagining was highly unusual, so it is unreasonable to assume that what was true of S. is true of most people. And because there may be large individual differences in imagery ability (Paivio, 1971), observations concerning one's own performance cannot establish a general principle. Yet it is general principles that we want in order to develop an understanding of imagery and a set of practical techniques that apply to many people.

Another problem is that what looks like an effect of imagery may in fact be the result of other factors. For example, the ancient orators may have used imagery extensively, but, given the importance of their speeches, they probably rehearsed their material repeatedly. Was it the imagery or the rehearsal that enabled them to remember their speeches? The anecdotal evidence that has been passed down cannot possibly answer this question. Nor can it tell us whether imagining always aids remembering or whether particular types of images work better than others.

What is needed to answer these questions is a systematic method of inquiry that enables us to assess the effects of imagery apart from other factors and to establish principles of broad scope. The method that cognitive psychologists use for these purposes is the scientific method, which has proven to be useful in many other disciplines. We now take a look at how one prominent cognitive psychologist, Gordon Bower of Stanford University, has used that method to test whether imagining aids remembering.

BOWER'S ANALYSIS

At the outset, we should note that Bower's approach is only one of many reasonable approaches. Bower's research is discussed here because it is a particularly clear and comprehensible illustration of how cognitive researchers attack a problem.

Bower (1972b) chose to study memory in a very simple task because the simpler the task is, the easier it will be to isolate the effects of a factor such as imagery. The task Bower used is called *paired-associate learning,* and it proceeded as follows. First, Bower presented a list of 20 pairs of nouns, for example, *dog - bicycle,* that referred to concrete, easily imagined objects. Each pair was shown for 5 seconds. Then he gave a memory test, called a cued-recall test, in which he presented the left-hand or stimulus word (the cue) of each pair and asked the subjects to recall the right-hand or response word. At the end of this test, Bower told the subjects what the correct responses had been. He then repeated the entire procedure four more times, using a different study list on each occasion. Following the presentation of all five lists, he gave a delayed memory test in which he presented the cue words from all five lists and asked the subjects to recall the response words.

The subjects in the experiment were college students who had been assigned on a random basis to one of two groups. The subjects in the imagery group were instructed to associate the two words in each pair by imagining the two objects interacting. For example, the *dog - bicycle* pair might have evoked an image of a dog riding a bicycle. In contrast, the subjects in the control group were left to their own devices, for they were told simply to learn the pairs of words.

The results, shown in Figure 1.1, were that the subjects in the imagery group achieved a much higher level of recall on both memory tests than did the subjects in the control group. At first glance, you might think that these results establish definitely that imagery aids memory. But reflection reveals some possible problems with this interpretation. For one thing, subjects do not always follow instructions exactly. It would be naive to assume that the subjects in the imagery condition learned only by forming images. Perhaps they rehearsed the pairs covertly, as one might do in trying to remember a phone number long enough to dial it. The superior performance of the imagery group may have been due to rehearsal rather than to imagery.

Bower clearly recognized this problem, and he set out to separate the effects of imagery from those of rehearsal. He recruited new subjects and assigned them to two groups, an imagery group and a rehearsal group, on a random basis. Both groups learned three lists of 30 pairs of nouns in a paired-associate learning procedure and then took a cued-recall test. The subjects in the imagery group were instructed to imagine the objects named by the nouns. The subjects in the rehearsal group were

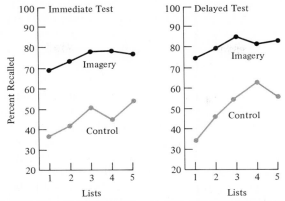

Figure 1.1 The level of immediate and delayed recall for subjects in the imagery group and the control group. (From Bower, 1972b.)

told to repeat each pair silently as it appeared. If the imagery instructions led the subjects to learn by rehearsing, then there would be no difference in the performance of the imagery group and the rehearsal group. In fact, however, the imagery group remembered the words better than the rehearsal group did. So the imagery instructions had effects that cannot be attributed solely to rehearsal.

Even these observations, however, fail to convince the clever skeptic who knows that subjects do not always comply with their instructions. After all, no direct evidence has been put forth showing that the subjects in the imagery group had in fact used imagery. Bower's next step, then, was to try to provide more direct evidence that the imagery instructions did lead to the use of imagery and that the use of imagery did influence memory. This task was difficult because he could not directly see or measure the images of his subjects. And he could not accept at face value his subjects' statements that they had been learning via imagery, for they might simply have been telling him what they believed he wanted to hear. For these reasons, Bower adopted the strategy of interfering with his subjects' images. If his subjects were in fact using imagery to remember, then interfering with their images should impair their performance on a memory test.

In order to interfere with the images of his subjects, Bower had his subjects perform two tasks simultaneously. One task involved learning a list of paired associates by forming images, as in the preceding experiments. The second task was to track with the first two fingers of one hand a wavy line that moved rapidly from side to side, as if a pen were being drawn erratically across a sheet of paper. On the basis of evidence obtained from other studies (Brooks, 1968), Bower knew that performance on a task requiring the use of imagery is impaired by the simultaneous execution of another visual task. It is as if we have a limited visual capacity that is strained by the demands of two visual tasks. If the imagery instructions actually led subjects to form visual images, then their performance should have been impaired by also performing the visual tracking task.

Bower also knew that imagery is disrupted little by the simultaneous performance of a nonvisual task. For this reason, he divided the subjects into two groups, both of which had been instructed to learn pairs of words by forming images. The visual group performed the visual tracking task described above while they learned the words. The tactile group performed a comparable tracking task by touch during learning; in particular, they tracked a piece of string glued to a sheet of paper with their first two fingers. Presumably, performing the tactile task does not interfere with visual imagery. If the subjects had learned the words by forming visual images, then the level of recall should have been higher for the tactile group than for the visual group. In fact, that is exactly what happened.

Taken alone, the outcome of each of these three experiments is open to several interpretations. But collectively, they all point toward a single conclusion: imagery can aid memory. Having established this point, Bower next examined whether all kinds of visual imagery facilitate retention equally.

In the preceding experiments, Bower had instructed his subjects to form images in which the two items were interacting, as in the example of a dog riding a bicycle. But we can also think of noninteractive images, for example, of a dog lying beside one wall of a room and a bicycle leaning against the opposite wall. Would such a noninteractive image facilitate recall as much as an interactive image does? In order to find out, Bower divided experimentally naive subjects into two groups and presented numerous pairs of nouns to each. He instructed the subjects in the interactive image group to form an interactive image of the items named by each pair of nouns. And he instructed the subjects in the noninteractive image group to form a noninteractive image of the items named by each pair of nouns.

This simple experiment had striking results: in a cued-recall test, the interactive image group recalled 71 percent of the items, whereas the noninteractive image group recalled only 46 percent of the items. Looking back at Figure 1.1, we see that the subjects in the noninteractive image group did as poorly on the retention test as had the subjects in the first experiment who had not been instructed to form images. So interactive images facilitate memory, but noninteractive images do not.

Bower's research on imagery did not end here, but we need not pursue the details further. Instead, we shall use this brief case study to highlight some of the chief characteristics of scientific activity and of the cognitive approach.

THE NATURE OF SCIENTIFIC INQUIRY AND KNOWLEDGE

The cornerstone of scientific inquiry is observation. In science, theories are evaluated through empirical testing, that is, through careful observation. For example, in judging the idea that imagery aids memory, Bower relied not on logic and personal belief but on careful observations made in the laboratory. In other words, he put the ideas to the empirical test, letting the observations guide his judgment. All good scientists follow this empirical approach in that they collect observations in order to test their theories. If the observations contradict a theory, then the theory will be modified or rejected in favor of a better one. This process of testing theories via observation is so fundamental in science that investigators abandon theories that cannot be tested. For example, many psychologists have abandoned Freud's psychodynamic theory because it made so few exact predictions that it could not be tested adequately.

Observation is fundamental also in the construction of scientific theories. The observations obtained from well-conceived experiments and naturalistic studies constitute the data base upon which theories are founded. For example, Bower observed that interactive imagery aided retention more than noninteractive imagery did. This observation needs to be explained, so it invites theorists to construct an illuminating account. Observations, then, provide the very soil in which scientific theories are rooted.

Of course, we rely on observations in many everyday activities, for example, in deciding whether one car gets better gas mileage than another. Yet everyday methods of observation are seldom as systematic and rigorous as the scientific method. Bower's approach was systematic in that he first thought of explanations of his data that did not involve imagery. Then he tried to rule out the nonimagery interpretations one by one. He succeeded in ruling out the nonimagery interpretations because he controlled his experiments rigorously, manipulating one factor at a time while holding other factors constant. For example, in the experiment concerning the effects of rehearsal, the only difference between the imagery group and the rehearsal group was the type of instruction that had been administered. This procedure allowed Bower to observe the effects of the instructions apart from other factors, such as the time of day at which the learning occurred or the types of words that were learned. In general, scientists conduct experiments in the laboratory so that they can simplify conditions and isolate factors such as the use of imagery. Needless to say, it is often difficult to isolate factors in the natural environment.

Our case study also shows that science is more than a passive body of knowledge—it is a dynamic, ongoing activity, a systematic search for new phenomena and explanatory principles. Scientists continually conceive of new experiments to answer important questions. And they seldom run out of important questions, for each experiment tends to raise as many questions as it answers. For example, Bower's findings concerning interactive images raise numerous questions. Why do interactive images work? Can noninteractive imagery ever aid memory? Do people who do not benefit by using imagery tend to form noninteractive images? Questions such as these lead inexorably to new experiments, which raise still other questions, and so on. Scientists pursue these questions for many reasons, among the noblest of which are unbridled curiosity and a passion for discovery and explanation.

Because science is an ongoing activity, scientific knowledge is tentative, not immutable. Theories that are widely accepted at a particular time seem to be irrevocably true. For example, before Einstein, space and time seemed to be absolute, unchanging aspects of Nature. But that theory, cherished though it had been, was eventually falsified by new observations, and Einstein's theory of relativity replaced it. Even the theory of relativity, however, is not immutable. If new observations contradict the theory, then the theory will have to be modified or rejected. Thus scientific theories are never true or proven in a final sense.

These comments have implications for the manner in which you should approach this text or any scientific literature. You should read with the understanding that the theories to be discussed are not immutably true and that no single experiment provides the final word on an issue. The science of cognition advances as people generate alternative interpretations of observations and think of ways to test them. By engaging in these activities as you read, you will achieve a deep understanding that cannot be attained by passive memorization.

A Look Behind the Method

In using a particular method, such as the scientific method illustrated above, investigators must make some assumptions. For example, scientists assume that they are studying lawful, orderly events and processes. If they did not make this deterministic assumption, it would be pointless to use the scientific method, which, after all, is designed to discover lawful, orderly events and relationships. For this reason, cognitive scientists assume that cognitive processes are inherently lawful and discoverable. But they also make assumptions that distinguish their approach from other approaches that psychologists have taken. Three of these assumptions deserve mention because they guide research. Understanding these assumptions should help you to see why cognitive psychologists propose the kinds of theories and questions that they do.

The first assumption is that introspection, looking inward on one's own thoughts, is limited as a method of analyzing cognition. One reason is that many cognitive processes are difficult if not impossible to introspect upon (Neisser, 1967; Nisbett and Wilson, 1977). As a simple illustration, look inward as you read and try to observe how you determine the meanings of the words. Through this exercise, you probably learned very little about how we determine the meanings of the words we read. Introspectively, the meanings seem to just come to us. In general, many cognitive processes are difficult to introspect upon. Consequently, they are best analyzed using nonintrospective methods. On the other hand, some aspects of cognition, for example, the steps we take in solving a crossword puzzle, can be introspected upon, and introspective evidence is often quite useful to investigators (Ericsson and Simon, 1980). But the point remains that the introspective method is limited in scope.

Another reason why the introspective method is limited is that we cannot observe directly the introspections of others. Rather, we infer the properties of others' introspections from what they say. Unfortunately, subjects may fail for numerous reasons to describe their introspections accurately. Consequently, their verbal reports may not always provide valid evidence concerning their cognitive processes. This kind of problem led early psychologists to abandon the method of introspection, and psychologists are still concerned about the problem today. Although contemporary researchers use introspective evidence under some conditions, they agree that nonintrospective methods such as those used by Bower are more powerful and less problematic.

The second assumption is that theories and research concerning cognition should be ecologically valid, that is, they should help to explain the everyday events that occur outside of the laboratory (Neisser, 1976; Tulving, 1979). In the laboratory, scientists often use simple procedures in which it is possible to isolate important factors. The potential danger in using simple procedures is that they may be artificial and distantly related to naturally occurring situations. If so, then the observations and the principles derived from the laboratory research will not generalize to natural settings. This is undesirable because scientists aim to discover principles that are as powerful and as general as possible. And surely we want a science that sheds light on the events we experience daily and that enables us to change these events for the better. For both theoretical and practical reasons, then, cognitive psychologists evaluate theory and research partly by judging ecological validity.

Fortunately, it is possible to conduct ecologically valid experiments under simple, well-controlled conditions. For example, Bower's studies were simple and well-controlled, and his observations have contributed to our understanding of some of the mnemonic devices that people have used for centuries (Bower, 1972b). In addition, his findings have some clear practical implications for how to improve memory.

The third assumption is that cognitive processes can be studied productively on a nonphysiological level. Cognitive psychologists believe that cognitive processes are based upon the physical events occurring in the nervous system, chiefly, the brain. And most believe that it is worth-while to analyze the psychological bases of cognition. But they also recognize that many cognitive processes are simply too complex to be adequately described, let alone explained, on the basis of our present knowledge and technology of neurophysiology. Further, much can be learned about cognitive processes without engaging in physiological analysis. For example, Bower helped to clarify the influence of imagery on memory, and he did so without taking a physiological approach. Equally important, Bower's nonphysiological approach has practical advantages. After all, it is relatively easy to improve someone's memory by instructing them to form interactive images. No one has devised physiological procedures for improving memory dramatically. And even if such procedures were available, they would probably be expensive and difficult to use in everyday settings. Whenever possible, we shall make use of the insights stemming from physiological analyses, but we shall be concerned mainly with nonphysiological research and theory.

These three assumptions are shared by most cognitive psychologists, and they constitute an important part of the definition of cognitive psychology. Yet cognitive psychology gains most of its distinctiveness from a fourth assumption: human cognition is a species of information processing. This assumption pervades most cognitive theorizing, so it merits special attention. In the following section, we trace the historical forces that shaped this assumption and contemporary theories of cognition.

HISTORICAL ORIGINS OF COGNITIVE PSYCHOLOGY

The study of cognition began long before the founding of psychology. The task of analyzing cognition fell to philosophers such as Aristotle and Plato, and later on to Descartes, Locke, and Kant, among others. These philosophers worked without the benefit of advanced scientific technology and knowledge. Nevertheless, they provided a rich legacy of ideas that guided the early psychologists and that live on today.

The Philosophical Background

EARLY GREEK PHILOSOPHERS
Plato and Aristotle contemplated an awesome number of subjects, including perception and memory. Plato proposed a copy theory in which he likened the mind to a block of wax, upon which perceptions and ideas make impressions. On this view, the mind forms direct copies or impressions of the objects it encounters. According to Plato, as long as an impression for a particular idea remains, so does our ability to remember that idea. Stated simply, Plato held that perception and memory are

passive processes in which outside objects and events are impressed upon us. Plato's influence lives on, for some contemporary theorists believe that our memories are like copies of external stimuli.

Aristotle's theory of mind is far too technical to explore here, but two of his enduring contributions require mention. First, Aristotle proposed that valid knowledge can be obtained through the senses. Other philosophers, including Plato, had distrusted the knowledge acquired by sight, touch, and so on, arguing that such knowledge may be distorted or may result from hallucinations. Aristotle's proposal that knowledge can be obtained through the senses constitutes the core of *empiricism*, a viewpoint that dominated psychology for many years.

Aristotle's second contribution was the proposal of laws of thought. He stated that thoughts become related by virtue of contiguity, similarity, and contrast. Contiguous ideas are ideas that occur close together in time. Once ideas have occurred in contiguity, they tend to occur together in the future. This is why thoughts tend to run from one to the other as they do. Likewise, ideas that are similar or that contrast tend to become related. In constructing these laws of thought, Aristotle provided the foundation for the intellectual tradition called associationism. This tradition has exerted a profound influence upon cognitive psychology, and the importance of factors such as contiguity continues to be recognized today.

DESCARTES

René Descartes (1596–1650) influenced psychology in two chief respects. Having distinguished between two substances, mind and body, he proposed that the body was a physical machine that could be understood through scientific analysis. Descartes himself provided mechanistic analyses not only of bodily functions, for example, digestion and circulation, but also of cognitive activities such as sensation and memory. In doing so, Descartes brought cognitive processes into the realm of sciences, and he planted the mechanistic seed that has blossomed so fully in contemporary computerlike models of cognition. Yet Descartes did not go all the way in his mechanism. He believed that humans have a nonphysical soul that permits conscious reflection, voluntary choice, and, hence, free will. The view that humans have both a mechanistic body and a rational, nonphysical soul is called mind-body dualism, Cartesian dualism or, simply, dualism. This dualistic outlook has had strong impact on philosophy and theology, and has worked its way into our legal and governmental institutions. With this dualistic theory, Descartes bequeathed to following generations a problem of major proportions. How can our nonphysical souls influence our physical bodies? This mind-body problem remains unresolved at present, and we shall encounter it in somewhat different clothing in subsequent discussions.

Descartes' legacy also includes his belief in innate ideas. He conceived of ideas such as infinity, God, and the axioms of geometry as innate since they seemed independent of experience. Although sensory experiences could activate or point to innate ideas, the innate ideas were not derived from experience but rather from the thinking of the soul. Because of his emphasis on innate ideas, Descartes may be called a *nativist*. Today, the nativist outlook continues to guide much cognitive research and theory (Chomsky, 1965).

LOCKE
Unlike Descartes, John Locke (1637–1704) asserted that knowledge derives from experience, not from innate ideas. Locke believed that at birth, the mind is like a *tabula rasa*, a blank sheet, which experience then writes upon. The positions taken by Descartes and Locke on whether knowledge is innate or based upon experience define the extremities of the nativism-empiricism controversy. Such radical positions have become less common today, but the controversy crops up in diverse guises in contemporary analyses of cognition.

Locke held that knowledge consists of ideas that are either simple or complex. Simple ideas are basic and unanalyzable, and they include ideas such as roundness, redness, and sweetness. Simple ideas may become connected or associated to form complex ideas. For example, the complex idea we call *apple* consists of the simple ideas of roundness, redness, and sweetness, among others. Locke's contentions that knowledge originates through experience and that complex ideas are ensembles of associated simple ideas prepared the way for the rise of associationism in Britain.

THE BRITISH ASSOCIATIONISTS
This group of philosophers included James Mill (1773–1836), his son John Stuart Mill (1806–1873), and Alexander Bain (1813–1903). Working in the empiricist tradition established by John Locke, Thomas Hobbes, David Hume, and George Berkeley, the British associationists articulated the associationistic outlook in an extreme, explicit form. They contended that human knowledge consists of associations that are established through experience. Because they asserted the primacy of experience, they fall squarely in the empiricist camp. They also proposed that contiguity was the chief mechanism whereby associations were formed. Presumably, ideas that occurred together in time became associated and, the more frequently those ideas occurred together, the more strongly associated they became. And once ideas have become associated, the occurrence of one calls forth the other. If one owned both a dog and a cat and had often experienced them at the same time, then the thought of the cat would call forth the thought of the dog (and vice versa), in the same way

that *salt* calls forth *pepper* and *man* calls forth *woman*. In this view, the stream of conscious thought flows along the routes defined by one's associations.

Like Locke, the associationists distinguished between simple and complex ideas, and they believed that complex ideas were built up from simple ideas that had occurred contiguously. For example, the idea of a cat is a complex idea composed of simple ideas such as our sensations of claws, fur, legs, tail, purring, and so on. Similarly, the meaning of *cat* consists of the simple ideas listed above and associated ideas such as pet, animal, and mammal. This view might tempt one to conclude that complex ideas and word meanings can be reduced to the sum of their constituents. Although many theorists concerned with concepts and meaning have succumbed to this reductionistic temptation, the British associationists themselves resisted it. Using a chemical analogy, John Stuart Mill argued that complex ideas do not reflect their simple components. Rather, complex ideas are compounds that, like water, have characteristics not found in the constituent elements. Mill proposed a sort of mental chemistry in which a whole complex idea consisted of more than the sum of its parts. In the psychology that developed later, there was to be much controversy over whether or not cognition has holistic, emergent properties not discernible in its constituents. If cognitions do have holistic properties, there are serious limitations on theories that analyze phenomena such as word meanings into elementary components.

KANT

While associationism flourished in Britain, radically different ideas related to those of Descartes emerged in Germany. Immanuel Kant (1774–1804) asserted that much human knowledge is imposed by the mind rather than provided directly by experience. He believed that it is the properties of the mind that permit us to be affected by experiences. In other words, the mind is the vehicle through which experience exerts its effects, and knowledge, even scientific knowledge, is equally the product of mind and experience. A somewhat oversimplified example may help clarify this point. We can comprehend and judge the truth or falsity of statements such as *All dogs are hairy*. We do this by relying partly upon our prior experiences with dogs. But we also use our understanding of the logical relationship specified by statements of the form *All _____are _____*. This relationship cannot be known entirely through experience, for one cannot possibly experience all dogs. Thus judging the latter type of statement requires something more than experience. Kant called that something an *a priori* concept—a concept the mind has before experience begins. Kant postulated many a priori concepts, including unity, space, time and causality. In asserting the importance of ideas not drawn from experience, Kant assumed a nativistic position. In claiming that the mind imposes order on the world and itself provides much of our knowledge, Kant took the position called *rationalism*. This position asserts that the mind is an active source of knowledge that must itself be understood if we are to understand the world around us. Similar views would subsequently arise in psychological analyses of cognition.

Associationism in Psychology

The exact point at which psychology branched off from philosophy is a matter of debate (Boring, 1950). But the separation was marked by a shift of method that marked the initiation of other sciences. The shift is from the method of logic and formal argumentation to the scientific method. It is one thing to establish a theory via plausible argument and demonstration and quite another to establish it empirically through rigorous observation and experimentation.

The founding of psychology as an experimental science is typically attributed to Wilhelm Wundt, the philosopher-scientist who established his laboratory in Leipzig, Germany, in 1879. Many of the experiments in Wundt's lab anticipated the cognitive research conducted today. For example, attention is presently the subject of intensive research, and studies at Leipzig were done to determine the size of the attention span, also called the span of apprehension or the span of immediate memory. A number of stimuli such as letters of the alphabet or words were flashed briefly upon a screen, and adult subjects were asked to recall the presented items. The result was that the subjects could recall around four to six randomly selected letters, and they did about as well with six-letter words as with letters. Thus the subjects recalled four to six units whether those units were small (single letters) or large (six-letter words). This result has been replicated many times.

Wundt's view of the proper definition and methods of psychology reflected the outlook and methods of the British associationists. For Wundt, psychology was the study of consciousness, but his approach was reductionistic. Using the method of introspection, Wundt hoped to break consciousness down into constituent elements and processes and their laws of connection, much as some associationists had tried to do. But Wundt gave the introspective method a different twist. The introspections Wundt was interested in were neither the casual reflections of laymen nor the systematic ones of philosophers. Rather, they were attempts to describe the elements of conscious experience, for example, the experience of an apple. Wundt gave his subjects long hours of training before he accepted their introspective data. Unsurprisingly, it was students of psychology who endured this training.

Despite heroic attempts of the early psychologists to ensure the accuracy and the reliability of their introspective data, their effort was doomed to fail, for reasons stated previously. Many cognitive activities could not be introspected upon. Furthermore, when introspection was possible, observers too often disagreed as to what the basic elements of their experiences were. Disagreements in science are common, and they can be productive, particularly in the realm of theory. But disagreements over the basic observations are intolerable; without reliable observations, there can be no science. The failure of the introspectionistic method to provide reliable data had widespread repercussions. It prepared the way for John Watson's radical proposal that psychology should study only behavior and reject introspection and the study of the mind. More important for present purposes, it prepared the way for the acceptance of a nonintrospectionist but experimental analysis of cognition. Just such an approach was independently undertaken by Hermann Ebbinghaus (1850–1909) well before the demise of introspective psychology.

Ebbinghaus' contemporaries were pessimistic about whether cognitive processes could be examined scientifically. Nevertheless, Ebbinghaus directed his keen mind and his commitment to science and associationistic philosophy toward his experimental odyssey into learning and memory.

EBBINGHAUS' METHOD

Ebbinghaus (1885) followed the British associationists in his belief that knowledge consists of associations acquired through experience, and he sought to discover the principles whereby associations are formed. One approach to this task would have been to study how associations are formed between pairs of familiar words, for example, *tree - ball*. But Ebbinghaus rejected this approach because subjects already have extensive knowledge about familiar words. How people learn pairs of words or passages of prose may reflect as much about their prior experiences as about the general process of forming associations. For example, in learning the *tree - ball* pair, you might imagine a large tree teeming with basketballs rather than leaves. Ebbinghaus viewed such activities as contaminating factors. In his eyes, they involved the use of existing associations, not the formation of new ones.

In order to avoid the "contamination" stemming from the intrusion of prior experience, Ebbinghaus constructed a list of 2300 nonsense syllables such as *JOQ* and *KOM*. Each syllable included a consonant, a vowel and another consonant and were later called CVC trigrams. Ebbinghaus believed that the syllables were relatively meaningless and lacked associations to the words of everyday language. By studying how long it took to learn lists of the nonsense syllables, he hoped to discover how new associations are formed, apart from the influence of previous experience.

One procedure Ebbinghaus used is called *serial learning*. Ebbinghaus would read a list of nonsense syllables item by item at a rapid, steady pace according to the beats of a metronome. He reread the list repeatedly until he felt close to mastery. Then he tested himself by looking at the first syllable and trying to recall the successive items in order. If he made an error, he reread the list and tested himself as before, and he continued reading and testing until he could repeat the list from memory without errors. As he learned a list, he measured how much time and how many repetitions had occurred.

Ebbinghaus was scrupulous in applying his method. Before learning a list, he tried carefully to eliminate distractions, and he tried to hold constant extraneous variables such as the time of day at which learning occurred, personal health, and mental attitude. To reduce sources of momentary bias and the effects of differences in the difficulty of various lists, he learned several lists in each experimental condition and based his conclusion upon the averaged data. In the course of his inquiry, he memorized virtually thousands of lists. Obviously, he had an incredibly high tolerance for nonsense! To his credit, Ebbinghaus published only when he had achieved a systematic and insightful analysis. His book, *Memory,* published in 1885, contained many observations that have withstood the test of time.

EBBINGHAUS' EMPIRICAL LEGACY

From our own experiences, we know that more work is required to remember more material. But exactly how much more work is required is perhaps less obvious, and Ebbinghaus helped illuminate this issue. He learned lists that included 7, 12, 16, 24, and 36 syllables to a criterion of one errorless recitation. The results, shown in Figure 1.2, were that as the list length increased, so did the number of repetitions, but the latter increase outstripped the former by far. Only a single repetition was required for a seven-syllable list, for seven syllables lie within the span of apprehension. Doubling the list length (and a bit more) to 16 syllables did not simply double the number of repetitions required from one to two. Rather, 30 repetitions were required for mastery of the 16-syllable list. Further, a five-fold increase in the number of syllables produced a 55-fold increase in repetitions. Learning involves much more than rote repetition, but to the extent that repetition contributes to learning, you should respect the relationship shown in Figure 1.2 in your own studies.

Ebbinghaus agreed with his associationist predecessors that contiguity is a fundamental determinant of memory. If contiguity contributes to memory, then the more frequently items occur together in time, the better the memory for those items should be. This frequency theory of memory was assessed in the following manner. Ebbinghaus rehearsed lists 16 syllables long from a few to 64 times. As he learned each list, he recorded the amount of time required for mastery, although he continued to re-

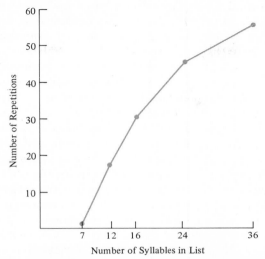

Figure 1.2   The effect of list length on the number of repetitions required for learning to a criterion of one errorless recitation. (Data from Ebbinghaus, 1885.)

hearse some lists (for example, the one rehearsed 64 times) far beyond the point of mastery. Next, he tested his memory for a particular list 24 hours after he had completed the original repetitions. The test consisted of a *relearning* task in which the list was learned to the criterion of one errorless recitation, and the time required for relearning the list was recorded. If the time required to relearn a list was less than the time required for learning it originally, that would indicate some memory for the material originally learned. What Ebbinghaus needed was a measure of how much remembering or forgetting had occurred, and to that end, he computed a *savings score* for each list. The savings score was expressed as a percentage defined according to this formula:

$$\text{Percent savings} = 100 \times \frac{(\text{original learning time} - \text{relearning time})}{\text{original learning time}}$$

Applying it to a concrete example, if it took 1200 seconds to learn a list originally and 900 seconds to relearn it, the percentage savings would be 25. The better a list is remembered, the faster relearning will be and the higher the savings score will be. How does the frequency of repetitions influence retention 24 hours later? Within the limits of the procedures used by Ebbinghaus, the frequency of repetition and retention bear a straight line or linear relationship to each other. Each repetition saved about 12 seconds in the relearning task 24 hours later. Thus the more the information was rehearsed, the better it was remembered. This is an important principle that you may use to improve your own retention, though the effects of repetition have turned out to be considerably more complex than Ebbinghaus envisioned.

The preceding study established the contribution of repetition to remembering, but it did not bear on a broader issue of memory: Once an association has been formed, how long is it remembered? To investigate this issue, Ebbinghaus first learned several lists. Then he relearned lists following intervals ranging from 19 minutes to 31 days. These intervals are called retention intervals because they are periods of time over which information must be remembered if performance in the retention test is to be successful. The results, shown in Figure 1.3, were that the level of retention, defined as the percentage of savings, declined sharply over retention intervals under two days. From two days onward, retention declined much more slowly. The curve shown is called a retention function, and many studies have reported retention functions similar in shape to that of Ebbinghaus. However, the Ebbinghaus function is odd in that it drops much more rapidly at short retention intervals than subsequently obtained functions do. The reason for the rapid initial forgetting observed by Ebbinghaus probably stemmed from the procedure of using himself as the subject. We know now that the forgetting of verbal items is fostered by the prior learning of similar items. This phenomenon is called *proactive interference*. As he learned more and more lists of nonsense syllables, Ebbinghaus became the very embodiment of proactive interference, and this was a source of bias in his experiments.

THE CONTRIBUTIONS OF EBBINGHAUS
The pioneering experiments of Ebbinghaus, despite the biases they may have included, yielded data that were truly remarkable in their orderliness and reliability. But his greatest contribution was not the body of information he obtained concerning learning and memory or even the novel method he devised. Rather, it was his rigorous experimental approach to the study of human mental processes. His work established beyond doubt that an experimental analysis could elucidate thinking and its causes, although the exact ways in which he applied the experimental method later proved to be flawed. Through his iron determination and impressive imagination, he established an experimental program that later became a dominant tradition in psychology.

TWENTIETH-CENTURY ASSOCIATIONISM
Standing on the experimental accomplishments of Ebbinghaus, many psychologists, particularly in the United States, took on the task of discovering the basic laws whereby associations are formed and remembered. In many respects, the associationistic movement of this century

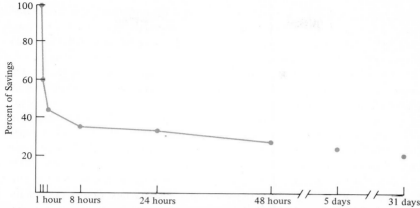

Figure 1.3   A retention function showing the relation between the level of memory and the length of the retention interval. (Data from Ebbinghaus, 1885.)

departed from the path forged by Ebbinghaus. For example, Ebbinghaus had recognized that his nonsense syllables were not all equally meaningless. Yet he was able to ignore the differences, probably because he was so disciplined in making himself learn by rote, without drawing relationships between the nonsense syllables and the words he knew. When other people served as subjects, however, large differences appeared among the nonsense syllables. *CAV* may lead one to think of *cave* or *calf*, whereas *ZUK* may not give rise to associated words so readily. To measure the differences between nonsense syllables, researchers devised scales of *meaningfulness* (Archer, 1960; Glaze, 1928). For example, Noble (1952) presented an item and asked the subjects to list all the words the item brought to mind. The average number of responses made to an item defined the meaningfulness of that item. By using methods such as this, investigators tried to define word meanings in an empirical, quantitative manner. And, having constructed measures of meaningfulness, they examined the effects of the level of meaningfulness upon learning and retention.

Associationistic research in this century also departed from the method of learning used by Ebbinghaus. For example, researchers began to use the paired-associate learning procedure which Bower had used rather than the serial learning procedure. The paired-associate procedure is advantageous because the items occur in specific pairs. This allows the experimenter to manipulate the contiguity of the stimulus and the response items. Additionally, the paired-associate procedure allows one to ask questions such as this: Does learning occur faster when only the stimulus words or only the response words refer to easily imagined objects? An experiment designed to answer this question might measure how rapidly people learn pairs such as *tree - fact* and *desk - soul*, in which only the stimuli refer to easily imagined objects, as opposed to pairs such as *truth - bike* and *fate - chef* in which only the responses refer to easily imagined objects. Note that the serial learning procedure could not be used to answer the question raised above. For in the serial learning procedure, each word is both a stimulus (for the following word) and a response (for the preceding word).

Using the paired-associate procedure, investigators analyzed whether associations formed gradually through contiguous occurrences of stimuli and responses or whether they formed in an all-or-none manner (Postman, 1963). Additionally, much attention was devoted to the effects of learning one set of associations upon the learning and memory of another set. Their efforts culminated in theories such as the interference theory of forgetting that appeared to be elegant, systematic, and broadly applicable. Up until the late 1950s and early 1960s, there was widespread faith that fundamental laws of thinking could be established through associationistic analyses of performance in simple procedures such as the paired-associate learning procedure.

The associationists, like Wundt and his followers, took a reductionistic approach to the study of thought. They believed that they could understand complex aspects of thinking if they first analyzed the simple components of thinking, namely, associations, and they showed great interest in factors such as contiguity and repetition. But they seldom asked how people were able to acquire associations in the first place. In other words, they did not inquire into the underlying cognitive capacities and mechanisms that made it possible for people to form and use associations. Needless to say, this approach conflicted with the tradition established by Descartes and Kant. It is unsurprising, then, that voices of dissent echoed even as associationism neared its zenith.

THE GESTALT COUNTERMOVEMENT

One dissenting voice came from Gestalt psychologists, particularly Max Wertheimer, Wolfgang Köhler, and Kurt Koffka. They reacted primarily against the structuralists, who, like Wundt, tried to break consciousness down into elementary components. But the Gestaltists also opposed the reductionistic approach of the associationists. The Gestaltists held that our perceptions and ideas have holistic properties and cannot be reduced to a set of constituent elements. As indicated by their famous slogan, *The whole is greater than the sum of its parts,* they believed that wholes have emergent properties that are indiscernible in the parts. For example, they recognized that a melody is more than a collection of individual notes. The notes seem to combine to form a higher-order pattern or Gestalt, as if a new structure had emerged as the notes were combined.

The Gestaltists also argued that structure and organization are actively imposed by the mind. This point is illustrated by the figure-ground phenomenon. In order to perceive an object such as a bird against the background of the sky, we must divide the region we are looking at into figure and ground. The figure is that which stands out from the background, and the ground is the background against which the figure is seen. In the previous example, the bird is the figure and the sky is the ground. That this figure-ground organization is actively imposed is illustrated by Figure 1.4, which shows an ambiguous figure. Initially, you tend to see a vase or goblet. But if you continue looking, the figure and the ground suddenly reverse, and you now see the profiles of two faces looking toward each other. What changed was not the picture you were looking at but the manner in which you organized the visual information into figure and ground. This example shows both that we actively organize incoming information and that how we organize the information determines what we perceive.

Because the Gestaltists believed that the whole is more than a collection of parts and that the mind actively imposes organization on incoming information, they departed from the associationistic research strategy. From the Gestalt outlook, it made no sense to study simple processes in hopes of eventually understanding complex ones. And it seemed far less important to study the formation of simple associations than to discover the basic principles whereby we organize information. Accordingly, the Gestaltists worked toward formulating the fundamental laws

Figure 1.4   An ambiguous figure showing figure-ground reversal. (From U. Neisser, *Cognitive Psychology*, © 1967, p. 90. Reprinted by permission of Prentice-Hall, Inc., Englewood Cliffs, N.J.)

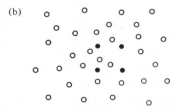

Figure 1.5   Two of the Gestalt laws of organization. (a) The law of proximity. (b) The law of similarity.

of organization, and they relied more on demonstration than experimentation.

Two of the Gestalt laws of organization are illustrated in Figure 1.5. According to the *law of proximity,* shown in panel (a), we tend to perceive nearby elements as a group. Instead of seeing a single row of dots or sets of three dots, we see distinct groups of two. Proximity does not always reign, however, as shown in panel (b). We perceive the closed circles as the corners of a square, despite the fact that each filled circle is closer to an open circle than to another closed one. This demonstrates the *law of similarity,* which states that similar elements will be perceived as belonging to a common group. These observations illustrate the importance of organization, and, in agreement with Kant, the active contribution of the mind to perception. Both of these themes transcended associationistic conceptions and subsequently formed part of the conceptual core of cognitive psychology.

BARTLETT'S RECONSTRUCTIVIST OUTLOOK

A second source of dissent against the associationistic approach came from Sir Frederick Bartlett. In *Remembering,* published in 1932, he criticized Ebbinghaus' attempt to eliminate meaning from the study of memory. Bartlett's own research led him to the opposing view that meaning is centrally important in memory. In order to see why Bartlett took this position, try reading the following passage twice, and then close your book and try to write out the entire passage.

The War of the Ghosts
One night two young men from Egulac went down to the river to hunt seals, and while they were there it became foggy and calm. Then they heard war-cries, and they thought: "Maybe this is a war-party." They escaped to the shore, and hid behind a log. Now canoes came up, and they heard the noise of paddles, and saw one canoe coming up to them. There were five men in the canoe, and they said:

"What do you think? We wish to take you along. We are going up the river to make war on the people."

One of the young men said: "I have no arrows."

"Arrows are in the canoe," they said.

"I will not go along. I might be killed. My relatives do not know where I have gone. But you," he said turning to the other, "may go with them."

So one of the young men went, but the other returned home.

And the warriors went on up the river to a town on the other side of Kalama. The people came down to the water, and they began to fight, and many were killed. But presently the young man heard one of the warriors say: "Quick, let us go home: that Indian has been hit." Now he thought: "Oh, they are ghosts." He did not feel sick, but they said he had been shot.

So the canoes went back to Egulac, and the young man went ashore to his house, and made a fire. And he told everybody and said: "Behold I accompanied ghosts, and we went to fight. Many of our fellows were killed, and many of those who attacked us were killed. They said I was hit, and I did not feel sick."

He told it all, and then he became quiet. When the sun rose he fell down. Something black came out of his mouth. His face became contorted. The people jumped up and cried.

He was dead. (Bartlett, 1932, p. 65)

The subjects were asked to reproduce the passages numerous times following retention intervals ranging from days to years. The subjects tended to recall ideas that were familiar and that fit in with their expectations about how people behave. For example, many subjects remembered that one of the young men had refused to go because "My relatives do not know where I have gone." Such familiar ideas were remembered even after long retention intervals. In the same way that the subjects often recalled the familiar, expected ideas, they tended to forget the unusual, inexplicable ideas. Many subjects failed to recall the significance of the ghosts and omitted the supernatural element entirely. Particularly at the longer retention intervals, the subjects tended to rationalize the mysterious events that Westerners find puzzling, and they introduced words and phrases that were familiar and expected.

Bartlett's observations led him to characterize the act of recall as an "effort after meaning" in which each subject related the story to his or her own outlook and understanding of the world. On this view, meaning is a crucial determinant of remembering, not a contaminating factor as Ebbinghaus had thought. Bartlett argued that studies involving nonsense syllables were too artificial to shed light on how people learn and remember in everyday settings.

Bartlett also argued against the view, implicit in much associationistic theory, that people remember mental copies of previously encountered items and events. He proposed instead that people recall events by reconstructing them, much as a detective reconstructs the events involved in a crime by combining fragments of evidence. You will gain an appreciation for this reconstructivist position if you take five minutes and try to remember what you did exactly one year ago today. At first, this task seems impossible, yet most people find that they can reconstruct what happened. This type of demonstration illustrates that, at least under some conditions, remembering is a highly active process.

Bartlett's proposals did not carry much impact initially, though they were rediscovered and became highly influential in the 1970s. Bartlett's emphasis on the importance of meaning and on the active nature of cognitive processes achieved widespread acceptance as psychology took the cognitive turn.

The Cognitive Turn

The decline of associationism occurred for several reasons. First, investigators made observations that were difficult to reconcile with associationistic theories. Second, theorists put forth effective arguments that associationistic theories were limited in principle. Simultaneously, new theories, based on research from areas outside of psychology, were introduced, and the new theories promised to succeed where associationistic theories had failed. In this section, we examine how these factors contributed to the decline of associationism and to the rise of the information processing approach or paradigm. This discussion draws upon the more detailed analyses provided by Lachman, Lachman, and Butterfield (1979) and by Chase (1978).

THE INFLUENCE OF HUMAN ENGINEERING

World War II brought about many advances in technology, and humans faced many difficult tasks such as detecting objects via radar and flying highly sophisticated aircraft. As you might expect, performance in these tasks was often less than optimal. To avert the drastic consequences of errors, psychologists were called to analyze and remedy the problems. In the process, they began to study phenomena that had previously been ignored for the most part. For example, divided attention, which had gone unexplored by associationists, became important in the study of flying. While landing, a pilot must divide his or her attention between watching the runway and operating the brake lever by touch. In some planes, this divided attention task proved to be very difficult, and crashes often occurred at landing. The problem was that the brake lever sat near the lever that retracted the landing gear. Being absorbed in the visual task of landing on the runway, pilots too often reached for the wrong lever and retracted their landing gear while in the very act of landing. Fortunately, the problem was resolved by redesigning the controls so

that very different arm movements were required for braking and re-
tracting the landing gear.

Working on these practical problems required psychologists to
move beyond the simplified laboratory procedures used to study verbal
learning and to analyze cognition in natural settings.

The analysis of phenomena such as divided attention forced psychologists to ask new questions about whether people can divide their
attention, and, if so, under what conditions. These kinds of questions
concerned the nature of human cognitive capacities, and they had not
been asked by the associationists. In an effort to explain their new observations, researchers proposed theories that departed radically from associationistic conceptions. Many of the most influential new theories came
from the study of communications engineering and information theory.

COMMUNICATIONS ENGINEERING AND INFORMATION THEORY

Communications engineering involves the design of efficient systems for
transmitting information, for example, by telephone. The paths along
which messages travel are called channels. Some types of channel have a
limited capacity, that is, they can transmit only so much information in a
particular period of time. Communications engineers in the 1940s
worked on the problem of how to transmit many messages in a communication system containing limited capacity channels. Having rejected the
costly approach of adding channels, they tried to find ways of using existing channels more efficiently by representing or coding information
efficiently.

The problem of achieving an efficient code is illustrated by a simple
example concerning Morse code. In order to send messages efficiently via
Morse code, one must consider that some letters occur in the English
language much more often than others. For example, the letter *E* occurs
very frequently, whereas Z occurs rarely. To send messages as rapidly as
possible, it pays to give frequently occurring letters a short code, such as
a single dot, that can be sent rapidly and to assign the longer codes to
infrequently occurring letters. To his credit, this is exactly what Samuel
Morse did in designing his code.

In general, a *code* is a symbolic representation for particular items
or events. In Morse code, a single dot represents or stands for the letter
E. Coding, also called *encoding,* refers to the processes involved in forming representations. As the preceding example shows, coding often involves transforming information from one form to another, for example,
from letters to dots and dashes. Encoding processes play a central role in
many aspects of cognition, and they will be discussed in numerous chapters of this book.

In the late 1940s, researchers constructed a new theory, called information theory, that helped to solve the problem of coding messages efficiently (Shannon, 1948; Shannon and Weaver, 1949). The theory defined the transmitted messages in terms of information, which was expressed mathematically and emphasized the importance not only of events that do occur but also of events that could have occurred. This aspect of information theory had far-reaching implications for psychology, as can be illustrated by an example.

Suppose you were in a room that was noisy because of construction going on outside. Another person whom you cannot see is in the same room and occasionally utters softly either *cold* or *dock*. You know that only these two words will be spoken, and your task is to say aloud the spoken word whenever one occurs. In this simple task, you expect to hear only *cold* or *dock*, so there is little uncertainty about which word will be spoken. But if the task were changed so that you might hear any of ten words, there would be greater uncertainty about which word will be spoken. And the greater the uncertainty in the task, the harder it would be to identify a particular spoken word, especially if the level of background noise is very high. In fact, experimenters using a similar procedure have reported that as the level of uncertainty increased, the accuracy of performance decreased (Miller, Heise, and Lichten, 1951). Thus performance depended not only on which word was spoken at a particular time but also on how many words the subjects knew could have occurred at that time. Other studies showed that the level of uncertainty influenced performance in a wide range of decision making tasks (Hyman, 1953; Leonard, 1958). Associationistic theories neither predicted nor explained the effects of uncertainty, for these theories concerned events that had actually occurred, not events that could have occurred. Unsurprisingly, then, theorists turned to information theory, which accounted for the effects of uncertainty and raised many new questions.

The new questions that researchers asked concerned the nature of human cognitive capacities. Investigators theorized about cognitive capacities by using concepts from information theory and communications engineering. Like communications systems, humans can be viewed as having a limited capacity. For example, in everyday life, we appear limited in how many stimuli we can attend to and how many activities we can perform at once. Many a wrinkled car fender has resulted from allocating too much attentional capacity to talking, to the detriment of driving performance. Like communications systems, we code incoming information, that is, we convert it from one form to another. In looking at a map of a city, we might code the visual information in a verbal form, providing ourselves with instructions such as "three blocks, turn right, then two blocks and look on the left." In this conception, human thought involves processes more active than the relatively passive formation and use of associations through contiguity, repetition, and exposure to the environment. Thought is viewed as an activity of a human information-processing system that has limited capacity, that actively converts information from one form to another, and that responds equally on the basis of its own internal knowledge and the external environment. This conception acquired greater appeal as associationistic theories encountered serious difficulties.

LINGUISTICS AND THE BOUNDARIES OF ASSOCIATIONISM

During the associationistic era, there was widespread faith that associationist theories applied to a broad range of phenomena. But around the time of the emergence of information-processing theories, the outlook for associationism took a sharp downward turn. One of the strongest associationist theories had been the interference theory of forgetting, which is discussed in Chapter 5. Many theorists assumed tacitly that interference theory could eventually be extended to provide a general theory of forgetting. This optimism was shaken when research began to turn up alarmingly frequent observations that contradicted interference theory (cf. Postman and Underwood, 1973).

At the same time, serious theoretical inadequacies were discovered, particularly in the study of language. Noam Chomsky, who helped revolutionize the study of linguistics in the late 1950s, argued persuasively that associationistic theories could not in principle account for ordinary language use. One of his arguments was that human language is characterized by *linguistic creativity*. Our language is creative in the sense that each of us has the ability to talk about novel events in novel ways, to go beyond what we have previously heard or said, in essence, to produce and comprehend an infinite variety of utterances. Associationistic theories of language viewed sentences as series of associated words. The problem with these theories is that to account for the ability to produce an infinite variety of sentences, they have to postulate an infinite number of associations, and such an account is very cumbersome. Furthermore, since they cannot predict which sequences of words do or do not qualify as grammatical sentences in a language, associationistic theories are incapable of accounting for our use of language.

A complementary argument put forth by Chomsky was that language has structure, and associationistic theories cannot account for complex linguistic structures. For example, the sentence *The ambiguous question confused the bright students* divides intuitively into two parts: *The ambiguous question* and *confused the bright students*. The words in each part seem to belong together, and the relations between words can be analyzed further, as shown in the treelike structure in Figure 1.6. The sentence has a hierarchical structure in that higher-order parts may be subdivided into several lower ones, and this is characteristic of the sentences of all natural languages. Associationistic theories, in depicting sentences as linear sequences of associated words, failed to describe these hierarchical relations and other aspects of linguistic structure. In stressing the centrality of structure, Chomsky developed a theme similar to that set forth by the Gestalt psychologists.

Chomsky also criticized associationism for its empiricistic outlook. He argued that when children acquire their native language, they do not simply say the things they have heard others say. For example, having produced the past tense form of regular verbs by adding an "ed" suffix, as in *talked* or *baked,* children often overextend the suffix to irregular verbs, thereby producing incorrect forms such as *comed* and *runned.* Apparently, children do not just passively reproduce verbal responses that have occurred previously in their environment, as some associationistic analyses had suggested. Rather, they learn in a highly active way, seeking regularities and underlying concepts. Furthermore, children in different countries seem to pass through a relatively fixed set of stages in mastering their language, and the languages that they eventually acquire have many underlying similarities. Chomsky proposed that the aspects of language found in many different cultures, which are called *linguistic universals,* reflect our biological heritage for language and do not arise from experience alone. In taking this nativist stance, Chomsky extended the tradition of Descartes and Kant, and he rode against the empirical tide of associationism. Ultimately, Chomsky's (1957, 1959, 1965) arguments carried the day. Before long, statements that associationistic theories were seriously limited in the realm of language appeared quite often (e.g., Bever, Fodor, and Garrett, 1968; Slobin, 1971).

Chomsky's success did not stand simply on the failure of associationism. His chief contribution has been an alternative theory of language called *transformational grammar,* which is discussed in Chapter 8. Because of the power and promise of this theory, psychologists

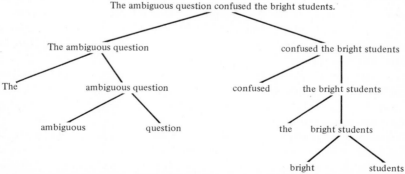

Figure 1.6   The hierarchical structure of the sentence *The ambiguous question confused the bright students.*

were eager to build new theories that incorporated the transformational theory, and the field of psycholinguistics was born. The psycholinguistic theories emphasized the innate, inner capacities of humans and their active role in various tasks. The psycholinguists, armed with the powerful transformational theory, sought to analyze the complexities of language directly rather than to simplify and control, as the associationists had done.

THE COMPUTER SCIENCE CONNECTION

The developments identified above encouraged psychologists to confront the complexities of human behavior head-on. What was needed next was a theoretical tool for conceptualizing complex processes. The digital computer provided just such a tool.

A computer is a system for processing symbolic information. Information may be fed into the machine through cards, through a teletype terminal, and so on. Through the process of encoding, the computer converts the incoming information into a usable format. Although computers form internal representations that are numerical, they can do much more than simply deal with numbers. For example, computers can process speech, pictures, written words, and many other types of symbolic information.

In the process of encoding, and in all of its operations, the computer is guided by a *program*. After information has been encoded, it may be *stored* or preserved in a *memory*. The memory may contain information that has been encoded recently or that has been stored for years, and it may also contain the results of previous operations by the machine. This stored information may be used in further machine operations. To be used, the information must be activated or called forth, and this process is called *retrieval*.

These operations may be illustrated by considering a simple program that computes the mean of a set of numbers. If the input were a set of 10 numbers, each number might first be encoded and then stored in memory. Next, the program might lead to the retrieval of the numbers, which would then be summed and divided by 10. The result could be stored for use in subsequent computations. Computers perform only a small number of operations in addition to encoding, storing, and retrieving information. Nevertheless, computers have performed some remarkable feats, including playing chess at the master's level and deriving some intricate mathematical theorems.

The computer is far more than an impressive technological achievement, for it provides a useful conceptualization of human cognition. In thinking, we engage in the same kinds of activities that computers do. In reading a book, we take visual information (printed words) and encode it in terms of its meaning. We remember much of the information we take in, and we may think of ourselves as storing information over time. In remembering, we call forth or retrieve previously learned information, and forgetting may be seen as the result of retrieval failures. In essence, then, it is possible to conceive of both humans and computers as systems for processing symbolic information. This is not to say that humans are nothing but computers of a particular kind or that present computers can do all that humans do, for these issues are far from being resolved. Yet it is useful for many purposes to think of human cognition in terms of information processing, by way of analogy with computers.

Psychologists adopted the information-processing conception for several reasons. First, the conception was useful in analyzing highly complex processes. For example, Newell, Shaw, and Simon (1958) devised a computer program that solved certain problems in roughly the same way that people did. That program constituted a theory of problem solving because it specified the steps and the processes involved in solving the problem, and it made new predictions. This type of theory promised to do what associationistic theories had not done, namely, clarify the complex cognitive activities that occur outside of simple laboratory tasks. By constructing theories of information processing, investigators hoped to achieve theories of greater generality and ecological validity.

The appeal of the information-processing conception also stemmed from the usefulness of the computer as a research tool. When a theory of cognition is embodied in a computer program, the program can be used to test whether the theory is complete, that is, whether it does all that it had been intended to do. For example, if a theory of how people comprehend language were stated in a computer program, the completeness of the theory could be evaluated by computer. If the computer produced an appropriate question in response to some sentences but produced gibberish in response to others, then a limit on the scope of the theory would have been established.

The usefulness of computers in research is also apparent in the field of *artificial intelligence,* the study of intelligent behavior of machines. Researchers in this field analyze what kinds of capacities computers have and how computers can be programmed to perform in intelligent ways. In learning how computers can or cannot perform particular activities, for example, reading, researchers get ideas about how humans perform that activity. Cognitive psychologists have obtained some of their most useful concepts from ideas that arose through research concerning artificial intelligence.

The information-processing conception caught on also because it incorporated many of the insights that had come from the theories of linguistics and communications engineering. Like the latter theories, theories of information processing emphasize inner events other than the formation and utilization of associations. And as we see in the next section, theories of information processing began to clarify the capacities and the architecture of the system that underlies complex cognitive processes.

OVERVIEW

By the end of the 1960s, many researchers believed that the human information-processing system consisted of three separate memory stores, as shown in Figure 1.7. This *multistore model*, which owes much to the research of Broadbent (1958) and Atkinson and Shiffrin (1968), has guided a large amount of research, and it continues to be influential. We consider it briefly here because it provides a convenient overview of information processing.

The Multistore Model

According to the multistore model, we process external stimuli in several stages. First, information enters the sensory memory store, which stores information in a raw, sensory form. For example, a visual stimulus is stored in sensory memory in a visual form consisting of physical properties such as color, brightness, shape, and lines. Similarly, an auditory stimulus is stored in sensory memory in an auditory form consisting of physical properties such as loudness and pitch. The sensory store retains large amounts of information, but the information weakens or decays in less than one second. The information in the sensory store can also be displaced by new visual information. Thus the information in sensory memory is forgotten very quickly unless it is transferred into the short-term store. In order to enter the short-term store, the information in sensory memory must be recognized. Pattern recognition involves matching

Human Processing System

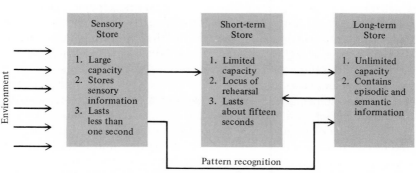

Figure 1.7   A multistore model of human information processing and the primary characteristics of each memory store.

information in the sensory store with information in the long-term store, assigning the information to well-learned categories. This process of pattern recognition sometimes involves attending to particular pieces of information in the sensory store but not to others. In summary, then, the sensory store retains large amounts of information briefly, allowing time for pattern recognition and attentional processes to occur.

After information has entered sensory memory and has been recognized or categorized, it may be passed on to the short-term store (STS). The short-term store is a limited capacity system that can hold about seven items (plus or minus two) at a time (Miller, 1956). For example, the items might be individual letters or familiar words. In either case, there are constraints on how much can be stored. The short-term store retains information for about 15 seconds, long enough, for example, to allow us to dial a phone number we have just looked up. Forgetting results from the gradual decay of information over time and also from the displacement of stored information by incoming information. By rehearsing, however, we can keep information in the short-term store indefinitely. Unlike the sensory store, then, the short-term store has limited capacity, it retains information for about 15 seconds, and it stores categorized information that can be rehearsed.

The information in the short-term store can be coded into an even more durable form by entering into the long-term store. The long-term store, unlike the short-term store, has no capacity limits and can retain information over long periods of time, perhaps even permanently. Nevertheless, the information in the long-term store can be forgotten, for we are often unable to retrieve the information stored in memory. Failures to retrieve information can stem from interference, as occurs when the recall of a person's name is blocked by the recall of other names. Retrieval failures can also result from the absence of retrieval cues, for example, the initials of a person's name.

The long-term store retains many kinds of information, two of which deserve mention here. One kind is *episodic information*, which concerns autobiographical events that we experienced at a particular time and place. Our memories for what we did yesterday, for what we ate for dinner two nights ago, and for our last visit with a friend all involve episodic information. In remembering episodic information, we recall particular events and the context in which they occurred. The second kind of information, called *semantic information*, includes our knowledge of facts and of the world. Our knowledge of how to speak and to write, of concepts such as space and time, and of the differences between mammals and birds is based upon semantic information. Unlike episodic information, semantic information is nonautobiographical and pertains to the world, not to our own past experiences (Tulving, 1972).

For this reason, semantic information is sometimes called world knowledge.

As you no doubt noticed, the multistore model includes not only three memory stores but also a set of processes for transferring information from one store to another. Atkinson and Shiffrin (1968) called these *control processes* because they control the flow of information within the system. Control processes are important because they govern the encoding, the retrieval, and the manipulation of information. They are also important because many of them can be activated voluntarily. For example, it is through the use of control processes that we deliberately rehearse or attend to items in an attempt to remember them.

The Present Approach: Processing and Knowledge

The multistore model guided research for over 20 years. But many researchers eventually abandoned the model, for reasons that are discussed in Chapter 4. One of the main reasons was that the model postulated a greater number of memory stores than was necessary (Craik and Lockhart, 1972). In order to provide a simpler account of memory, theorists began to emphasize the stages and the kinds of processing executed by a single memory unit, sometimes called the central processor. This emphasis is reflected in the present text, which is less concerned with memory stores than with the processing that occurs during activities such as attending, encoding, and problem solving. This emphasis is also reflected in our terminology. For example, we shall speak of sensory memory as an early stage of processing, not as a separate memory store.

The first half of this text is concerned with some of the basic cognitive processes. In Chapter 2, we examine pattern recognition, the process in which incoming stimuli are matched with information already stored in the memory system. Through pattern recognition, we acquire information about events in the environment. In Chapter 3, we continue our analysis of the processes through which people acquire information. We shall see that the acquisition of new information is often limited because at any particular moment, we can attend to only so many stimuli. Some of the stimuli we attend to remain in our conscious awareness for about 15 seconds; this brief retention is called immediate memory. As we shall see, the limits on our attention and our immediate memory can often be overcome through training.

In order to remember the information in immediate memory over long periods of time, we must encode the information into a durable form. Encoding processes are featured in Chapter 4, which concerns remembering. We will see that people are highly flexible encoders and can adjust their codes to suit the task at hand. For example, if the task involved remembering a phone number long enough to dial it, we might encode the information in a verbal format that allowed for rehearsal. Or, if we had to remember the directions provided by a map, we might encode the information in a visual format that indicated the important spatial relationships shown on the map. Through encoding, then, we construct internal symbolic representations that are useful in performing particular tasks. The theme of Chapter 4 is that the manner in which we encode an item determines whether we will remember that item. For example, if you encode a word by relating it to other words, as occurs in forming an interactive image, then you will remember the word well. But if you encoded a word without relating it to other words, you would remember the word less well.

Whereas Chapters 2, 3, and 4 concern the acquisition of information, Chapter 5 concerns the retrieval of information. We will see that forgetting often results from retrieval failure and that forgetting can be reduced by presenting contextual cues. The effects of retrieval cues are familiar to everyone who has heard a favorite song from the past and felt a flood of emotion-inducing memories. Cues are believed to aid memory partly by guiding a search of stored information or knowledge.

The second half of this text is concerned with the kinds of knowledge people have. In Chapter 6, we inquire into concepts, the building blocks of our world knowledge. In Chapter 7, we analyze the manner in which conceptual and semantic knowledge is represented in the memory system. The question of how knowledge is represented is crucial in cognitive psychology. Without knowing how knowledge is represented in memory, we cannot possibly discover the manner in which people use their knowledge to make inferences, to produce sentences, and so on. In Chapter 8, we investigate the knowledge and the processing that occurs when we comprehend language, as in reading. We will see that comprehension is based upon knowledge of grammar or sentence construction, of word meanings, and of the events in the world. People use this knowledge as if solving a problem, the problem of communicating clearly. In the final chapter, we examine the manner in which people use their knowledge to solve problems.

In concluding this brief overview, we should recognize a potential hazard that arises in using the vocabulary of cognitive psychology. Cognitive terms are highly metaphorical and have taken on theoretical meanings that diverge from their meanings in everyday language. For example, psychologists say that concepts may be stored in the information-processing system. This statement may seem akin to an everyday statement asserting that boxes may be stored in the garage. The problem is that boxes are static physical objects (or so we think of them) that occupy space and may be moved physically from one location to another, but this is not necessarily true of concepts or of images, information, and other cognitive constructs. Concepts cannot be seen or touched or moved around. Additionally, they may consist of dynamic processes that change steadily. To avoid confusion, it is wise to regard terms such as *concept* and *image* as theoretical constructs that are no more tied to a particular location in space than are mathematical constructs such as infinity. Keeping these hazards in mind will help you to avoid some oversimplified concepts of cognition.

• *Summary.* Cognitive psychology is the science of human information processing. Its aim is to identify the cognitive processes and the knowledge that underlie the everyday activities of attending, perceiving, remembering, learning, comprehending, and problem solving. Cognitive psychologists pursue this aim by studying behavior in controlled experiments. They use data obtained from introspective and physiological methods, but they do not rely on these methods exclusively.

Cognitive psychology has been shaped by ideas from many disciplines. The contemporary approach reflects the views of early nativistic philosophers such as Descartes and Kant. But the most direct philosophical influence has been the intellectual tradition called associationism. Associationistic philosophers analyzed the mind in terms of associations derived through experience, particularly through temporal contiguity. This view guided the work of Hermann Ebbinghaus, whose pioneering research established that mental processes were lawful and subject to an experimental analysis. Ebbinghaus hoped to formulate basic laws of association formation and retention by examining memory for nonsense syllables in simple conditions that minimized the influence of prior learning. The impressive rigor and empirical successes of his approach led to extensive studies of verbal learning and verbal association, and his methods influence research today.

The associationistic outlook and methods prevailed for over fifty years. But in the 1950s, associationism began to decline from its position of dominance. Associationistic theories failed to explain new observations, and linguists showed that associationistic theories were incapable of explaining complex phenomena such as language. In World War II, some psychologists had studied topics in human engineering that were not clarified by associationistic theories, and new theories and methods were devised. The new theories drew upon novel insights from the fields of communications engineering and information science. By analogy, humans were viewed as information-processing systems that actively coded or transformed incoming information into a usable form and deliberately allocated their limited attentional capacity in accord with their goals and expectations. Psychologists soon became concerned less with the determinants of association formation than with the inner capacities and processing mechanisms of humans. Following new advances in computer technology, the computer became a sufficiently complex symbol-manipulating system to provide a physical model psychologists could use to conceptualize cognition. Both computers and people may be thought of as processing systems that encode, store, retrieve, and manipulate information. Associations came to be seen as a small part of the entire cognitive story.

Contemporary theories of information processing are concerned with cognitive processes such as encoding, storage, and retrieval, and with the knowledge that enables us to make inferences, to comprehend language, and to solve problems. The first half of this book concerns the basic cognitive processes. The second half concerns the nature and the use of complex aspects of knowledge.

Chapter 2
From Stimulation to
Pattern Recognition

Pattern recognition is the process by which we categorize incoming information by matching it up with that in our long-term memories. Essentially, this is a process of interpreting or assigning meaning to the world around us. Without pattern recognition, the world would appear as a meaningless buzz of confusion, an endless parade of unfamiliar stimuli. This process is crucial because in order to survive and to reproduce, we must recognize food items, potential mates, oncoming cars, and so on. Pattern recognition contributes to many cognitive activities, including the reading activity in which you are now engaged.

In order to illustrate the processes discussed in this chapter, consider how recognition occurs as we read a book. First, the light reflected from a page enters our eyes and stimulates the visual receptors in our retinas, the rods and the cones. The resulting visual information is retained briefly, and this initial stage of processing is called sensory memory. From this information, we separate figure and ground, with the result that we see lines of print standing out against the background of the page. We then analyze the features of the sensory information, detecting local features such as the curved and straight lines that letters are composed of and global features such as the overall shape of the words on a line. By matching these local and global features with the features we have learned previously, we recognize particular letters or even entire words. This type of processing is called *data driven processing* because it is guided by the incoming sensory data.

Pattern recognition is also influenced by our expectations and our prior knowledge. As an example, assume you were reading a story about Mary driving a car and you read the words *Reflexively, Mary jammed on. . . .* In this context, the next words would probably be *the brakes.* Expecting to see those words next, you might begin to pay attention to the global features of those words, looking, for example, for the overall shape of the word *the.* This is an instance of *conceptually driven processing* because your processing was guided by your prior knowledge and concepts concerning driving. This example shows that pattern recognition is in part a highly active process of search and interpretation.

During reading and other activities, data driven and conceptually driven processing often occur simultaneously and in a continuous flow. For the sake of clarity, however, we shall examine these types of processing separately. We begin by analyzing data driven processing, focusing on sensory memory and the analysis of features. Then we explore conceptually driven processing and the effects of context. Next, we look into speech perception, which for many years appeared to involve unique recognition processes. We conclude by discussing the effects of practice on pattern recognition. Throughout the chapter, we will be concerned chiefly with the recognition of visual and auditory stimuli, for more is known about vision and audition than about the other sensory modalities.

SENSORY MEMORY

Many of the stimuli we encounter in our environment persist in time, and this aids perception, for perception requires time. Many other stimuli are very short-lived, lasting well under half a second, but these brief stimuli may be very important to perceive. Lightning on a dark night might briefly illuminate the landscape and permit us to detect and avoid an imminent hazard. A brief auditory stimulus such as the snap of a nearby twig might alert us to the presence of an unseen predator or intruder. Recognizing such brief stimuli is obviously important. But how can we respond to stimuli that are so brief that perception cannot occur in their presence? Nature's solution to this problem is *sensory memory,* the initial stage of a processing in which incoming information is retained for about half a second.

Iconic Memory

The phenomenon of visual sensory memory, also called *iconic memory*, was examined by Sperling (1960) in a now classic experiment. Sperling used a tachistoscope, which is a device for presenting visual stimuli for very brief periods of time, to present arrays of letters such as the following:

```
M   T   F
K   Q   V
D   L   N
```

He presented the array for 50 milliseconds (one-twentieth of a second) and asked the adult subjects to recall as many letters as possible. Since this procedure required the recall of the whole array, it was called the *whole report procedure.* The results were that the subjects accurately reported only about four or five letters, on the average, even when the presented array contained as many as 12 letters. This result is consistent with the observations made in Wundt's laboratory that were described earlier. Presumably, the ability to report only four or five letters results from the limited capacity of immediate memory, to be discussed in the following chapter.

But Sperling questioned whether the limited memory span accurately indicated how many items the subjects had seen. Perhaps they had seen more than they could report. Sperling investigated this possibility by using a *partial report procedure,* which required the recall of only one row in the presented array. Immediately after the array was shown, the subjects heard a high, medium, or low tone, and the tones signalled the subjects to report either the top, middle, or bottom rows, respectively. Thus in a trial, an array could be flashed for 50 milliseconds (msec) followed by the sounding of, say, a low tone. That would signal the subject to recall the letters in the third row only. On other trials, other tones would have signalled the recall of the first or second rows, and which row was signalled was varied irregularly from trial to trial. They key point is that the subjects did not know which row to report until after the array had been presented. In order to report accurately, then, the subjects had to rely upon their memory of what they had seen.

The results from the partial report procedure were that the subjects were able to successfully report the letters from any row that was signalled. For example, when the array had included nine letters, the subjects recalled an average of about 2.7 items correctly from any row. Since any row could be reported accurately, all three rows, a total of around eight letters, must have been available in memory. As Figure 2.1 shows, performance in the partial report procedure continued to improve as the

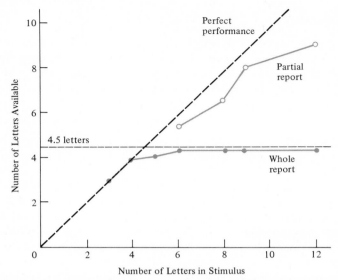

Figure 2.1   The number of letters that can be recalled in the partial and the whole report procedures for displays of various sizes. (After Sperling, 1960. Copyright 1960 by the American Psychological Association. Reprinted by permission.)

number of letters presented was increased. In contrast, performance in the whole report procedure did not improve with increases in the number of presented letters. The results from the partial report procedure show that the subjects remembered most of the presented items, even when as many as 12 had been presented, but they were unable to report more than four or five in a trial.

Why could the subjects report only four or five letters even when they had twice that number available? To answer this question, Sperling altered the partial report procedure by imposing brief delays between the stimulus array and the recall signal. Figure 2.2 shows that the percentage of letters that could be reported accurately decreased systematically as the recall signal was delayed progressively longer. In fact, when the recall cue followed the array by 1.0 second, the subjects in the partial report condition performed no better than subjects had previously in the whole report condition. These observations suggest that the subjects retained information about the entire array for a short time, between 250 and 500 msec, but only long enough to report several letters accurately. This interpretation is consistent with the introspections of the subjects. They said they "saw" the entire array for a short time but that the image faded before they could report all of the items. Phenomenally, the image is like a mental snapshot that resembles the presented array, so the name "iconic memory" (Neisser, 1967) seems fitting. The conception of iconic

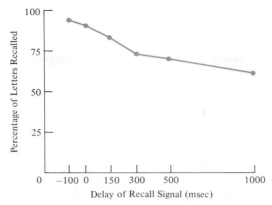

Figure 2.2   The effects of the delay between the stimulus array and the recall signal upon performance in the partial report procedure. (After Sperling, 1960. Copyright 1960 by the American Psychological Association. Reprinted by permission.)

memory that we shall arrive at, however, shall outstrip this notion of a passive image. Developing our conception of iconic memory requires analysis of its duration, the nature of the information involved, and the sources of the phenomenon. Each of these is now examined.

ICONIC PERSISTENCE

When researchers measure aspects of cognition such as the duration of iconic memory, they use the *method of converging operations* (Garner, Hake, and Erikson, 1956). Ideally, this method involves measuring the phenomenon of interest using two independent procedures. If two independent procedures for measuring iconic memory yielded similar estimates of how long iconic memory lasts, then we would have reason to believe that we had attained a valid estimate of the duration of iconic memory.

Achieving such converging results is important because the results of any single procedure might reflect the particular properties of that procedure rather than the general properties of the phenomenon under study. A concrete example should clarify this point. Sperling observed that iconic memory lasts for 500 msec or less, and this observation has been replicated many times. But Sperling's procedure required that the subjects report several items on each trial. Perhaps the recall of one item interfered with the recall of subsequent items, a phenomenon called *output interference*. Conceivably, a different estimate of how long iconic memory lasts might be obtained if the subjects reported only one item in a trial. What is needed is a different, converging measure of the duration of iconic memory that minimizes the effects of output interference.

Fortunately, Averbach and Coriell (1961) have provided such a

Step 1. Present 16-letter
array for 50 msec.

Step 3. Present bar marker
above where *E* had been.

Step 2. Delay period;
screen is blank.

Step 4. Recall period;
screen is blank.

Figure 2.3   The procedure of the experiment by Averbach and Coriell. In this example, the bar marker signalled the subjects to recall *E*.

measure. They told their subjects to stare at a particular point on a screen and flashed an array of 16 letters for 50 msec. Then, following a delay that ranged from 0 msec to 500 msec, they presented a bar marker just above the position in which one of the letters had occurred, as shown in Figure 2.3. The task of the subjects was to name the letter that had appeared in the position beneath the bar marker. The results were that the subjects recalled between 65 percent and 80 percent of the items correctly when there was no delay between the presentation of the array and the marker. But the percentages of correct responses decreased gradually as the delay between the array and the marker increased. This decrease ended after about 250 msec, which suggests that the sensory information had been available for approximately one quarter of a second. This estimate is slightly lower than that obtained by Sperling. But overall, the results agree that iconic memory lasts somewhere between 250 and 500 msec.

VISUAL INFORMATION

Evidence that iconic memory involves visual information comes from studies of visual masking. Averbach and Coriell (1961) used a procedure like that described in Figure 2.3, using a circle rather than a marker as a recall cue. The circle was sufficiently large that if it had been presented at the same time as the letters, it would have surrounded the cued letter without touching it. When the delay between the letter array and the circle was very brief, for example, 100 msec, the percentage of correct responses was very low, far lower than had occurred when the bar marker had served as the cue. Apparently, the circle masked or erased the letter that had appeared in the same location. These results show that information in iconic memory may be forgotten not only through decaying or fading over time but also through masking or interference from other stimuli.

Note that the masking resulted from the presentation of another visual stimulus, the circle. In contrast, the tones that Sperling had used to signal recall did not produce masking (also see Scarborough, 1972). Masking, then, occurs when the two stimuli (for example, the letter and the circle) are of the same sensory modality. Visual masking may be important in many activities, for example, in reading. If in scanning across a line of print, incoming visual information were superimposed on the information already in iconic memory, the incoming letters and words would be unresolvable. This suggestion is speculative, and the exact varieties and functions of masking are not well known (Turvey, 1978). For now, the important point is that the masking of iconic information by visual stimuli indicates that iconic information is visual.

PRECATEGORICAL AND CATEGORICAL INFORMATION

Initially, advocates of the multistore model believed that the sensory memory store differed from other memory stores because it contained raw, unprocessed information. Presumably, that information concerned simple physical properties—size, location, brightness, and so on. Because sensory memory held raw information that had not been recognized, sensory information was said to be preperceptual or *precategorical information.* In contrast, the other memory stores contained information that had been recognized or categorized. That *categorical information* concerned more abstract properties such as the names of letters, the meanings of words, and the identity of external objects. This difference was one of the chief reasons why theorists postulated a separate sensory memory store.

Sperling (1960) presented some of the evidence that suggested that sensory memory involved only precategorical information. Recall that Sperling had previously compared performance in partial report and in whole report procedures. When the subjects were asked to recall the items that had occurred in one particular row, performance was much better than in the whole report condition, in which the subjects were asked to recall all of the presented items. This partial report advantage indicated the existence of a brief sensory memory.

Sperling used a similar experimental design to test whether iconic memory contained only precategorical information. In the whole report condition, an array of letters and digits was presented briefly, and the subjects then reported as many of the items as possible. In the partial report condition, the same type of array was presented briefly, and the subjects then received a signal to report the items from one of the two categories, for example, from the category of letters. The rationale was that if iconic memory contained categorical information that distinguished letters from numbers, then a partial report advantage would occur. Yet that is not what happened: the level of recall was equal in the two conditions, suggesting that iconic memory did not contain categorical information.

Many subsequent experiments have used the same type of design in order to determine the kind of information in iconic memory. A partial report advantage has occurred when the partial report cues instructed the subjects to recall items of a particular brightness, location, size (von Wright, 1968, 1970), shape (Turvey and Kravetz, 1970) or color (Banks and Barber, 1977). But, in general, no partial report advantage has occurred when the cues instructed the subjects to recall items of a particular category, for example, letters or digits (von Wright, 1968). Collectively, these observations indicated that iconic memory involves only precategorical information.

Recent evidence, however, shows that under some conditions, iconic memory does involve categorical information. For example, Merikle (1980) presented an array containing four letters and four digits randomly arranged in a circle. The array was presented for 50 msec. Then, following a brief delay ranging from 0 msec to 900 msec, the number *one, two,* or *three* was spoken. These numbers instructed the subjects to report only the letters, only the digits, or all of the items, respectively. Thus *one* and *two* were partial report cues, while *three* was a whole report cue. Surprisingly, the percentage of items recalled was higher in the partial report conditions than in the whole report condition. And the magnitude of this partial report advantage decreased as the delay between the presentation of the array and the report cue increased. When the delay was 900 msec, performance was equal in the partial report condition and the whole report condition. These results show that the information required to distinguish between letters and numbers is available immediately following stimulus presentation. These results militate against the view that iconic memory involves only precategorical information.

Why did Merikle observe that iconic memory includes categorical information whereas Sperling did not? The answer lies in the procedural differences between the two investigations. In Sperling's experiment, the whole and the partial report procedures differed with regard to cue uncertainty. In the whole report procedure, the subjects always knew well in advance of a trial that they were to recall as many items as possible. So no uncertainty existed as to which recall cue would occur. But in the partial report condition, the subjects did not know which recall cue would occur until a trial had begun. So cue uncertainty existed in the partial report procedure but not in the whole report procedure. This difference between the partial report and the whole report procedures did not occur in Merikle's experiment. In the latter experiment, the subjects never knew until after stimulus presentation whether they were to provide partial or whole report. Thus, when the partial and the whole report conditions are equated with respect to cue uncertainty, the evidence suggests that iconic memory involves categorical information. This outcome reminds us of how important it is to look for converging operations and to avoid reliance on the results of any single procedure. This outcome also shows just how subtle the confounding of variables can be in an experiment. The partial report and the whole report procedures used by Sperling seemed to differ only with respect to the number of items that the subjects were asked to recall. But Merikle's experiment demonstrates elegantly that the two procedures contained subtle differences in cue uncertainty.

We may conclude that categorical information is involved in iconic memory, at least under certain conditions. This conclusion conflicts with the traditional view that iconic memory is a separate memory store that contains raw, unprocessed information. The conclusion also questions the appropriateness of the term *sensory memory*, for the remembered information need not be entirely sensory. But this is not a call to abandon the concept of iconic memory altogether. Iconic memory may still be thought of as an early stage of processing in which information persists briefly beyond the time of stimulus presentation (Breitmeyer, 1980; Di-Lollo, 1980).

SOURCES OF ICONIC MEMORY

Cognitive and physiological inquiry most often proceed independently. But combining the insight from both levels of analysis often leads to a deeper understanding of a phenomenon, and iconic memory is a case in point. Some recent research indicates that iconic memory has separate sources in the rods and the cones. As you probably know, the rods are active in low levels of illumination and are insensitive to color differences. In contrast, the cones are active at high levels of illumination and are sensitive to color differences.

In one experiment (Sakitt and Long, 1979), dark-adapted subjects were shown briefly two successive slides, each containing a red dot on a gray background. The red dot on the first slide was presented in the center of a screen. Then, following a delay, called the interstimulus interval, the second slide was presented. The red dot on the second slide was either above or below or to the left or the right of the position of the first dot. The task of the subject was to indicate the position of the second dot relative to the first. Since the two dots were not presented simultaneously, the task required visual memory for the dot positions. The duration of this memory was evaluated by measuring the level of performance at various interstimulus intervals.

To isolate the contribution of the rods and cones, three conditions were examined. In the cone contrast condition, the contribution of the rods was eliminated or sharply reduced. This was accomplished by arranging the illumination levels of the dots and their surrounds so that the levels were matched for the rods but not the cones. In this condition, the rod system could not detect the dots whereas the cone system could. The second condition, the rod contrast condition, did just the opposite of the first. The illumination levels of dot and surround were adjusted so that they matched for the cones but not for the rods. In this condition, the rod system could detect the dots on the basis of illumination differences but the cone system could not, although the cone system could detect the dot by its color. In the third condition, the rod and cone contrast condition, both the rod and the cone systems could detect the dots on the basis of differences in illumination.

The results of the experiment, shown in Figure 2.4, show that the rods and cones make different contributions to iconic memory. The top curve, which reflects the contribution of both the rods and the cones, provides evidence of relatively long-lasting iconic memory. The long duration probably occurs because the subjects were dark-adapted and the illumination was dim. Other studies have shown that estimates of the duration of iconic memory are influenced by lighting conditions (Dick, 1974). The bottom curve of Figure 2.4 shows performance in the cone contrast condition in which only the cones were operative. When the rod system was neutralized, the shape of the iconic memory curve was altered substantially, and the icon lasted less than 200 msec. As Sakitt and Long put it, if you spare the rod, you spoil the icon. In keeping with this

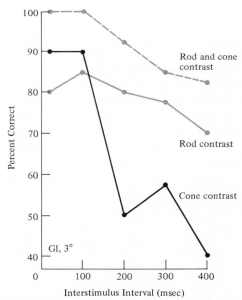

Figure 2.4   The level of retention for the dot locations at various interstimulus intervals. (From Sakitt and Long, 1979. Copyright 1979 by the American Psychological Association. Reprinted by permission.)

view, the middle curve obtained in the rod contrast condition shows that when the rod system was operative, the icon was relatively durable. In summary, there appear to be separate rod and cone icons, with the latter persisting less than 200 msec and the former lasting considerably longer.

Additional research has shown that brief cone icons and longer lasting rod icons occur under daytime illumination conditions as well as the conditions of dim illumination in the preceding experiment (Sakitt and Long, 1978, 1979). Moreover, durable iconic memory has been observed in an individual who is color-blind and sees only with the rod system (Sakitt, 1975, 1976). Taken together, these observations suggest that iconic memory has separate rod and cone sources and that the rods are responsible for iconic storage over longer intervals. If the rods are indeed responsible for memory beyond 200 msec, this would establish that iconic memory is mediated by events occurring at the peripheral level of the receptors rather than by events occurring at a central level in the brain (Sakitt, 1976).

This picture portraying a brief cone and a long rod icon is not supported by all of the evidence available. For example, Banks and Barber (1977, 1980) have observed retention for color information beyond 200 msec. The color-blind rods could not be responsible for this effect. It remains for future research to determine the exact contributions of the rods and the cones to iconic memory.

A PROCESSING VIEW

Initially, theorists conceived of iconic memory as a passive storage phenomenon. But several observations challenge this view. For example, Treisman, Russell, and Green (1975) briefly presented an array of moving disks and asked their subjects to indicate the direction of motion of either all the disks or a signalled subset of them. Performance in the latter, partial report condition exceeded that in the whole report condition, suggesting that information concerning motion was retained briefly. This observation is important because motion is believed to be detected by movement-sensitive analyzers—movement detectors—in the brain. Perhaps iconic memory is best thought of not as a passive storage phenomenon but as the early stages of analysis of features such as movement, brightness, color, and so on (DiLollo, 1980; Turvey, 1978).

This process view contrasts sharply with the passive view initially proposed by multistore theorists. The conception of an iconic memory store leads us to interpret observations of iconic memory as manifestations of a single underlying structure. But a process view leads us to think of iconic memory as the outcome of numerous processes such as the analysis of features and the persistence of neural activity in the visual receptors and path to and in the brain. The process view is preferable, chiefly because it accommodates the diverse processes involved in iconic memory (Coltheart, 1980).

Auditory Sensory Memory

Sensory memory which occurs in the auditory modality is called *echoic memory* (Neisser, 1967). Like iconic memory, echoic memory serves to keep incoming information available long enough for the occurrence of pattern recognition.

Echoic memory is believed to contribute to everyday activities, particularly the perception of speech. For example, when someone says the word *bat*, the first sound we perceive is a *ba* sound. Yet the initial sound waves that reach our ears do not produce that sound. Rather, the physical information leading to the *ba* sound is distributed over time throughout a substantial portion of the word. Without memory for the initial portion of the speech stimulus, it might be difficult to interpret correctly the later portions, thereby impairing the perception of the speech sound.

The existence and the duration of echoic memory have been documented by using partial and whole report procedures analogous to those used to analyze iconic memory (Moray, Bates, and Barnett, 1965). In one experiment (Darwin, Turvey, and Crowder, 1972), subjects listened simultaneously to three lists of letters and digits. The three lists were presented rapidly, in about one second, via stereophonic headphones. One list was presented to only the left ear, another was presented to only the right ear, and the third list was presented to both ears simultaneously and sounded as if it were coming to the middle of the head. The subjects in the whole report condition were asked to report as many of the items as possible. The subjects in the partial report condition were asked to report the items from one of the lists. Which list they were to report was signalled by one of three lights arranged in a row. The left, center, and right lights signalled the subjects to recall the lists heard on the left, in the center, or on the right, respectively. Thus, ear location in this study parallels row location in Sperling's experiments. The light cue was presented either 0, 1, 2, or 4 seconds after the lists had been presented.

The results, shown in Figure 2.5, were that a small but reliable partial report advantage occurred when the report cue followed the lists by 0, 1, or 2 seconds. But no partial report advantage occurred when the report cue followed the lists by 4 seconds. Apparently, then, the auditory information persisted, but only for about 2 seconds. These results provide clear support for the existence of echoic memory.

The same authors next investigated whether echoic memory involves only precategorical information. Their procedure matched the one described above in all but one respect. The partial report cues now indicated whether the letters or the numbers should be recalled. As had

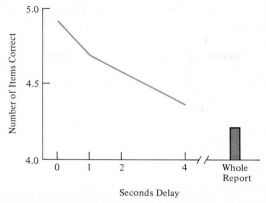

Figure 2.5   The partial report advantage in echoic memory. (From Darwin, Turvey, and Crowder, 1971.)

occurred in Merikle's study of iconic memory, performance in the partial report procedure exceeded that in the whole report procedure. This outcome suggests that echoic memory does involve the categorical information that is required to distinguish between letters and numbers.

These observations lead to the view that echoic memory, like iconic memory, involves the momentary persistence of information beyond the time of the stimulus presentation. But they do not support the traditionally held view that the echoic memory involves only precategorical information (Crowder and Morton, 1969). In closing this brief discussion, however, it should be pointed out that very little is known about echoic memory at present. Many different procedures have been used to study echoic memory (Crowder, 1978), but the results of those procedures show an unnerving lack of convergence. The most that can now be said with confidence is that echoic memory does exist, but its exact properties remain to be identified by future research.

RECOGNIZING VISUAL PATTERNS

Each day, we recognize many visual patterns, but we seldom pause to appreciate the importance, the magnitude, and the complexity of this task. Pattern recognition is important because in order to survive, we must recognize food and water, dangerous persons and situations, oncoming cars, and so on. In light of the tremendous number of different patterns that we recognize daily, it is remarkable how effectively and effortlessly we recognize the things around us. Our skill in recognizing patterns appears striking when you consider how variable the members of our perceptual categories are. The letter *A*, for example, occurs in innumerable shapes, sizes, thicknesses, and orientations. Yet we recognize an *A* as an *A* whether we are reading the large, standardized print of traffic control signs or the idiosyncratic, barely legible scribbles of a friend. How this occurs is one of the chief problems that theories of pattern recognition must explicate.

In this section, we begin our inquiry into the events that occur largely beyond the stage of sensory memory. We shall focus initially on the analysis of simple features. Then we examine more global aspects of processing. This will lead into an examination of conceptually driven processing and the effects of context.

Feature Analysis

Visual patterns are composed of numerous features put together in particular ways. For example, the letters of the alphabet can be analyzed in terms of features such as horizontal, vertical, and diagonal lines, and closed and open curves (Geyer and DeWald, 1973; Gibson, 1969). One of the most influential and pervasive ideas in the literature on pattern recognition is that detecting the features of a pattern contributes to the recognition of that pattern (Lindsay and Norman, 1972; Rumelhart and Siple, 1974; Selfridge and Neisser, 1960). If the presented pattern were a letter, for example, it might first be represented in sensory memory, and perceptual processes might begin by analyzing features. When all the features had been resolved, the pattern would be recognized. The validity of this account will be assessed as we proceed.

BEHAVIORAL EVIDENCE

Evidence that feature detection contributes to pattern recognition comes from numerous sources. In one experiment (Kinney, Marsetta, and Showman, 1966), a series of letters and digits was presented visually, and the subjects were asked to identify the items that had been shown. Most errors of identification, called confusion errors, involved letters having common visual features. For example, if a presented item had been *B* and the subject erred in recalling that item, the error often consisted of an item such as *8*, which has some of the same visual features as *B*. In contrast, the subjects seldom confused items such as *A* and *S* that have few visual features in common. Theoretical analyses have indicated that the greater the number of visual features two items have in common, the greater are the chances that those two items will be confused (Geyer et al., 1973; Gibson, 1964).

Additional behavioral evidence for the occurrence of feature analysis comes from studies of performance in high-speed search tasks. As an example, quickly scan each of the columns in Figure 2.6 and identify the letter Z in each column. In an experiment that used this procedure (Neisser, 1964), subjects found the target letter Z faster in columns such

ODUGQR	IVMXEW
QCDUGO	EWVMIX
CQOGRD	EXWMVI
QUGCDR	IXEMWV
URDGQO	VXWEMI
GRUQDO	MXVEWI
DUZGRO	XVWZEI
UCGROD	MWXVIE
DQRCGU	VIMEXW
QDOCGU	EXVWIM

(1)   (2)

Figure 2.6   Lists used to study feature analysis in a high-speed search task. (From "Visual Search" by U. Neisser. Copyright © 1964 by Scientific American, Inc. All rights reserved.)

as column one than in those such as column two. The apparent reason is that the nontarget letters in column one have few features in common with the target letter Z, whereas the nontarget letters in column two have several features in common with Z. Thus the letters in column two must be examined more carefully than those in column one. Incidentally, Neisser's subjects improved their scanning times substantially over ten days of practice. The effects of practice upon pattern recognition will be discussed further in a subsequent section.

The preceding observations suggest that subjects do engage in feature analysis. But we cannot conclude that these observations are explained by theories of feature analysis. The reason is that the features are defined largely on the basis of the observed confusion patterns, so it is logically circular to say that the confusions resulted from the subjects analyzing just those features. That would be a bit like saying "Mary is eating because she is hungry" when the only evidence that she is hungry is that she is eating. If a noncircular explanation is to be achieved, the explainer (feature analysis or hunger) cannot be inferred from the observation to be explained (confusions and eating). What is needed is evidence for feature analyzers or detectors independent of the observations to be explained by feature analysis.

PHYSIOLOGICAL EVIDENCE
Fortunately, there is independent physiological evidence of feature detectors in the brain regions that are involved in processing visual stimuli. The visual cortex of cats and monkeys contains single neurons that respond selectively to line orientation (Hubel and Wiesel, 1962, 1964). For example, when vertical lines are presented to an anesthetized monkey, some of the neurons in the monkey's visual cortex fire rapidly, as measured by tiny electrodes implanted in the brain. The responding of these

neurons decreases substantially when the orientation of the line is shifted even 15 to 20° from the upright position. Other cortical neurons respond selectively to horizontal lines, 45° lines, moving lines, and so on.

The procedure described above cannot be used on people, so other methods have been devised for identifying feature detectors in humans. An example is the *selective adaptation procedure*, which involves three steps. First, harmless electrodes are attached to the subject's skull. These electrodes measure the cortical evoked response, which indicates the activity of large numbers of cortical neurons. Second, the experimenter presents an adapting stimulus, for example, a vertical line, repeatedly or continuously. The rationale is that with repeated stimulation, the feature detectors that respond selectively to the vertical line will fatigue and respond less. The third step is to present various test stimuli—in this case, lines of various orientations—and to measure the cortical evoked response. If there is in fact a feature detector that responds selectively to vertical lines, then the evoked response should be weak when the test stimulus is a vertical line. Further, the magnitude of the evoked response should increase when test stimuli other than vertical lines are presented. In fact, both predictions have been confirmed, thereby indicating the existence of detectors for particular orientations (Campbell and Maffei, 1970).

Other studies that used the selective adaptation procedure have established that we also have detectors for color and motion (Eimas and Miller, 1978). Overall, these observations suggest that feature analysis does play a role in pattern recognition.

THE LIMITS OF FEATURE ANALYSIS

Theories of feature analysis help to explain how we recognize many different patterns, including novel ones. For example, we may recognize a novel letter as an *A* because that letter activates the same feature detectors that had been activated by *A*s we had seen previously.

Yet analyzing features cannot be all that is involved in recognizing patterns. For one thing, patterns consist not only of features but also of relationships between features. Both *L* and *T*, for example, contain a horizontal line and a vertical line, but the letters are distinguished by the relationships between those features. A complete theory of pattern recognition must go beyond feature detection and explain how we process relationships between features.

Theories of feature analysis are limited also because they cannot explain the interpretative aspects of the pattern recognition process. As an illustration, look at Figure 2.7a. At first glance, most people read the forms as *the cat*. Notice that the middle symbols in both words are identical and should therefore activate the same feature detectors. Yet we recognize one symbol as an *H* and the other as an *A*. In essence, we interpret the middle symbol according to the surrounding context. How we do so is unexplained by theories of feature analysis.

Taking a more extreme example, look at Figure 2.7b and try to recognize the object shown. It may help to know that the picture shows a peppered moth resting on a bark-covered tree. The moth becomes easy to see only when you know what to look for. We recognize the moth through a process of interpreting the information in the picture, not by detecting features alone. Both examples show that pattern recognition consists of much more than passively registering the physical information around us.

Feature analysis may even fail to provide the best account of performance in simple tasks involving letter recognition (Bouma, 1971). For example, subjects often confuse letters on the basis of their overall shape

THE CAT

(a)

(b)

Figure 2.7   The role of interpretation in pattern recognition. (a) The middle symbol in both words is the same, yet one is interpreted as *H* and the other as *A*. (From "Pattern recognition by machine" by O. E. Selfridge and U. Neisser. Copyright © 1960 by Scientific American. All rights reserved.) (b) Try to find an object in this picture. (Rogers, DPI)

rather than the particular features they share (Lupker, 1979). This suggests that pattern recognition may proceed via global analyses, which we now examine.

Global Processing

One type of global processing that leads to pattern recognition consists of comparing the incoming stimulus with a holistic representation of a category. For example, when we see an animal we have never seen before, we may recognize the animal as a dog by comparing the novel stimulus with the internal representation we have of a prototypical dog. This idea is the core of the *prototype theory* of pattern recognition.

PROTOTYPES

Many natural categories seem to have best or most typical instances (Reed, 1978; Rosch, 1978). A typical pattern belonging to the category *dog* would be about 2.5 feet high, have four legs, hair, two eyes, a relatively long nose, sharp teeth, and so on. An atypical pattern might be 8 inches high, bald, with a short snout, stubby tail, and small teeth. The average or most typical member of a category is called the *prototype*. A prototype may be a representation of a pattern seen before, but more often, it is abstracted from experience with different members of the category. By comparing stimuli to this abstracted, average member of a category, we may come to recognize patterns.

Some evidence in support of the prototype theory comes from experiments in which people learned three categories of random-dot patterns such as those shown in Figure 2.8 (Posner and Keele, 1968; Posner, 1969, 1970). The stimuli included three prototype dot patterns and four distortions of each that were generated by making small, random displacements of the dots in the prototypical pattern. For each category of four distortions, the prototype represented the central tendency of the category. In Phase 1 of the experiment, adults learned to assign the distortions to the three categories, but the prototypes were never presented. In Phase 2, the subjects were asked to classify a variety of stimuli into the categories learned in Phase 1. The stimuli included some of the distortions from Phase 1, some novel distortions of the prototypes, and the actual prototypes, which the subjects had never seen before. The novel distortions and the prototypes were equally similar to the stimuli that had been presented in Phase 1.

The chief result was that the subjects classified the prototypes very accurately, indeed, as accurately as they had classified the patterns in Phase 1. This observation suggests that the subjects had abstracted the prototypes in Phase 1 even though the prototypes had not actually been presented. Following a delay of one week, the accuracy in classifying the

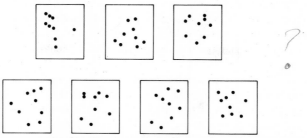

Figure 2.8   Examples of random-dot patterns. The top row includes three prototypes and the bottom row shows four distortions of the right-most prototype. (From Posner, 1969.)

prototypes did not decline, whereas the accuracy in classifying the distortions of the prototypes did decline. Furthermore, the accuracy in classifying the novel distortions depended on how similar the novel patterns were to the prototypes. In particular, the subjects seldom erred in classifying patterns that resembled the prototypes closely, which suggests that they classified the novel patterns by comparing them to the prototypes they had abstracted.

Additional experiments (Franks and Bransford, 1971; Reed, 1972) have established that we recognize stimuli such as schematic faces by comparing them to prototypes, and the prototype model has been shown to predict performance better than its rivals. To some extent, models of prototype matching may be combined with models of feature analysis, for a stimulus may be compared with a prototype by comparing the features of the two. By the same token, however, it should be remembered that our knowledge of prototypes consists of more than knowledge of a group of elementary features. Prototype models are discussed further in our subsequent examination of concepts. For now, the important point is that the construction and use of prototypes is one holistic process that may contribute to pattern recognition.

WHOLES AND PARTS

The discussion of feature analysis pointed out that patterns may be thought of as a set of independent features that stand in a particular configuration. But this is not the only way that patterns may be thought of. As we saw previously (see pages 20–22), the Gestalt psychologists asserted that the whole is more than the sum of its parts, and they called the organized wholes we perceive *gestalts*. In this view, recognizing patterns is a process not of detecting independent features but of apprehending whole, integrated structures that have emergent properties not found in the component parts. Thus, dot groups such as . . . . . and :: are perceived not as four independent dots but as a straight line and a square, respectively. Despite the many contributions of the early Gestaltists, Gestalt theory was based chiefly on demonstrations that, while convincing, did not establish experimentally the primacy of wholes or the mechanisms for perceiving them. Fortunately, this situation is now being remedied.

Several recent studies have examined whether we directly perceive the component features or the larger, holistic aspects of patterns (Lupker, 1979). In one experiment (Pomerantz, Sager, and Stoever, 1977; also see Williams and Weisstein, 1978), subjects were required to discriminate rapidly the presence of a feature when the feature was presented alone or in the context of another feature. In the no-context condition, the subjects discriminated between the parenthesis features) and (. In each of numerous trials, one of these two stimuli was flashed briefly on a screen. The subjects moved a switch backward when the stimulus was) and forward when it was (. The time elapsing from the stimulus presentation to the subject's response—the reaction time—was measured. In the context condition, the procedure was identical except that the stimuli were)) and ( ). Since these stimuli differ only with respect to the left-hand feature, the context condition required discrimination of) and (, just as the no-context condition did. The difference was that in the context condition, the discrimination was made in the context of another feature, namely). The rationale was that the patterns)) and ( ) were gestalt-like and could be perceived as integrated units rather than the separate features) and (. If holistic, gestalt-like patterns can be perceived more directly than the individual features, then the subjects should discriminate faster between)) and ( ) than between) and (. In fact, that is exactly what happened. In at least some conditions, then, we seem to detect wholes rather than component parts, in keeping with Gestalt theory.

These observations do not, however, show that the global aspects of a stimulus are always processed before the elementary features. Patterns consist of both large, holistic units and small, elementary units or features. Experimentation is required to determine which units we actually process, that is, which units are functional. So far, research has revealed several factors that may determine what the functional units are. One factor is the nature of the attributes of the presented stimuli. Some combinations of features seem to fit together readily to form a coherent, higher-order unit, whereas others do so less readily (Garner, 1974; Palmer 1980; Treisman and Gelade, 1980). Features or dimensions that fit together readily, as hue and brightness do, are said to be integral because they are likely to be processed as an integrated unit. Experience may also determine what serves as a functional unit; for example, features that often occur together may come to be processed as a unit (LaBerge, 1976).

A third determinant is the type of procedure used. If target and nontarget patterns can be distinguished by their global shapes, then the overall shape may be used as the functional unit of processing. But if the items differ only with respect to a particular feature, then that feature may become a functional unit of processing. Thus what serves as a functional unit of processing may vary according to the task (Hoffman, 1980). Therefore, it is inappropriate to ask what are *the* units of processing. Whether processing is based upon global or elementary units depends upon many interacting factors.

THE CYCLE OF PROCESSING

According to simple models of feature analysis, the process of pattern recognition begins with the detection of elementary features. The cycle of processing moves from the perception of parts to the constructive synthesis of wholes. This conception, however, is too simplistic. As the Gestalt psychologists pointed out, we must distinguish between figure and ground before we perceive particular features or objects. For example, in looking at the ambiguous figure shown on page 21 (Figure 1.4), we perceive features such as throats and noses only after we have distinguished the heads as figure and the white area as ground. The process of distinguishing between figure and ground is global, and it precedes the processing of local details. The same occurs in our everyday perceptual activities. For example, recognizing a printed word or a person standing at a distance down a street requires first separating figure and ground and then analyzing detailed parts of the figure. These considerations suggest that processing proceeds from the global to the local level, and some of the experimental evidence supportive of this view shall now be examined.

The procedure of one ingenious experiment (Navon, 1977) may be illustrated by looking at the right-hand side of Figure 2.9 and deciding quickly which letter you see. In the experiment, there were two conditions, global and local. In the global condition, letters such as those shown in Figure 2.9 were presented and the subjects were instructed to respond to the large letter by pressing one key if they saw an *H* and another key if they saw an *S*. The local condition was similar, except the subjects were instructed to indicate whether the smaller letters were *H* or *S*. On some trials, the large and the small letters matched (for example, all were *H*s), whereas on other trials, they did not match, as in panel (b) of Figure 2.9. The principal results were that the subjects responded significantly faster in the global condition than in the local condition, suggesting they recognized the global letter first. Furthermore, the subjects in the global condition were able to ignore the small letters, for their reaction times were the same whether the large and small letters matched or not. In contrast, the subjects in the local condition responded much slower when the large and the small letters mismatched than when they

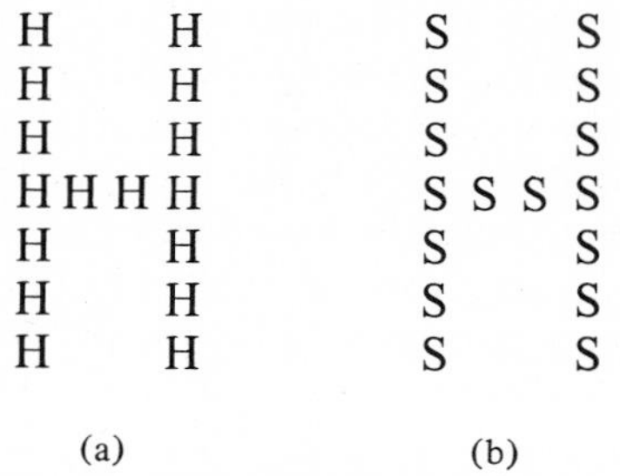

```
H    H        S      S
H    H        S      S
H    H        S      S
H H H H       S S S S
H    H        S      S
H    H        S      S
H    H        S      S
```

(a)   (b)

Figure 2.9   The types of letters used in the global condition of the experiment by Navon (1977). (a) The large and the small letters match. (b) The large and the small letters do not match.

matched. Thus the subjects responding to the local letter were unable to ignore the global letter. Processing the global letter seemed to occur automatically and interfered with processing the local letter. Taken together, these results suggest that the global processing preceded the local processing. Accordingly, numerous theorists have suggested that, in general, perceptual processing begins at global levels and proceeds to more local levels (Broadbent, 1977; Navon, 1977).

This suggestion has not gone unchallenged. One contradictory observation comes from a study involving letter displays such as that shown in panel (b) of figure 2.9 (Kinchla and Wolfe, 1979). The procedure used was the same as that described above, except that the subjects were sometimes shown letter displays that were much larger than those that had been presented in the preceding experiment. The largest display was somewhat smaller than a piece of typing paper held at arm's length. The results were that when small displays were presented, the subjects responded faster to the global letter than to the smaller component letters, as in the preceding experiment. In contradiction to the global-to-local model, however, when large displays were presented, the subjects responded faster to the component letters than to the global letter. This outcome did not result from an inability to see the global letter, for the subjects did respond correctly to the global letter.

The overall picture that has developed thus far is that perceptual processing is sometimes global-to-local and at other times local-to-global. This is really not too surprising, for the path of processing may vary according to the viewing conditions (Hoffman, 1980). For example, when we see a figure inside a dimly lit restaurant or theater, information concerning minute visual features is sparse, so we might respond first to the global information. If the global analysis suggests that the figure is someone we know, we might then focus our attention on particular details. Under other conditions, however, processing might proceed from the local toward the global level. For example, when a large display of letters is shown, the small letters may be focused upon the fovea, the area of greatest acuity, whereas the global letter stimulates the peripheral areas of the retina. Because of this acuity difference, we might detect the small letters faster than the global letters. An important question, unanswered by the preceding experiments, is whether the flow of processing is invariably global-to-local when the entire display falls on the fovea.

In conclusion, perceptual processing is highly flexible and adjusts to the diverse demands placed upon us by our environments. It is oversimplified to suggest that processing invariably follows either the global-to-local or the local-to-global routes. In fact, we may follow both routes simultaneously, and the results at one level of analysis may influence events at the other. In everyday tasks such as recognizing a person walking at a distance, we seem to take an initial global look, then focus in on particular details, then return to a more global level, and so on. In this sense, perception involves cyclic processes (Broadbent, 1977; Neisser, 1976). This theme shall find support in our analysis of context.

Context and Pattern Recognition

The world we live in is highly structured and predictable, for particular events are far more likely to occur in some contexts than others. In everyday settings, we form expectations about what things we are likely to see in various contexts, and these expectations may influence how we recognize patterns. For example, Palmer (1975) showed adults two pictures in succession. The first was a context drawing of a scene such as a kitchen. The second was a briefly presented drawing of a target object, for example, a mailbox or a loaf of bread. When the target drawings were consistent with the preceding context, as in the kitchen-bread pair, the subjects identified the target drawings much more often than when the target object was inappropriate to the context. Thus the context influenced pattern recognition, just as it did in the demonstration provided earlier concerning the moth and *THE CAT* (see Figure 2.7).

In order to gain a first-hand appreciation of the effects of context, try reading a nontechnical book or magazine upside down for about 15 minutes. Initially, you may find it slow going. But as you practice and rely more fully upon your expectations about what the next words are likely to be, your reading speed should improve markedly. This demonstration is not entirely artificial. For the speed of normal reading, about 300 to 600 words per minute on the average, results partly from our use of contextual information (Norman, 1976).

DATA DRIVEN AND CONCEPTUALLY DRIVEN PROCESSING

When we process stimuli such as sentences, we may begin by analyzing the global and the local features of individual words. At later stages of processing, we might analyze the meaning of the words and then identify the relationships between the meanings of the different words, thereby determining the meaning of the sentence. In this scenario, processing began with the analyses of the sensory data and then proceeded to deeper, conceptual or semantic analyses, and the output at one stage of processing served as the input for the next. Because all of the processing is initiated or driven by the incoming sensory data, this type of processing is called data driven processing.

Data driven processing contrasts with conceptually driven processing, in which the recognition process is guided by our expectations, which in turn are based upon our conceptual knowledge and contextual information. For example, if you were reading a story about a hospital and had just read the words *The patient was examined by the*, you would probably expect the next word to be *doctor*. That expectation is based upon your knowledge of what happens in hospitals and of what doctors usually do to patients. Because of that expectation, you might begin to search for the global shape of the word *doctor* or the features of the letter *d*. This is an example of conceptually driven processing because the pickup of new information is guided by the outcome of semantic and conceptual analyses. Figure 2.10 illustrates the difference between data driven and conceptually driven processing.

In many tasks requiring pattern recognition, data driven and conceptually driven processing work in unison. For example, as we read, our eyes fixate upon visual stimuli and we begin to analyze the features of words and letters and then determine the meanings of the words. We then use these meanings and our expectations about which words will probably occur next to guide our analysis of the next words we fixate upon. These analyses provide the input that leads to the formation of additional expectations, which in turn guide new feature analyses, and so on. Pattern recognition, then, may involve continual interactions between data driven and conceptually driven processing. In the next section, we examine some of the processes through which conceptually driven processing influences pattern recognition.

MECHANISMS OF CONTEXTUAL INFLUENCE

Context may affect performance in numerous ways, and some of these do not, strictly speaking, involve perception. Suppose subjects were asked to rapidly identify a briefly presented target word, *cat*. If the target were preceded by a sentence such as *The dog chased the* _____, performance might be better than when the target word was presented alone with no context (Tulving and Gold, 1963). Although the sentence context may have facilitated the perception of the target words, it may simply have allowed the subjects to guess the target word without recognizing it at

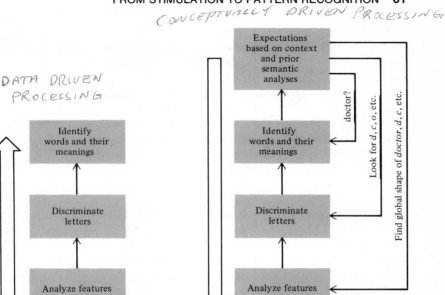

Figure 2.10   Two ways of processing the word *doctor* in the context of the sentence *The patient was examined by the doctor.* Panel (a) shows data driven processing, in which sensory analyses precede semantic ones, and the flow of processing is from bottom to top. Panel (b) shows conceptually driven processing, also called top-down processing, in which semantic analyses and expectations influence lower-level analyses.

all, for it is common knowledge that cats are often assailed by dogs. Alternatively, the subjects may have detected the first letter of the target word and then guessed the rest on the basis of the contextual information. This is just the sort of thing we do in trying to read illegible handwriting and in speed reading. This account of contextual influence is called the sophisticated guessing model and posits a combination of data driven and conceptually driven processing. Another account states that the context biases the subjects in favor of producing words appropriate to the context. The same perceptual events might occur in the presence or absence of context, but the context might lower the threshold for producing the target word. Both the guessing and bias models point to the effects of context on responding, not on processing. Both accounts must be ruled out in any demonstration that context affects the perceptual processing involved in pattern recognition (cf. Baron, 1978).

One way in which context may influence perceptual processing is by allowing a partial and selective analysis of the features of the stimuli to be recognized (Rumelhart, 1977; Rumelhart and Siple, 1974; Smith and Spoehr, 1974). For example, in processing the sentence *The dog chased the cat*, we expect to see the word *cat* by the time we reach the end of the sentence. Consequently, we may analyze only a few of the features in *cat* to confirm our expectation. This account resembles the response bias model mentioned above. The difference is that in the present case, the context biases perceptual analyses rather than the mechanisms involved in response production. This selective perceptual processing based upon context probably occurs when the quality of the stimulus information is poor, as it is when we read road signs in the distance or in dim light.

Context may also influence perception without engendering selective processing. For example, in the act of recognizing words, we may in some instances process most of the stimulus information and recognize each letter. However, this complete or full processing may be speeded by appropriate contextual information, perhaps by priming particular feature detectors (LaBerge, 1976) or by enhancing the accessibility of semantic information in long-term memory (Meyer, Schaneveldt, and Ruddy, 1975). This suggestion is consistent with the idea advanced earlier that in some instances, the features or parts of patterns may be processed faster in the context of the whole pattern than when they occur alone (Pomerantz et al., 1977). But the studies discussed previously involved unusual stimuli such as) and)), so it is appropriate to examine some of the evidence from studies involving more natural stimuli.

Numerous experiments have shown that letters are recognized faster when presented in the context of words than when presented alone or in the context of nonwords (Baron, 1978; Wheeler, 1970). In a seminal experiment by Reicher (1969), each trial involved two steps. First, the subjects were shown briefly either a word such as *WORD*, an anagram containing the same letters such as *OWRD*, or a single letter such as *D*. Second, target letters such as *D* and *K* were presented, and the experimenter measured how long it took the subjects to decide which letter had occurred in the first step. The target letters were chosen in such a way that either could have made a word on word trials (*WORK* or *WORD*) or a nonword on nonword trials. The target letter occurred with equal frequency in all four positions of a word or nonword, so the subjects could not have known where to look before the stimuli had been presented. The results were that the subjects identified which target letter had been presented better when the letter appeared in a word rather than a nonword or alone.

This outcome, called the *word superiority effect*, shows that words can be recognized as wholes. The exact mechanisms involved in the word superiority effect are unclear. But it is known that the effect occurs in an impressive variety of conditions, including those that rule out the guessing and the response bias interpretations (Baron, 1978). The effect is important because seeing whole words quickly could advance one's reading speed. Consistent with this idea, good readers show a large word superiority effect, whereas poor readers do not (Mason, 1975). Overall, these observations attest to the effects of context upon the perception of written words. In the next section, we see that context also influences the perception of spoken words.

RECOGNIZING SPEECH

The capacity for language is one of the most important of all our cognitive capacities, for language is the basis of human communication and cooperation. Additionally, many theorists believe that our capacity for language sets us apart from other animals, making us biologically unique (Chomsky, 1972; Lenneberg, 1967). For these reasons, it is important to understand how we perceive speech.

Categorical Perception

In spoken language, words having different meanings are, except for homonyms and the like, distinguished by different speech sounds. The smallest parts of language that lead to differences in word meanings are called *phonemes*. The words *pin* and *bin* differ in meaning, and the two words are distinguished only by their initial sounds. Accordingly, these different initial sounds are said to belong to separate phonemes designated as /p/ and /b/. These same phonemes also distinguish many other pairs of words such as *pat* and *bat,* and *pill* and *bill.* Of course, the phonemes that distinguish between words having different meanings do not always occur in the initial position in the words, as shown by *but* and *bet, top* and *ton,* and *run* and *ran.*

The phonemes that occur in English do not occur in all languages. For example, English contains the /l/ - /r/ distinction (as in *late* and *rate*), but Japanese does not, and Japanese people tend not to hear the difference between those sounds (Miyawaki, Strange, Verbugge, Liberman, Jenkins, and Fujimura, 1975). It is understandable, then, that native speakers of Japanese who are learning to speak English often have difficulty mastering the /l/ - /r/ distinction. Similarly, the initial sounds of *keep* and *cool* do not belong to different phonemes in English but they do in Arabic, and we would probably experience difficulty in mastering that distinction in learning Arabic. In general, then, speakers of a language tend not to notice the difference between two speech sounds unless those sounds belong to different phonemes in their language. In other words, speakers perceive the sounds of their language in terms of the phonemic categories of their language. In order to show this clearly, we must first consider some physical properties of speech.

SPEECH STIMULI

When we speak, we produce sound waves. Two important properties of these waves are frequency and amplitude. The frequency of the sound waves determines their pitch, whereas the amplitude of the waves determines their loudness. To study the acoustic properties of speech, a device called a speech spectrograph is used. Simply put, a speech spectrograph converts acoustic patterns of speech into a visible record which shows the frequency and the amplitude of the speech stimulus over time. Figure 2.11 shows the spectrogram of the word *bib*. In this spectrogram, the frequency is represented on the vertical dimension, the duration is represented on the horizontal dimension, and the amplitude is shown by the darkness of the record. The three darker regions of the spectrogram are areas of high energy concentration called *formants;* formants carry much of the information that is required for speech perception (Massaro, 1975; Pisoni, 1978). The importance of formants and other acoustic properties of speech may be assessed by producing synthetic speech stimuli, varying a particular acoustic property such as the presence or absence

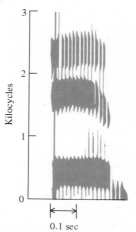

Figure 2.11   A speech spectrogram for the word *bib*. (After Strange and Jenkins, 1978.)

of a particular formant, and observing how people perceive the sounds. Just this approach has been used to analyze how we perceive stop consonants such as /b/, /d/, and /g/.

CATEGORICAL PERCEPTION OF STOP CONSONANTS

In an early experiment (Liberman, Harris, Hoffman, and Griffiths, 1957), 14 syllables were synthesized in such a way as to sound like *ba, da,* or *ga.* The stimuli contained two formants and differed only with respect to the direction and the extent of the transitions of the upper or second formant. Schematic spectrograms of the 14 stimuli are shown in Figure 2.12a. In the series of 14 stimuli, the physical differences between adjacent stimuli were equal. For example, the physical difference between stimuli 2 and 3 was equal to that between stimuli 4 and 5 or between 10 and 11. When the stimuli were presented one at a time in a random order, adults identified the stimuli as shown in Figure 2.12b. Stimuli 1 through 3 were identified as /b/, 5 through 9 were identified as /d/, and 10 through 14 were identified as /g/. Note that the categories did not gradually fade into the adjacent ones. Rather, the shifts from one category to the next were abrupt, suggesting that the stimuli were not perceived as a continuous series but as members of only three discrete categories.

The preceding results show how subjects assigned the phonemic labels, but the question remained whether the subjects could actually hear the differences between stimuli that were given the same label. After all, we may label numerous visual stimuli *red* even though we can discern their differences. To decide whether the subjects could discriminate the differences between the stimuli they labelled the same, an ABX test of discrimination was given. In each trial, three stimuli were presented briefly one after another. The first two (designated A and B) always differed, and the third stimulus (X) matched one of the first two. The subjects' task was to indicate whether the third stimulus matched the first or the second stimulus. If the subjects can discriminate between the first two stimuli, then they should correctly indicate on a large percentage of trials which of the first two stimuli matched the third one. But if they failed to discriminate between the first two stimuli, then they would have to guess and could make the correct response on only about 50% of the trials. By presenting all possible pairs of the 14 stimuli, the experimenters determined which pairs of stimuli the subjects could or could not discriminate between.

The results of the discrimination procedure were in striking agreement with the results of the preceding identification procedure. For example, the subjects classified stimuli one and three as belonging to the /b/ phoneme, and in the discrimination procedure, they failed to discriminate between these stimuli. In contrast, discrimination accuracy

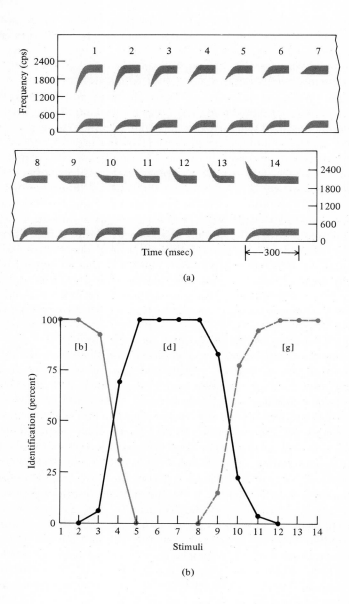

Figure 2.12 The identification of the syllables *ba, da,* and *ga.* (a) Schematic spectrograms of the stimuli that were classified. (b) The identification functions for the /b/, /d/, and /g/ sounds. (After Liberman, Harris, Hoffman and Griffith, 1957. Copyright © 1957 by the American Psychological Association. All rights reserved.)

was high at the boundaries between phonemes. For example, the subjects discriminated accurately between stimuli three and five, which belonged to the phonemes /b/ and /d/, respectively. Overall, the subjects discriminated between stimuli from different phonemes but not from the same phoneme, even when the acoustic differences between the stimuli were about equal. Apparently, the subjects heard the differences between phonemic categories but not within particular categories. This phenomenon is called *categorical perception.*

Further research has established that many different consonants are perceived categorically, whereas vowels tend not to be (for reviews, see Pisoni, 1978; Studdert-Kennedy, 1974). But even in consonants, categorical perception arises from a combination of perceptual and nonperceptual factors. For example, the ABX procedure described above requires subjects to remember the A and B stimuli while comparing them to the X stimulus. Perhaps the categorical perception observed in the ABX procedure arises in part from the memory demands implicit in the task. In keeping with this suggestion, the perception of consonants appears to be less categorical in tasks that relax the memory demands of the ABX task (Pisoni, 1978). For example, if the subjects hear two rather than three stimuli on a trial and simply indicate whether they are the same or different, they do show some ability to discriminate the differences between stimuli within a phonemic category (Pisoni and Tash, 1974).

Memory-related factors may also influence performance in studies of categorical perception by virtue of the fact that many procedures require the subjects to label the stimuli, for example, as *ba* or *da* (Massaro, 1975; Rep, Healy, and Crowder, 1979). Conceivably, the subjects do notice the differences among the stimuli within a particular category but treat them as the same because they have a common label. Yet this account cannot explain all aspects of categorical perception. For example, categorical perception has been observed in preverbal infants who have not developed the skill of labelling (cf. Eimas, 1978). Overall, then, categorical perception of consonants does seem to be a genuine perceptual phenomenon (Ades, 1977; Pisoni, 1978).

THE ORIGIN AND UNIQUENESS OF CATEGORICAL PERCEPTION

In categorical perception, as in many aspects of cognition, both biological and experiential factors play an important role. The contribution of experience is shown by the differences in speech perception among adults who speak different languages. As mentioned previously, Americans discriminate easily between /l/ and /r/, as in the words *late* and *rate,* whereas Japanese do not. Moreover, Americans perceive the /l/ - /r/ distinction categorically (Miyawaki et al., 1975). Similarly, English and Thai speakers both perceive *ba* and *pa* sounds categorically, but they locate the phonemic boundary in different places. Additionally, Thai speakers distinguish three phonemic categories whereas we distinguish only two (Abramson and Lisker, 1970; Lisker and Abramson, 1964).

These between-language differences in the number and the location of phonemic categories probably arise from the different linguistic experiences of the subjects. This interpretation is suggested by the results of several developmental studies (Strange and Jenkins, 1978). For example, Kikuyu children begin learning to speak English as a second language when they are about 8 years old. Although at age 7 they do not distinguish between *ba* and *pa* as speakers of English do, they do come to make that discrimination with increased age and experience (Streeter and Landauer, 1976). Moreover, adults can be trained to discriminate between stimuli drawn from the same phonemic category (Carney, Widin, and Viemeister, 1977).

The effects of experience are pervasive, but they are not the only basis for categorical perception. For one thing, infants as young as 1 month old discriminate categorically some of the same speech sounds as adults (Eimas, 1978; Morse, 1978). At that early age, infants neither produce nor comprehend words. And since they have had limited exposure to language, their ability to discriminate categorically probably arises from biological factors. A more convincing result along similar lines is that infants from Spanish-speaking environments make some of the same categorical distinctions that infants from English-speaking environments do, even if those distinctions are not made in Spanish (Lasky, Syrdal-Lasky, and Klein, 1975). Since the infants had no exposure to English, these results are probably attributable to biological factors. This type of observation raises the possibility that we are born with particular built-in sensitivities to speech that are then confirmed or modified by our experience. It seems clear that both biological and experiential factors influence speech perception but we know little about how the two interact, and their underlying mechanisms are obscure.

Much of the interest in the categorical perception of speech arose because many simple auditory stimuli are not perceived categorically, and speech perception appeared unique. Subsequent studies, however, have demonstrated categorical perception of complex nonspeech sounds such as the musical sounds made by either plucking or bowing a violin (Cutting and Rosner, 1974; Miller, Wier, Pastore, Kelly, and Dooling, 1976). Apparently, categorical perception is not the sole privilege of speech stimuli. Nor does categorical perception appear unique to humans. For example, nonverbal animals such as chinchillas have been trained to discriminate between sounds from the /d/ and /t/ categories. Following training, they classified novel stimuli into the categories in much the same way adult humans do (Kuhl and Miller, 1975). Rhesus monkeys also show some ability to perceive speech sounds categorically and as humans do (Morse and Snowdon, 1975; Waters and Wilson, 1976).

Unlike humans, however, monkeys can discriminate accurately between stimuli belonging to the same category. Whether this difference between the performance of humans and nonhumans would disappear following extended training is unknown. At any rate, these results suggest that categorical perception may arise from general features of mammalian auditory systems rather than only from our particular biological specializations for language.

Context and Speech Perception

The recognition of speech stimuli, like the recognition of visual stimuli, is influenced extensively by context. Warren (1970), for example, presented adults with a recording of this sentence: *The state governors met with their respective legi°latures convening in the capital city.* The asterisk indicates that the initial *ess* sound in *legislatures* was deleted and replaced with the sound of a cough. Surprisingly, not one of the 20 subjects recognized that the *ess* sound had been deleted. They reported hearing the appropriate sound even though it had not been presented physically. This phenomenon, called the *phonemic restoration effect,* demonstrates compellingly that the context in which a sound occurs determines how that sound is perceived. Because of the effects of context, we may fail to even notice the mispronunciations that occur in everyday speech (Cole, 1973; Marslen-Wilson and Welsh, 1978).

The extensive influence of context attests to the importance of conceptually driven processing in the perception of speech. Speech perception involves much more than passively detecting acoustic cues—it is an act of construction guided by our expectations and our knowledge (Neisser, 1967; Pisoni, 1978). This idea has provided the basis for the development of computer programs that recognize speech (Reddy and Newell, 1975). Although researchers in the field of artificial intelligence have not designed machines that can recognize speech nearly as well as humans do, the success of machine recognition systems, like that of the human recognition system, seems to depend on how well they use contextual information.

SERIAL AND PARALLEL PROCESSING

Up to this point, we have seen that we recognize patterns by analyzing elementary features and holistic units and that both the incoming data and our expectations guide the flow of processing. But we have not considered one of the fundamental questions to be asked about any processing mechanism: does processing occur serially or in parallel? *Serial processing* involves analyzing one item at a time, whereas *parallel processing* involves analyzing numerous items simultaneously.

The question whether perceptual processing occurs serially or in parallel is important in part because it pertains to the widely held view that we have limited processing capacity. The relationship between capacity limitations and the type of processing is illustrated by an analogy. Factory workers who assemble engines have a limited capacity for work—they can do only so much in a particular period of time. By working on only one engine at a time, they devote full capacity to each engine on the line. This serial processing approach allows for the assembly of each engine without exceeding the limited capacity of the worker. If a worker were required to assemble three engines simultaneously and in a short period of time, the capacity of the worker would be strained, and full assembly would be impossible. The same points apply to perceptual processing. If our processing capacity is limited, then we might have to process incoming items serially. In that way, sufficient capacity would be devoted to each item to allow for recognition. If, on the other hand, our processing capacity were unlimited, then we could engage in parallel processing. Capacity limitations are mentioned here in order to show the broader implications of the question whether processing occurs serially or in parallel. In the following chapter, we shall discuss capacity limitations in detail. For now, we shall concentrate on whether pattern recognition involves serial or parallel processing and on the effects of practice.

Evidence from Studies of Reaction Time

One way to determine whether serial or parallel processing occurs in pattern recognition is to see whether adults can search for numerous targets in a display as well as they can search for one. If the subjects can find any of three targets as fast and as accurately as they can find one, that would suggest the occurrence of parallel processing. On the other hand, if searching for three targets took three times longer than searching for one, that would suggest that the subjects had searched serially for one target after another. Following similar logic, serial or parallel processing might be detected by varying the number of nontarget items in the stimulus array. If processing were serial rather than parallel, more time should be required to find a target in a ten-item array than in a five-item array. The reason is that it takes time to search for each item, and there are twice as many items to search for in a ten-item array than in a five-item array.

In an extensive set of experiments, Schneider and Shiffrin (1977; Shiffrin and Schneider, 1977) examined the effects of both the number of targets and the size of the array being searched. The exact procedures used were very complicated, and a simplified version is presented here for the sake of clarity. In one experiment, arrays containing either letters or digits were presented for 160 msec. The task of the subjects was to indicate as quickly as possible whether the array contained a predesignated target item. The number of items in the stimulus array was varied systematically across trials. For example, the array that was presented on one trial might have contained the letters Z and F, and the target letters might have been Z and Q. On other trials, the subjects might have searched for the targets Z and Q in an array containing four rather than two letters. If serial processing were occurring, then it should take longer to find the targets in a four-item array than in a two-item array. In this experiment, the number of target items was also varied over trials. For example, the subjects sometimes searched for one target and sometimes searched for four targets in an array of four letters. Once again, the prediction was that if serial processing were occurring, then it should take longer to find each of four targets than only one target.

The results of the experiment confirmed both predictions: it took longer to find the targets in larger stimulus arrays than in smaller ones. And it took longer to search for four targets than for only one target. Both outcomes indicate that the subjects scanned the arrays serially, processing one item at a time.

Serial processing is not inevitable, however, as shown by the results of a second experiment. The procedure matched that described above with two exceptions. First, the stimulus arrays contained both letters and digits, and the target items and the nontarget items belonged to different categories. On some trials, the target items were letters and the nontarget items were digits, whereas the reverse was true on other trials. Second, the items that were used as targets in some trials served as nontargets in other trials. The results of this experiment contrasted dramatically with those of the first experiment. The subjects searched large arrays as fast as small arrays, and they searched for four targets as fast as they searched for one target. These results show that the subjects processed the items in a parallel rather than a serial manner.

The results of these two experiments and many others (Shiffrin, 1976) establish that there is no single answer to the question whether pattern recognition involves serial or parallel processing. Serial processing occurs under some conditions, whereas parallel processing occurs under other conditions. The question that arises now is what kinds of factors lead to the occurrence of serial and parallel processing. Part of the answer to this question lies in the effects of practice, which we now examine.

The Effects of Practice

When people initially search for targets in arrays of items, they take longer to search for multiple targets than for a single target, which suggests that they had been processing serially. But following extended practice in the same task, they often search for many targets as rapidly as they search for one (cf. Rabbitt, 1978). In fact, Neisser, Novick, and Lazar (1963) observed that well-practiced subjects searched effectively for as many as ten targets as fast as they searched for one. Apparently, then, subjects initially engage in serial processing, but, following additional practice, they switch over to parallel processing. This type of switch also occurs in pattern recognition tasks outside of the laboratory. For example, try scanning newspapers for information concerning the price of gold. Because you have not had extensive practice, you probably searched slowly, scanning one column or even one line at a time. In contrast, professional news scanners search thousands of words each minute, scanning numerous columns in parallel.

AUTOMATICITY

One way in which extended practice might influence performance in tasks requiring pattern recognition is by allowing the recognition process to become automatic. An automatic process is one that is executed smoothly, effortlessly, and without conscious guidance. Automatic processing is involved in many everyday activities such as walking and eating. For example, we have had so much practice at walking that we now walk in a coordinated manner without jerking and swaying. And although we do have to think consciously about where we are walking, we do not have to think about how to walk, for example, about how to move our arms or to place one foot in front of the other. In much the same way, practice might enable us to recognize patterns automatically without effort or conscious control.

One implication of this view is that once items have come to be processed automatically, it will be difficult to ignore them even if processing them interferes with performance. Since the items are processed without conscious control, they cannot be ignored intentionally. This implication has been tested by Schneider and Shiffrin (1977). In the first phase of their experiment, adults searched for four target letters in briefly presented arrays of two letters. The targets were consonants from one half of the alphabet, and the nontarget items were consonants from the other half. Phase one continued for 1500 trials, long enough to allow for the development of automatic recognition. The results, shown by the solid line in Figure 2.13, were that performance became much more accurate following extended training than it had been initially. Additionally, the reaction times decreased markedly during training.

In the second phase of the experiment, the target and the nontarget items were reversed. Otherwise, the procedure matched that of the first phase. If in phase one the subjects had learned to detect the targets automatically, then their performance in phase two should have suffered ini-

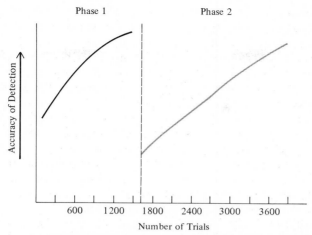

Figure 2.13   Idealized data from the experiment by Schneider and Shiffrin (1977), showing the effects of practice on pattern recognition.

tially. Presumably, the targets from phase one would continue to be recognized automatically, thereby interfering with the detection of the new
targets in phase two. As shown by the lighter line in Figure 2.13, performance did suffer initially when the target and the nontarget items
were reversed. For example, the level of accuracy during the first 600
trials of phase two was lower than it had been on the very first trials of
phase one. Further, it took over 2100 trials for performance to rise in
phase two to the high level that had been achieved in 900 trials during
phase one. At least in the initial stages of phase two, then, the subjects
failed to ignore the targets from phase one.

Overall, these results suggest that continued practice leads to automatic processing over which the subjects have little or no conscious control. The concept of automatic processing will be examined further in
our discussion of attention. For now, the chief point is that the development of automatic processing may allow for the occurrence of parallel
rather than serial processing.

PRACTICE AND THE UNITS OF PROCESSING

In concluding this section, we should note that practice may enable subjects to process relatively large or global units, and the results may mimic
those which occur through parallel processing. For example, LaBerge
(1973) presented two stimuli briefly and successively, and he asked subjects to indicate as quickly as possible whether the two stimuli matched.
On some trials, familiar stimuli such as the letters *b* and *q* were presented. On other trials, unfamiliar stimuli such as ⌐ and ⌐ were presented. The results were that early in the experiment, the subjects re-

sponded much faster to familiar than to unfamiliar stimuli. After five days of practice, however, the subjects came to match familiar and unfamiliar stimuli equally fast.

These results are subject to two different interpretations. One is that the unfamiliar patterns were initially analyzed serially, one feature at a time. But added practice led to the occurrence of parallel processing of the features, thereby reducing the reaction times. A second interpretation is that the subjects initially processed the individual features of the unfamiliar patterns in a serial manner. But following added training, the stimuli came to be processed as coherent units. As a result, the subjects could perform the task by comparing two global units rather than a larger number of smaller, elementary units. In turn, comparing fewer units could have reduced the amount of processing time. So the decreased reaction times that occurred could indicate a changeover from serial to parallel processing or a modification in the size of the unit of processing. Of course, both changes may have contributed to the results, though additional experiments are required to settle the issue.

Collectively, these observations show clearly that it is inappropriate to cast humans as either serial or parallel processors or to dispute whether we process in global or local units. Cognition is flexible and may change through experience, and the theories we construct must accommodate these facts.

• *Summary.* In order to survive, we must recognize many different stimuli. Some stimuli are present too briefly to allow for the occurrence of recognition. Fortunately, incoming stimuli are remembered in a relatively simple form for a brief period of time. This initial stage of processing is called sensory memory, and its function is to preserve incoming information long enough to allow pattern recognition and further processing to occur. When visual stimuli are presented, the contents of sensory memory may include information regarding the physical properties of the stimulus such as its size, shape, color, brightness, and motion. Sensory memory also contains some categorical information, for example, the information that distinguishes between the categories of letters and digits. Both the rods and the cones contribute to visual sensory memory, also called iconic memory. Sensory memory was initially conceived of as a passive storage phenomenon. The conception now emerging, however, is that sensory memory is the outcome of diverse processes that occur in the initial stages that lead to pattern recognition.

Recognizing patterns involves numerous processes that may proceed simultaneously and in a continuous flow under everyday conditions. Behavioral and physiological evidence indicates that we may recognize patterns such as letters in part by detecting their elementary features, such as vertical, horizontal, and curved lines. Feature detection alone, however, fails to tell the entire story of pattern recognition. Stimuli may be perceived in a holistic manner by matching them with a stored representation of the best example of a category; this is the essence of the prototype theory. Additionally, some simple stimuli seem to go together perceptually, and a growing body of evidence shows that we can process higher-order global, integrated units. Some models emphasize holistic processing, whereas others stress piecemeal analysis. However, pattern recognition, like many aspects of cognition, cannot be made to conform to oversimplified dichotomies. Holistic and partwise analyses may alternate in the cycle of processing. Which type of analysis predominates depends upon factors such as the types of stimuli presented and how well-practiced the subjects are.

Pattern recognition does not come about solely through processing the stimuli in the immediate environment. In a particular context, some patterns are more likely to occur than others, and our expectations about what is likely to occur may influence how incoming information is processed. If we expect to see a particular word in a particular place in a sentence, we might look specifically for the particular global characteristics we know the expected word has, and we might process the entire word as a single unit. Alternatively, we might select some elementary features for analysis while neglecting others. Context influences which aspects of the sensory data before us we process, but it may also determine how those data are perceived. Identical features of stimuli may be interpreted in different ways depending upon the context. And in perceiving speech, we may hear particular speech sounds appropriate to a particular context even when no physical sound waves occurred. These observations indicate that pattern recognition is often an active, interpretative process in which internal representations are constructed.

We may perceive some types of biologically important patterns through unique processes. Early research concerning categorical perception suggested that speech perception involved unique processes. We say that we perceive speech categorically because we do not normally hear the differences between physically different sounds belonging to a category, such as the category of *ba* sounds. But we do hear the differences between two sounds from different categories such as *pa* and *ba*, even though the latter two sounds are no more different physically than are the two sounds from within the *ba* category. Categorical perception has both genetic and experiential determinants, and the categories heard by speakers of one language may not be heard by the speakers of a different language. Categorical perception has turned out to be less unique than it initially appeared to be, for it has been observed in nonhumans listening to speech stimuli and in humans listening to nonspeech stimuli.

The effects of experience are evident also in studies of serial and parallel processing. In serial processing, one item at a time is analyzed, whereas in parallel processing, numerous items are analyzed simultaneously. Early in training, serial processing often occurs, for subjects take longer to search for multiple targets than for a single target. Following extended practice, however, multiple items may be processed automatically and in parallel. These effects of practice attest to the flexibility of cognitive processing.

Chapter 3
Attention and Immediate Memory

Attention is a familiar process, closely related to the acquisition and the retention of information. Consider, for example, the commonplace activity of looking up a phone number. As we scan a page of telephone listings, we concentrate on particular names and numbers, and the remaining items on the page remain a hazy blur on the fringes of our conscious awareness. Having found the correct name, we read the corresponding number, thereby acquiring the desired information. As we concentrate on the number, the number stands clearly in our minds, and it occupies our awareness for a short period of time, long enough to dial the number. Yet several minutes later, the number will be difficult to recall. It is as if the number had faded away after we had stopped attending to it. As this example shows, attending to an item establishes that item in memory, but only for a brief period of time. This brief memory, which usually lasts under half a minute, is called *immediate memory*. It differs from sensory memory in that the information in immediate memory has been fully recognized and can be maintained indefinitely through rehearsal.

The link between attention and immediate memory is particularly apparent in the results of studies that have measured the *span of appre-hension,* the number of briefly presented items that can be recalled im-mediately. The procedure used in these studies can be illustrated by an example. Read the following string of digits at the rate of about one per second, then look away and try to recall the digits in order:

7 9   1   4   0

Now do the same with regard to this string of digits:

2   6   5   8   9   3   1   4   7   0   5   3

Most likely, you recalled the first string completely but recalled only part of the second string, perhaps about seven digits. Many studies that have used this type of procedure have shown that the span of apprehension, also called the span of immediate memory or simply the memory span, is usually limited to about seven items, give or take two (Miller, 1956; Woodworth, 1938). You may recall that this limitation occurred in Sperling's studies of iconic memory, for the subjects in the whole report condition recalled only five or so items correctly. Sometimes, the span of apprehension is thought of as the number of items that can be attended to simultaneously. At other times, it is thought of as the number of items that can be held in immediate memory. The two conceptions are com-patible because immediate memory and attention overlap extensively.

In everyday situations, we sometimes attend selectively by pro-cessing some items fully while ignoring other items or processing them partially. In the first section of this chapter, we examine models of selec-tive attention, which, historically, have shaped the direction of research. The early models held that selective attention occurred at a particular stage of processing. For example, one influential model stated that the physical features of all incoming stimuli are analyzed (Broadbent, 1958). But because of our limited capacity for processing, we attend selectively to one stimulus by filtering out or rejecting the competing stimuli. Sub-sequent research, however, revealed problems with this conception. For one thing, we can sometimes attend to two tasks at the same time, as we do when we walk and talk simultaneously. This observation and many others is accounted for best by the *model of resource allocation.* This model states that people have a limited processing capacity, that is, lim-ited processing resources, that can be used in a flexible manner to satisfy the demands of various tasks. The model is so useful that it provides our definition of attention: attention is the process of allocating cognitive re-sources. Using the model as an organizational framework, we shall exam-ine selective attention, divided attention, and the effects of practice upon the development of attentional skills and automaticity.

In the second section of this chapter, we extend the model of re-source allocation to the topic of immediate memory. We shall investigate the phenomena pertaining to organization, forgetting, and retrieval in immediate memory. Because our processing resources are limited, the capacity of immediate memory is limited to about seven units of information. Through practice, however, we can organize many individual items into seven larger chunks of information. As a result, we can increase our memory span substantially. Nevertheless, forgetting continues to occur. We will see that some forgetting results from the passage of time. But forgetting also results from failures to retrieve information and to allocate sufficient resources to the task of remembering. In the final section of the chapter, we examine retrieval processes, in particular, the processes through which the information in immediate memory is searched.

ATTENDING

The term "attention" applies to many different phenomena. When someone is consciously aware of one stimulus but not of others, we say that the person is attending selectively to the first stimulus. But attention is not always selective. Skilled drivers can drive in light traffic and engage simultaneously in a casual conversation. In cases such as this, we say that divided attention occurs. Further, attention does not always occur consciously. For example, in driving, we are not always consciously aware of what we are doing, yet we are in a sense attending to driving. In this section, we seek to unite these phenomena—selective attention, divided attention, and nonconscious attention—into a unified framework.

Selective Attention

Selective attention pervades many everyday activities. As you try to follow a difficult lecture, you focus your concentration on the meaning of the words spoken by the lecturer, but you do not notice the sounds of the traffic outside, the positions of your feet, or the movements of those around you. Similarly, in carrying on a conversation at a crowded, noisy party, you attend specifically to the conversation in which you are engaged and ignore other conversations. But even when our attention seems riveted, it may remain flexible. If we hear our name or an important topic arise in another conversation, we may try to follow both conversations by switching attention back and forth between the two.

Beneath the simplicity of these examples lie a number of complex issues. What cues do we use to separate and to attend selectively to one input rather than others? Do we recognize all of the incoming stimuli and then attend selectively to one input, or does selection occur before pattern recognition has been completed? Is our processing capacity so strictly limited that we are forced to attend to only one stimulus at a time?

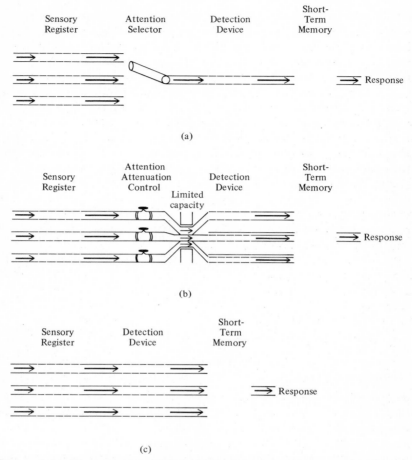

Figure 3.1   Three models of attention. (a) A filter model in which information from a single channel is analyzed. (b) The attenuation model in
which inputs can be attentuated at an early stage of analysis. (c) The
model of late selection. (From Shiffrin, Craig, and Cohen, 1973.)

In order to answer these questions and others, investigators have
used the *dichotic listening procedure,* which simulates listening at a
party. In this procedure, two auditory messages are presented simultaneously, one to each ear, by means of stereophonic headphones. The listener is instructed to attend to only the information presented to one ear.
To ensure that the subject in fact attends to that message, the subject
shadows the message by repeating each word aloud as soon as it occurs.
If no shadowing errors occur, then the subject must have attended to the
shadowed message.

Using the results of the dichotic listening procedure, investigators constructed and tested numerous models of attention, all of which have contributed to our present conceptions of attention. We now examine the filter model, the attenuation model, and the model of late selection.

THE FILTER MODEL

Cherry (1953) used the dichotic listening procedure to determine which, if any, aspects of the unshadowed message were noticed by the subjects. He had subjects shadow recordings of passages from a newspaper that were presented to one ear. To the other, nonattended ear, he presented recordings of a steady tone, normal English spoken by a male or a female, or speech played backwards. Later, he questioned the subjects about the unshadowed message. The results were that the subjects almost always reported correctly whether a tone had been presented and whether a male or a female had been speaking. In contrast, they failed to identify either the particular words from the unattended message or the language that had been spoken. Apparently, then, the subjects attended to the gross physical properties but not to the semantic properties of the un- shadowed message. It was as if they had rejected all but the physical as- pects of the unshadowed message. Similar observations were made by Moray (1959), who reported that subjects failed to recall the words from the unshadowed message even when those words had been repeated 35 times.

Broadbent (1958) explained these observations within the context of an overall processing model that provided the outlines of the multistore theory that was discussed briefly in Chapter 1. He proposed that the processing system acts as a single communication channel that has a lim- ited capacity. Because of the limited capacity, only one message at a time can receive the extensive processing required to determine the meaning of the message. Which of the numerous inputs receive attention is determined by a selective filter that permits only one message to pass. As shown in Figure 3.1a, the information in the sensory store is selected by means of a selective filter that can be directed at any one of several input channels. Only the information in the selected channel is analyzed semantically and transmitted to the short-term store. The details of Broadbent's overall theory are not of primary concern here. The impor- tant point is that he proposed that filtering is accomplished by analyzing and distinguishing between messages on the basis of their gross physical characteristics.

This filter model explains why Cherry's subjects had recognized whether a tone or a male or a female voice had occurred in the unshad- owed message. Presumably, the subjects had analyzed the physical properties of both the shadowed and the unshadowed messages. They then filtered out the unshadowed message and devoted full capacity to the shadowed message. Because they filtered out the unshadowed message at an early stage of analysis, they never identified the words in that message.

The central claim of the filter model is that we fully attend to and analyze the meaning of only one message at a time. How, then, can we understand two simultaneous conversations, as we do at parties? According to the filter model, we do so by switching back and forth rapidly between them. In this manner, we give the appearance of analyzing two messages simultaneously. But at a particular point in time, we attend fully to only one message. Through this approach, we monitor several events without overtaxing our limited capacity.

THE ATTENUATION MODEL

The filter model asserted that we select one message for full attention by analyzing the physical features of incoming messages. Subsequent studies, however, showed that selection can occur at numerous levels of analysis, including semantic levels. For example, Treisman (1964) instructed subjects to shadow a message presented to one ear. As the subjects shadowed, she presented the same message following a time lag to the other ear. The results were that the subjects detected that the two messages were identical. Further, bilingual subjects detected the identity of the two messages even when the messages had been spoken in two different languages. In a similar vein, Moray (1959) observed that subjects who were shadowing one message sometimes noticed the presentation of their names in the unshadowed message. Taken together, these observations show that people do process the meaning of information in the unshadowed message. These observations contradict the filter model, which held that people process the physical properties but not the meanings of items in the unshadowed message.

In order to account for these observations, Treisman (1964) proposed an *attenuation model* that stated that incoming messages are subjected to a series of tests. The first tests analyze the physical properties of the messages; the second tests analyze patterns of syllables and particular words; the third tests analyze the meanings of the words. All three tests are not always executed, for the analysis ends at whichever level distinguishes between the two messages. Assume, for example, that you had been instructed to shadow the message coming to only your left ear and that the messages presented to your left and right ears had been spoken by a male and by a female, respectively. Because the two messages can be distinguished by their physical properties, only the first-level tests are conducted. But if the first tests had failed to distinguish between the two messages, then the second tests would have been executed, and so on. The level at which selection occurs, then, depends on how the two messages differ.

The attenuation model diverges from the filter model in two respects. First, the filter model held that attentional selection occurs on the basis of physical analyses and that the meaning of the unattended message is not analyzed. Treisman's model, on the other hand, held that attentional selection can occur on the basis of numerous analyses, even semantic ones, and that the meaning of the unattended message is processed on some occasions. In Treisman's model, then, the analyses that guide attentional selection, called *preattentive analyses* (Neisser, 1967), may be more complex than the simple physical analyses emphasized by the filter model. Second, the filter model held that the selective process occurred in an all-or-none manner by means of the switching of the filter. In contrast, Treisman proposed that selection occurs through a process of attenuation, as illustrated in Figure 3.1b. The information from all of the channels is analyzed and transmitted to the short-term store. But the information has been attenuated or reduced because of limited processing capacity. On this view, the unattended information is not filtered out entirely but may be processed less fully than the attended information.

EARLY AND LATE SELECTION

The attenuation model provided a more complete account of the data discussed above than the filter model did. Yet the attenuation model had a serious flaw: it was too complex. The attenuation model was proposed at a time when theorists already had a complex processing model, the multistore model. The notion of filtering during the early stages of processing did not add much complexity to the overall model of processing, for filtering involved the analysis of simple physical features. But the attenuation model proposed that selection can occur at one of several levels, thereby adding a substantial degree of complexity to the overall model. In hopes of simplifying the theory of information processing, some investigators began to ask whether it is necessary to postulate a complex attentional mechanism that operates at the early stages of processing. Could the selection of information occur at a later stage of analysis, for example, at the stage of short-term memory?

Numerous theorists answered this question affirmatively (Deutsch and Deutsch, 1963; Norman, 1968; Shiffrin and Gardner, 1972). Although they proposed various models, they agreed that selection occurs at a late stage of analysis, as shown in Figure 3.1c. This model of late selection rejects the notion of an early attentional mechanism. All incoming information is transmitted in parallel to the short-term store. Because the short-term store has a limited capacity, it can neither store all of the incoming information nor transmit it to the long-term store. As a result, a selective process occurs: some information is lost from the short-term store when the capacity of the store has been exceeded, whereas some information is retained. One advantage of this model is that it allows for the occurrence of selection without adding a complex attentional mechanism to an already complex model of processing.

The chief difference between the model of late selection and the attenuation model concerns the stage at which attentional selection occurs. The attenuation model is a model of early selection since it holds that selection occurs in the early stages of processing, often before pattern recognition has occurred. The model of late selection, on the other hand, holds that all incoming information is recognized and that selection occurs at the stage of short-term memory. For this reason, the model of late selection predicts that all incoming information will be recognized, even if the information is presented in the unshadowed message in a dichotic listening procedure.

In one experiment that tested this prediction (Lewis, 1970), subjects were told to shadow lists of words presented to one ear and to ignore the words presented to the other ear. Some of the words that were presented to the unattended ear were synonyms of the words that were presented to the attended ear. For example, *large* might have been presented to the unattended ear just before *big* had been presented to the attended ear. The experimenter measured the shadowing latency, the amount of time that elapsed from the presentation of a word to the subject's response of saying the word. The results were that it took the subjects longer to shadow a word (*big*) when a synonym (*large*) had just been presented to the unattended ear than when a semantically unrelated word (*hat*) had just been presented to the unattended ear. Clearly, the subjects had processed the meaning of the words presented to the unattended ear. Further, they had processed the semantic relationship between the words that had been presented to the two ears. The occurrence of such extensive semantic processing supports the model of late selection but not the model of early selection. The model of late selection is also supported by the observation, discussed earlier, that people can search for numerous targets in parallel. Apparently, incoming items are not attenuated before pattern recognition has occurred.

At this point, we see that there is some empirical support for the models of both early selection and late selection. Which model is correct? This question has been difficult to answer, for it has been all but impossible to do a crucial experiment that falsifies one model and supports the other decisively. The difficulty of determining the stage at which selective attention occurs led many investigators to re-examine their assumptions. In asking at which stage selection occurs, they had been assuming that processing can be divided into a sequence of stages:

sensory memory - feature analysis - recognition - short-term memory

The trouble is that this conception emphasizes data driven processing rather than conceptually driven processing. But we saw earlier that se- mantic and conceptual analyses influence the processing of incoming in- formation. Further, this conceptually driven processing can occur at the same time as data driven processing. Thus it is inappropriate to ask whether attention precedes or follows semantic analyses, for semantic analyses can occur throughout all phases of processing. This view is part of the foundation of the model of resource allocation.

Attention as Resource Allocation

The evidence discussed above shows that we often attend selectively to one task at a time. Yet in many everyday situations, we seem to be able to divide our attention between two tasks. For example, as you drive along a familiar road in little traffic, it is easy to carry on a conversation with a friend. Similarly, we often walk and talk simultaneously with no interfer- ence between the two activities. A complete theory of attention must explain why selective attention occurs under some conditions whereas divided attention occurs under others.

One useful conception that applies to both selective and divided at- tention is the model of resource allocation, though it is less a formal model than a framework that guides research. According to Kahneman (1973) and to Norman and Bobrow (1975), the developers of the model, we have a limited pool of cognitive resources that we use in processing information. We attend to a task such as learning a list of words by allo- cating resources to that task. If the task is difficult, it engages most of our processing resources, so few resources are available for performing an- other task simultaneously. In this type of condition, selective attention will occur. For example, carrying on a deep conversation might occupy so many of our processing resources that we have to choose between driving and talking. If, however, the task is simple, it engages few of our processing resources, so sufficient resources are available for performing other tasks simultaneously. In this type of condition, divided attention can occur. For example, carrying on a casual conversation occupies few resources, so we have the resources required to simultaneously drive a car.

The resource allocation model holds that we use our limited re- sources in a flexible manner (Kahneman, 1973). For example, if we were dissatisfied with our performance on a task such as reading, we could increase our effort, thereby devoting additional resources to the task. The manner in which we allocate our resources depends partly upon situational factors. While driving in light traffic, we might allocate some resources to driving and other resources to thinking. But if a child suddenly ran into our path, we would allocate almost all of our resources to driving. As a result, we would have to stop thinking about other matters. Thus the model depicts attention as a flexible process, a process of allocating resources.

The resource allocation model makes numerous predictions. First, it predicts that we can perform two tasks concurrently without interference, provided that the combined demands of the two tasks do not exceed our limited resources. Second, it predicts that the performance of one task will interfere with the simultaneous performance of another task when the two tasks combined demand more processing resources than are available. Third, it predicts that subjects can tailor their allocation policy in accordance with the demands of the task. We next examine evidence bearing on all three points.

EVIDENCE OF FLEXIBLE RESOURCE ALLOCATION
Posner and Boies (1971; Posner and Klein, 1973) asked subjects to perform two simultaneous tasks involving letter matching and tone detection. In each trial of the letter matching task, a warning signal, a cross, was presented on a screen for half a second. Then a letter such as A was flashed on the screen for 50 msec. Following a delay of one second, a second letter was presented on the screen. The subjects' task was to indicate whether the two letters were identical or different by pressing one of two buttons as quickly as possible. The subjects were told to devote their attention primarily to the letter matching task, the primary task. In the tone detection task, the secondary task, a tone was presented via headphones, and the subjects tapped a key as quickly as possible when they heard a tone. The tones were presented at various positions within the trials, as illustrated in Figure 3.2a. The tones were also presented in between trials. The logic behind this procedure was that performance on the tone detection task provided a measure of how much processing capacity was devoted to the primary task. If a tone came on when no letters were being processed, the subjects could devote all of their resources to detecting the tone. But if a tone came on when the letters were being processed, then the two tasks might compete for limited resources, and performance on the tone detection task would suffer.

As shown in Figure 3.2b, the time required to detect the tones depended on the time at which the tone occurred. Point 1 shows how long

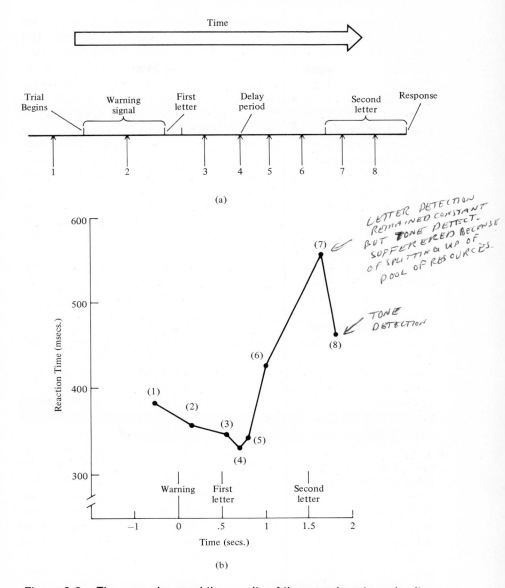

Figure 3.2   The procedure and the results of the experiment on simultaneous letter matching and tone detection. (a) The sequence of events in a single trial. The numbers designate the points at which tones were presented intermittently. The subjects responded to the tones as they performed the letter matching task. (b) The time required to detect the tones at various points during the trials. (From Posner and Boies, 1971. Copyright 1971 by the American Psychological Association. Reprinted by permission.)

it took to detect the tones that occurred in between trials, and it provides a baseline or point of reference against which the reaction times from within the trials may be compared. Note first that the subjects detected the tones faster when the warning signal was on (Point 2) than during the time in between the trials (Point 1). That outcome probably reflected a temporary increase in the level of alertness or arousal. According to Posner (1978), *alertness* is a nonspecific state of readiness in which one is prepared to perceive all new inputs and to perform various tasks. For example, when a race director says *Runners on your mark, get ready,* the runners enter a state of heightened alertness in which they are prepared to perceive all stimuli (including the word *Go!*) and to run as fast as possible. The effects of alertness are consistent with the resource allocation model, which assumes that as the level of alertness increases, more resources become available and are utilized, thereby improving performance (Kahneman, 1973).

When the tones occurred within 300 msec of the presentation of the first letter, as at Points 3, 4, and 5, the reaction times stayed at the low level that had occurred during the warning signal. Yet during those 300 msec, the subjects processed and recognized the first letter. Because the first letter had been presented for only 50 msec, it must have been processed during either that time or, more likely, in the following 250 msec in which it was retained in sensory memory. Since the reaction times did not increase as the first letter was processed for recognition, we may conclude that the subjects had sufficient resources that they were able to process the letter and to detect the tone simultaneously and without interference. This observation, then, confirms the prediction that we can do two things effectively at once when the combined demands of both tasks do not exceed the number of available resources.

When the tones occurred at Point 6, before the second letter had been presented, the reaction times increased. At that time, the subjects may have been rehearsing the first letter so that it would be fresh in their minds when the second letter appeared. A more dramatic increase in the reaction time occurred at Points 7 and 8, the times during which the subjects compared the two letters. The large increase in reaction time indicates that the comparison of the two letters required a significant number of available resources. Apparently, the combined demands of the comparison process and the detection process were so great that the performance on the detection task suffered. In contrast, the reaction times on the primary task, the letter comparison task, remained constant, regardless of the position at which the tones had been presented.

These results support the notion that performance suffers when the combined demands of two tasks exceed the total number of available resources. They also support the notion that subjects can tailor their allocation policy in accordance with the demands of the task. Because the reaction times varied on the secondary task but not on the primary task, we may conclude that the subjects allocated their resources in a manner that permitted them to maintain a high level of performance on the primary task. Collectively, these observations constitute impressive support for the resource allocation model.

The view that people can allocate their processing resources in a flexible manner has important practical implications. For example, if a first-grader were having difficulty in all aspects of learning, the teachers might be tempted to think that the child had a very low capacity for learning. If the teachers adopted that belief, they might lower their expectations about the child and contribute unwittingly to the child's poor performance. In fact, the child may have the resources required to learn at the usual rate. But he or she might not be allocating resources in the manner required to learn easily and quickly. Because performance often improves when additional resources are devoted to a task, one cannot infer a limitation of capacity from the performance that occurs under one set of conditions. Before conclusions can be made about the child's capacity, steps must be taken to encourage the child to devote additional resources to learning. The same point applies to studies conducted in the laboratory. Before concluding that processing capacity is too limited to allow people to perform two tasks simultaneously without interference, one must examine performance under diverse conditions designed to encourage subjects to use their resources in a more efficient manner (Norman and Bobrow, 1975).

EVALUATION OF THE MODEL

Having discussed the model and some of the evidence that supports it, we are now in a position to evaluate it. One of the principal advantages of the resource allocation model is that it accounts for the occurrence of both early selection and late selection in dichotic listening experiments. For example, late selection can occur when the primary task, the shadowing task, is relatively easy and there are sufficient resources available for analyzing simultaneously the meaning of the unshadowed message. In contrast, early selection might occur when the shadowing task is relatively difficult and there are too few resources available for analyzing simultaneously the meaning of the unshadowed message. Consistent with this view, Johnston and Heinz (1978) observed that more resources are required to distinguish between two messsages on the basis of semantic cues than on the basis of physical, sensory cues. In essence, the model holds that attention is a flexible process that cannot be pinned down to one particular stage of processing. The point at which selection occurs depends upon many factors, including the difficulty of the primary task, the number of resources available, and the allocation policy used by the subjects.

A related advantage is that the model disavows the idea that processing occurs in a fixed sequence of stages, beginning with sensory analyses and ending with semantic analyses. The model allows for the occurrence of this kind of data driven processing. But it also allows for the occurrence of conceptually driven processing in which expectations and semantic analyses influence the processing of incoming information (Norman, 1979). Thus the model encourages the view that processing proceeds not through a fixed sequence of stages but through the ongoing interaction between simple, physical analyses and sophisticated, semantic analyses.

The model is advantageous also because it encompasses diverse facets of attention. The models of early and late selection concerned the selection of incoming information. But that is only one facet of attention. As an illustration, try to remember what happened at the first party you attended in high school. As you recalled that episode, you probably felt your attention focus on past events and turn away from present events and incoming information. In other words, you were attending selectively to remember information. This example of selective attention is beyond the scope of the models of early and late selection, but it can be accommodated readily by the model of resource allocation. In remembering past events, we may use many resources, so many that we cannot simultaneously process present events. Thus the model applies to selective attention to both internal and external events. Further, the model can account for divided attention and for the effects of alertness. The major achievement of the model is that it unites these diverse aspects of attention around a single concept, resource allocation.

These advantages notwithstanding, the model leaves a number of fundamental questions unanswered. For example, what exactly are resources and how can they be measured? Because this question has not yet been answered, the model remains somewhat vague and difficult to test precisely.

The lack of a precise definition of resources makes it difficult for the model to explain fully why interference occurs between some tasks but not others. The model assumes that the performance of a primary task will interfere with the simultaneous performance of a secondary task when the combined demands of the two tasks exceed the available resources. Yet some observations suggest that there may be different kinds of resources, for example, resources that are used specifically to execute visual tasks. Interference can occur when two visual tasks use up the available visual resources, even though many resources may be available for use in nonvisual tasks. For example, Treisman and Davies (1973) measured performance on two simultaneous search tasks that were both visual (for example, searching lists of written words) or both auditory. A third condition, the mixed condition, included one auditory and one visual task. Much more interference occurred in the first two conditions in which the two tasks involved a single modality than in the mixed condition, in which the two tasks involved different modalities. The importance of devising measures of resources will become even more apparent in the following discussion of automaticity and the effects of practice.

Capacity, Skills, and Consciousness

The preceding discussion focused on the theory that attention is a process of allocating resources from a limited central pool. Yet this is only one conception of attention. For example, some investigators reject the assumption that our processing capacity or resources are limited. Investigators also disagree over the relation between attention and conscious awareness. Some equate attention with conscious awareness, whereas others argue that attention and awareness do not overlap completely. In this section, we probe further into the appropriate definition of attention. We begin by analyzing skills of divided attention as a means of examining the view that our processing capacity is limited. Then we inquire into automaticity and the relationship between attention and conscious awareness.

ARE PROCESSING RESOURCES LIMITED?

One of the central assumptions of the resource allocation model is that our processing resources are limited. This assumption of limited capacity agrees with the observations, described above, that performance on one task can suffer when we try to perform another task simultaneously. The assumption also agrees with our everyday observations. For example, we seem to be capable of performing a very simple task such as rocking in a rocking chair while reading. But most of us seem to be incapable of reading at our usual levels of speed and comprehension at the same time we perform another complex semantic task, for example, comprehending a news broadcast. We can, of course, switch attention back and forth rapidly between the two tasks. The point remains, however, that most of us do not perform both tasks simultaneously. You can verify this point for yourself by trying to do both things simultaneously and without switching.

We may be inherently limited in our capacity to perform two complex semantic tasks simultaneously. Yet it is possible that through extensive practice, people could perform two complex semantic tasks simultaneously and without interference (Hirst, Spelke, Reaves, Caharack, and

Neisser, 1980; Neisser, 1976). In order to test this hypothesis, Hirst et al. tried to train two adults to read and to take dictation simultaneously. The reading task involved reading short stories and taking frequent comprehension tests that consisted of questions about the general theme of the stories and about specific events that had been mentioned. The dictation task involved writing simple sentences such as *Spot got free* or *A fire alarm went off* that were dictated at a rate of 25 to 30 words per minute. The experimenters did not instruct the subjects to try to understand the dictated material. Yet the dictation task encouraged semantic processing because people can take dictation more accurately when they understand the sentences they are copying. Each experimental session was divided into a series of two kinds of trials. During the reading-only trials, the subjects performed only the reading task. During the reading-dictation trials, the subjects read and took dictation simultaneously. By comparing reading speed and comprehension on the reading-only trials and on the reading-dictation trials, the experimenters determined whether the subjects had become capable of reading as well while taking dictation as while reading alone.

The results were that in the initial sessions of training, taking dictation interfered with reading, even when the dictated material consisted of short numbers, for example, 346. But following continued training, the two subjects read at the same levels of speed and comprehension whether they were taking dictation simultaneously or not. As the subjects became more proficient in performing both tasks at once, the experimenters increased the length of the dictated sentences gradually. After 114 training sessions, one subject had learned to take dictation on five-word sentences with no loss in reading speed or comprehension. After 62 training sessions, the other subject had learned to take dictation on three-word sentences with no loss in reading speed or comprehension.

Following the completion of training, the experimenters tested whether the subjects had understood the dictated material. As the subjects were reading, the experimenters dictated sets of three sentences that described an episode, as in *The rope broke. Spot got free. Father chased him.* Then they presented three test sentences, for example (1) *Spot got free,* (2) *Spot's rope broke,* and (3) *Spot chased father.* The subjects classified each sentence as either familiar (dictated previously) or unfamiliar (not dictated previously). They also used a six-point scale to rate whether they were very confident, moderately confident, or uncertain that their responses were correct. The rationale was that if they had understood the episode described by the three dictated sentences, they would rate test sentence (2) as more familiar than sentence (3). For the meaning of (2) was consistent with the episode described by the dictated sentences, whereas the meaning of (3) was not. In fact, the results confirmed this prediction. Even on the very first test, which the subjects had not expected, the subjects gave higher familiarity ratings to sentences such as (2) than to sentences such as (3). Additionally, the subjects continued to read at the same levels of speed and comprehension whether they had been taking dictation simultaneously or not. We may conclude, then, that people can perform two complex semantic tasks simultaneously.

Based on these observations, Hirst et al. proposed that our processing capacity has virtually no limits and that we can learn to perform any two tasks at once, barring obvious physical limitations, for example, the limit on running and riding a bike simultaneously. This proposal is intriguing, but it has not yet been tested adequately. After all, the observation that two individuals learned to read and to take dictation simultaneously does not establish that anyone can learn to execute any two or more tasks simultaneously. Much more research is needed to decide whether the apparent limits on our processing capacity are surmountable. It should also be pointed out that the observations of Hirst et al. are consistent with the model of resource allocation. Perhaps the people who could read and take dictation simultaneously had limited processing resources but had learned through practice to use those resources efficiently.

This view emphasizes the importance of using one's resources in a skilled, efficient manner. One way in which practice might lead to the efficient use of the available resources is by producing large units of processing. Through practice, processes that had once been separate and sequential become amalgamated into holistic actions in which we do two or more things at once. This point is illustrated by an analogy with a physical skill, driving a car having a manual transmission. In order to slow down quickly, the driver executes four steps: braking with the right foot, depressing the clutch with the left foot, shifting to a lower gear, and releasing the clutch. The unskilled driver tends to execute these four steps one after another, as if each one had a separate identity. And the novice driver executes the steps in a poorly coordinated manner. Through practice, however, the driver learns to execute the steps as a single, well-coordinated action in which some steps, for example, braking and depressing the clutch, occur simultaneously. It is as if the steps have lost their individual identity and have fused into a holistic unit of action. Similarly, practice in performing two mental tasks simultaneously leads to the development of holistic attentional skills. In the early stages of practice, we may be forced to switch back and forth between two difficult tasks. But through practice, we might learn to perform both tasks as a single action. This outlook, which suggests that skilled performance involves the efficient use of processing resources, helps to clarify automatic processing.

AUTOMATICITY REVISITED

As discussed earlier, automatic processing is a highly skilled activity that occurs effortlessly and without conscious guidance. Activities that are performed automatically are probably so well learned that they require very few resources. If we think of activities as varying along a continuum of resource allocation, as shown in Figure 3.3, automatic processing falls at the end of the continuum at which the fewest resources are used. Because they require so few resources, these activities can be performed at the same time other activities are executed. This analysis agrees with the observation that, following extensive practice, people perform tasks such as recognizing letters automatically (see pages 71–74). As the processing of letters becomes automatic, it requires fewer and fewer resources. The result is that people can process letters in a parallel rather than a serial manner.

The view that automatic processing requires few resources illuminates the functions of automatic processing. As performance on a task becomes automatic, more and more resources become available for performing other tasks. In an emergency, having extra resources available can make the difference between life and death. For example, when scuba divers encounter danger and must rise to the surface quickly, they must remove their 15-pound weight belt. But when gripped by the panic induced by a sudden loss of air or by the arrival of sharks, divers sometimes concentrate on matters other than removing their weight belts. In one tragic case (Egstrom and Bachrach, 1971), an inexperienced diver drowned while diving for golf balls in only 12 feet of water. In a flood of panic, she had failed to remove her weight belt, and, even in death, she clung to a heavy bag of golf balls. This fatality could have been avoided if the diver had practiced removing her belt so that the action would have been executed automatically and with fewer resources. Because of ex-

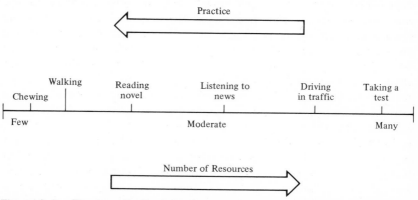

Figure 3.3   The hypothetical continuum of resource allocation and the demands of some everyday activities.

tensive training, skilled divers can perform several lifesaving maneuvers automatically, thereby avoiding such dire consequences. For similar reasons, pilots, fire fighters and paramedics receive extensive practice so that they perform their specialized tasks automatically.

AUTOMATICITY AND CONSCIOUSNESS

The phenomenon of automaticity has important implications for the appropriate definition of attention. We often think of attention and conscious awareness as identical processes, partly because both involve channeling our concentration in some directions rather than others. And we tend to think that we are aware of the stimuli that we process at a particular moment. Yet attention and consciousness should probably not be equated. Even though we perform some tasks without conscious attention, we must in some sense be attending to them. Otherwise, we would be unable to perform them. This line of thinking leads to the distinction between two types of attention: conscious attention and automatic attention. Broadbent (1977) suggested the distinction, using the terms *active attention* and *passive attention*. Conscious attention is under active, deliberate guidance, whereas automatic attention occurs involuntarily, without conscious guidance.

The distinction between conscious and automatic attention also agrees with the observation that our conscious control over what we attend to is complete. In an early experiment by Stroop (1935), subjects were asked to name the colors of various stimuli. Some stimuli were colored chips; other stimuli were names of colors printed in colored ink. The color words named one color but were printed in a different color. For example, the word *green* might have been printed in red ink, or the word *yellow* might have been printed in blue ink. The results were that it took almost twice as long to name the colors of the printed words than of the colored chips. This outcome has been called the *Stroop effect.* Apparently, the subjects had been unable to avoid reading the words, even though the words were not relevant to the task of naming colors. Reading the words may have interfered with the perception of the colors. Alternatively, reading the words may have evoked a tendency to say the word names, thereby competing with the correct response of saying the color names (Dyer, 1973). For our purposes, the important point is that the subjects read the words automatically, as if their attention had been beyond conscious control.

The dominance that automatic processing sometimes exerts over conscious processing probably contributes to our ability to survive. For example, if you consciously focused all of your resources on an activity such as running fast, you might fail to notice important stimuli such as swerving cars. This point was made clear to the author while pitching in a softball game. My conscious attention was focused entirely upon pitching the ball to a particular location when the hitter smashed a line drive at my head. Fortunately, automatic processes detected the oncoming ball, and I ducked before my head was reshaped by the ball. This example testifies to the value of being unable to consciously devote all of our resources to one event.

Although conscious and automatic attention seem to be rivals in some instances, as in Stroop's experiment, they often work together in harmony. For example, sleeping parents can detect automatically the first whimper of a sick child, thereby enabling them to attend consciously to the child's needs. Apparently, the automatic attentional processes had guided the parents' conscious attention. Similarly, in reading, automatic analyses that divide the page into figure and ground precede and guide conscious attention to particular words (Neisser, 1967).

The view that processing can occur automatically and can guide our conscious awareness emphasizes that we do not always control what we do consciously. But this view does not imply that conscious attention is unimportant. After all, we can in many instances choose consciously to attend to some things rather than others. By attending to items consciously, we take deliberate control over the manner in which we solve problems, form images, or compose sentences. And, as the following section documents, attending to items consciously enables us to take control over what we remember.

IMMEDIATE MEMORY

Attention and memory are closely related, so much so that they are indistinguishable in some instances. When we attend to an item it becomes part of the immediate present, the currently apprehended chunk of time that seems fresh in our minds and that stands out against the background of the remembered past. The item remains part of the immediate present for a short time, less than half a minute, and can be recalled easily during that time. But as time passes, the item seems to fade away and to be forgotten, unless active steps are taken to remember it. As an everyday example, when you look up a new phone number, the number is fresh in your mind initially and is easy to recall. In the absence of rehearsal, however, the number seems to fade out of the immediate present and to be forgotten. As this example shows, items that enter our conscious attention thereby become memorable for a short period of time.

William James (1890), one of the pioneers of modern psychology, called this type of brief memory primary memory, and he distinguished it from memory over long periods of time, which he called secondary memory. According to James, the information in primary memory has never left consciousness and can be recalled easily. In contrast, the information in secondary memory has been absent from consciousness for a time, and it is recalled via an effortful search of our memories of the past.

James' distinction between primary and secondary memory was based chiefly on introspective evidence. Almost 70 years passed before psychologists studied primary memory in the laboratory using well-controlled procedures (Brown, 1958). In one experiment (Peterson and Peterson, 1959), a set of three consonants such as MVK was presented briefly to the subject. Immediately following the presentation of the consonants, the subject heard a number, for example, 491. The subject's task was to count backwards by threes from the number until the experimenter presented a recall cue. The cue signalled the subject to stop counting and to recall the three consonants. This sequence of events constituted a single trial, and the experiment included many trials. On some trials, the time between the presentation of the consonants and the time of recall—the retention interval—was short, for example, 3 seconds. On other trials, the retention interval was longer. During all of the retention intervals, the subjects counted backwards by threes. The task of counting backwards is called a distractor task because it was intended to prevent the subject from attending to and rehearsing the consonants. If the subjects had been allowed to rehearse the items, to say the items to themselves over and over, no forgetting would have occurred (Brown, 1958).

The results, shown in Figure 3.4, were that the level of retention decreased gradually over time. At the 3-second retention intervals, the subjects recalled over 50 percent of the items correctly. But at the 18-second retention intervals, the subjects recalled fewer than 10 percent of the items correctly. These observations confirm James' proposal that we remember the information which we have attended to for a short period of time, around 15 seconds. This type of temporary memory has been given many names, including primary memory, short-term memory, and immediate memory. We shall use the term *immediate memory* to emphasize that the remembered information belongs to the psychological present.

In this section, we inquire into the properties of immediate memory, postponing the question whether it is useful to postulate the existence of a short-term store, as in the multistore model of memory. Regardless of the validity of the multistore model, the phenomenon of immediate memory remains worthy of investigation. We begin by examining the constraints on immediate memory and the manner in which the constraints can be reduced through practice, organization, and encoding. Then we examine the topics of forgetting and retrieval.

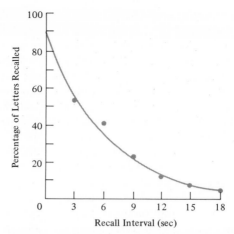

Figure 3.4   Short-term retention for sets of three consonants. (From Peterson and Peterson, 1959. Copyright 1959 by The American Psychological Association.)

Organization and Encoding

As shown by studies of the span of immediate memory, most people have a limited ability to remember briefly-presented items. Presumably, the limitation on the memory span reflects the limits on our processing resources. We saw previously that practice leads to the use of fewer resources. Accordingly, we might expect that practice in remembering will also lead to the use of fewer resources. As additional resources become available, they can be devoted to remembering additional information. In this conception, practice should improve immediate memory. Recent research on memory for chess positions encourages this conception.

MEMORY AND SKILL IN CHESS

Chess masters have truly impressive ability to remember the configurations of chess pieces that occur in games (de Groot, 1965, 1966). Masters can play several different games of chess simultaneously, even while blindfolded, and this task requires accurate memory for many positions and moves. As a result of the extensive amount of time they have devoted to chess—about 50,000 hours of playing time—masters remember a vast number of board positions, moves, and even entire matches.

Chase and Simon (1973) evaluated the immediate memory skills of the chess master by using the following procedure. On each of a series of trials, they showed the masters a chessboard containing a configuration of pieces that could occur in the middle of a regulation game. After 5 seconds, they removed the board from view and asked the master to take a group of chess pieces and to assemble them on a blank board into the configuration that had just been shown. When the master had recalled as many of the positions as possible, a new trial began, and the procedure was repeated. This memory task was given not only to masters but also to Class A players, who play very well, and to novices.

As Figure 3.5a shows, the masters recalled about 16 pieces on the first trial, twice as many pieces as the Class A players recalled. In turn, the Class A players recalled twice as many pieces as the novices. The level of immediate memory for chess positions, then, depended upon the level of skill and on the amount of prior practice at playing chess. Over trials, all three groups came to remember the board with equal accuracy. But the masters achieved a high level faster than the Class A players, who achieved a high level faster than the novices.

Did the advantage of the masters occur because chess masters have a greater memory capacity than other people do? In order to find out, Chase and Simon conducted a second experiment identical to that described above except that the boards that they presented contained pieces that had been placed at random. If the masters had greater attentional capacity than the others, then the masters should have outperformed the others in this experiment just as they had in the first experiment. The results, shown in Figure 3.5b, were that the masters recalled no more pieces than the less skilled subjects did on the first trial. And on the subsequent trials, the masters recalled fewer pieces than the others did. So the masters did not have greater capacity than the less skilled players. The masters showed superior immediate memory capacity for only the kinds of positions that they had previously had extensive practice on. Taken together, these observations establish that through extensive practice, the span of immediate memory can be increased substantially. They also show that the effects of practice are specific to the types of stimuli that had been processed during practice.

Through additional analyses, Chase and Simon discovered that practice produces effects in addition to an increase in the length of the memory span. By measuring how long the subjects had taken to place the pieces on the blank board in the first experiment, they observed that the subjects had recalled the pieces in specific groups. For example, a master might have paused for several seconds and then placed a rook, a knight, and a king on the board in rapid succession. Following another pause of several seconds, the master might have placed a few pawns on the board in rapid succession. Thus the subjects recalled the pieces in large groups or chunks. Chase and Simon observed that the masters' chunks contained more pieces than did those of the less skilled players. The advantage of remembering items in large chunks will become apparent in the following section.

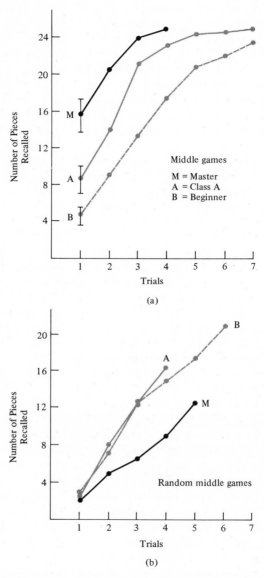

Figure 3.5 Memory for chess positions. (a) Memory of positions of the kind that occur in actual games. (b) Memory for random board positions. (From Chase and Simon, 1973.)

CHUNKING AND CAPACITY

Miller (1956) coined the term *chunking* in his classic paper concerning the capacity of immediate memory. Miller asked subjects to remember strings of digits such as 0110100111001101001111. In keeping with what is known about the usual span of apprehension, the subjects recalled only about seven digits correctly. Miller also showed that people can remember a greater number of digits by organizing the digits into higher-order groups or chunks. In one experiment, he taught subjects to organize sets of three binary digits (0s and 1s) into single numbers according to the following rules:

000 = 0	100 = 4
001 = 1	101 = 5
010 = 2	110 = 6
011 = 3	111 = 7

Using this scheme, subjects processed strings such as 110100011111 in the following manner. First, they divided the string into four groups of three digits: 110, 100, 011, and 111. Then they converted each group into a single digit by applying the rules, namely 110 = 6, 100 = 4, 011 = 3, and 111 = 7. By remembering the four digits 6437, then, they remembered the entire string of twelve 0s and 1s. Following extensive practice using this method, the subjects remembered many more than seven digits. Indeed, one subject learned to recall sequences of up to 40 binary digits. These observations show that organization exerts strong effects on immediate memory.

Miller argued that the chunking method worked by allowing the subjects to use their limited capacity in an efficient manner. Having reviewed a large amount of literature, he concluded that the capacity of immediate memory is limited to seven items, plus or minus two. But he also argued that the seven items could be individual digits or well-learned chunks such as groups of three digits or familiar words, for example, *the*. On this account, organizing the binary digits had not actually increased the capacity of immediate memory. The organizational method increased the digit span because the subjects had learned to remember seven large chunks rather than seven individual digits.

Miller's work on chunking was important historically because it kindled the emerging conception that humans may be viewed as processing systems having limited capacity. But the estimate that the capacity of immediate memory is seven chunks is best viewed as a rough approximation. For one thing, chunks have not been defined precisely, and it is of little help to define a chunk as that which adults can remember seven of. Further, because the capacity of immediate memory reflects the limits on our attentional capacity and because the number of resources available can vary depending on the type of task, the level of fatigue, and so on, the capacity of immediate memory can vary across situations (Baddeley, Thomson, and Buchanon, 1975). For these reasons, the most we can say is that the capacity of immediate memory is limited but not fixed and that organization facilitates immediate memory.

ENCODING BY REDUCTION AND BY ELABORATION

Encoding is the process through which we represent information inside the processing system. In encoding information, people often transform the presented information. For example, through the process of *reduction coding*, people transform the presented information into a smaller, more manageable amount. By definition, organizing items into chunks is an instance of reduction coding because organizing reduces a number of individual items to a smaller number of chunks.

CHUNKING

Another way in which people transform the presented information is called *elaboration coding*, which consists of adding to the presented information (Baddeley and Patterson, 1971). As an example, you might encode the notes on the musical scale (E, G, B, D, F) by rehearsing the sentence *Every Good Boy Does Fine.* Although the sentence adds to the information to be remembered, it seems to be an effective mnemonic device. Like reduction coding, elaboration coding can produce dramatic effects on immediate memory. Truly striking results occur when subjects use reduction and elaboration coding in unison.

In one study (Ericsson, Chase, and Faloon, 1980), an undergraduate (S.F.), who had average memory ability and intelligence, participated in a memory-span task for three to five hours a week over a period of one and a half years. A string of digits was read to S.F. at the rate of one per second and he then recalled the string. If S.F. recalled the entire string correctly, the experimenters added a digit to the next string. Otherwise, they removed a digit. On half of the trials, S.F. described what he had done to remember the digits. In the first few days on the memory task, S.F.'s performance was unremarkable, for he recalled only about seven digits correctly. Astonishingly, though, his digit span increased to about 80 digits following 230 hours of practice. So there is hope yet for those of us who suffer from chronic forgetfulness.

Analysis of S.F.'s verbal reports indicated that he had learned to use several strategies involving elaboration coding. Being a distance runner, S.F. categorized many three- and four-digit groups as running times for various races. For example, he encoded the string 3492 as "three minutes and 49 point 2 seconds, near world-record mile time." Similarly, he categorized digit groups as ages, for example, by transforming 893 into "89 point 3, very old man." Both examples also demonstrate that encoding items for immediate retention often involves making mnemonic associations, that is, relating the incoming information to information that had already been learned. The importance of elaboration coding was evaluated by presenting strings that were very difficult to encode as running times. When that was done, S.F.'s performance fell almost to the beginning level. Conversely, his performance improved markedly when all of the strings were easy to encode as running times.

As the length of the presented strings increased, S.F. began using reduction coding. In particular, he grouped several sets of four items, each of which had been encoded as running times, into a single supergroup. For example, he might have encoded a string of 48 digits into 12 groups of four-digit running times. Then he might have grouped the four-digit groups into four supergroups, each of which contained twelve digits, as in the following arrangement:

444 444 444 444

This process of organizing the groups into supergroups reduced the number of higher-order units from twelve to four, thereby reducing the demands on his processing capacity.

The fact that S.F. used a combination of elaboration and reduction coding demonstrates that adults are flexible encoders. They do not fixate entirely on any single strategy, and they adjust their strategies to meet the demands of the task. These observations also establish two other points. First, encoding processes have profound effects upon memory. Second, the effective use of encoding strategies is an acquired skill. Given the appropriate amounts of and kinds of practice, we may be able to overcome most of the usual limits on the memory span. In order to improve your own immediate memory skills, you should practice using various kinds of encoding strategies on diverse types of material. Despite our best efforts, however, we will probably never escape the problem of forgetting, our next topic.

Forgetting

Most people have had the frustrating experience of looking up a new phone number and then forgetting the number before dialing it. It is as if the number had faded from consciousness as a result of the passage of time. This view, which agrees with the popular notion that the passage of time leads to the occurrence of forgetting, is central to the *decay theory* of forgetting. According to the decay theory, forgetting is a passive process in which information spontaneously weakens or decays over time.

An alternative to the decay theory is the *interference theory* of forgetting, which states that forgetting results not from the passage of time but from the events that occur as time passes (McGeoch, 1942). By analogy, the writing on a gravestone fades over time, but the fading results not from the passage of time but from the abrasive action of the wind and the rain that inevitably occur as time passes. According to the interference theory, forgetting can be produced by the events that either precede or follow the presentation of the items that the subject is to remember. *Proactive interference* occurs when the recall of learned information is impaired by the events that preceded the learning episode. For example, your memory for a phone number you have just looked up may be impaired by spontaneously remembering other numbers you had learned previously. *Retroactive interference* occurs when the recall of learned information is impaired by the events that followed the learning episode. For example, your memory for a phone number you have just looked up could suffer if, before dialing the number, you heard someone else say a different number.

In this section, we examine both theories of forgetting. We begin with the interference theory because understanding the effects of interference is a prerequisite for testing the decay theory.

PROACTIVE INTERFERENCE

Recall that in the experiment by Peterson and Peterson (1959), the subjects heard three consonants, counted backwards by threes during the retention interval, and then recalled the consonants. The chief result was that as the length of the retention interval increased, the amount of forgetting increased (see Figure 3.4). At first glance, this outcome suggests that the forgetting had resulted from the passage of time. Yet the forgetting could also have resulted from proactive interference. The Petersons' experiment had included many trials. Thus, the retention of the items presented on the twentieth trial, for example, could have been hindered by proactive interference from the items that had been learned on the first nineteen trials.

If proactive interference from items learned in preceding trials had produced forgetting, then little forgetting should occur on the very first trial, for the first trial had not been preceded by experimental events that would have produced proactive interference. For two reasons, the Petersons' data did not indicate how much forgetting had occurred on the first trial. First, the Petersons had given the subjects two practice trials. Including practice trials served to familiarize the subjects with the experimental procedure, but the trials could have provided a source of proactive interference. Second, the Petersons had averaged together the subjects' performance over many trials. Averaging is useful for showing overall trends and for minimizing the influence of momentary fluctuations in performance resulting from inattentiveness. Averaging, however, may also be hazardous. What happens in the initial trials may differ from what occurs in the later trials, and the average performance over all trials can obscure the differences.

Keppel and Underwood (1962) tested whether forgetting occurred

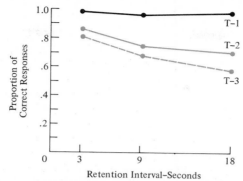

Figure 3.6 The role of proactive interference in the Brown-Peterson procedure. T-1, T-2, and T-3 show performance on the first, second, and third trials, respectively. (From Keppel and Underwood, 1962.)

on the first trial of the Petersons' procedure. Three groups of subjects were exposed to a first trial that had a retention interval of 3, 9, or 18 seconds, respectively. The subjects also participated in two trials following the first. As Figure 3.6 shows, no forgetting occurred on the first trial, even at the 18-second retention interval. On the second and third trials, however, a considerable amount of forgetting occurred, indicating that proactive interference built up over trials. These observations show that forgetting over short periods of time can result from proactive interference, not from decay alone.

Subsequent studies have shown that the amount of proactive interference that occurs depends upon the degree of similarity between the items learned in previous trials and the items that the subject is currently trying to remember (Wickens, 1972). Wickens, Born, and Allen (1963) exposed subjects to four successive trials in which the retention interval was 15 seconds. The control group was asked to remember sets of three consonants on each trial. The experimental group was asked to remember sets of three digits on the first three trials and a set of three consonants on the fourth trial, as shown in Figure 3.7a. Note that both groups learned the same items on the fourth trial. But the control group received similar items on all four trials, whereas the experimental group received similar items on the first three trials and different items on the fourth trial.

The results for the control group were that the level of retention decreased over trials, reaching the lowest point on the fourth trial (see Figure 3.7b). In other words, proactive interference built up over the four trials. Proactive interference also increased for the experimental group, but only over the first three trials. When dissimilar material was introduced in the fourth trial, retention rose to the same high level that had been achieved on the first trial. It was as if the proactive interference

	Trial 1	Trial 2	Trial 3	Trial 4
Experimental	948	671	253	MRG
Control	XKV	NTY	ZBL	MRG

(a)

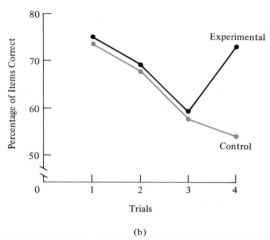

(b)

Figure 3.7   Release from proactive interference. (a) The design of the experiment. (b) Idealized data showing a release from proactive interference, the increased level of recall by the experimental group on the fourth trial.

built up over the first three trials had dissipated. This outcome, called *release from proactive interference* (Wickens, 1972), shows that the amount of proactive interference depended upon the similarity of the events that occurred over trials.

The occurrence of proactive interference in studies of immediate memory results partly from failures to retrieve information. In one experiment (Gardiner, Craik, and Birtwhistle, 1972), the subjects were exposed to three successive trials in which the to-be-remembered items were names of domestic flowers, for example, *pansy* and *rose*. The items presented on the fourth trial were names of wildflowers such as *dandelion* and *daisy*. The control group was not told of the shift in category from domestic flowers to wildflowers. The experimental group, however, was told about the category shift at the time of recall. The results for the control group were that the level of retention declined over all four trials; there was no release from proactive interference. But in the experimental group, the level of retention declined over only the first three trials and rose sharply on the fourth. Thus the experimental group showed a release from proactive interference on the fourth trial. Because retrieval cues can produce a release from proactive interference, proactive interference stems at least partly from problems in retrieving information.

One possible way in which proactive interference may occur is that previously learned items compete with the items that the subject is currently trying to remember. Consistent with this idea, subjects do sometimes err by recalling the items that had been presented previously (Loftus and Patterson, 1975). But the question then becomes why did the old items compete with the new ones? Baddeley (1976) has suggested that proactive interference involves a failure to discriminate between the items presented on different trials. As the subjects learn items over trials, the items get lost in a mass, as occurs when many boxes are piled up in a warehouse. In order to discriminate the current items from the mass of old items, the new items must be distinctive; otherwise, competition will occur. This *discrimination hypothesis* agrees well with the observation that little proactive interference occurs when the current items are very different from and stand out from the old items. The hypothesis also agrees with the observation that the presentation of retrieval cues reduces proactive interference. This is because retrieval cues add distinctiveness to the items that they cue.

RETROACTIVE INTERFERENCE

Using a novel procedure called the probe procedure, Waugh and Norman (1965) showed that the events following the to-be-remembered items produce interference. In their procedure, the subjects heard a list of 16 digits. Then they heard a tone together with a probe digit that had occurred earlier in the list. The subjects' task was to name the digit that had followed the probe digit initially. For example, the items presented in one trial might have been:

4 9 1 6 2 5 0 7 3 8 2 7 6 1 3 9, tone 5

In this example, the probe digit is 5, and the target response would be 0 since 0 followed 5 in the list. By varying where the probe digit occurred in the list, Waugh and Norman examined whether the amount of forgetting (indicated by the number of incorrect responses) depended upon how many digits intervened between the target and the end of the list.

The results were that the earlier the target digit had occurred in the list, the more likely it was to be forgotten. In other words, as the number of digits following the target digit increased, so did the amount of forgetting. As Figure 3.8 shows, more forgetting occurred when five digits followed the target than when only one or two followed it. This suggests that the number of digits following the target determined the amount of interference and forgetting. But note that another interpretation is pos-

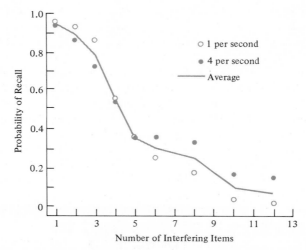

Figure 3.8   Retroactive interference in the probe procedure. The greater the number of items that followed the probe digit, the more forgetting occurred. (From Waugh and Norman, 1965. Copyright 1965 by the American Psychological Association. All rights reserved.)

sible. The digits had been presented at a rate of one per second. When five digits followed the target, at least 5 seconds passed between the presentation of the target and the signal to recall it. But when one digit followed the target, only one or so seconds passed between the presentation of the target and the signal to recall it. We would expect more decay to occur when five digits followed the target. So the results could have been due to decay, not interference.

Waugh and Norman tested the decay interpretation by examining what happens when the list of digits is presented four times faster, at a rate of four digits per second. The results were very similar to those which had occurred at the slower rate of presentation (see Figure 3.8). For example, when five digits followed the target, equal amounts of forgetting occurred in the fast-presentation and the slow-presentation conditions. Yet in the slow-presentation condition about four times as much time passed between the presentation of the target and the signal to recall it. This outcome militates against the decay interpretation and shows the importance of interference.

The amount of retroactive interference depends upon the complexity of the distractor task that the subject performs during the retention interval (Posner and Rossman, 1965). For example, Crowder (1967) gave subjects five words to remember. During the retention interval, the subjects performed a distractor task that involved rapidly pressing keys in response to flashing lights. In the control condition, there was a simple relationship between the lights and the keys: the first light signalled the subject to press the first key, the second light signalled the subject to press the second key, and so on. In the experimental condition, the distractor task was more complex. The order of the lights differed from that of the keys. For example, the first light might have signalled the subject to press the seventh key, the sixth light might have signalled the subject to press the second key, and so on. Unsurprisingly, more forgetting occurred in the experimental condition that had involved the more complex distractor task.

A plausible account of these observations can be given by the model of resource allocation. It is reasonable to assume that the more difficult the distractor task is, the greater is the number of resources that the subject must allocate to the task, and in turn, the fewer the resources that are allocated to the task of remembering the presented items. On this account, forgetting occurs because subjects devote few processing resources to the memory task, too few to allow the subject to rehearse, to organize, and to remember the items. This analysis agrees with the view that attention and immediate memory are related facets of the process of resource allocation.

DECAY

Determining whether decay produces forgetting has proven to be an exceedingly challenging task. The ideal way to evaluate the effects of decay would be to have subjects learn several items and then to do absolutely nothing during the retention interval, thereby eliminating the effects of retroactive interference and preventing rehearsal. Of course, no one has ever done this ideal experiment, for it is virtually impossible to do nothing during the retention interval. Additionally, it is difficult to induce the subjects not to rehearse during the retention interval. Most subjects want to appear intelligent and to remember well in memory experiments. Consequently, they often rehearse items covertly even when they have been told not to (Reitman, 1971, 1974). Because rehearsal retards forgetting, the occurrence of rehearsal can potentially mask the effects of the passage of time.

Some of the most convincing evidence that decay produces forgetting comes from an experiment by Shiffrin and Cook (1978; also see Reitman, 1974; Wingfield and Byrnes, 1972). In order to minimize the subjects' tendency to rehearse items, they told each subject that they were studying how well people can forget, not how well people can remember. Specifically, they said they were studying whether performing a tone detection task would facilitate forgetting. Their experiment included many trials, each of which lasted approximately 40 seconds. During the trials, tones were presented against a background of white noise (a moderately loud *shhhh* sound), and the subjects were paid according to how many tones they detected. Each trial began with at least several seconds of tone detection. Then a series of five consonants was presented for 2.5 seconds. The subjects had been instructed to say the letters aloud and to then put them out of mind and to continue with the tone detection task. The trials were of two kinds. On long-delay trials, the letters were presented early in the trial, 32.5 seconds before the end of the trial and the signal to recall the letters. On the short-delay trials, the letters were presented late in the trial, 12.5 seconds before the end of the trial. The two kinds of trials were intermixed throughout the experiment. If forgetting results from decay, then more forgetting should have occurred in the long-delay trials than in the short-delay trials, for a greater amount of time intervened between learning and recall in the long-delay trials.

The results were that the subjects forgot about 20 percent of the letters on the short-delay trials, whereas they forgot about 30 percent of the letters in the long-delay trials. The occurrence of more forgetting at the longer delay suggests that the forgetting resulted from decay. But the decay interpretation cannot be accepted fully unless alternative interpretations have been ruled out. The forgetting probably did not result from retroactive interference because the events that occurred during the retention interval had little resemblance to the target letters. Further, the results could not be explained in terms of rehearsal. The subjects had little reason to rehearse, and the performance of the tone detection task probably required too many resources to allow for rehearsal. Moreover, if the subjects had been rehearsing, they would have recalled the items equally well on the long-delay and on the short-delay trials, for rehearsal prevents forgetting.

A more serious problem is that proactive interference probably built up over trials. Fortunately, other studies have examined the effects of decay in the absence of proactive interference. For example, Baddeley and Scott (1971) tested subjects on only one trial, which prevented the development of proactive interference. Nevertheless, more forgetting occurred as the retention intervals increased. Collectively, these observations converge on the conclusion that decay does produce forgetting over short intervals of time, though the effects of decay have consistently been small.

Historically, the theories of decay and interference have been rivals. Yet we should recognize that decay and interference processes often work together and interact (Baddeley, 1976). As information decays over time, it probably becomes less distinctive. As noted previously, the loss of distinctiveness leads to interference by making the information difficult to retrieve. In this conception, decay and interference are separated by a very thin and somewhat arbitrary line, and a complete theory of forgetting must unite the two factors.

Retrieval

After items have become part of the immediate present, that is, part of immediate memory, we can process them in various ways. As discussed earlier, we can deliberately organize or rehearse the remembered items. We can also search among and compare different items. Search and comparison processes are probably important in many everyday tasks. For example, if someone asked you which of two remembered houses were more attractive, you might imagine the two houses side by side and consciously scan and compare the two.

The manner in which people search and compare items in immediate memory has been studied extensively in a memory scanning task devised by Sternberg (1966). Sternberg presented a series of digits for one or two seconds. The series of digits, called the memory set, varied in size and included from one to six digits. Two seconds after the presentation of the memory set, a test digit was presented. On some trials, the test digit belonged to the memory set, whereas on other trials, it did not. The subjects' task was to indicate by pressing buttons whether or not the test digit belonged to the memory set for that trial. For example, if the memory set were 7 3 8 1 and the test digit were 8, the correct response would be a press of the "Yes" button. If the test digit had been 2, the correct response would have been a press of the "No" button. In this type of task, errors are rare, and performance is assessed by measuring the reaction time, that is, the amount of time required to respond to the test stimulus.

The results, shown in Figure 3.9, were that the more digits there were in the memory set, the longer it took subjects to respond. Each addition of another digit to the memory set resulted in an increase in the reaction time by a particular amount, about 38 msec. At each set size, "Yes" and "No" responses occurred at nearly equal speed. Similar observations have been reported in many experiments, whether the presented items were digits, letters, or words (Sternberg, 1975). These orderly observations have generated considerable theoretical interest, and we next examine some models of performance in Sternberg's procedure.

THE SERIAL-EXHAUSTIVE MODEL

Sternberg (1969, 1975) has proposed that performance in the preceding task involves four stages of processing. First, the test digit must be encoded. Second, the test digit must be compared mentally with the digits in the memory set. Then a decision must be made as to whether a match occurred. Finally, the overt response must be made. In Sternberg's experiment, the test digit was presented in the same way in every trial, so one may assume that the time required to encode the test digit remained constant over trials. In other words, the differences in reaction times shown in Figure 3.9 did not stem from differences in the time required to

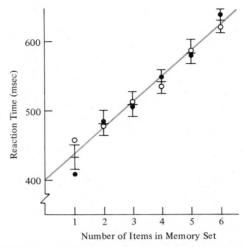

Figure 3.9   The mean reaction time for positive responses (filled circles) and negative responses (open circles) for memory sets of various sizes. (After Sternberg, 1966. Copyright 1966 by the American Association for the Advancement of Science.)

encode the test digit. Similarly, the time required to execute the overt response after a decision had been made was probably constant over trials. The increase in reaction times shown in Figure 3.9 must have occurred because when more digits were presented in the memory set, the subjects had more items in memory to compare with the test digit. Following this line of reasoning, Sternberg set forth a model of how comparisons are made in memory.

Sternberg (1966, 1969, 1975) proposed that subjects compare the test digit to digits in the memory set serially, one after another. This proposal is consistent with the observed increase in reaction times that occurs when digits are added to the memory set. If the comparisons were made serially and each took some time, then increasing the number of comparisons would increase the reaction time. Consider on the other hand what would have happened if the comparisons had been made in parallel, that is, simultaneously. If the comparison process occurred in parallel, then five comparisons could be made as fast as one, and the reaction times should not increase as more and more digits are added to the memory set. Because reaction times did increase as digits were added to the memory set, Sternberg concluded that the mental scanning or comparison process is serial rather than parallel in nature.

Sternberg also considered how long the scanning process continued within trials. Intuitively, it makes sense that the subjects would compare the test digit to all the items in the memory set on trials in which the correct response was "No." The subjects could be sure that the correct response on a trial was "No" only if they had scanned the entire memory set. On "No" trials, then, the test digit must be compared to every item in the memory set; this type of scanning is called *exhaustive*. We would not expect exhaustive scanning to occur on trials in which the correct response is "Yes." Consider what might happen on a trial in which the memory set were 8 2 9 5 7 1 and the test digit was 2. In scanning the memory set, subjects might first compare 2 and 8, and since no match occurred, they might continue scanning. Next they would compare 2 and 2, which obviously match. It would be reasonable for the subjects to end the scanning process at this point and make the "Yes" response. This type of scanning that terminates when a match is made is called *self-terminating*. Thus we might expect exhaustive scanning on "No" trials and self-terminating scanning on "Yes" trials. We could determine if this occurred by examining the slopes of the reaction time functions for "Yes" and "No" responses in Sternberg's procedure. On "Yes" trials, the digit that matched the test digit would on the average occur in the middle of the memory set. For this reason, only half the items in the memory set would have to be scanned on "Yes" trials if the scanning were self-terminating. Since only half as many items would be scanned on "Yes" trials as on the "No" trials in which exhaustive scanning occurs, the slope of the function for "Yes" responses would be half that of the function for "No" responses.

In fact, Sternberg found evidence for exhaustive scanning on both "Yes" and "No" trials. Looking back at Figure 3.9, we see that the slopes of the functions for "Yes" and "No" responses were equal. This means that scanning occurred in the same way on "Yes" and "No" trials. Because scanning must have been exhaustive on "No" trials, and because the slopes were equal on "Yes" and "No" trials, Sternberg concluded that the scanning was exhaustive on both "Yes" and "No" trials. Although this conclusion is consistent with the observations, it is certainly counterintuitive. Why should subjects continue scanning after they have already found a match between the test digit and an item in the memory set? One possibility is that comparing items with the test digit can be done very rapidly, whereas the decisions to respond "Yes" or "No" are much slower. Subjects could perform their task by comparing item 1 with the test digit, deciding whether to respond "Yes" or"No," comparing item 2 with the test digit, deciding again whether to respond "Yes" or "No," and so on. But this would require a long time since numerous slow decisions are made. By scanning exhaustively, the subjects can make all of the fast comparisons quickly and then make only one slow decision. Overall, this exhaustive scanning strategy could lead to faster reaction times than would occur following a self-terminating strategy.

PROBLEMS WITH THE SERIAL-EXHAUSTIVE MODEL

One difficulty encountered by the serial-exhaustive model is that there is no direct evidence indicating that comparisons can be made faster than decisions can. Without this evidence, the serial-exhaustive model is plausible, but so are some alternative models. For example, Sternberg's observations can be explained not only by serial processing models but also by particular parallel processing models (Corcoran, 1971; Townsend, 1971, 1974). Assume that the subject has limited processing resources and that the available resources are divided equally among several items which are processed at the same time. When few items are in the memory set, a relatively large number of resources are devoted to each item. Consequently, the items can be processed rapidly and simultaneously. But when more items are in the memory set, a relatively small number of resources are devoted to each item, and the items are therefore processed more slowly. Although the items are processed in parallel in both cases, the reaction time should increase as the size of the memory set increases. In this way, the results shown in Figure 3.9 can be explained via parallel processing. As it turns out, parallel processing models have limited generality (Sternberg, 1975). By the same token, however, there are limits on the generality of the serial-exhaustive model, and these are discussed next.

In our discussion of pattern recognition, we saw that unpracticed subjects often scan items in sensory memory serially. Following extensive practice, however, subjects come to scan items automatically and in parallel. In Sternberg's procedure, similar practice effects occur, and well-practiced subjects can scan for several targets as fast as they can for one or two (Simpson, 1972). At one time, researchers hoped that studying performance in tasks such as that used by Sternberg would clarify whether mental scanning is fundamentally a serial or a parallel process. With the benefit of retrospect, however, we now see that it is inappropriate to ask whether scanning is serial or parallel. Scanning can and does occur in many ways that depend in part on the subject's history of practice.

Another troublesome finding is that serial position effects occur in memory scanning experiments (Burrows and Okada, 1971; Clifton and Birenbaum, 1970; Raeburn, 1974). For example, when the test item matches the last item in the memory set, the reaction time is faster than it is when the test item matches an item from the middle of the memory set. This type of effect, called a serial position effect, is not readily accounted for by the serial-exhaustive model.

The serial-exhaustive model also has difficulty explaining the effect of repeating items in the memory set. Baddeley and Ecob (1973) examined the scanning of memory sets that either contained repeated items, as in the set 2 9 5 2 3, or contained no repeated items. They found that the reaction times were very short when the test item matched a repeated item, for example, the digit 2 in the preceding example. But the reaction times were longer when the test item matched a nonrepeated item.

Perhaps the most serious problem with the serial-exhaustive model concerns its ecological validity. Many investigators believe that the memory scanning task is artificial and unlike the tasks that people perform in everyday situations. Because the model has not been shown to apply to a wide range of tasks, it may lack the broad generality that we want models to have.

THE FAMILIARITY-SEARCH MODEL

In order to account for the effects of factors such as repetition and to provide a general model of retrieval, Atkinson and Juola (1973, 1974) proposed an extension of the serial-exhaustive model. In their familiarity-search model, which is presented here in simplified form, they assumed that the items that are presented in a memory scanning task can vary along a continuum of familiarity. As shown in Figure 3.10, items that have been presented infrequently will seem quite unfamiliar to the subject, whereas items that have been presented frequently will seem to be highly familiar. Each presentation of an item boosts the familiarity of that item, moving the item toward the right-hand end of the continuum.

The model states that two separate processes can influence performance in the memory scanning task. In deciding whether a test item belongs to the memory set, the subject first checks the level of familiarity of the item. This familiarity-checking process occurs rapidly and does not involve scanning memory serially. The process of familiarity check-

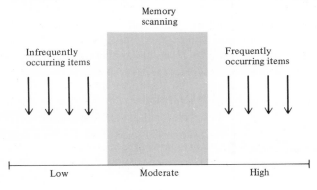

Figure 3.10   The familiarity-search model of recognition in immediate memory. The items inside the shaded region are scanned serially and exhaustively. The items outside the shaded region are responded to quickly on the basis of a rapid familiarity check.

ing is illustrated by what occurs when someone shows you a picture of a friend. Quite often, we experience a strong feeling of familiarity, and we recognize the friend immediately, without having searched memory. The friend is so familiar that there is no need to conduct a memory search. According to the model, if the test item is very high in familiarity, the subject decides quickly that the item had occurred in the memory set and responds "Yes." Similarly, if the test item is very low in familiarity, the subject decides quickly that the item had not occurred in the memory set and responds "No." If, however, the test item seems moderately familiar, then the subject will be uncertain about whether the test item had occurred in the memory set. As a result, the subject will deliberately compare the test item to each item in memory. Specifically the subject executes a serial, exhaustive scan, which occurs more slowly than the process of familiarity checking.

The model is summarized in Figure 3.10. The test items that fall on either side of the shaded region are evaluated by the rapid process of familiarity checking. The test items that fall inside of the shaded region are evaluated by the slower process of serial and exhaustive scanning.

The familiarity-search model has numerous advantages. Because the model includes a process of serial, exhaustive scanning, it can explain all of the data that Sternberg's model explained. Additionally, the model explains observations that had been troublesome for Sternberg's model. For example, it explains why subjects respond very quickly to test items that match items that had been repeated in the memory set. As items are repeated, they become more familiar and move into the high-familiarity portion of the familiarity continuum. Consequently, the repeated items can be evaluated on the basis of the rapid process of familiarity checking rather than the slower process of serial, exhaustive scanning.

The chief advantage of the model, however, is that it can account for many observations concerning the recognition of well-learned items, the items said to be in long-term memory (Banks and Atkinson, 1974). In other words, the model has a substantial amount of generality. No doubt the model achieves generality in part because it emphasizes that there is no single way in which people recognize items. Depending upon the conditions of the experiment, recognition may occur through a rapid process of familiarity checking or through the slower process of serial and exhaustive scanning. As illustrated in this section, models of cognition must come to grips with the flexibility of human information processing.

* *Summary.* Attention and memory are closely related, for items that have been attended to can be recalled during a period of approximately 15 seconds. This type of brief retention is called immediate memory. The central theme of this chapter is that both attention and immediate mem-

ory are clarified by the model of resource allocation, which grew out of research concerning selective attention.

Selective attention involves processing some stimuli but not others at a particular moment. Selective attention has been studied extensively using the dichotic listening procedure, in which two different messages are presented, one to each ear, and the subject shadows or repeats one message. Early research indicated that subjects remember little of the unshadowed message, and they notice only its gross physical characteristics. This observation led to the filter model, which stated that the unattended message is filtered or blocked at an early stage of analysis. The filter model, and the models of early selection that succeeded it, held that people fully attend to and analyze the meaning of only one message at a time. Yet some research showed that people do process the meaning of information presented to the unshadowed ear. Consequently, theorists constructed a model of late selection, which stated that all incoming information is analyzed semantically and that attentional selection occurs at a late stage of analysis.

Eventually, many theorists abandoned the models of early and late selection because both models concerned data driven rather than conceptually driven processing. Further, the stage models did not explain the effects of practice, nor did they provide a broad account of both selective and divided attention. Many theorists found it useful to reconceptualize attention as a process of allocating processing resources. According to the resource allocation model, people have limited processing resources (also called limited capacity) that can be used in a flexible manner. When a sufficient number of processing resources are available, people can successfully perform two tasks simultaneously. But when one task requires most of the available resources, only one task can be performed, and selective attention occurs.

An important but unresolved question is whether our processing resources are limited. Through extensive practice, some people have learned to read and to take dictation simultaneously, as if practice had expanded their processing resources. Yet it is possible that practice leads to the development of skilled performance and to a reduction in the number of resources required to perform a particular task. Practice also leads to the occurrence of automatic processing, which indicates that attention cannot be equated with conscious awareness. In everyday situations, the direction of attention is determined by both automatic processing and deliberate, conscious processing.

The limitations on our supply of processing resources are reflected in the limited capacity of immediate memory. If a string of items, for example, digits, is presented briefly, most people recall only about seven items, the span of immediate memory. Because practice leads to more effective use of resources, practice can facilitate immediate memory. For example, if people practice organizing single items into larger groups or chunks, they can increase their memory span dramatically. Organizing items into chunks is a process of reduction coding, which functionally reduces the number of items to be remembered. Immediate memory can also be facilitated by elaboration coding, which involves adding well-remembered information to the information to be remembered. Both kinds of coding illustrate that encoding is an active process that entails transforming the presented information.

Forgetting in immediate memory results partly from the passage of time, that is, through a process of gradual weakening or decay. Forgetting also results from interference, that is, from the processing of items that are similar to the items that are to be remembered. Proactive interference occurs when previously learned items impair the retention of items presented later. Proactive interference stems from problems in retrieving information, for example, from the failure to discriminate the items that are to be remembered from previously learned items. Interference can also occur retroactively, as when the processing of items at one time impairs the retention of previously learned items. Retroactive interference stems in part from the failure to allocate sufficient resources to the task of remembering. In many situations, decay and interference probably interact. For example, as items decay over time, they may become less distinctive and more difficult to discriminate from the items that had been learned previously, thereby facilitating the occurrence of proactive interference.

Most studies of retrieval from immediate memory have used a high-speed recognition procedure in which a test item is presented and the subject indicates quickly whether the test item matches one of a set of remembered items. Under some conditions, subjects perform this task by searching or scanning the remembered items serially and exhaustively. In particular, they compare the test item to each remembered item one at a time. But when the remembered items are either highly familiar or highly unfamiliar, the subjects do not execute a memory search. Rather, they evaluate the level of familiarity of the test items. So retrieval, like many aspects of cognition, is a highly flexible process.

Chapter 4
Encoding and
Remembering

Immediate memory is important in many situations, yet it is too temporary to satisfy all of the demands of everyday life. Nowhere is this more evident than in the case of a man known in the clinical literature as H.M. (Milner, 1966; Milner, Corkin, and Teuber, 1968).

H.M. was a motor winder in his late twenties who suffered severe epileptic seizures that interfered with his work and presented a major health hazard. To reduce the seizure activity, H.M. allowed surgeons to remove the internal part of the temporal lobes of his brain, which contains the hippocampus, the amygdala, and other structures that are known to play a role in remembering.

The surgery controlled his epilepsy and did not impair his intelligence. But the operation did impair H.M.'s memory. He remembered events from early in life but did not remember the events from one or two years just before the operation. The larger problem, however, was that H.M. had difficulty learning and remembering information about the events that followed the operation. In most instances, he remembered new information for only seconds or a few minutes. He and his family moved following the operation, but even after a year, H.M. had not learned the new address. When he had to find his own way home, he often returned to the house in which he had lived prior to the operation. He read and reread the same magazines, showing no signs of boredom. And he told the same jokes repeatedly without recognizing that he had told them before. He even had to be reminded each day to shave. Overall, H.M. lived as a creature trapped in the immediate present, unable to remember for long.

The case of H.M. is admittedly extreme. Yet it demonstrates the importance of long-term memory. Without the capacity for forming new long-term memories, we would be unable to learn and to benefit from our previous experiences.

This chapter concerns the processes involved in remembering new information over relatively long periods of time. We begin by analyzing the multistore model of memory, which stated that the memory system contains separate short-term and long-term stores. According to the model, incoming information is retained in the short-term store, a temporary storage system. By rehearsing or by encoding the information, the information is transferred to the long-term store and can be retained over long periods of time. The multistore model guided research concerning remembering for almost 20 years. The model is no longer accepted widely, but it still merits our attention. By understanding the model and its limitations, we gain insight into current research and theory, much of which arose as either an extension of or a reaction against the multistore model.

In the second section of this chapter, we inquire into current conceptions of remembering, which stress the importance of encoding processes. Craik and Lockhart (1972) argued persuasively that remembering was best seen as the product of encoding processes rather than of retention in several memory stores. They proposed that people can analyze incoming information on numerous levels. On the simplest level of analysis or, as they called it, level of processing, the person analyzes the physical properties of the stimulus. For example, if the stimulus were a printed word, one might notice whether the word was capitalized or uncapitalized, long or short. On a deeper level of processing, the semantic level, one might determine the meaning of the word. Craik and Lockhart suggested that memory depended upon the level of processing: the more deeply the information had been processed, the longer it would be remembered. This conception, which is called the *levels of processing model*, abandoned the idea that there are separate short-term and long-term stores. We shall examine this model in detail because it reshaped the direction of research and because its offshoots are highly influential at present.

The levels of processing model initially assumed that processing occurs in a fixed sequence of stages. When this assumption ran aground, theorists modified the model by emphasizing the effects of the elaborateness, not the depth, of processing. An item can be processed elaborately by relating it to other items, for example, by joining various words in a sentence. Or the item can be analyzed further in isolation, for example, by noting that the word *bat* has several meanings rather than a single meaning. According to the revised model, the more elaborately an item is processed, the better it will be remembered. Using this idea as our conceptual framework, we shall examine the effects of organization and of mnemonic systems upon retention.

One of the central themes of the chapter is that people can encode information in a variety of ways, and they often tailor their coding strategies to satisfy the demands of the task at hand. For example, in studying for a multiple choice test designed to evaluate your memory for specific facts, you would probably memorize many specific facts, perhaps by using the strategy of rehearsing the facts repeatedly. You would no doubt study differently for an essay test that required you to evaluate and to integrate concepts rather than to memorize passively. As this example indicates, people have extensive knowledge of how to encode in order to remember different kinds of information. In other words, they know how to remember. This knowledge is called metamnemonic (pronounced meta-ni-mön-ic) knowledge, though we shall often use the simpler term *metamemory* (Flavell and Wellman, 1977). In the last section of this chapter, we explore the metamnemonic knowledge that people use in selecting and in evaluating their strategies for remembering.

THE MULTISTORE MODEL

Extending the theoretical work done by Broadbent (1958) and by Waugh and Norman (1965), among others, Atkinson and Shiffrin (1968) proposed one of the most detailed and influential multistore models. They viewed the processing system as a set of three *memory structures:* the sensory store, the short-term store, and the long-term store. They stated that these structures are permanent, built-in components of the system that do not vary from one situation to another.

Having discussed sensory memory, we will concentrate in this section on the short-term store and the long-term store. According to the model, the short-term store retains information temporarily, for about 15 seconds, and it has a capacity for holding about seven chunks of information. Items can be lost from the short-term store through both decay and interference. In contrast, the long-term store retains information for long periods of time, perhaps permanently, and it has an unlimited storage capacity. The information in the long-term store could decay. But forgetting resulted primarily from the failure to retrieve the stored information.

The model also included a set of control processes, which are operations that people use to manipulate the information within a memory store or to transfer information between stores. Two of the most important control processes were rehearsal and coding. According to the model, rehearsal both maintains items in the short-term store and transfers items to the long-term store. Presumably, the more we rehearse an item, the more likely it is that we will remember that item over long periods of time. The second control process, coding, involves transforming the information in the short-term store in ways that facilitate storage in long-term memory. For example, a four-digit number retained in the short-term store might be transformed into a running time, as in the case of S.F. discussed earlier.

Control processes, unlike the memory structures, can be used in flexible ways. For example, a person might choose to rehearse some items rather than others, and the person could even choose not to rehearse at all. Further, some people might prefer to learn information by engaging in rehearsal, whereas other people might prefer to form images or to organize information. The control processes, then, add flexibility to the processing system.

The model of Atkinson and Shiffrin illustrates the multistore model, but our chief concern is with the features that are common to various models. In general, multistore models have two important features in common. First, they posit the existence of separate short-term and long-term stores. Second, they hold that rehearsal maintains information in the short-term store and transfers information to the long-term store. In this section, we examine the cases for and against both assumptions. When we speak of the multistore model, we refer to a generic model that makes these two assumptions.

Evidence in Favor of the Model

Some of the evidence that suggests that there are separate short-term and long-term stores comes from studies of people who have suffered brain damage. Drachman and Arbit (1966) evaluated the span of immediate memory of people who, like H.M., had sustained injuries to the temporal lobes of the brain. They presented sequences of digits that varied in length, and they repeated each sequence until the patient had recalled it correctly. They observed that the patients' span of immediate memory was about the same as that of individuals who had not sustained brain damage. But the patients took many more trials than the undamaged people to learn sequences of digits that exceeded their memory span. Thus the patients showed a deficit in learning new information, yet their capacity for immediate memory was normal. Further, they showed normal intelligence and remembered events that had occurred prior to the brain injury. In terms of the multistore model, the brain damage had left the memory stores of the patients intact but had impaired the ability to transfer information from the short-term store to the long-term store. This interpretation applies also to the case of H.M., described at the beginning of this chapter.

Studies of people who suffer from Korsakoff's syndrome have produced similar observations. *Korsakoff's syndrome* is produced by chronic alcoholism, which, over a period of years, leads to vitamin deficiencies and eventually to brain damage. In many cases, hospitalization and treatment follow an acute drinking phase or binge that renders the alcoholic confused and amnesic. The patients show severe retrograde amnesia in that they forget the events that had occurred several months prior to the last drinking binge. The patients also show marked anterograde amnesia, the failure to remember events that had occurred after the last binge. Patients suffering from Korsakoff's syndrome show a normal span of immediate memory but show an impaired ability to remember lists of words over long periods of time (Zangwill, 1946).

Overall, these observations suggest that people have separate short-term and long-term stores and that damage to the brain, particularly to the temporal lobes, impairs the ability to transfer information from one store to the other. Although these observations support the multistore model, it is desirable to obtain converging evidence of separate memory stores from studies of undamaged individuals. In fact converging evidence has been adduced from studies of memory capacity, coding, and free recall.

CAPACITY DIFFERENCES

In the preceding chapter, we saw that the span of immediate memory is usually limited to about seven chunks. On the other hand, no one has discovered limits on our capacity for remembering over long periods of time. In our lifetimes, we learn a tremendous number of words, places, faces, and events. These observations have suggested to many theorists that we have two memory stores that differ in their storage capacity. Presumably, the span of immediate memory is limited because the short-term store can retain only about seven chunks. After the short-term store has been filled up, new items cannot be stored, so they will not be remembered. If a new item were allowed to enter the short-term store, that item would displace one of the previously stored items, which would then be forgotten. Unlike the short-term store, the long-term store has unlimited capacity and can retain an indefinitely large amount of information.

PHONEMIC VERSUS SEMANTIC CODING

Evidence from studies of coding has also been used to argue that separate short-term and long-term stores exist. For example, Conrad (1964) observed that people remember items over a short period of time by encoding the items verbally. He presented sequences of six letters such as *B* and *S* aurally against a background of nonverbal noise at a rate of one letter every three-quarters of a second. The subjects' task was to write down the letters they had heard. The results were that the subjects often erred by recalling items that sounded like the presented items. For example, when *B* had been presented, the subjects often erred by recalling *C* or *V*, which sound like *B*. But they seldom erred by recalling the letter *F*, which looks like *B* but does not sound like *B*. Overall, the greater the phonemic similarity (similarity in sound) between two letters, the more often those two letters were confused by the subjects. Because the subjects confused letters that sounded alike but not those that looked alike, Conrad concluded that the subjects had encoded the letters verbally. Conrad obtained highly similar results when he repeated the experiment but presented the letter sequences visually. Regardless of whether the letters had been presented visually or aurally, then, the subjects encoded the items verbally. This outcome suggested that the short-term store retained information only in a verbal format. Because the code contained information concerning the sounds of the items, the code may be called a phonemic code.

In contrast, the long-term store seemed to retain semantically coded information. For example, Sachs (1967) read her subjects stories, one of which concerned Galileo. One of the sentences in the middle of the story was *He sent a letter about it to Galileo, the great Italian scientist.* Without advance warning, Sachs stopped reading the story either 0, 80, or 160 syllables following the reading of the sentence. She then presented one of four test sentences:

Identical: He sent a letter about it to Galileo, the great Italian scientist.
Semantic change: Galileo, the great Italian scientist, sent him a letter about it.
Syntactic change: A letter about it was sent to Galileo, the great Italian scientist.
Formal change: He sent Galileo, the great Italian scientist, a letter about it.

The subjects' task was to indicate whether the test sentence had occurred verbatim in the story. Only the first test sentence had actually occurred in the story. The other test sentences differed from the original with regard to either meaning or grammatical structure.

When the memory test occurred immediately after the reading of the sentence in the story, the subjects responded accurately to all four kinds of test sentences. So they must have remembered the exact wording of the sentence for at least a short time. But when 160 syllables had intervened between the reading of the sentence and the memory test, the subjects responded accurately only to the test sentence labelled "semantic change." Thus they remembered the meaning of the sentence but not its exact wording or grammatical form. This observation suggested that the information in the long-term store had been encoded semantically. Overall, then, it appeared that the short-term store retained phonemic information, whereas the long-term store retained semantic information.

SERIAL POSITION EFFECTS

One of the most commonly used procedures for studying memory is the *free recall* procedure. In a typical free recall task, the experimenter presents a list of, for example, 15 words at a rate of one word every 3 seconds. The subjects' task is to recall the items in any order. The results of this type of procedure, shown by the gray solid line in Figure 4.1, were that the level of recall was highest for the words that had been presented at the beginning and end of the list (Glanzer and Cunitz, 1966). This outcome is called the *serial position effect* because the retention of an item depended upon the position in which it had been presented. The serial position effect is so large and easy to replicate that it has attracted extensive attention since Ebbinghaus' time. In general, the effect consists of two components. The high level of retention for the first few items is called the *primacy effect*; the high level of retention for the last few items is called the *recency effect.*

Many investigators believe that the primacy effect reflects the output of the long-term store, whereas the recency effect reflects the output of the short-term store. One of the chief reasons is that some variables in-

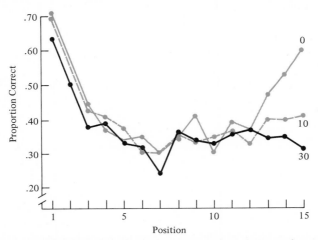

Figure 4.1   The serial position effect in free recall. Interposing a delay of 10 or 30 seconds between the presentation of the list and the test of retention reduced the recency effect but did not influence the primacy effect. (From Glanzer and Cunitz, 1966.)

fluence the recency effect but not the primacy effect. For example, Glanzer and Cunitz (1966) presented a list of 15 words followed by a retention interval of 0, 10, or 30 seconds. During the 10- and 30-second retention intervals, the subjects performed a counting task that was intended to prevent rehearsal. As Figure 4.1 shows, the size of the recency effect depended on the duration of the retention interval. Indeed, the 30-second retention interval eliminated the recency effect. Presumably, the last few items had been retained briefly in the short-term store but had been forgotten because of decay or interference during the retention interval. But when retention was tested immediately, the subjects could recall the last few items at the beginning of the test, before the items had been lost from the short-term store. In fact, the subjects did tend to recall the last few items first and then recall the initial items from the list. Figure 4.1 also shows that the length of the retention interval did not influence the primacy effect. According to the multistore model, the first few items were in the long-term store, so retention of those items was not influenced by the length of the retention interval.

Whereas some factors influence the recency effect but not the primacy effect, other factors do the reverse. For example, Glanzer and Cunitz (1966) presented a 20-item list to three different groups of subjects at a rate of 3, 6, or 9 seconds per word. They then asked the subjects to recall the list immediately. The results were that the rate of presentation did not influence the size of the recency effect, but it did influence the size of the primacy effect. In particular, the slower the rate of presentation had been, the higher the level of recall was for the first five or so items in the list. Glanzer et al. suggested that the slower the rate of presentation, the more the subjects rehearsed the initial items in the list. The extra rehearsal facilitated retention by transferring the items to the long-term store. This account is consonant with the idea that the primacy effect reflects the output of the long-term store.

This interpretation of the primacy effect draws additional support from experiments in which rehearsal was measured directly. Rundus and Atkinson (1970) presented 11 lists of 20 unrelated nouns at a rate of one word every 5 seconds. The subjects were asked to rehearse aloud the word that was being shown and any of the other words from the list. Following the presentation of each list, a test of free recall was administered. As shown by the solid line in Figure 4.2, the usual serial position effect occurred: there were large primacy and recency effects. Figure 4.2 also shows how many times the words at each position in the lists were rehearsed. For all but the last three items in the list, there was a marked correspondence between the number of rehearsals and the level of retention. Thus the primacy effect seems to depend upon the amount of rehearsal, suggesting that the effect is a long-term storage phenomenon. This observation supports the view that rehearsal leads to the transfer of

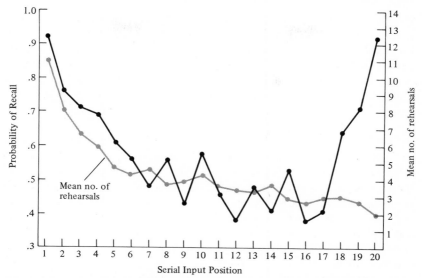

Figure 4.2   The role of rehearsal in the serial position effect. The black line shows the level of recall of the items at various input positions. The gray line indicates how many times each item had been rehearsed. (From Rundus and Atkinson, 1970.)

information from the short-term store to the long-term store. The results also show that the recency effect does not depend on the amount of rehearsal, presumably because the last few items were retained in the short-term store without extensive rehearsal.

Overall, the multistore model provides a coherent account of the serial position effect. The subjects rehearse the initial items frequently, thereby transferring the items to the long-term store. This long-term storage accounts for the primacy effect. The subjects retain the last few items in the short-term store and recall those items first in the retention test, before the items have been lost from the short-term store. This accounts for the recency effect. The items in the middle of the list are recalled poorly for at least two reasons. First, they are so far from the end of the list that they are not in the short-term store at the beginning of the retention test. Second, the subjects did not rehearse them extensively because only a few items can be rehearsed at a time. If the subjects had rehearsed all of the items equally, they might have failed to rehearse any of the items enough times to allow for long-term storage. By rehearsing the initial items extensively, the subjects managed to transfer at least a few items to the long-term store.

As you can see, the multistore model accounted for a wide range of observations. The model was attractive partly because of its simplicity and its clarity. It defined the processing system in terms of three concrete memory stores, each of which stored and processed information in a unique, well-specified manner. Additionally, the model specified clearly how information was transferred throughout the system. For a time, some theorists believed that they could achieve a relatively complete account of cognition by simply working out the details of the model. Further research, however, shattered this optimistic outlook.

The Case Against the Model

One major problem that the model faces concerns the manner in which information is encoded. Initially, the multistore model held that the short-term store retained only phonemic information. But numerous experiments established that visual coding also occurs in immediate memory tasks. In one experiment (Kroll, Parks, Parkinson, Bieber, and Johnson, 1970), subjects shadowed a series of letters read in a male voice. As they shadowed, a test letter was presented. In the auditory condition, the test letter was read in a female voice. In the visual condition, the test letter was flashed briefly on a screen. The subjects' task was to shadow without errors but also to remember the test letter during a retention interval that lasted 1, 10, or 25 seconds. The rationale was that if the subjects had encoded the test letter phonemically then the shadowed letters, which had to be encoded verbally, would retroactively interfere with the test letter. The results were that the subjects in both conditions recalled around 96 percent of the items following the 1-second intervals. But following the 25-second intervals, the level of recall was much higher in the visual condition than in the auditory condition. Thus the shadowed letters interfered with the aurally presented test letter. This suggests that the subjects in the visual condition had encoded the test letter in a visual format, thereby reducing the interference from the phonemic input from the shadowing task.

Other experiments showed that semantic information can also be retained in the short-term store (Shulman, 1972). Apparently, then, people are flexible encoders. Under some conditions, perhaps when verbal rehearsal will facilitate the performance of a task, people encode the incoming information phonemically. But under other conditions, they can encode information visually or semantically. In their initial form, multistore models were too rigid to accommodate this flexibility.

Of course, multistore models could be liberalized so as to allow for the retention of visual, phonemic, and semantic information by both the short-term store and the long-term store. But this modification adds complexity to the model. Additionally, it removes one of the clearest distinctions between the short-term store and the long-term store. Neither problem is fatal, but both problems decrease the attractiveness of the model.

LONG-TERM RECENCY EFFECTS

As discussed above, the model stated that recency effects occur because the last few items in a list are retained in the short-term store at the beginning of the recall period. On this view, the recency effect is short-lived and does not occur following retention intervals longer than about 15 seconds. Contrary to this position, Bjork and Whitten (1974) observed that recency effects can occur over longer periods of time. They presented 10 pairs of words and interposed a 12-second delay between the presentation of successive pairs. Additionally, they interposed a 20-second delay between the presentation of the last pair and a retention test in which the subjects attempted to recall all 10 pairs. During the delay periods, the subjects performed an arithmetic task designed to prevent rehearsal. Because of the length of the delay periods, the subjects should not have been able to recall any items from the short-term store. Nevertheless, a large recency effect occurred: the level of recall for the last three or four words that had been presented was very high. On the other hand, the level of recall for the words that had been presented in the middle of the list was quite low.

Many other experiments have documented the occurrence of long-term recency effects (Baddeley and Hitch, 1977; Glenberg, Bradley, Stevenson, Kraus, Tkachuk, Gretz, Fish, and Turpin, 1980). They have also tested whether the long-term recency effect reflects the output of the short-term store. If it did, then the effect should be influenced by the difficulty of the distractor task that the subjects perform during the retention interval. In performing a difficult distractor task, the subjects must use a substantial amount of the limited capacity of the short-term store. As a result, little capacity would remain for storing the last few items in a list, and the size of the recency effect would decrease. In fact, however, the difficulty of the distractor does not alter the long-term recency effect (Glenberg et al., 1980). Taken together, these observations challenge the position that recency effects indicate the existence of a separate short-term store. One could argue that the multistore model explains short-term but not long-term recency effects. But the point remains that the model fails to provide a general account of serial position effects. As the model lost its generality, it became less attractive.

CAPACITY: STORAGE OR PROCESSING LIMITS?

The multistore model attributes the limits on our cognitive capacity, for example, the limits on the span of immediate memory, to the limited storage capacity of the short-term store. Usually, theorists have assumed that the storage capacity of the short-term store was about seven items or chunks. Craik and Lockhart (1972) criticized this view, noting that experimental estimates of the number of words retained in the short-term store have ranged from two to twenty. Conceivably, the subjects in these experiments could have been remembering a constant seven chunks of information. After all, subjects can probably group several words such as *Haste makes waste* into a single unit. Unfortunately, the advocates of the multistore model never defined chunks clearly. Chunks were defined as whatever the subjects remembered seven of. Because predictions cannot be made using this type of after-the-fact account, the account is uncompelling.

Craik and Lockhart (1972) argued that our cognitive limitations reflect limitations on processing capacity, not on storage capacity. This position can account for the observations that the multistore model explained in terms of storage capacity. In the preceding chapter, for example, we saw that the limits on our processing resources can account for the limits on the span of immediate memory.

Using the concept of limited processing capacity as outlined in the preceding chapter, Craik and Lockhart were able to explain many observations concerning immediate memory. And they did so without postulating a separate short-term store. In essence, they showed that it is necessary to assume the existence of only one memory store. This position is simpler than the multistore position, which assumed the existence of separate short-term and long-term stores. Simplicity is desirable since the more complex the theory, the more difficult the theory is to use. Moreover, a theory that makes few assumptions but explains many observations is powerful and elegant, whereas a theory that makes many assumptions and explains the same body of observations is less so. In general, then, theorists want to assume the existence of as few memory stores as possible. As we shall see, the proposal of Craik and Lockhart eventually carried the day.

REHEARSAL REVISITED

The multistore model required a mechanism for transferring information from the short-term store to the long-term store. Otherwise, the model could not explain the occurrence of relatively permanent learning and retention. Initially, rehearsal was viewed as one of the primary transfer mechanisms. The effects of rehearsal appeared unequivocal, particularly in analyses of the primacy effect. This added credibility to the model. But as research continued, rehearsal proved not to be a straightforward transfer mechanism (Jacoby and Bartz, 1972).

To illustrate, consider a clever experiment by Rundus (1977), who told subjects he was studying immediate memory for numbers. In each of a series of trials, he presented two numbers that the subjects were to remember during a retention interval of 4, 8, or 12 seconds. Then he read a word which the subjects repeated aloud once per second during the retention interval. He told the subjects that the word repetition task was designed to prevent rehearsal of the numbers. In fact, however, Rundus really wanted to know whether the number of times a word was rehearsed influenced the retention of that word. At the end of the experiment, the subjects were asked to recall all of the words they had rehearsed. The results were that the number of rehearsals (4, 8, or 12) had no effect on the level of recall. Thus increased rehearsal does not always facilitate long-term retention.

These observations discredited the notion that rehearsal is a straightforward process that invariably transfers information to the long-term store. No doubt the multistore model could have been modified in order to account for the complex effects of rehearsal. But that modification would have increased the complexity of the model even more. And the model was in trouble on other grounds, as discussed above. Eventually, a number of small problems added up and led theorists to reject the assumption of separate short-term and long-term stores. Today, theorists such as Shiffrin (1976), who had helped formulate the multistore model, envision short-term memory as the product of activating a portion of a single memory store.

Many laypeople think that scientists reject a model only if the model has been disproven. But this view is incomplete, if not incorrect (Kuhn, 1970). Scientists often abandon a model because it no longer seems to point toward the important questions, because it has become unwieldy and difficult to test, or because a simpler, more interesting model has evolved. All of these factors contributed to the decline of the multistore model. For example, the observations concerning rehearsal suggested that there may be different kinds of rehearsal, or different types of processing. These observations were intriguing, yet the multistore model neither explained them nor guided research into them. But Craik and Lockhart soon proposed a new conception, the levels of processing model, that accounted for the new observations and guided research into the effects of different types of processing. Their model became dominant during the 1970s, and its offshoots are still highly influential.

DEPTH, ELABORATION, AND MEMORY

The research reviewed above showed that people encode information in a flexible manner. And the weight of the evidence indicated that people tend to remember phonemically coded information for relatively short periods of time, whereas they remember semantically coded information for relatively long periods of time. The levels of processing model united these insights into a coherent framework.

Levels of Processing

The levels of processing conception was proposed initially as a framework for guiding research (Craik and Lockhart, 1972). But because it has been used by many authors as an explanatory account, we shall call it a model.

The model, like some models of attention, builds on the idea that incoming information is analyzed in stages. In the initial stages, physical or sensory features are analyzed. In the intermediate stages of processing, pattern recognition occurs, and the incoming items can be labelled. The later stages of analysis involve the abstraction of meaning. For example, having recognized and named the word *dog,* you might process that word semantically by analyzing the features that most dogs have, by thinking of associated words such as *cat,* or by forming an image of your own dog.

In this model, processing proceeds through a series of stages or levels, and a greater degree of cognitive or semantic analysis occurs at each successive stage. In other words, the stages vary with respect to the *depth of processing,* where greater depth implies a greater degree of conceptual or semantic analysis. Using this terminology, the semantic level of processing is the deepest level of processing, and the level at which naming occurs is deeper than the level at which physical features are analyzed. As Figure 4.3 shows, these levels can be thought of as lying on a continuum ranging from shallow, physical analyses to deep, semantic analyses. The greater the depth at which information is processed, the farther down on the continuum it moves.

Perception and memory have long been seen as closely related processes (Köhler, 1947). The model embodies this position, stating that

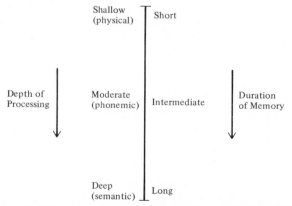

Figure 4.3 The levels of processing model. The model states that items can be processed at various depths, and the deeper the processing, the longer the items will be remembered.

memory is a by-product of perceptual analyses. As shown in Figure 4.3, the deeper the level of processing, the longer the processed information will be remembered. This thesis accounts for the retention of phonemic and semantic information in the following manner. We remember phonemic information for a moderate amount of time because that information has been processed at a moderately deep level. Similarly, we remember semantic information over long periods of time because that information has been processed at a deep level. Note that the model accounts for retention without postulating several memory stores.

Capacity limitations, according to the model, arise from constraints on our processing capacity, not on our storage capacity. The span of immediate memory is limited because only so many items can be processed at a particular time. The items that are being processed at a particular moment are said to belong to primary memory. As you can see, this view agrees with James' conception of primary memory and also with the position outlined in the preceding chapter.

TYPE I AND TYPE II PROCESSING

Because information can be maintained in immediate memory through rehearsal, Craik and Lockhart proposed that capacity can be used to recirculate information at one level of processing. This type of recirculatory processing, called *Type I processing*, maintains information in primary memory. But since it does not process information at progressively deeper levels, it does not facilitate retention once attention has been withdrawn. For example, when you mindlessly rehearse a phone number in order to remember it long enough to dial it, you are engaging in Type I processing. In contrast, *Type II processing*, which involves processing information at progressively greater depths, does lead to longer lasting retention. In concrete terms, Type I processing maintains items at a particular point on the continuum diagrammed in Figure 4.3, whereas Type II processing moves toward the deeper end of the continuum. Type I and Type II processing correspond roughly to the short-term storage and the long-term storage posited by the multistore model. The difference is that the levels of processing model posits only one memory store and emphasizes processing rather than storage factors.

The distinction between Type I and Type II processing accounts for the observations concerning rehearsal that had posed problems for the multistore model. Rehearsal that serves only to maintain items in primary memory, sometimes called maintenance rehearsal (Craik and Watkins, 1973), entails Type I processing. Rehearsal that aids long-term retention, sometimes called elaborative rehearsal, entails Type II processing. Thus the model holds that rehearsal per se does not influence memory. What matters is the type of processing that the subjects engage in as they rehearse. If they are thinking of new associations to a word or relating the meanings of different words as they rehearse, then rehearsal will appear to have aided memory. But if they are processing information at a particular level while rehearsing, then rehearsal will appear to have had no influence on memory.

Unlike the multistore model, the levels of processing model emphasizes the flexibility of human information processing. We can process information at various points along the continuum of depth, and we can maintain information at any point along the continuum. This conception agrees with the observation that people can encode information in various ways. Equally important, it calls attention to the importance of encoding processes and of processing operations as determinants of memory. Although the model built upon ideas that had been available for some time, it constituted a radical departure from the multistore model.

SEMANTIC VERSUS NONSEMANTIC PROCESSING

The model asserts that information processed at deep, semantic levels will be remembered better over a relatively long period of time than information processed at shallow, nonsemantic levels. The obvious way to test this assertion is to tell some subjects to process information at a shallow level and to tell others to process information at a deep level. Subsequently, a test of retention could be given. The trouble, however, is that if the subjects were told they were participating in a memory experiment and were asked to process at one particular level, they might secretly process the information in whatever ways they think will aid retention. After all, most people want to perform well and to appear intelligent.

In order to control the manner in which subjects process information, investigators use *incidental learning* procedures. Specifically, the subjects are deceived into thinking that the goal of the experiment is to examine how they perform a plausible cover task when in fact the purpose is to study memory. This type of procedure was used by Craik and Tulving (1975). They told their subjects that the experiment concerned perception and the speed of reaction. In each of 60 trials, a question was presented and then a word was flashed for 200 msec. The subject's task was to answer the question about the word as rapidly as possible. The questions were designed to induce the subjects to encode the words in particular ways. To induce the subjects to encode the physical characteristics of a word such as *table,* the experimenters asked a question such as "Is the word in capital letters?" To induce phonemic coding of a word such as *crate,* the experimenters asked a question such as "Does the word rhyme with WEIGHT?" Semantic encoding was induced by asking a question such as "Would the word fit the sentence: 'They met a _____ in the street'?" Following the series of questions and answers, the subjects were unexpectedly given a recognition test for the words. The recognition test consisted of 180 words, including the 60 original words and 120 lures or distractors. The subjects' task was to indicate which words had been presented originally.

As predicted, the level of encoding determined the level of retention, as Figure 4.4 shows. Retention was poorest for the words that had been encoded on a physical level. Retention was greatest for the words that had been encoded on a semantic level. And retention was intermediate for the words that had been encoded phonemically. This pattern of observation showing better retention for semantically processed information has occurred in many experiments with many different tasks and stimuli (Bower and Karlin, 1974; Bransford, Nitsch, and Franks, 1977; Dooling and Christiaansen, 1977; Fisher and Craik, 1977; Lockhart, Craik, and Jacoby, 1976). Collectively, these results support the levels of processing model. They also agree with observations from our daily activities. As an example, we may remember the theme of our favorite novel for many years but rapidly forget what color shirt was worn by the stranger who sat beside us on the bus yesterday. Once again, semantic encoding leads to longer retention than shallower encoding.

The model would be impoverished if it accounted only for observations from incidental learning procedures. In activities such as shopping and studying for tests, people try intentionally to remember information. Fortunately, the model does apply to intentional learning. It states that the level of retention depends upon the depth of processing regardless of whether the processing occurs incidentally or intentionally. On this assumption, the level of retention should be as high following incidental semantic processing as following intentional learning.

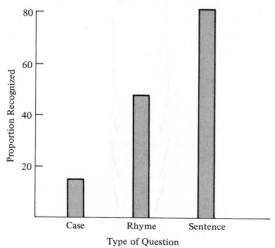

Figure 4.4   The effects of the level of encoding upon retention. (From Craik and Tulving, 1975. Copyright 1975 by the American Psychological Association. All rights reserved.)

Evidence concerning this assumption comes from an experiment by Hyde and Jenkins (1969), who read a list of 24 words to adults at a rate of 2 seconds per word. The subjects in the intentional learning condition were told they would later be asked to recall the words. The subjects in the other conditions, the incidental learning conditions, were not told they would have to remember the words. Instead, they were deceived as to the actual purpose of the experiment and were asked to perform one of several orienting tasks. In one orienting task, the subject indicated whether each of the 24 words contained the letter *E*. In another orienting task, the subjects rated each word on a scale of pleasantness and unpleasantness. These orienting tasks required subjects to process the words in very different ways. For example, rating the pleasantness of a word requires analyzing its meaning. But looking for an **E** does not require semantic processing. As predicted, the subjects who had rated the pleasantness of the words recalled as many words as the subjects in the intentional learning condition did. Significantly fewer words were recalled in the letter detection condition. A similar pattern of results has been obtained in many other studies (Hyde and Jenkins, 1973; Walsh and Jenkins, 1973). Collectively, these observations show that the intention to learn per se is not among the chief determinants of memory. What is most important is how the subjects encode information—how they operate upon it. Semantic processing leads to a high level of retention regardless of whether it was undertaken intentionally or incidentally.

These observations increased the credibility of the model. The model was attractive also because it was conceptually simple and because it accommodated many of the observations that had been troublesome to the multistore model. During the 1970s, the levels of processing model virtually reshaped the study of memory. Nevertheless, the model encountered problems, some of which were discovered by its chief proponents.

The Limits of Levels

The model stands largely on the observation that semantic processing leads to better retention than nonsemantic processing. But this outcome is not universal. For example, Morris, Bransford, and Franks (1977) asked subjects questions designed to induce phonemic or semantic processing, as Craik and Tulving had. Phonemic processing was induced by asking the question"_____ rhymes with legal?" Semantic processing was produced by presenting statements such as "The _____ had a silver engine." A target word was read following each sentence, and subjects indicated whether the sentence rhymed or was meaningful, but they did not know they would be asked to remember the words. Two types of retention test were given. One was a standard recognition test including an equal number of target words and novel foils. The second was a rhyming recognition test that included foils and words that rhymed with the target words. The subjects' task in the rhyming recognition test was to indicate which words rhymed with the target words.

Surprisingly, opposite results occurred in the two tests. In the standard test, retention was superior for the semantically processed words. But in the rhyme test, retention was superior for the phonemically processed words. This outcome contradicts the model, yet similar observations have occurred in numerous studies (Bransford, Franks, Morris, and Stein, 1979; Stein, 1978). These observations underscore the importance of using more than one type of test in studies of memory.

On a deeper level (sorry!), these observations indicate that the value of a particular activity depends upon the type of task one is performing. Semantic processing aids retention, but only if the semantic processing is appropriate to the retention test that is administered. If a rhyme test will be administered, then semantic processing will be less useful than phonemic processing.

Another problem confronting the levels of processing model concerns the degree of expertise or knowledge of the subject (Bransford et al., 1979). For example, we are all experts in recognizing the sounds of our native language. We remember the sounds of many words and the voices of many speakers over long periods of time. Similarly, we are skilled readers. Kolers and Ostry (1974; Kolers, 1979) have shown that people can remember over long periods of time the type of print they have read. The model fails to explain how people remember physical properties over long periods of time. Of course, one could argue that they do so by processing the physical information deeply. But this argument breaks down the distinction between nonsemantic and semantic processing. Additionally, it is difficult to measure exactly the level at which processing occurred. This problem is examined next.

THE PROBLEM OF DEFINING DEPTH

In most experiments, the depth of processing is defined by the type of incidental learning task that the subject performs. For example, if the task requires phonemic processing, then it is assumed that the subject engages in phonemic processing. The problem with this assumption is that the subject may engage not only in phonemic processing but also in semantic processing (Nelson, 1979; Postman, Thompkins, and Gray, 1978). Because of our extensive experience in processing words semantically, for example, in the act of reading, we may automatically process words at the semantic level even in tasks that require only phonemic processing. So it is unwise to define the level of processing in terms of the requirements of incidental learning tasks.

In the absence of an adequate method of measuring the level of processing, we may be tempted to infer the level of processing from the observed level of retention. High levels of retention might indicate the occurrence of semantic processing, whereas low levels of retention might indicate the occurrence of nonsemantic processing. But taking this step robs the model of its explanatory power. If we attribute the high retention to deep processing, when the only evidence of deep processing is the high retention, we are trapped in a vicious circle (Baddeley, 1978; Eyesenck, 1978; Nelson, 1977; Postman, 1976).

To eliminate the problem of circularity, we need to define the level of processing without referring to the level of retention. Investigators have tried hard to formulate such a definition. Some have examined whether deeper processing is indicated by relatively long processing times (Craik and Tulving, 1975; Kunen, Green, and Waterman, 1979) or by the extensive use of processing resources (Eyesenck and Eyesenck, 1979; Tyler, Hertel, McCallum, and Ellis, 1979). Others have tried to define depth by subjective ratings of the level of processing (Seamon and Virostek, 1978). Yet these attempts have met with little success. For now, the problem of defining levels empirically remains unsolved.

TWO KINDS OF REHEARSAL?

The model asserted that Type I processing, also called maintenance rehearsal, maintains information at a particular level of processing but does not improve retention. Type II processing, also called elaborative rehearsal, analyzes information at progressively deeper levels, thereby improving retention. We saw previously that some observations support this distinction. For example, the number of times subjects rehearsed words, supposedly as part of a distractor task, did not influence the level of recall (Rundus, 1977). This outcome seems to indicate that maintenance rehearsal does not improve retention.

Other experiments, however, have shown that maintenance rehearsal can improve retention (Geiselman and Bjork, 1980; Glenberg and Adams, 1978; Maki and Schuler, 1980; Nelson, 1977; Woodward et al., 1973). Glenberg et al. (1978) presented numbers to be remembered in each of a series of trials in an immediate memory task. During the retention intervals, the subjects repeated particular words, supposedly as a means of preventing rehearsal. At the end of the session, the subjects were asked unexpectedly to recall all of the words. As Rundus had observed, the number of rehearsals of a word did not influence the level of recall. But a test of recognition showed that rehearsal did facilitate recognition. Using a similar experimental procedure, Rundus (1980) observed that if the rehearsal occurred over a period of 60 seconds, a longer period than had been used in earlier studies, then rehearsal facilitated recall by a small but significant margin.

These observations initially seem to oppose the view that maintenance rehearsal does not affect retention. But owing to the problems involved in defining levels of processing, these observations are difficult to interpret. Perhaps the subjects in the preceding experiments engaged in elaborative rehearsal even though the task did not demand it. If elaborative rehearsal did in fact occur, then these results pose no problem for the model. Yet it is difficult to tell whether the subjects had engaged in maintenance rehearsal, elaborative rehearsal, or both.

In light of this uncertainty, it is unsurprising that theorists disagree about whether there are two different kinds of rehearsal. Some have argued in favor of retaining a modified version of the distinction, claiming that the two types of rehearsal influence retention through different processes (Geiselman and Bjork, 1980; Rundus, 1980). Specifically, elaborative rehearsal may involve processing items at progressively deeper levels and relating the meanings of the various items that are being processed. Maintenance rehearsal, on the other hand, involves linking the rehearsed items with the external or internal contextual cues that are present. For example, as a word is rehearsed, it may automatically become associated with the sights and the sounds in the experimental room, with the subjects' feelings of hunger, and so on. If those cues are present in the retention test, then they may facilitate the retrieval of the rehearsed words. Other theorists, however, contend that a strict dichotomy between two kinds of rehearsal is untenable (Craik, 1979; Craik and Jacoby, 1979; Jacoby, Bartz, and Evans, 1978). They favor replacing the dichotomy with a continuum of rehearsal activities that influence retention in various degrees. Additional research must decide which of these conceptions is most useful.

STAGES RECONSIDERED

A major problem of the model was that it envisaged a fixed sequence of processing stages that began with physical analyses and terminated with semantic analyses. As was shown in the discussion of attention, however, we often process in a conceptually driven manner in which deep semantic analyses precede and guide the analysis of physical features. For example, in reading the sentence *The name of our planet is 'earth,'* we may begin processing semantic information pertaining to our planet before actually seeing the word *earth*. And when our eyes encounter *earth*, we may process at a semantic level and use the results to guide the analysis of the physical features of the word. In conceptually driven processing, deeper analyses precede and guide shallower analyses. This processing sequence is just the opposite of the sequence proposed by the model.

These problems necessitated the revision of the model. The revised model disavowed the concept of a fixed sequence of processing stages, yet it retained much of the flavor of the initial model. We now examine the revised model, which centers around the concept of the elaborateness of processing.

Elaboration, Organization, and Mnemonics

The revised model states that retention depends not on the depth of encoding but on the elaborateness or the spread of encoding (Craik and Tulving, 1975). The elaborateness of encoding refers to the extent to which items are related to or organized with other items. For example, in learning a list of words that includes *grief, love, forgotten,* and *spinster,* you could encode *spinster* in a relatively elaborate manner by relating it to the other words, perhaps by making up a story that included all of the words. You might encode *spinster* in a less elaborate manner by analyzing the meaning of that word without relating it to the meaning of the other words. This definition of elaborateness emphasizes the relationships between different items.

Elaborateness also refers to the extent to which an individual item is analyzed, regardless of the level at which the processing occurs. For example, *spinster* has numerous semantic attributes or features, including *female, unmarried,* and *old.* The more attributes we encode, the more elaborate our memory representation is. Whereas the first definition emphasized between-item elaboration, this definition stresses within-item elaboration. These definitions point out that information can be elaborated in at least two ways, both of which occur by adding information to the internal representation.

One reason behind the emphasis on elaborateness is that the elaborateness of processing affects retention apart from the level of processing. Craik and Tulving (1975) asked subjects whether briefly presented words such as *watch* made sense in various sentences, for example, *He dropped the* _____ and *The old man hobbled across the room and picked up the valuable* _____ *from the mahogany table.* Both sentences require processing at the semantic level. But the latter sentence requires richer, more elaborate encoding because it provides more semantic context than the former sentence. The results of an unannounced memory test showed that the more elaborately the words had been processed, the higher the level of retention was. This kind of observation has convinced many theorists that retention depends less on the level of processing than on the elaborateness of processing (cf. Cermak and Craik, 1979).

The elaborateness concept is preferred also because it avoids the notion of a fixed sequence of processing stages (Craik and Tulving, 1975). Phonemic analyses can occur before physical analyses have been completed, and semantic analyses can occur before phonemic analyses have

been completed. For example, in reading an article about the chimpan-
zee, you might process the physical and the phonemic features of the
word *chimp* minimally, while processing the semantic features elaborately. After all, in reading, we attend primarily to the meaning of
words rather than to their physical and phonemic properties. Under
other conditions, for example, in evaluating the rhythm of a poem, you
might process the physical features of the words elaborately while processing the meanings minimally.

Unlike the initial model, this conception states that elaborate processing facilitates retention regardless of whether the processing involves
physical, phonemic, or semantic analyses. Indeed, if the physical processing is more elaborate than the semantic processing, as occurs in evaluating the rhythm of a poem, this conception predicts that the physical
information will be remembered better than semantic information. Nevertheless, this conception retains the central idea that the manner in
which information is encoded determines the level of retention. Keeping
this similarity in mind, we now examine the effects of the elaborateness
of processing on retention. We begin with a discussion of between-item
elaboration and return subsequently to within-item elaboration.

ORGANIZATION IN FREE RECALL

One way to process an item elaborately is to group that item with other
items, that is, to organize the items. As a demonstration, read the following list of words at a slow rate, about 2 to 3 seconds per word. Then close
the book and write down as many of the words as possible in any order.

> Bear, cucumber, fox, chair, turnip, dog, stool, radish, bed, sofa, squash,
> rabbit, tomato, monkey, carrot, lamp, cow, broccoli, table, mouse, let-
> tuce, dresser, desk, horse

In recalling this type of list, most people recall the words by category.
You probably tended to recall the animals together, the vegetables together, and the furniture items together. This phenomenon, which was
studied by Bousfield (1953), is called *categorical clustering.* It shows that
we tend to organize items into groups as we learn.

Early experiments tested whether organization facilitated retention.
For example, Tulving (1962) presented a list of 16 two-syllable nouns at a
rate of one word per second. The words in the list were unrelated in that
they did not belong to similar categories, and they were not highly associated. When the list had been presented, the subjects were asked to recall the words in any order. Then a second trial began, and the procedure
was repeated except that the words were presented in a different order.
This procedure continued over ten trials. Tulving measured the degree
of organization by measuring the extent to which pairs of words were re-

called together across trials. The rationale was that if a subject recalled two words, for example, *building* and *cent*, one after another on successive trials, then one could assume that the subject had organized those words in a stable group.

Over trials, both the number of words and the level of organization increased. Because the words in the list were not related in any obvious way, the subjects may have imposed organization on the list as they learned it. This phenomenon, called *subjective organization*, is consistent with the Gestalt outlook that learning is a process of actively imposing structure upon incoming stimuli. Equally important, this observation suggests that organizing facilitates remembering. Of course, a positive correlation between the level of organization and the level of retention does not imply that increased organization causes improvements in retention.

In an effort to obtain stronger, noncorrelational evidence, investigators have examined the effects of inducing organization. One way to induce organization is to present the items in a manner that calls attention to the semantic relationships between the items. For example, Bower, Clark, Lesgold, and Winzenz (1969) asked subjects to remember 112 words that belonged to one of four conceptual hierarchies. One of the hierarchies included the names of minerals, as shown in Figure 4.5a. This type of arrangement is called a conceptual hierarchy because it contains

Minerals

	Metals			Stones
Rare	Common	Alloys	Precious	Masonry
platinum	aluminum	bronze	sapphire	limestone
silver	copper	steel	emerald	granite
gold	lead	brass	diamond	marble
	iron		ruby	slate

(a)

Brass

	Ruby			Gold
Granite	Steel	Lead	Iron	Sapphire
minerals	limestone	metals	masonry	alloys
emerald	rare	precious	aluminum	diamond
copper	stones	slate	common	platinum
	silver		bronze	marble

(b)

Figure 4.5   The hierarchies presented by Bower et al. (1969). (a) The conceptual hierarchy for "minerals." (b) A random arrangement of the words in (a).

conceptually related groups of items arranged in such a manner that each higher-level category subsumes the categories beneath it. The subjects in the organization group saw the words arranged on cards as in Figure 4.5a. This type of arrangement was intended to call attention to the relationships between the words and to encourage the subjects to organize the words. The subjects studied four different hierarchies, each of which included 28 words, for 56 seconds in each of four trials. An identical procedure was followed for the control group, except that the words on each card had been placed randomly in a hierarchy, as in Figure 4.5b. This arrangement did not highlight the conceptual relations between items.

The results were that following the first study period, the subjects in the organization group recalled 73 of the 112 words. But the subjects in the control group recalled only about 20 words. Following four trials, the subjects in the organization group recalled all 112 words, whereas the subjects in the control group recalled only half that number. Additionally, the recall profiles showed that the subjects in the organization group recalled the items in a highly organized manner. They usually started at the top of the hierarchy and then worked downward branch by branch of the hierarchy. For example, they tended to recall *minerals, metals,* and *rare* before recalling *platinum* and *silver.* This organized pattern of recall was not apparent in the recall profiles of the subjects in the control group. These observations establish that organization does facilitate memory. Many other observations agree with this conclusion (Bower, 1972).

There are numerous reasons why organization aids memory. As pointed out in the preceding chapter, encoding items into groups reduces the burden on our limited processing resources. As resources are freed, we can find or construct new relations between the items to be remembered and the information we already remember (Mandler, 1979). The eventual outcome is improvements in learning and retention.

Three other reasons concern the retrieval of information. First, when several items have been combined into a single group or chunk, retrieving one member of the group may make the others more accessible. A physical analogy is that finding one book in a library provides access to other related books nearby. Second, when items have been encoded in a group, there may be multiple retrieval paths into the group (one path per item), and this might enhance the retrievability of the information. Third, when items have been organized into a hierarchy, as in the preceding experiment, the hierarchical structure can be used as a plan that guides the retrieval of each branch of the hierarchy. The elaborateness of encoding, then, may influence retention largely by facilitating retrieval. This interpretation emphasizes the close relation between encoding and retrieval.

MNEMONICS

Additional evidence concerning the effects of the elaborateness of encoding comes from studies of mnemonic systems, devices designed to aid memory. For example, Bower and Clark (1969) instructed subjects to learn lists of ten words by making up a story that linked the words together. The subjects managed to connect the words in stories, as in this example:

> A LUMBERJACK DARTed out of a forest, SKATEd around a HEDGE past a COLONY of DUCKS. He tripped on some FURNITURE, tearing his STOCKING while hastening toward the PILLOW where his MISTRESS lay.

Subjects in a control group had not been instructed to use the story mnemonic, but they studied the lists for the same length of time. Following the learning of 12 lists, the subjects were asked to recall all of the words that they had studied. Impressively, the subjects in the story group recalled 93 percent of the words, whereas the subjects in the control group recalled only 13 percent of the words.

An alert skeptic might argue that these observations can be explained in terms of the depth of processing rather than the elaborateness of processing. Perhaps the subjects in the story group had processed the words semantically whereas the subjects in the control group had processed the words nonsemantically. The results of other experiments, however, have reduced the plausibility of this account (Battig and Belleza, 1979). Belleza, Richards, and Geiselman (1976) presented a list of words and asked subjects to use each word in a separate, meaningful sentence. The subjects in the story group were asked to weave their sentences into a continuous story. The subjects in the control group used each word in a sentence but did not try to combine the sentences into a story. Both tasks required semantic processing. Yet the subjects in the story group recalled a greater number of words than the subjects in the control group. So the effects of using the story mnemonic are better explained by the elaborateness of processing than by the depth of processing.

Another mnemonic that involves elaborate processing is called the *keyword system* (Atkinson, 1975). This system, which was designed to facilitate the learning of the vocabulary of a second language, consists of two steps. The first is to associate a vocabulary word with a rhyming English word called a keyword. For example, if the vocabulary item presented were *pato,* the Spanish word for *duck,* one could use *pot* as the keyword. Having associated *pato* and *pot,* one would then form an image of the keyword interacting with the English translation of the vocabulary item. One might imagine a duck swimming in a large pot or perhaps a duck marching around with a pot on its head. In summary, the keyword system involves associating a vocabulary word with a rhyming English word, the keyword, and then imagining the keyword and the English translation word interacting.

This system, like many mnemonics, may seem like the long and hard way of doing things. Yet the system has been shown to be highly effective (Presley, Levin, Hall, Miller, and Berry, 1980). Atkinson (1975) asked subjects to learn 120 Russian words. Half the subjects learned and used the keyword system, whereas the other subjects received no formal instructions. The two groups received equal numbers of study sessions. The results were that the subjects who used the keyword system recalled the meaning of 72 percent of the Russian words, but the other subjects recalled the meanings of only 46 percent of the words. On a surprise test given six weeks later, the subjects who had used the keyword system continued to outdo the others.

The keyword system probably aids performance by encouraging elaborate phonemic and semantic processing. Elaborate phonemic processing occurs by associating a vocabulary item with the similar sounding keyword. This phonemic processing is particularly useful because learning to pronounce words correctly is often one of the largest obstacles to learning foreign vocabulary. Elaborate semantic processing occurs while imagining the object named by the keyword interacting with the English translation of the vocabulary item. In forming an interactive image, one relates different items to each other. On this view, the benefits of forming interactive images, as in the method of loci that was discussed in the first chapter, stem from the occurrence of elaborate processing.

As we learn more about memory and about why elaborate processing is so effective, we should be able to invent useful new mnemonics and to improve existing ones. It is hoped these will help to advance our educational practices and to reduce the frequency of forgetting. Some educators object to the use of mnemonics because many mnemonic systems resemble tricks that do not promote comprehension of underlying concepts. But this seems less a constraint on mnemonic systems than on our ingenuity, for carefully designed mnemonics can stimulate the elaborate semantic processing that educators have always tried to encourage.

Elaborateness and Distinctiveness

We now turn to the effects of within-item elaboration, that is, the extent to which an individual item is analyzed. The memory codes we form may be thought of as groups of attributes or features from numerous dimensions (Bower, 1967; Nelson, 1979; Underwood, 1969; Wickens, 1972). For example, if you encountered the word *skyscraper,* you might process the sound and the meaning of the word, thereby forming a memory code containing phonemic and semantic attributes. The greater the number of attributes of an item you have analyzed, the more elaborately you have encoded that item.

If the elaborate processing aids memory, then an analysis of several attributes of an item should lead to better retention than an analysis of only one attribute. In order to test this prediction, Battig and Einstein (1977; also see Battig, 1979) asked subjects to rate words along one, two, or three dimensions. For example, one of the dimensions concerned the pleasantness of words; the subjects used a six-point scale to indicate the degree of pleasantness or unpleasantness of the words. Two days later, the subjects were asked to recall the words they had rated. As predicted, the subjects recalled a greater number of the words they had rated on three dimensions than of those they had rated on one or two dimensions. These observations suggest that the degree of within-item elaboration influences retention.

DISTINCTIVENESS

As discussed previously, elaborate processing may aid memory by facilitating the retrieval of information. Many investigators believe that elaborate processing makes items distinctive or discriminable from other items and that the increased distinctiveness aids retrieval (Eyesenck, 1979; Jacoby and Craik, 1979). A physical analogy clarifies this view. If a coach asked you to get a particular basketball from a storage room, you would be more likely to find the correct ball if you had a complete description rather than a partial one. The complete description would provide information that distinguished the desired ball from the others. Similarly, an elaborate memory code provides a relatively complete description of the remembered item. For this reason, the item is relatively distinctive and easy to discriminate from other remembered items. As a result, the item can be retrieved more accurately than a less distinctive item can be.

Eyesenck (1979) examined the effects of distinctiveness by inducing either distinctive or nondistinctive coding at the phonemic level of processing. In the nondistinctive condition, the task was to pronounce a series of words in the usual manner. The words were nouns, for example, *glove,* that could be pronounced in the usual manner (gluv) or in an unusual manner (glōve, which rhymes with *cove*). In the distinctive condition, the task was to pronounce the words in the unusual manner. On a subsequent recognition test, the subjects remembered a greater number of words from the distinctive condition than from the nondistinctive condition. Distinctive processing at the phonemic level, then, increased retention.

In further experiments, Eyesenck showed that distinctive processing at the phonemic level can lead to the same high level of retention that results from semantic processing. Thus the distinctiveness of encoding can override the effects of the level of encoding. This type of observation poses problems for the initial levels of processing model. Now that we have examined the revisions of that initial model, we may reinterpret some of the observations discussed earlier.

DEPTH EFFECTS RECONSIDERED

In a typical study of levels of processing, subjects are induced to encode information at either of two levels, for example, the phonemic and semantic levels. As you know, semantic processing often leads to superior retention. This outcome may be due to the depth of encoding, but it may also be due to differences in the elaborateness and distinctiveness of encoding. In particular, semantic processing may give rise to more elaborate and distinctive encoding than phonemic processing does (Anderson and Reder, 1979; Moscovitch and Craik, 1976). Because we belong to a literate society, we have all had extensive practice in processing words semantically and remembering themes. Reading, for example, requires that we discern the semantic relationships between words in sentences, between sentences, and so on. As well-practiced readers, we may encode semantic information elaborately with little effort or conscious thought. In contrast, we are seldom called upon to process the sounds of the words we hear elaborately. Consequently, in a study of levels of processing, adults may automatically encode semantic information elaborately and nonsemantic information nonelaborately. Consistent with this view, semantically processed words tend to be recalled in organized clusters, whereas nonsemantically processed words tend not to be (Hyde and Jenkins, 1973).

This account, which stresses the importance of prior experience and elaborate encoding, makes interesting predictions. Presumably, people such as poets who have had extensive experience in discerning the relationships among the sounds of printed words would automatically encode elaborately on the phonemic level. These individuals should remember phonemically processed words as well as semantically processed words. Following similar logic, professional musicians might be expected to remember the physical features of songs better than laypeople do. To the knowledge of the author, no one has tested these predictions. But studies should be conducted to determine the relationship between practice and the effects of the elaborateness of encoding.

Semantic processing may also give rise to more distinctive, elaborate encodings because of the nature of the tasks often used in studies of levels of processing. Answer each of the following questions. Do *bear* and *bare* rhyme? Do *distill* and *remove* have the same meaning? Answering the first question required the comparison of two sounds, and there is little if any reason to process elaborately. But the second question calls for some elaborate processing. Words have many senses and shades of meaning, and the second question can be answered accurately only when all possible meanings have been analyzed. In short, question two requires elaborate processing whereas question one does not. Although this particular comparison is extreme, the point applies to many other examples. Tasks that induce different levels of processing may also induce different degrees of elaboration, and it may be the latter that influence memory.

The view that elaborate processing facilitates memory is useful and is currently guiding extensive research. Yet this view must overcome several obstacles. We lack adequate measures of elaborateness and distinctiveness. Consequently, it is difficult to determine the exact relationship between elaborate processing and retention. Similarly, we cannot say exactly how elaborateness and distinctiveness are related. Theorists have only begun to test the hypothesis that elaborate processing aids retention by increasing the distinctiveness of the remembered information. But research along these lines is now under way, and this should increase our understanding of remembering.

METAMEMORY

Remembering often occurs as a by-product of incidental processing. But in many situations, remembering results from deliberate, conscious efforts. For example, we write notes to remind ourselves what to buy while shopping, and we place particular items near the door in order to remember to take them with us when we leave. Similarly, in studying for a history test, we may intentionally rehearse key dates, imagine pivotal episodes, organize events according to temporal sequence, and so on. These examples show not only that we often remember intentionally but also that we know how to remember. This knowledge or awareness of how to remember is called metamemory or metamnemonic knowledge (Flavell and Wellman, 1977).

Our metamnemonic knowledge is important because it enables us to tailor the manner in which we process to the demands of the task. Most adults have many different strategies for encoding information, but not all of the strategies are equally appropriate in a particular task. For example, if the task were to read and remember the theme of a novel, then a semantic coding strategy would be more effective than a phonemic coding strategy. Without metamnemonic knowledge, people would fail more frequently than they already do to use appropriate coding strategies. As a result, they would be more forgetful and would appear less intelligent. Because of the importance of metamemory, this section focuses on our knowledge of how to remember and analyzes where this knowledge comes from.

Broadly speaking, metamemory includes our knowledge about our memory skills, about the determinants of our performance in memory tasks, and about how to monitor and modify our activities so as to remember. These and other components of metamemory are best thought of as components of problem solving (Brown and DeLoache, 1978). In this instance, the problem is how to remember something. Accordingly, we shall group the components of metamemory into categories corresponding to the broad steps involved in solving a problem: defining the problem, planning a strategy for solving it, and monitoring and adjusting performance in accord with the outcomes. In this section, we focus on the first two steps since they have been studied extensively.

Awareness of the Mnemonic Problem

The mnemonic problem, the possibility that we may forget something worth remembering, is pervasive in everyday life. Who has not had the experience of walking into a test confident of remembering the critical information only to leave feeling shell-shocked and deflated? Recognizing the mnemonic problem requires awareness of the goal of remembering something and assessing whether special effort is needed to meet the demands of the present memory task. In turn, making this assessment requires considerable knowledge of our own memory skills and knowledge and of the factors that make a memory task difficult (Flavell and Wellman, 1977). As we shall see, this knowledge arises through experience; its absence is often conspicuous in young children and inexperienced adults.

KNOWLEDGE OF PERSON VARIABLES

Awareness of a memory problem can arise from knowledge about the scope and limits of one's own memory and of human memory in general. Through our experiences, we know the difficulty of remembering large amounts of poorly learned information. Yet the limits on the span of immediate memory are not so apparent to young children. In one experiment (Yussen and Levy, 1975), 4-, 8-, and 20-year-olds were shown a set of ten pictures and were asked to estimate how many they thought they could recall on an immediate retention test. As shown in Figure 4.6, the youngest children were quite inept in predicting their actual memory span. For the 20-year-olds, on the other hand, there was little discrepancy between the predicted and the actual memory span. Having such accurate knowledge enables the adults to discern memory problems that the 4-year-olds would not have noticed. Although 4-year-olds do recognize the memory problem in some situations (Acredolo, Pick, and Olsen, 1975), their knowledge of their own memory skills is understandably limited.

The adults' knowledge of their actual memory span may have arisen

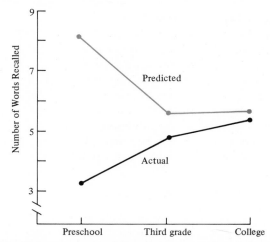

Figure 4.6 Predicted and actual memory spans of people at various ages. (Data from Yussen and Levy, 1975.)

from the understanding that, in general, the span of immediate memory is limited to about seven items. Each of us acquires extensive knowledge about the general properties of human memory, even in the absence of formal instruction in psychology. We learn in school that all students must study in order to remember the presented information. We learn from our families that the elderly are often forgetful, that the young cannot be expected to know their exact memorial abilities, and so on. This knowledge of the memory skills of large groups of people can help us discriminate memory problems in ourselves as well as others.

Some of the most important metamnemonic knowledge we have pertains to our own memorial idiosyncrasies and propensities. For unknown reasons, some people can effortlessly remember names and faces, whereas others must struggle to remember names but have impressive memories for numbers. Some people, such as the preoccupied "absent-minded professor" find themselves so forgetful that they fastidiously take notes (which they promptly lose) on almost every important event. These examples illustrate long-term or dispositional memory characteristics. As we learn more and more about our own characteristics, we become aware of and anticipate the memory problems we face in various situations. In addition to knowing our long-term characteristics, we know about the effects of short-term conditions upon our memory. Through our unique experiences, we may learn that lack of sleep begets a general forgetfulness or that we tend to forget things heard in a moment of indisposition. This knowledge may also help us to identify and anticipate memory problems.

KNOWLEDGE OF TASK VARIABLES

Adults in our culture have extensive knowledge about the variables that influence the difficulty of a memory task. We know that long retention intervals produce more forgetting, and that large quantities of information are more difficult to remember than small quantities are. Similarly, we know that retention depends on the type of memory test. Specifically, recall of the gist or theme of a passage is usually easier than verbatim recall. The differences in the difficulty of various types of test are particularly well known to students. Some students have even been known to use the type of test as a criterion for choosing courses. Without a doubt, this knowledge of task variables enables adults to discriminate the occasions on which memory problems are likely to occur.

Knowledge of the task variables that influence memory is hardly restricted to adults. In one type of study (Kreutzer, Leonard, and Flavell, 1975; Myers and Paris, 1978), children were told a story about a girl who had been asked to listen to a record so that she could later repeat what the record said. The story ended by the girl asking whether she could tell the story in her own words or had to recall it word for word. The children were asked whether verbatim recall or recall of the gist would be easier. Selection of gist recall as easier than verbatim recall increased sharply from kindergarten through fifth or sixth grade. Also, the fifth- and sixth-graders were able to say why the girl in the story had asked about the type of test. These results raise the possibility that increased experience in school leads to increased metamnemonic knowledge.

Another important type of task variable concerns the characteristics of the stimuli to be remembered. Adults recognize readily that it is easier to learn a list of familiar words than a list of unfamiliar nonsense syllables. Similarly, we know that a list of words divided into obvious semantic categories such as *fruit* and *names* is easier to remember than a list of semantically unrelated words. This knowledge is particularly interesting because it pertains to learned characteristics of the stimuli, not to external characteristics. The ability to judge the extent of our internal knowledge rather than simply assess external variables arises through experience. For example children often fail to predict that semantically related words will be better remembered than semantically unrelated words will be (Kreutzer et al., 1975; Moynahan, 1973). Ability to make such predictions increases as children receive more experience in school.

At present, we do not know exactly how schooling and other aspects of experience lead individuals to discriminate which task variables influence retention. We should recognize, however, that parents, teachers, and peers often provide instructions concerning which task variables influence memory. Parents tell us to make a list of the items needed at the store because "there are too many things to remember." Teachers often tell students that the tests given so far have been easy but that future tests will require verbatim retention and will be much harder. Instructions such as these may increase the child's awareness of the task variables associated with memory problems. Equally important, the instructions point out that active steps must be taken to avoid forgetting. This instruction probably helps children to learn to plan a strategy for remembering.

Planning a Mnemonic Strategy

Becoming aware that a particular memory problem exists is only the first step toward deliberately alleviating the problem. In order to take effective action, one must also know that what one does can alleviate the problems. That is, one must realize that one's own cognitive activities can prevent or minimize forgetting. In addition, one must be able to plan a course of action, to choose an appropriate strategy, that will overcome the memory problem.

The difference between these two facets of planning a strategy is illustrated by the following experiment (Appel, Cooper, McCarrell, Sims-Knight, Yussen, and Flavell, 1972). Children were shown a series of pictures following either of two types of instructions. The memory instructions indicated that there would be a retention test for the pictures. The other instructions told the children to look at the pictures since doing so would facilitate performance on a subsequent task. The two types of instructions led 11-year-olds to engage in very different activities and to recall the picture better following the instructions to remember. In contrast, 4-year-olds did not respond differently to the two sets of instructions, and they recalled an equal number of items in the two conditions. Seven-year-olds recalled about the same number of pictures in the two conditions, but the instructions did have some effect. The memory instructions led the 7-year-olds to name the stimuli often, whereas the instructions to look did not have that effect. Apparently, the 7-year-olds knew they had to do something to prevent forgetting, but the activities they chose were ineffective. So knowing that one must plan a course of action and choosing an effective strategy are two different things.

THE VARIETY AND APPROPRIATENESS OF STRATEGIES

Choosing an effective strategy for overcoming a particular memory problem depends partly on having various strategies to choose from. Adults do have many strategies, and these may be divided into two categories: internal and external (Kreutzer et al., 1975). Internal strategies involve engaging in internal activities such as imaging and rehearsing to facilitate memory. External strategies involve acting on the external environment in ways intended to facilitate memory. We use external strategies when we write lists of things to remember, when we put objects in places where we will probably see and remember them, and when we ask others to remind us to do particular things. As you might expect, young children often have fewer mnemonic strategies at their disposal than older children and adults do (Kreutzer et al., 1975). No doubt this difference in knowledge of strategies contributes to the performance differences between children and adults on both memory and metamemory tasks.

A second prerequisite for adopting an effective mnemonic strategy is the ability to distinguish between strategies that are appropriate or inappropriate to the tasks at hand. If the task called for remembering many intricate, briefly presented pictures, a strategy involving verbal coding and rehearsal would probably fail. That same strategy, however, might be useful in remembering a telephone number for a short time. In general, judging the appropriateness of a particular strategy requires knowledge about stimuli, task variables, one's own knowledge, and, of course, one's skill in using the strategy.

STRATEGY DEVELOPMENT AND APPLICATION
As discussed above, choosing an effective strategy demands that several strategies be available and that the individual recognize which strategies will succeed. Two key questions concern how adults acquire various strategies and how they recognize which strategies will work in which tasks. Researchers have not yet answered these questions, but some useful information has come from studies of rehearsal in children.

There are marked developmental differences in the knowledge and use of rehearsal strategies (Ornstein and Naus, 1978). Children of 5 years and under seldom rehearse spontaneously, whereas 7-year-olds and older children do so readily (Flavell, Beach, and Chinsky, 1966). Differences occur not only in the amount or frequency of rehearsal but also in the type of rehearsal. When second-graders rehearse, they tend to repeat one item at a time, with little apparent effort at relating the various items that have been presented. In contrast, sixth-graders rehearse items in groups of three or four; this elaborative rehearsal leads to a high level of retention (Ornstein and Naus, 1978; Ornstein, Naus, and Stone, 1977). Similarly, 13-year-olds rehearse the members of a particular category together, whereas 8-year-olds and younger children do not (Ornstein, Naus, and Liberty, 1975).

The failure of young children to rehearse does not stem from an inability to do so. Young children do rehearse when they are explicitly instructed to do so, and the increased rehearsal does improve retention (Keeny, Cannizo, and Flavell, 1967; Ornstein et al., 1977). Why is it, then, that young children do not usually rehearse on their own? The answer to this question is unknown, but spontaneous rehearsal is unlikely to occur unless the following two conditions have been met earlier in the child's lifetime. First, rehearsal must have been made to occur. Second, the memorial consequences of rehearsal must have been effective in maintaining the rehearsal activity.

Both of these conditions seem to be satisfied in formal educational settings. Before children in our society have entered school, they probably have not had extensive memory demands placed on them. The demands they do face can often be satisfied through the use of strategies other than rehearsal. For example, the task of remembering to bring a baseball to the playground can be performed by putting a baseball near the front door. Indeed, young children tend to think of such external strategies rather than internal ones such as rehearsal (Kreutzer et al., 1975). In school, however, external strategies are often prohibited; when taking tests, we are expected to rely on our internal resources. Further, many of the stimuli we are told to remember in school are verbal and well-suited for rehearsal (how else is one to remember multiplication tables?). These factors, together with the strong incentives that teachers and parents provide for remembering in school, set the stage for the use of the rehearsal strategy.

Children often begin rehearsing as the result of what teachers do. For example, the author learned to rehearse in the course of learning the familiar alphabet rhyme in first grade. The teacher would begin the jingle, encourage the students to follow along, and to practice saying it to ourselves. We were also told that we could remember the alphabet by simply repeating the rhyme. So, schooling seems to be important for inducing people to use internal verbal strategies. This conclusion is supported by cross-cultural research, which has shown that the use of verbal mnemonics such as organizing words semantically is correlated with the extent of formal education (Cole and Scribner, 1977).

When rehearsal has been induced, beneficial consequences may follow. The child who rehearses the alphabet and subsequently recalls the alphabet correctly might receive a high grade, the approval of the teacher and the parents, and so on. These positive consequences may lead the child to rehearse in future situations. Similarly, positive social consequences are often applied to teach the child the relation between rehearsing and remembering. For example, a teacher might ask a young girl how she plans to remember the names of the state capitals. If the girl said she planned to say them to herself over and over, the teacher might express his or her approval. This type of training might help children learn to observe their own activities and to intentionally plan particular strategies for remembering.

Continuing in the same vein, the social consequences of mnemonic activities may help teach the child to choose an appropriate strategy. Having learned to use the rehearsal strategy, the child may tend to apply it to tasks for which it is unsuited. The negative results might include poor performance on a retention test, a low grade on a test, and parental disapproval. By applying a particular strategy successfully in some situations but not others, children may learn to discriminate when the strategy will or will not work. These comments also apply to how adults come to recognize the appropriateness of various strategies.

As these comments indicate, cognitive strategies are molded by their consequences, and they operate in the service of social needs. Ultimately, cognition is both a product and a mainspring of social interaction.

• *Summary.* For nearly 20 years, the multistore model guided research concerning memory. The multistore model assumed that there are separate short-term and long-term memory stores. The short-term store had limited storage capacity and retained information for about 15 seconds. On the other hand, the long-term store had unlimited storage capacity and retained information for long periods of time, perhaps permanently. Through rehearsal, information was maintained in the short-term store and was transferred to the long-term store.

Numerous observations supported the assumption of separate short-term and long-term stores. Some people who had suffered brain damage had normal memory spans but often failed to remember new information over the long run. This observation suggested the existence of a separate short-term store. The two memory stores also seemed to differ with respect to coding. In immediate memory tasks, most subjects encoded information phonemically, that is, by sound. But in studies of long-term retention, subjects encoded information semantically. Additionally, in studies of free recall for lists of words, people remembered the first few and the last few words much better than they remembered the other words. The superior retention for the last few items, the recency effect, disappeared when a 30-second delay was imposed between the presentation of the list and the test of recall. But the superior retention of the first items, the primacy effect, was not influenced by the delay. It appeared that the primacy effect reflected long-term storage, whereas the recency effect reflected short-term storage. Consistent with this account, the subjects rehearsed the first few items more often than the last few items, suggesting that rehearsal transferred items from the short-term store to the long-term store.

The multistore model failed eventually. Investigators discovered that people retain not only phonemic information but also semantic and visual information in immediate memory. This observation undercut the coding distinction between the two stores. Other studies reported long-term recency effects. Experiments concerning rehearsal suggested that there were two kinds of rehearsal. Maintenance rehearsal maintained information in immediate memory but did not enhance long-term retention. Elaborative rehearsal, which involved relating the rehearsed items to one another, did enhance long-term retention. These results showed that rehearsal was not a simple transfer mechanism and that there may be different types of processing.

The multistore model was superseded by the levels of processing model, which disavowed the notion of separate short-term and long-term stores. The model stated that incoming information is analyzed in stages, beginning with the analysis of physical features and ending with the analysis of meaning and conceptual relations between items. The succession of stages is called depth of processing, where greater depth implies a greater degree of cognitive or semantic analysis. The thesis of the model is that the deeper the level of processing, the higher the level of retention. Consistent with this view, words that have been encoded semantically are remembered better than are words that have been encoded phonemically. Unlike the multistore model, the levels of processing model attributed the limited span of immediate memory to the limits on our processing resources, not to limits on the storage capacity of a short-term store. Further, the model held that there are two kinds of processing. Type I processing recirculated items at a particular depth of processing and did not aid retention, whereas Type II processing analyzed items on a deeper level and did aid retention. This conception allowed the model to account for the effects of the two kinds of rehearsal.

The levels of processing model encountered several problems. First, the notion of a fixed sequence of processing stages was too rigid. Second, the levels of processing were difficult to define, and the model was therefore difficult to test. Third, in retention tests that assessed memory for phonemic information, the level of retention was sometimes as high following phonemic processing as it was following semantic processing. Fourth, maintenance rehearsal was observed to increase the level of recognition, thereby questioning whether Type I processing had no influence on memory.

The subsequent revision of the model emphasized that retention depends on the elaborateness rather than the depth of processing. Elaborate processing can occur by relating incoming items to other incoming items or to remembered information. In studies of free recall, people spontaneously organize words into groups, and this elaborate processing is correlated with high levels of retention. Further, retention can be facilitated by inducing elaborate processing, for example, by making the organization of a list noticeable, by instructing the subjects to form interactive images or to link items together in a story. Elaborate processing can also occur by analyzing a greater number of features of an individual item, for example, by noting the different shades of meaning of the word *radical*. This type of elaboration can also aid retention, perhaps by providing a relatively complete description of the encoded item. In turn, the complete description makes the item distinctive and more retrievable. This emphasis on elaborateness has the advantage of avoiding the concept of a fixed sequence of processing stages while retaining the idea that the type of encoding determines the level of retention. This theme continues to be the dominant force in analyses of remembering.

Studies of the effects of coding on remembering show that people can encode information in a variety of ways, and they often adjust their coding strategies to meet the demands of particular tasks. This adjustment process is guided by the knowledge of how to remember, called metamemory. Metamemory consists of three related components that serve to detect and to resolve a memory problem, the possibility that we might forget something important. First, one must become aware that a memory problem exists; this requires knowing what one does and does not know, what one is likely to forget, and what the demands of the task are. Second, one plans a strategy such as rehearsing, imaging, or writing oneself a note for preventing forgetting. Effective planning requires having various strategies available and judging the appropriateness of particular strategies to the task at hand. Third, one monitors one's performance to determine whether the strategy should be continued, modified, or replaced. Skill in each of these areas arises through experience, particularly through training received in school. Of course, being aware of a memory problem and of how to solve it does not necessarily enable us to act accordingly. Although we view conscious thought as our guide, thought and action are separated by a gap too wide and significant to ignore.

Chapter 5
Retrieval Processes

We have all had the frustrating experience of being unable to recall a particular name or word even though we are certain we know it and feel on the verge of recalling it. This phenomenon, called the *tip-of-the-tongue phenomenon* (Brown and McNeill, 1966), can be particularly excruciating when taking a test under pressure.

Brown and McNeill induced the tip-of-the-tongue state by giving adults dictionary definitions of rare words and asking them to recall the word that had been defined. One of the definitions presented was "a navigational instrument used in measuring angular distances, especially the altitude of the sun, moon and stars at sea." Subjects who heard the definition and who claimed to be in the tip-of-the-tongue state were asked numerous questions about the target word. In particular, they were asked how many syllables the word had, what the first letter was, what the word sounds like, and which other words have a similar meaning.

The results were that the subjects accurately described numerous aspects of the target word even when they were unable to recall it. For example, they correctly identified the initial letter 57 percent of the time, and they identified the exact number of syllables 63 percent of the time. Quite often they were able to pick out words that resembled the target word in sound or meaning. For example, the subjects given the definition stated above indicated that the target word was related conceptually to *astrolabe* and *compass* and sounded like *secant* and *sextet*. In case you are in the tip-of-the-tongue state yourself the target word is *sextant*. These observations indicate that the subjects knew the target words even if they failed to recall them. Quite often, the subjects recalled the target word in a burst of relief following a period of entrapment in the tip-of-the-tongue state.

This simple experiment demonstrates that the information that is available or stored in memory may become inaccessible or difficult to retrieve. When people fail to retrieve information that is stored in memory, we say that they have forgotten the information even though they may be able to remember it eventually. In the first section of this chapter, we analyze the forgetting of well-learned information over periods of time longer than those spanned by immediate memory. We shall see that interference, amnesias, and emotionally-induced forgetting result primarily from failures to retrieve information.

Fortunately, retrieval failures can often be remedied by the presentation of retrieval cues. In one experiment (Tulving and Pearlstone, 1966), subjects learned a list of 48 words that contained four words in 12 different categories. The words were grouped by category, and the name of each category was presented, as follows:

FRUIT — apple, pear, orange, banana
VEHICLE — car, truck, bus, plane

In a test of free recall, the subjects were asked later to recall all of the words. Then they were given a test of cued recall in which the names of the categories (FRUIT, VEHICLE) were presented and the task was to recall the words that had been studied. The results were that the subjects performed much better in the test of cued recall than in the test of free recall. Thus retrieval cues can enhance the accessibility of stored information.

The effectiveness with which cues aid memory is also apparent from our everyday experiences. Upon visiting the homes of relatives or the neighborhood we grew up in, our consciousness is flooded by memories of events from our childhood days. Similarly, the melody of a song brings back emotion-laden memories of past experiences and companions. Because retrieval cues influence remembering and forgetting, the second section of this chapter inquires into the conditions under which cues facilitate retrieval. The chief theme will be that in both recognition and recall, cues aid retrieval if they had been processed at the time of encoding.

Retrieval often involves the process of searching memory. As an illustration, take several minutes and try to remember what you did on December 28, 1979. This task may seem hopeless at first, but if you try, you will probably be surprised at your success. Most people begin this task by using their general knowledge, for example, the knowledge that "I must have been at home or visiting relatives since that is what I always do over the Christmas–New Year holidays." This information isolates temporal landmarks and provides contextual cues that enable you to search memory for specific episodes. For example, you might form an image of yourself at home and scan the imagined scene to see who is present. Or, if you remembered having received a bicycle for Christmas that year, you might imagine yourself riding to various places. In this manner, you retrieve additional information about the context of your activities, and the contextual cues help you to search for and to retrieve the stored information concerning the episodes that had occurred. You probably did not perform this task by retrieving an exact copy of the episode from memory. As this example illustrates, retrieval is sometimes a process of reconstructing past events using our world knowledge. In the last section of this chapter, we examine the reconstructive processes that occur in remembering stories and pictures.

FORGETTING AS RETRIEVAL FAILURE

In this section, we analyze the role of retrieval failures in interference, amnesia, and emotionally induced forgetting. At the outset, however, we should recognize that retrieval failure is not the sole cause of forgetting over relatively long periods of time. Forgetting may also stem from decay. Recall that Ebbinghaus had reported that as time passed following the learning of a list, more and more forgetting occurred. This observation and others like it led theorists working at the turn of the century to believe that the passage of time determines forgetting (Thorndike, 1914).

Despite its intuitive appeal, the decay theory has not fared well. For one thing, no one has devised a method for testing the effects of decay over long periods of time. This is unsurprising since it is extremely difficult to eliminate all sources of interference during a long retention interval. And historically, there were several strikes against the decay theory. McGeoch (1932) argued that the passage of time per se is not a cause. For example, metal rusts as time passes. But rusting results not from the passage of time but from the oxidation process that occurs as time passes. Similarly, forgetting may result not from the passage of time but from the interfering events that occur as time passes. Indeed, in our previous discussion of immediate memory, we noted that forgetting often results from interference rather than decay.

McGeoch's criticisms gained strength from the results of early studies of whether the events that occur following learning produce forgetting. In one study (Jenkins and Dallenbach, 1924), adults learned a list of 10 nonsense syllables, followed by a retention interval that lasted 1, 2, 4, or 8 hours. During this interval, half of the subjects slept while half remained awake. If forgetting results from the passage of time, equal amounts of forgetting should have occurred in the sleeping and the waking conditions. In fact, however, much more forgetting occurred in the waking condition than in the sleeping condition. Thus forgetting was influenced more by the events that occurred as time passed than by the passage of time per se. Some forgetting occurred in the sleeping condition, suggesting that the passage of time without any intervening activity also produced forgetting. The trouble with this view is that we dream while we sleep, and dreaming could have produced the forgetting that had occurred (Ekstrand, 1972). Overall, then, these observations failed to provide impressive support for the decay theory. The stage was set for a theory that attributed forgetting to the events in the retention interval. The interference theory answered this call.

Retroactive and Proactive Interference

Retroactive and proactive interference have been analyzed extensively in studies of paired-associate learning. The standard experiment on retroactive interference involves two groups of subjects, as shown in Figure 5.1a. The experimental group learns two paired-associate lists designated as A-B and A-D; this design is called the A-B, A-D paradigm. The capital letters refer to particular sets of words. Different letters such as "A" and "B" refer to different sets of words. In the A-B, A-D paradigm, the two lists contain the same stimulus items (the "A" items) and different re-

Condition	Step 1	Step 2	Step 3
Experimental	Learn A–B	Learn A–D	Recall A–B
Control	Learn A–B	Perform distractor	Recall A–B

(a)

Experimental	Learn A–B	Learn A–D	Recall A–D
Control	Perform distractor	Learn A–D	Recall A–D

(b)

Figure 5.1   Interference paradigms in paired-associate learning. (a) The retroactive interference paradigm. (b) The proactive interference paradigm.

sponse items (the "B" and "D" items). For example, the A-B list might include *JOF-bright* and *KEV-round*, and the A-D list might include *JOF-filthy* and *KEV-lame*. The experimental group first learns the A-B list and then the A-D list. Following a retention interval, during which the subjects perform a distractor task designed to prevent rehearsal, memory of the A-B list is tested by presenting the "A" items and asking the subjects to recall the appropriate "B" items. The control group learns the A-B list and then performs a distractor task such as solving simple arithmetic problems or learning a second list, called a C-D list, that is unrelated to the A-B list. Then the control group is asked to recall the A-B list. For both groups, the same amount of time intervenes between the learning of the A-B list and the recall of that list. Therefore, differences in the performance of the two groups must be attributed to the learning of the A-D list, not to decay. If the experimental group recalls fewer "B" items than the control group does, then retroactive interference is said to have occurred. Usually, a large amount of retroactive interference occurs in the A-B, A-D paradigm (Postman, 1961, 1971).

As shown in Figure 5.1b, the proactive interference paradigm matches the retroactive interference paradigm in all but two respects. First, retention of the A-D list is tested, usually following a brief retention interval during which the subjects perform a distractor task designed to prevent rehearsal. Second, the control group learns the A-D list rather than the A-B list. The typical result of this paradigm is that the experimental group forgets many more items than the control group does (Postman, 1961, 1971). This outcome indicates that the learning of the A-B list by the experimental group had proactively interfered with the recall of the A-D list.

Historically, proactive and retroactive interference were explained by numerous processes, some of which we now consider.

RESPONSE COMPETITION

McGeoch (1942) proposed that retroactive interference resulted from competition between responses at the time of recall. For example, in the A-B, A-D paradigm, the subjects associate two different responses with the "A" stimuli. Suppose one of the A-B pairs was *KOJ-14* and the corresponding A-D pair was *KOJ-26*. In the retention test for the A-B pairs, the subjects would be shown *KOJ*, which might elicit both *14* and *26*. The association between *KOJ* and *26* might be stronger than that between *KOJ* and *14* since the *KOJ-26* pair was learned more recently. Hence, the subjects might recall *26* rather than *14*, as if the recall of *26* blocked or competed with the recall of *14*. Most of us have experienced this sort of response competition. For example, in trying to recall the title of one movie, we may consistently come up with another. This incorrect title can block or dominate over the correct one, thereby producing forgetting.

Melton and Irwin (1940) tested whether interference stems from response competition. The subjects first learned a list of 18 nonsense syllables. Next they studied the items of a different list on each of 5, 10, 20, or 40 trials. Finally, the subjects were asked to recall the items from the first list, and their performance was compared to that of control subjects who had learned only the first list. If retroactive interference results from response competition, then the subjects who had learned two lists should err in recalling the first list by recalling items from the second list. In other words, there should be intrusions from the second list.

The results of the experiment provided only partial support for the response-competition hypothesis. As Figure 5.2 shows, extensive retroactive interference occurred, particularly when 20 trials had been devoted to the second list. As predicted, intrusions from the second list did occur. But the curve showing the number of intrusions did not match the curve showing the amount of retroactive interference. In fact, following 40 trials of exposure to the second list, very few intrusions occurred, whereas a substantial amount of interference occurred. Response competition, then, accounts for only a portion of the observed retroactive interference. The interference left unexplained by response competition was attributed to unlearning (Melton and Irwin, 1940; Underwood, 1948).

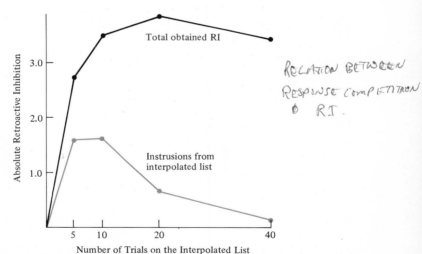

Figure 5.2   The relationship between the amount of response competition (as indicated by the number of intrusions) and the amount of retroactive interference. The absolute amount of retroactive interference is defined as the difference in recall for the experimental group and a control group that learned only one list. (From Melton and Irwin, 1940.)

UNLEARNING

In the standard A-B, A-D procedure, the subjects first learn associations between the A and B items. Those associations might intrude in the learning of the A-D list. When this occurs, the "B" responses are incorrect and are extinguished or unlearned; this idea is called the unlearning hypothesis. On this account, subjects who have learned the A-B and A-D lists fail to recall the "B" items subsequently because the A-B associations were unlearned during the learning of the A-D list.

Barnes and Underwood (1959) tried to test whether the A-B associations were unlearned as a consequence of learning the A-D list. They had their subjects learn an A-B list and then study an A-D list for 1, 5, 10, or 20 trials. In an effort to reduce the effects of response competition, they modified the retention test used in the standard procedure. Specifically, they presented the "A" items and asked the subjects to recall the responses from both lists rather than from only the first list, as in the standard procedure. Since there was an opportunity for both the "B" and the "D" responses to occur, competition between the "B" and the "D" responses should, presumably, have been minimal. With response competition minimized, the inability to recall the "B" items would be due to unlearning. The results of the experiment, illustrated in Figure 5.3, were that as the number of trials on the second list increased, fewer and fewer items were recalled from the first list. In contrast, more and more items from the second list were recalled, thus reducing the amount of response competition. According to the unlearning hypothesis, more trials on the

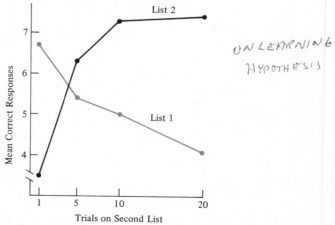

Figure 5.3   The number of words recalled from both the A-B list (List 1) and the A-D list (List 2) as a function of the number of trials on the A-D list. (From Barnes and Underwood, 1959. Copyright 1959 by the American Psychological Association. Reprinted by permission.)

A-D list increased both the strength of the A-D associations and the degree of unlearning of the A-B associations.

The unlearning hypothesis, however, encountered serious problems. Subsequent experiments showed that spontaneous recovery does occur in the A-B, A-D paradigm. But the effect has been too weak and short-lived to explain the occurrence of proactive interference (Brown, 1976). Additionally, some evidence contradicts the unlearning hypothesis. For example, in the retroactive interference paradigm, the subjects are usually asked to recall the "B" responses in the presence of the "A" item. Postman and Stark (1969) modified this procedure by giving a recognition test rather than a recall test. Specifically, an "A" item was shown with a set of "B" items, as in a multiple-choice test, and the subjects had to pick the correct "B" item. Surprisingly, retroactive interference failed to occur in the A-B, A-D procedure when the recognition test was used. This shows that the "B" responses had not been unlearned but merely had become difficult to retrieve.

This type of observation led Postman and Stark to conclude that the subjects had not unlearned the individual "B" responses but had suppressed the entire set of responses. They called this idea the hypothesis of *response set suppression.* Because this hypothesis concerned entire sets of responses rather than single stimulus-response associations, it departed from traditional associationistic concepts. It also added a new concept to the interference theory, thereby making the theory more complex. As research continued, theorists had to add still more new concepts to the theory (Postman, 1976; and Postman and Underwood, 1973). Gradually, the theory became too complex and unwieldy.

More devastating, theorists began to believe that the theory applied only to laboratory experiments concerning the learning of artificial lists (Tulving and Madigan, 1970). They doubted that the theory could ever explain how we remember and forget factual, semantic information. For these reasons, most theorists abandoned the interference theory and adopted the view that forgetting results from retrieval failures. The advantage of this view was that it applied not only to the forgetting of lists of words but also to the forgetting of the semantic information we use in many everyday situations.

CUE-DEPENDENT FORGETTING

If retroactive interference involves a failure to retrieve information, then the interference effect should be reduced by giving the subjects retrieval cues in the retention test. In order to test this prediction, Tulving and Psotka (1971) asked subjects to learn six different word lists. Each list included 24 words that belonged to six different categories. When each list was presented, the words from each category were grouped together to

make the categories noticeable. An example of part of one list is as follows: *zinc, copper, aluminum, bronze, orange, apple, pear, melon, hut,
cottage, tent, hotel.* . . . Each list was presented three times in succession,
and a free recall test was then given for that list. When the six lists had
been learned and retention had been tested for each, two tests of overall
retention were given. The subjects' task in each overall test was to recall
all of the words from all of the lists. One overall test involved a free recall
procedure. The other involved a cued-recall procedure in which the
subjects were given the names of all the categories that the presented
words belonged to.

First consider the results of the overall test of free recall, shown in
Figure 5.4. The level of recall was high for the words that had appeared
in the sixth list that had been learned. Since the subjects learned no lists
following the sixth (that is, there were no interpolated lists), there would
have been little or no retroactive interference for the words in that list.
In contrast, the words in the first list should have been subject to much
retroactive interference, for the subjects had learned five lists following
the first. As expected, few words were recalled from the first list. In general, the level of retention decreased as the number of interpolated lists
increased. Impressively, the retroactive interference was virtually eliminated when the retrieval cues were provided. Each list was recalled
about as well in the overall cued-recall test as in the test that had followed the original learning. Tulving (1974) concluded that retroactive

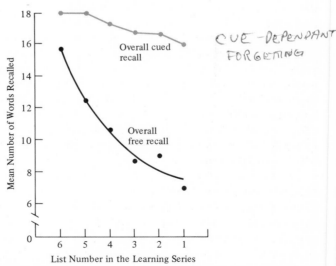

Figure 5.4   Cue-dependent forgetting. The forgetting that occurred in
the overall test of free recall was eliminated when retrieval cues were
provided. (After Tulving, 1974.)

interference is an instance of cue-dependent forgetting, forgetting that results from the absence of effective retrieval cues.

These observations have important practical implications. They suggest that we should be able to minimize the occurrence of retroactive interference by using learning methods that provide effective retrieval cues. Mnemonic systems such as the method of loci do just that. Recall that the method of loci involves imagining the items to be remembered in particular well-learned locations, for example, the rooms of your home. You retrieve the items by taking a mental walk through the house, imagining each room and its contents. In essence, the mnemonic provides a stable retrieval plan, the mental walk, and each imagined room provides cues that aid the retrieval of the items.

Bower and Reitman (1972) showed that interference can be minimized by using the method of loci. Subjects learned five lists of words using a single set of locations. Thus each imagined room would have contained five imagined items from five different lists. The results were that no retroactive interference occurred: the subjects remembered the words from all five lists accurately. We may conclude that retroactive interference is an instance of retrieval failure and that it can be prevented through the use of learning methods that provide retrieval cues.

PROACTIVE INTERFERENCE

Recall that in the proactive interference paradigm, the subject learns the A-B list, then learns the A-D list, and then attempts to recall the A-D list. Initially, the interference theory had attributed proactive interference to competition with the "D" responses from the previously learned "B" responses that recovered spontaneously as time passed. But when the unlearning hypothesis had been discredited, this account was rejected. Subsequently, interference theorists proposed the *list differentiation hypothesis,* which states that proactive interference results from a failure to discriminate which list had been learned most recently (Underwood and Ekstrand, 1967; Underwood and Freund, 1968). This hypothesis is plausible in that successful recall of the A-D list in the A-B, A-D paradigm requires distinguishing between the two lists on the basis of the times at which they occurred.

Underwood and Freund (1968) tested the list differentiation hypothesis by varying the amount of time that intervened between the learning of the A-B and the A-D lists. The rationale was that a long delay between the two tasks would make the respective times of occurrence more discriminable, thereby reducing the amount of proactive interference. This prediction was confirmed. Postman and Gray (1977) also tested whether increasing the degree of list differentiation reduced the amount of proactive interference. As their subjects learned the A-D list, they recalled the responses from both the "B" and the "D" lists, thereby keeping the two lists distinct. In keeping with the list differentiation hypothesis, little proactive interference occurred in this procedure.

As you may have noticed, the list differentiation hypothesis is roughly equivalent to the discrimination hypothesis that was discussed in connection with proactive interference in immediate memory. Both hypotheses attribute proactive interference to the failure to discriminate between recently learned items and previously learned items. In turn, this failure to discriminate impairs the retrieval of the recently learned items. Thus proactive interference, like retroactive interference, results from the failure to retrieve information. A complete explanation of interference effects, then, must come not from associationistic theories of interference but from cognitive theories of retrieval.

The practical importance of this conclusion is that we can reduce proactive interference by encoding the items learned at different times in a distinctive manner. For example, we can construct distinctive images or stories, and we can look for distinctive cues that might facilitate retrieval. These comments remind us of the intimate connection between encoding and retrieval processes.

Amnesia and Retrieval

Beyond the shelter of the laboratory, people sometimes suffer head injuries as the result of car accidents, fights, and so on. One frequent consequence of traumatic incidents is *retrograde amnesia,* the forgetting of events that preceded the trauma. Almost all patients who are interviewed shortly after the traumatic incident show retrograde amnesia, and the degree of amnesia tends to increase as the severity of the trauma increases (Russell and Nathan, 1946). But subsequent interviews reveal an intriguing change: over time, the patient's memories return, with the older ones returning first. Several years following an injury, only a few islands of forgetting remain (Russell, 1971).

The clinical observations, though suggestive, are difficult to interpret. The shrinkage of forgetting over time, for example, may be illusory. How do we know that the gaps in the patients' memories were not filled in through conversations with friends and witnesses? And how do we know that the doctors' expectations did not bias the patients' statements during the interviews? An objective test is needed to circumvent these problems. Studies of the effects of electroconvulsive shock (ECS) have answered this call.

ECS

People who suffer severe depression sometimes receive electroconvulsive therapy, in which a series of shocks are administered to the brain. The ECS produces convulsions, unconsciousness, and retrograde amnesia, be-

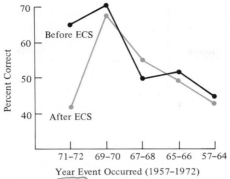

Figure 5.5   The effects of ECS on memory for popular TV shows aired between 1957 and 1972. (From Squire, Slater, and Chase, 1975. Copyright 1975 by the American Association for the Advancement of Science.)

sides relief from the depression (Cronholm, 1969; Dornbush and Williams, 1974). In order to assess the effects of ECS on forgetting, Squire, Slater, and Chase (1975) prepared an objective test of memory for well-known television programs that had been aired between 1957 and 1972 (the experiment was conducted in 1974). The test consisted of multiple-choice questions, for example: Which of the following was a TV show? (a) Wagons Westward, (b) Ozzie and Harriet, (c) The Whiz Game, and (d) The Breakfast Show. The subjects were 16 patients who were about to undergo electroconvulsive therapy. The patients received one form of the test before the first ECS treatment. They also received another, equally difficult, form of the test following their fifth ECS treatment.

As shown in Figure 5.5, the ECS produced forgetting of the most recent memories, but not of the older ones. When Squire et al. administered another memory test one to two weeks following the ECS therapy, they observed that the memory for the recent programs had recovered almost fully. These observations agree with the clinical observations of Russell and Nathan. More important, they show that the trauma had not erased the forgotten information from memory. Rather, the trauma had made the information irretrievable for a period of time. Of course, the crucial question is why did the information become more retrievable as time passed? This question has not been answered yet, and it poses an interesting challenge for future research.

RETRIEVAL CUES AND AMNESIA
The role of retrieval processes is apparent also in studies of the effects of Korsakoff's syndrome and of surgically induced lesions of the hippocampus (recall the case of H.M.), which produce anterograde amnesia, impairment of the ability to remember new information.

Marslen-Wilson and Teuber (1975) studied the long-term memory of a group of Korsakoff patients, of a group of normal subjects, and of H.M. They presented photographs of people who had been famous during various periods between 1920 and 1970. The photographs were of faces that the subjects had probably seen before the onset of amnesia and of faces they had probably seen after the onset of amnesia. The subjects' task was to name each picture. If the subject failed to recall a particular name, the experimenter presented a retrieval cue, for example, the initials of the person or a brief statement such as "she was an actress in the 1940s."

The results were that, in the absence of the retrieval cues, H.M. and the Korsakoff patients recalled faces from the distant past (the preamnesic period) as well as did the normal subjects (see Figure 5.6). But H.M. and the Korsakoff patients did much worse than the normal subjects in recalling the names of people who had become famous in the 1960s, well after the onset of amnesia (in the 1950s). This is the phenomenon of anterograde amnesia.

Radically different results occurred when the experimenters provided the retrieval cues. As shown in Figure 5.6, H.M. recalled 80 percent of the names of the people who had become famous during the 1960s. Similarly, the Korsakoff patients recalled 83% of the names, and the normal subjects recalled almost all of the names. Although H.M. and the Korsakoff patients showed deficits relative to the normal subjects, they nonetheless remembered many faces that they had seen following the onset of amnesia. Thus, anterograde amnesia does not involve a com-

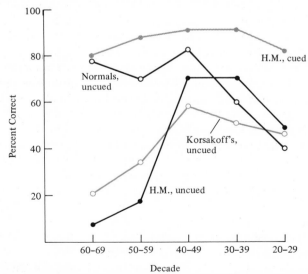

Figure 5.6   Long-term recognition of the faces of famous people from various decades. (Data from Marslen-Wilson and Teuber, 1975.)

plete inability to remember new information over long periods of time. And contrary to the multistore model, it does not stem from problems in transferring information from a short-term store to a long-term store. Rather, anterograde amnesia stems largely from problems in retrieving information.

Of course, the failure to retrieve old information may also influence the manner in which new information is encoded. Some research has shown that amnesic patients are slow in retrieving semantic information (Cermak, Reale, and Baker, 1978). The slowness of or difficulty in retrieving semantic information may lead Korsakoff patients to avoid elaborate semantic processing, which may in turn impair retention (Cermak and Reale, 1978). This conception is speculative at present. But additional studies of the interaction of retrieval and encoding should clarify the nature of amnesia.

Emotion and Retrieval

Failures to retrieve information often stem from the lack of appropriate retrieval cues, but retrieval failures may also be brought about by emotional factors. The psychiatric literature contains numerous well-documented cases of fugues, in which a person runs away from his problems or conflicts by taking on a new identity or escaping from the present environment. Persons in the fugue state are often amnesic in that they remember little of their former identity and life (Nemiah, 1969).

William James described one of the best-documented cases, the case of Rev. Ansel Bourne. Bourne was a 30-year-old preacher who throughout life had been subject to headaches, depressions, and brief periods of unconsciousness. One day he drew money from his bank in his home state of Rhode Island, paid some bills, and stepped into a horsecar (the year was 1887). This was the last episode he remembered. Two months later, he awakened in fear and asked the people in his house to tell him where he was and what had been happening. It turned out that he was in Norristown, Pennsylvania, where he was known as A. J. Brown. Under the identity of Brown, he had rented and run a small candy store, but he had done no preaching, and his behavior had seemed normal to others. Bourne was quite astonished at all this, for he remembered nothing of his life in Norristown. Indeed, he had refused initially to believe that two months had passed. Eventually, Bourne was referred to William James, who used hypnosis to induce the recall of the Norristown episode. Under hypnosis, Bourne recalled the details of his life as A. J. Brown, but he recalled little of Ansel Bourne and failed to recognize his wife. It was as if the Brown and Bourne personalities were dissociated from each other. Information about both personalities had been stored, but the information about one was not retrievable while the other dominated consciousness. Despite James' best efforts, he was unable to fuse the two personalities. Hilgard (1977) has provided a provocative account of many additional cases of fugues and other types of dissociation.

Sigmund Freud (1957) is perhaps the one most responsible for documenting and popularizing the view that emotional factors can lead to forgetting. Freud's theory of forgetting centered around the concept of *repression*, one of the pivotal concepts in his theory of personality (Brenner, 1957; Erdelyi and Goldberg, 1979). Repression is a type of motivated forgetting in which painful or anxiety-arousing memories are unconsciously blocked and kept out of consciousness. Although repressed memories are not in consciousness, they remain in the memory system. Freud believed that repressed information would become manifest in behavior such as slips of the tongue (for example, a member of the student government might intend to say *We adore our Dean* and instead say *We abhor our Dean*), which presumably reveal the speaker's true feelings and motives. More important, Freud argued that repressed information can lead to neurotic patterns of behavior, particularly excessive defensive reactions.

Through extensive clinical studies, Freud and others presented evidence that repression does occur. But the clinical evidence has been difficult to interpret, and psychoanalysts have, understandably, been concerned more with alleviating their clients' problems than with determining the exact causes of forgetting. Further, it has been difficult to reconstruct in the laboratory the complex events that are believed to cause repression (Erdelyi and Goldberg, 1979; Holmes, 1974). Aside from the issue of repression, however, there is evidence that emotional factors can produce forgetting.

Glucksberg and King (1967) had subjects learn a list of paired-associates in which the response items were common words. Then shock electrodes were attached to their fingers, and a second list of words was presented. Some of the words were accompanied by a mild but unpleasant electric shock, whereas others were not. The subjects' task was to say each word as it appeared and to indicate whether the word was safe or paired with shock. This test continued until the subjects correctly anticipated shock or no shock for each word. What the subjects did not know was that the words on the second list were associates of the words that had been learned in the first list. For example, one shock-paired word from the second list was *tree*, an associate of the word *fruit*, which had appeared in the first list. Published norms of word associations indicate that *fruit* tends to evoke the associate *apple*, which in turn evokes *tree*, as in this chain of associations: *fruit - apple - tree*. Because of the intermediary link (*apple*), *fruit* and *tree* are said to be remote associates. If *tree* had become aversive because it had been paired with shock, the learned aversiveness might generalize to remotely associated words such as *fruit* and make them difficult to retrieve.

This prediction was supported by the results of a retention test for the words in list one. Retention for the words whose associates had been paired with shock was five times lower than for words whose associates had not been paired with shock. When the subjects were questioned, none of them recognized any specific connections between the shock-paired words from list two and the remote associates from list one. Further, no subjects identified the purpose of the experiment, so it is unlikely that they had simply been acting as if they had forgotten the words from list one in an effort to please the experimenters.

Before concluding that words such as *fruit* were remembered poorly because of their emotional unpleasantness, some alternative interpretations must be considered. The poor retention for words such as *fruit* could not be attributed to a low level of initial learning since all the words in list one had initially been learned to about the same level. Another possibility is that words such as *fruit* were subject to more retroactive interference than the other words in list one were. This is plausible since shock-paired words such as *tree* were better learned than the words that had not been paired with shock. And it is known that higher degrees of list two learning can produce more retroactive interference (Melton and Irwin, 1940). To evaluate this possibility, Glucksberg and King repeated their experiment but paired some words from list two with money or shock in different groups. The money-paired words were learned as well as the shock-paired words. Yet the remote associates of the money-paired words were remembered better than the remote associates of the shock-paired words. Apparently, then, the associates of shock-paired words were poorly remembered because they had become aversive, not because they had been subject to more retroactive interference.

We may conclude that emotion-induced forgetting did occur in the study by Glucksberg and King. These results show that unpleasant information can be difficult to retrieve, but they also establish a point of broader significance. Cognition and emotion are often analyzed separately, but in everyday life, thinking and feeling occur together and influence each other. To fully understand cognition in the natural environment, we must understand how cognitive and emotional factors interact.

CONTEXT AND RETRIEVAL

When we acquire new information, we do so in a particular context. For example, the words we read occur in the context of phrases and sentences, the sentences occur in the context of paragraphs, and so on. Through conceptually driven processing, the context influences how we encode the stimuli before us (Jenkins, 1974). The word *bat*, for example, might be encoded very differently in the context of an article about the

World Series than about the gruesome affairs of Count Dracula. In this example, retrieval influences encoding, for the processing of the new information was guided by the information that had been retrieved from memory.

The retrieval of information also occurs in a context, which determines the accessibility of the desired information. We have seen repeatedly that retrieval cues provide a context that can facilitate retrieval and prevent forgetting. Because remembering often results from the presentation of effective retrieval cues, it is important to discover what makes cues effective or ineffective. In this section, we examine the theory of encoding specificity, which clarifies the conditions under which cues facilitate retrieval. Then we shall use our understanding of the effects of context to analyze the relationship between recognition and recall.

Encoding Specificity

The theory of encoding specificity states that a cue will aid retrieval if it provides information that had been processed during the encoding of the target information (Thomson and Tulving, 1970; Tulving and Thomson, 1973; Tulving, 1979).

The original evidence in favor of the encoding specificity theory came from an experiment by Thomson and Tulving (1970). They asked subjects to learn lists containing 24 target words. Each target word was presented with a context word or cue word that was strongly or weakly associated with the target word. An example of part of one of the lists is as follows:

CUE WORDS		*TARGET WORDS*
ground	—	COLD
want	—	NEED
sky	—	BLUE
swift	—	GO

The cue words are on the left, and their associated target words are on the right. *Ground* and *swift* are weak associates of their respective target words, whereas *want* and *sky* are strong associates of their target words. The subjects were told to remember only the target words, but they were also told that attending to the cue words might help them in their task.

The subjects learned three successive lists. Following the learning of each of the first two lists, there was a cued-recall test in which the cue words were presented and the subjects recalled the associated target words. This procedure was designed to induce the subjects to use the cue words in their task of learning and remembering.

Following the learning of the third list, a different recall procedure was used. Specifically, some of the cues that were presented at the time of recall differed from the originally presented cues. Recall for the items that had been paired initially with weak cues (for example, *COLD* had been paired with *ground*) was tested sometimes with the same weak cues but at other times with strong-associate cues (for example, *hot*, which is a strong associate of *COLD*) that had not been presented before. Similarly, recall for the items that had been presented initially with strong cues (for example, *sky* — *BLUE*) was tested sometimes with the same strong cue and sometimes with a weak, novel cue (for example, *pretty*, a weak associate of *BLUE*). According to the encoding specificity theory, the only effective retrieval cues should be those that had been present and processed at the time of encoding and at the time of recall.

As predicted, the level of recall was high when the cues that had been presented at the time of retrieval had also been present at the time of encoding. As Figure 5.7 shows, when both input and output cues were strong associates of the targets, over 80 percent of the target words were recalled. When both cues were weak associates of the target words, 73 percent of the target words were recalled. In contrast, the level of recall was low when the retrieval cues had not been presented at the time of encoding. This is surprising in that one might expect strong associates to invariably aid retrieval. After all, the word *hot* tends to make one think

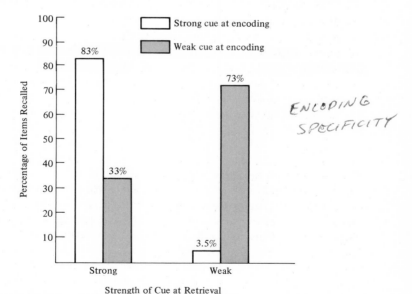

Figure 5.7   The phenomenon of encoding specificity. A high level of recall occurred only when the encoding cues and the retrieval cues matched (strong-strong or weak-weak). (Data from Thomson and Tulving, 1970.)

of *cold*, which was one of the target words. Nevertheless, the strong associates of the target words facilitated recall only when they had been present during both encoding and retrieval. The strength of the retrieval cue did have a small effect since the two bars on the right of Figure 5.7 are lower than those on the left. But this effect was small by comparison to whether the encoding and retrieval cues matched.

These observations show that contextual cues facilitate recall if they have been processed during both encoding and retrieval. We expect forgetting to occur when the contextual cues present at the time of retrieval are not the same as the cues that had been present and processed at the time of encoding.

INCIDENTAL CUES

The preceding experiment concerned external cues that were obviously related to the target words. Can recall also be aided by cues that bear no obvious relation to the target words? The context in which retrieval occurs includes many incidental features that seem unrelated to the information to be retrieved. If we were trying to remember the Battle of Hastings during a history test, the appearance of the examination room, the time of day, and feelings of hunger would be incidental features of the context. Common sense might suggest that retrieval would be facilitated by the presence of pertinent contextual features but not by incidental ones. But this view has been shown to be false; it does not matter whether the information present at the time of retrieval is pertinent or incidental. What matters is whether the information present at the time of retrieval had been processed at the time of encoding.

In one experiment, Smith (1979) tested whether retention is better when the overall study and test contexts match than when they differ. Two groups of subjects learned a list of common nouns in the same room, room A. Each group received a recognition test on some of the items they had learned. The purpose of this test was to make the subjects think that they no longer had to remember the words, thereby reducing rehearsal following the test. What the subjects did not know was that they would subsequently be asked to recall the words. In the second part of the experiment, the subjects were taken to a novel room, room B, and were asked to draw the room from different perspectives. The actual purpose was simply to familiarize the subjects with room B. After ten minutes of drawing, the subjects were taken to a waiting room for several minutes. Then they were taken to a test room where they were asked to recall all the words they had learned initially. One group of subjects, called the same-context group, was tested in the room where they had learned the words initially. The other group, called the different-context group, was tested in room B where they had engaged in drawing but not word processing.

The results were that the same-context group recalled 25 percent more words than the different-context group did. The advantage of the same-context group did not stem from being tested in a familiar room, for both groups were familiar with their test rooms. It therefore seems unlikely that the subjects in the different-context group did poorly because they were anxious or distracted by virtue of being in a test room that differed from the study room. Disruption from moving from one room to another just before taking a test can lead to poor retention. Yet both groups had been equally disrupted by being taken to the waiting room before taking the retention test. The most appropriate conclusion, then, is that the same-context group recalled more words because they had access to contextual cues that had been present at both encoding and retrieval. The different-context group was tested in an environment that lacked the contextual cues that had been present at the time of encoding, and their performance suffered accordingly.

These results help to extend the encoding specificity theory in two ways. First, the theory applies not only when the retrieval cues bear an obvious meaningful relation to the target information. In the preceding experiment, features of the rooms used had no obvious relation to the words that the subjects learned. Nevertheless, those incidental cues acted as effective retrieval cues, provided that they had been processed during the learning of the list. Second, the theory is not restricted to situations in which the subjects are told that the cues present during learning will later be useful in recalling the words. In Smith's experiment, the subjects had not been instructed to attend to features of the room as they learned the list, and it is unlikely that they deliberately attended to the features of the room. Whether contextual cues are processed intentionally or incidentally, the encoding specificity theory applies. Cues that are processed at the time of encoding act as effective retrieval cues.

SELF-GENERATED CONTEXT

Up to this point, we have concentrated on contextual cues provided by the environment. External stimuli are influential determinants of remembering and forgetting, but our cognitive processes are not bound strictly to the immediate environment. We can generate our own contextual cues internally and use the self-generated context to prevent forgetting. For example, Smith (1979) showed that the use of self-generated context can reduce the forgetting that occurs in the different-context condition described above. Three groups of subjects learned a list of words in room A and were asked later to recall the words in room B, with which they had been familiarized. At the time of recall, one group, called the picture group, was shown slides of room A and instructed to use their memory of room A to help them recall the words. Another group, called the covert-context group, was told to remember room A and to use their memories of room A to help recall the words. The instructions given to these groups would have had little effect if the subjects had not remembered the features of room A. To encourage the subjects to try to remember room A, the subjects were asked before the retention test to write down ten things they remembered seeing in that room. The third group, called the irrelevant-context group, was told to think about a room at home in order to warm up mentally for remembering the words.

The chief results were that the picture group and the covert-context group recalled equal numbers of words, and both groups recalled more than the irrelevant-context group. Thus, recall was facilitated by the instructions to remember the learning room and to use the covert context to remember the words. The covert context generated by the subjects was helpful only when that contextual information matched the contextual information present at the time of learning. Since performance was equal in the covert-context group and the picture group, we may conclude that the overt contextual information provided by the slide had little effect. Apparently, covert context can be as effective as overt context. Indeed, Smith showed in the same report that the covert-context group recalled as many words as a same-context group that learned and recalled the words in the same external environment. Imagined context then, can facilitate retrieval as much as external context can.

The effects of covert context upon recall have important practical implications. Many students have had the unfortunate experience of learning information thoroughly and then drawing a blank upon entering the test room. No doubt this stems in part from anxiety. But, as we have seen, being in a test environment that differs from the study environment can contribute to retrieval failures. Fortunately, retrieval failures are not inevitable. In taking a test, you can improve your retention by remembering the context in which you studied and by using that context to retrieve the learned information.

We can also use the same principle in the opposite direction. While studying in one's room or in the library, we should imagine being in the test room and recalling the information. By doing this, we provide ourselves with cues at the time of encoding that will be present at the time of retrieval. According to the encoding specificity theory, this is exactly what leads to good retention. This conception may help explain why the method of loci mnemonic involves encoding information concerning the context of an imagined, well-known location. No matter where we are, we can remember the encoded information by imagining the appropriate locations. This amounts to generating covertly the mental context that had been present at the time of encoding. Consequently, the level of retention is high. Through practice in using covert context, we stand to improve our own skill in retrieving information.

STATE-DEPENDENT RETRIEVAL

The effects of covert context can also be seen in connection with the use of drugs, including marijuana, amphetamines, barbiturates, and alcohol (Eich, 1977; Overton, 1972; Swanson and Kinsbourne, 1979).

Heavy drinking produces a distinctive mental state or covert context, and what has been learned while intoxicated may be best remembered while intoxicated (Eich, 1977; Overton, 1972). This phenomenon is called *state-dependent learning* or *state-dependent retrieval.* Many studies have reported that retention is higher when a person who had been intoxicated at the time of encoding was intoxicated rather than sober at the time of retrieval (cf. Eich, 1977). Indeed, retention was often as high when subjects were intoxicated at both encoding and retrieval as when they were sober at both. Blackouts and other instances of forgetting may occur in part because of the change in internal context that occurs when one sobers up after being intoxicated. Forgotten information may become retrievable when the drinker returns to the initial context by drinking. Thus some of the effects of alcohol upon memory may be understood in terms of the theory of encoding specificity and the effects of internal context.

MOOD AND RETRIEVAL

The internal context provided by strong emotions also influences retrieval. In some ingenious experiments by Bower (1981) and his associates, subjects were hypnotized and were asked to get themselves into either a happy or a sad mood by remembering past episodes that had made them feel happy or sad. They learned one list of words while they were happy and then learned a second list while they were sad. Then they were asked to recall the first list while either happy or sad. The results were that the level of recall was high when the subjects recalled the first list while in the same mood they had been in while learning that list. For example, if they had been happy while they had learned list one and they were also happy at the time of the recall test, then the level of recall was high. But if they had been happy while they had learned list one and they were sad at the time of the recall test, then the level of recall was low. Thus, when the subjects were in a particular mood, they tended to remember episodes that they had experienced previously while they had been in a similar mood.

This observation is consistent with many observations from natural settings (Bower, 1981). For example, depressed people tend to remember sad or depressing episodes, and this can intensify the depression. As another example, Sirhan Sirhan, who assassinated Bobby Kennedy in 1968, had no conscious recollection of the murderous episode. One possible reason was that Sirhan committed the murder in a highly agitated state. Because that state differed greatly from his usual emotional state, he was unable to remember the episode. While under hypnosis, Sirhan became agitated, and he recalled the episode so vividly that he screamed the death curses, "fired" the shots, and choked as he recalled the attack of the Secret Service bodyguard. Curiously, Sirhan showed no conscious recollection of the murder, suggesting that the episode was retrievable only when he was in the mood he had been in when he had committed the crime. Of course, repression may also have contributed to the lack of conscious recollection, but the point remains that moods can influence memory. This effect of internal context, together with the effects of external and self-generated contexts, indicates the broad range of the theory of encoding specificity.

The Relationship Between Recall and Recognition

So far, we have discussed recognition and recall as methods to study retrieval processes. But we can ask penetrating theoretical questions about recognition and recall per se. Do recognition and recall involve similar processes? Or do they require different retrieval processes? In order to examine these issues, we next inquire into the relationship between recognition and recall.

When asked whether recognition or recall is easier, most students reply that recognition is easier. Unfortunately, this view has led some students to choose courses in which the instructor gives multiple-choice (recognition) tests rather than essay or fill-in (recall) tests. This view might lead one to believe that the amount of or the strength of the information in memory required for recognition is less than that which is required for recall. On this view, recognition and recall are fundamentally similar processes.

Theorists have evaluated this sort of view by examining whether a particular variable, for example, the level of processing, has similar effects on recognition and recall. A variable should have similar effects if recall and recognition involve similar processes but not if they involve different processes.

DETERMINANTS OF RECOGNITION AND RECALL

We have seen previously that retention in both recognition and recall procedures is influenced by retroactive interference and by the level at which information is processed. Another factor that affects recognition and recall similarly is the presence of contextual information both at the time of encoding and at the time of retention. As discussed earlier, recall is facilitated by the presentation of cues that had been processed at the time of encoding. The same can be said of recognition. In one experiment (Light and Carter-Sobell, 1970), subjects studied a list of adjective-noun pairs, for example, *strawberry - JAM*. Each of the nouns had two meanings (*jam* can refer either to a food or to a traffic snarl), and the adjective provided a context that biased the subject to encode one particular meaning of the noun (the food meaning in this example).

Subsequently, the subjects received a recognition test in which the nouns were presented with the adjective that had been presented during the study phase (as in *strawberry - JAM*), alone (as in *JAM*), or with an adjective that suggested the other meaning of the noun (as in *traffic - JAM*). The percentages of nouns that were recognized correctly were 64 percent, 43 percent, and 27 percent, respectively. So recognition was facilitated by the presentation of the adjective that had been presented at the time of encoding but not by a different adjective. These observations suggest that similar processes underlie recognition and recall.

There are, however, variables that influence recognition and recall in opposite ways. One such variable is the frequency with which words occur in our language, as indicated by frequency counts in books and magazines (Kucera and Francis, 1967). In general, rare words (*squab, portal, gimp*) are recognized better than common words (*girl, water, fact*), but just the opposite is true for recall (Hall, 1954; Kinsbourne and George, 1974; McCormack and Swenson, 1972). Similarly, rehearsing words in a nonelaborative manner often improves the level of recognition but has little effect on the level of recall (Mandler, 1979; Woodward et al., 1973).

Another variable that affects recognition and recall differently is organization. Subjects who learn highly organized word lists (for example, lists that contain items from three or four obvious categories) recall more words than subjects who learn word lists that are not highly organized. On the other hand, the level of list organization has no effects on performance in a recognition test (Kintsch, 1968, 1970). Some studies have shown that performance in a recognition test is affected by the level of list organization (Mandler and Boeck, 1974). Yet closer analysis has revealed that the effect of organization occurred when the subjects recalled the target items in the act of recognizing them. Thus it appears that organization influences recall, not recognition. Collectively, these observations suggest that to some extent, different processes contribute to recognition and recall.

THE GENERATION-RECOGNITION MODEL

The preceding kinds of observations have led many theorists to propose that recognition and recall involve both similar and different processes (Anderson and Bower, 1972; Brown 1976; James, 1890; Kintsch, 1970; Müller, 1913). The models that incorporate this view vary with respect to details and the names assigned to the hypothesized processes. But since the models are similar, they will be referred to here collectively as the generation-recognition model.

The generation-recognition model states that two processes underlie recall, whereas only one process underlies recognition. In particular, recall involves both generation and recognition processes, as is illustrated by a simple demonstration. Try to recall who your teacher was in second grade. In performing this task, many people generate several possible names of teachers and then try to recognize which of the generated names is correct. The generation process involves searching through memory in a systematic manner and retrieving potential target items. For example, when you were asked who was your teacher in second grade, the phrase *teacher in second grade* provided a cue that may have facilitated the retrieval of the name of a particular teacher. Because of your previous experiences in school, the name of one teacher is associated with the names of other teachers. As a result, the name of the first teacher triggers the retrieval of the names of other teachers, and each generated name cues the retrieval of other, associated names. The result is a chain of associated names of teachers. Generating words in this manner is a directed search process in which the generation of one item serves as a cue for retrieving associated items.

As you generated various names, you probably tried to judge whether each one was correct. This recognition process probably occurred by evaluating contextual information that you retrieved together with each particular name. For example, the name Ms. Kellam might evoke an image of the classroom in which Ms. Kellam had taught and of the students who had sat beside you in that room. If that contextual information strongly indicated that the name was that of your teacher in second grade, then you would accept that name as correct and produce it overtly. Thus recognizing an item can occur by assessing the contextual information associated with that item. The recognition process can also occur by assessing the familiarity value of an item, as in the familiarity-search model discussed earlier in connection with immediate memory. If a generated item appeared highly familiar, then you would recall the item overtly. This generation plus recognition process continues until your attempt at recall has been completed.

In more sophisticated versions of the model (Anderson and Bower, 1972, 1974), recall occurs through a somewhat different process than that described above. Each item in memory is assumed to be associated with or tagged by a list marker. If *tomato* occurred in study List 1, then the stored representation of tomato would be marked by a "List 1" tag. For this reason, the generation-recognition model is said to be a type of tagging theory. The details of how information is represented in a tagging theory are not our concern here. The important point is that in learning a list of English words, the subjects are not learning the words from scratch; rather, they are learning that the words occurred in a particular context, the context described as "the first list presented in experimental setting X." Generating the words from List 1 involves gaining access to the memory items bearing a "List 1" marker. When one item from List 1 has been accessed, the others can be generated by following the associative pathways bearing List 1 tags. Recognizing a generated item requires deciding whether the item is associated with a sufficient number of contextual cues that are also associated with other list items and markers.

The crux of the generation-recognition model is that recall involves both the generation and the recognition processes, whereas recognition involves only the latter process. This conceptualization helps explain how a variable such as organization can have different effects upon recall and recognition. When organization occurs during learning, numerous associations are formed between the items in a list. The more highly organized the list is, the more obvious are the relations between items and the stronger are the interitem associations. In recalling the items, the generation process proceeds by following the associative pathways between the items and will proceed most effectively when the level of organization is high. Thus, organization improves recall by facilitating the generation process. In this account, organization is assumed not to influence the recognition process, which does not involve following associative pathways established during learning. This idea is consistent with the observation that organization tends not to influence performance in recognition tasks. Following similar logic, the model can account for the opposing effects of other variables upon recall and recognition.

The model can also account for the similar effects that some variables have on recall and recognition. For example, retroactive interference may impair both recognition and recall by impeding both the generation and the recognition processes. This account clarifies why more retroactive interference occurs in recall procedures than in recognition procedures. Retroactive interference can impair only the recognition process involved in recognition tasks. But retroactive interference can impair both the generation and the recognition processes that are involved in recall. Consequently, there is a greater overall amount of retroactive interference in recall than in recognition tasks.

Much of the explanatory power of the model derives from the postulation of the two separate processes that may be affected in similar or opposing ways by particular variables. In evaluating the model, it is important to measure each process separately (Anderson and Bower, 1972). One strategy for accomplishing this is to instruct subjects to generate and recognize items overtly rather than covertly, as in the following experiment (Rabinowitz, Mandler, and Barsalou, 1979). The subjects were shown a series of 50 words, which they assigned to particular categories. They then were asked to recall the list by saying the name of a category and then naming all the items they could think of that belonged to the category, regardless of whether the words belonged to the list. They were also asked to say whether each generated word had occurred in the list. Other subjects were simply asked to recall the list words.

The results were that the subjects who had been told to generate and recognize words recalled many more words than did the subjects who had received the standard recall instructions. Presumably, the former subjects had generated more words by searching thoroughly through the categories. Another important result was that the subjects who had been instructed to generate and recognize produced many old words that they erroneously called "new," The fact that they failed to recognize many of the words they had generated suggests that generating and recognizing are different processes, as stated by the model.

The model can also account for some counterintuitive observations concerning a phenomenon called recognition failure.

WHEN RECOGNITION FAILS

Research concerning encoding specificity turned up some observations that were troublesome for the early versions of the generation-recognition model. According to the model, subjects should not be able to recall words that they have failed to recognize previously. When the recognition process fails, attempts at recall should be unsuccessful since the recognition process is also involved in recall. Yet studies of encoding specificity have shown that unrecognized items can be recalled subsequently.

In one experiment (Tulving and Thomson, 1973), which is outlined in Figure 5.8, subjects learned a list of target words. Each target word (*LIGHT, NEED*) was paired with a cue word (*head, bath*) that was a

Step 1 Study List		Steps 2 and 3 Free Association and Recognition Test					Step 4 Cued-Recall Test	
Cue ↓	Target ↓	Strong associate of targets ↓					Cues from Step 1 ↓	
head	LIGHT	dark	*night*	*light*	*(black)*	*room*	head	*light*
bath	NEED	want	*need*	*desire*	*wish*	*get*	bath	
pretty	BLUE	sky	*sun*	*cloud*	*blue*	*open*	pretty	*blue*
grasp	BABY	infant	*child*	*mother*	*love*	*(baby)*	grasp	
whiskey	WATER	lake	*water*	*smooth*	*river*	*ocean*	whiskey	*water*
cabbage	ROUND	square	*(round)*	*flat*	*circle*	*corner*	cabbage	*round*
spider	BIRD	eagle	*eye*	*mountain*	*bird*	*high*	spider	
glue	CHAIR	table	*chair*	*desk*	*lamp*	*top*	glue	*chair*

Figure 5.8 The procedure of an experiment concerning recognition failure. The handwritten words are the responses of a hypothetical subject. Recognition failure occurred when the subject recalled words (*blue, water*) in Step 4 that had not been recognized in Step 3. (From Tulving, 1974.)

weak associate. After learning the list, the subjects were given strong associates of the targets. For example, *dark* was a strong associate of *LIGHT*. As in a test of free association, the subjects wrote down the words that were called to mind by the strong associates. The strong associates usually evoked the target words that had been learned previously; for example, *infant* evoked *baby*, and *eagle* evoked *bird*. Following the free association test, the subjects were asked to examine the words that they had generated and to circle target words from the list that they had learned in Step One. This was a recognition test. Subsequently, the cue words from Step One were presented and the subjects were asked to recall the appropriate target words. This was a cued-recall test.

The results were that in the recognition test, the subjects failed to recognize many of the target words that they had generated in the free association task. Surprisingly, many of the words that had not been recognized were recalled later in the cued-recall test. In other words, the subjects recalled many of the target words they had failed to recognize. This outcome is called *recognition failure*.

Recognition failure has been observed in numerous kinds of procedures (Bowyer and Humphreys, 1979; Flexser and Tulving, 1978; Wiseman and Tulving, 1975, 1976). Yet there are indications that the effect occurs with some types of words but not with others, so the generality of the effect is uncertain (Rabinowitz, Mandler, and Barsalou, 1977; Salzberg, 1976). Nevertheless, the phenomenon of recognition failure has attracted attention for two reasons. First, it runs counter to our intuitions that recognition is easier than recall and that people should therefore be able to recognize words that they can recall. More important, the phenomenon contradicted some early versions of the generation-recognition model, which state that the items that are recalled must also be recognizable.

This apparent contradiction has been resolved in more recent versions of the generation-recognition model (Light, Kimble, and Pellegrino, 1975; Martin, 1975). These models integrate what is known about encoding with the generation-recognition conception of retrieval. Specifically, remembered words are viewed not as unitary items but as collections of semantic, phonemic, and other attributes or features. For example, when the word *jam* is presented in the context of the phrase *strawberry jam*, subjects may process only the food-related attributes of *jam*. Strictly speaking, they do not remember the word *jam*; they remember only the food-related attributes that they had encoded. The word *jam* is recalled or recognized only if the attributes that had been encoded were activated in the retention test. In this example, *jam* will not be recognized if it is presented in the context of *traffic jam*, for the context provided by *traffic* will not activate the food-related attributes of *jam*.

This view agrees with the observation that subjects who had studied *jam* in the context of *strawberry jam* recognized *jam* in the context of *strawberry* but not in the context of *traffic* (Light and Carter-Sobell, 1970).

Consider how this view explains the recognition failure that occurred in the experiment outlined in Figure 5.8. In Step One, the cue words biased the subjects toward encoding particular attributes of the target words. For example, the word *whiskey* may have led the subjects to encode *water* as a mixer. Indeed, the subjects may have encoded the *whiskey - WATER* pair by forming an image of themselves indulging in a mixed drink containing whiskey and water. In the free association task, the subjects generated the word *water* but failed to recognize it as a target word. This might have occurred because the context of the recognition test differed from that of the initial learning phase. Looking at Figure 5.8, we see that in Step Two, *water* occurred in the context of *lake, smooth, river,* and *ocean.* This context concerns bodies of water, so the drink-related attributes of *water* were not activated. As a result, the subjects failed to recognize that *water* was a target word. In the cued-recall test, the cue words (for example, *whiskey*) were presented, and the subjects recalled words that they had failed to recognize. Apparently, the cues provided access to the attributes of the target words that had been encoded in Step One.

This account predicts that the level of recognition for particular words should equal or surpass the level of recall for those words if both the recognition and the recall tests provided the contextual cues that had been processed during encoding. Wallace (1978) has done this by presenting the cue words from Step One in both the recognition and the recall tests. As predicted, the level of recall did not surpass the level of recognition. Thus, when the effects of context are incorporated into the generation-recognition model, the model can accommodate the phenomenon of recognition failure.

LIMITS OF THE GENERATION-RECOGNITION MODEL

The generation-recognition model, despite its ability to accommodate many observations, confronts numerous problems (Tulving, 1976). For example, it is difficult to measure precisely the generation and recognition processes. This makes the model difficult to test and reduces its predictive power. A more serious problem is that the model may lack generality. For example, when subjects are explicitly instructed to recall items by generating and then recognizing them, they recall more words than do subjects who are simply told to recall the items (Rabinowitz et al., 1979). But if the retention test occurs a week after learning, just the opposite occurs: the subjects who overtly generate and recognize items recall fewer words than the subjects who received the standard free recall instructions. This means that subjects do not typically recall words by generating and recognizing them. If this interpretation proves to be correct, the generation-recognition model would be of limited generality. Generating and then recognizing items may be only one among many strategies that subjects use in recalling information (Rabinowitz et al., 1979).

The emphasis upon retrieval strategies puts the question of how recognition and recall are related in a new light. If there are numerous strategies for retrieving information, there may be no one fundamental relationship between recognition and recall. This view conflicts with the generation-recognition model, but it makes sense in light of the diverse ways in which recognition and recall may occur. Retrieval in some instances seems to require no search process and little evaluation of contextual information. When someone asks what your name is, you hardly have to conduct a memory search by generating names and recognizing your own. But in trying to recall the name of someone whom you have not seen for years, you may conduct a search by generating various plausible names. Similarly, recognizing the names of our relatives may occur on the basis of a familiarity check, with no assessment of context. But recognizing a person in a picture may require searching memory for information concerning the context in which we might have encountered the person. Exactly how retrieval occurs on a particular occasion will depend upon the properties of the stimuli, the requirements of the task, and the knowledge the subjects have. Before we can understand fully the various ways in which recognition and recall are related, we need to discover the various retrieval strategies humans use and to define the conditions in which they are likely to occur.

ENCODING SPECIFICITY AND INDEPENDENT RETRIEVAL INFORMATION

A very different view from those discussed above has arisen from research concerning encoding specificity. Recall that the hypothesis of encoding specificity states that a cue will facilitate retrieval if it provides information that matches the previously encoded information. Theorists have applied this hypothesis to both recognition and recall (Flexser et al., 1978; Tulving, 1976). In particular, they have argued that in both recognition and in cued recall, there is a single retrieval process whereby the information extracted from a retrieval cue provides access to a particular memory trace. In a cued-recall test, the cue is the context that had been presented along with the target word during learning. In a recognition test, the cue is the target item itself, and the subject's task is to recall the context in which the target item had occurred. This conception makes sense in that we often recognize words and people by recalling the context in which we have previously seen them. In a recognition test, then, the target words serve as cues for the retrieval of contextual information.

If recognition and recall involve the same process, why are items that are sometimes recognized not recalled, and vice versa? One possibility, which Flexser and Tulving (1978) have developed in a quantitative model, is that subjects use different retrieval information in recognition and cued-recall tasks. This proposal is illustrated in a simplified form in Figure 5.9. A cue-target pair that has ten features or attributes may be encoded in a particular situation in terms of seven attributes, indicated by the checked boxes in panel (a). In a recognition test, the target word itself is the retrieval cue. Retrieval cues, like any processed items, may be encoded in terms of several attributes; typically, only some of the possible attributes will be encoded. As shown in panel (b), the target word might be encoded in terms of six attributes, not all of which match the attributes encoded initially. Only features 2, 5, and 9 will be useful in recognition since they are the only features that match the originally encoded features. As shown in panel (c), the real cue (the context word) might be encoded in terms of five features. Of those five features 3, 5, 7, and 10 match features of the initial memory trace. Notice that four features of the recall cue match features in the memory trace, whereas only three features of the recognition cue (the target word) match features in the memory trace. Since retrieval depends upon the degree of overlap between the features of the retrieval cue and the features in the memory

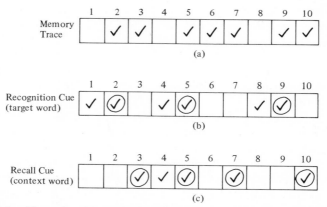

Figure 5.9   The role of retrieval in recognition and in cued recall. (a) The attributes of encoding for a hypothetical cue-target pair. The checks indicate which attributes have been encoded. (b) The attributes of encoding for the target word that is presented in a recognition test. The circles indicate the attributes that match the features of the memory trace. (c) The encoded features for the context word presented in a cued-recall test. Note that different features can be retrieved in the recognition and the recall tests. (After Flexser and Tulving, 1978. Copyright 1978 by the American Psychological Association. Reprinted by permission.)

trace, the level of recall in this case would exceed the level of recognition.

The crux of this model is that recognition and recall may be based upon different retrieval information. Although the same features may be involved in both recognition and recall, there is little correlation between the features used in the two instances of retrieval. In other words, recognition and recall are based upon independent information. Building on this idea, Flexser and Tulving gave a precise account of the degree of recognition failure.

This conception may be too rigid in that it asserts that retrieval cues provide direct and automatic access to stored information. We no doubt recall some information, for example, our names, via direct access and without an extensive search of memory. On some occasions, however, we do retrieve information by engaging in an extensive search of memory, as suggested by the generation-recognition model.

Nevertheless, the Flexser and Tulving model incorporates the important idea that different information may be used in recognition and recall. This view is supported by numerous observations (Brown, 1976; Underwood, 1972). In one experiment (Carey and Lockhart, 1973; also see Barlota and Neely, 1980), subjects encoded information in anticipation of a recall test. After learning and recalling several lists, they learned a list and then took an unexpected recognition test. Performance in the recognition test was lower and qualitatively different than the performance of subjects who had expected a recognition test during learning. Apparently, subjects encode different information when they expect a recall test rather than a recognition test. Additional insights into the nature of retrieval may come from an analysis of the different kinds of information that support recognition and recall.

RETRIEVING THROUGH RECONSTRUCTING

Most studies of memory have concerned verbatim (word for word) retention for relatively simple verbal materials, for example, lists of words. There are several reasons behind the interest in verbatim retention. First, many theorists, from Plato to the associationists of this century, have viewed remembering as a process of forming memory traces that are replicas or copies of the presented information. From this perspective, it makes sense to say that people remember words only if they can reproduce or recognize those words in the exact form in which they had been presented. Second, it is easier to measure retention when responses are scored as correct only if they match the presented items exactly. For example, if a presented word were *wolf* and the subject recalled *fox*, how would we know whether the recall of *fox* reflected memory for particular attributes of *wolf?* Third, historical precedent has encouraged the study of verbatim retention. Following Ebbinghaus' research, many investigators studied verbatim retention of lists of words. In order to relate current observations to those made in the past, it is necessary to use methods that resemble those used in the past. For this reason, the study of verbatim retention has, rightly or wrongly, become deeply entrenched in psychology.

The study of verbatim retention is justifiable in that verbatim retention occurs in some everyday situations. For example, most people remember the exact wording of the punchlines of their favorite jokes. This is unsurprising since jokes can fall flat when they are told improperly. Verbatim retention also results from schooling, for many schoolchildren have had to memorize passages such as Hamlet's "To be or not to be" soliloquy and the national anthem. Even years following the learning episode, people remember the exact wording of such passages (Rubin, 1977). Indeed, the author remembers the exact wording of many passages and songs that he would prefer to forget.

Verbatim retention can result from incidental learning as well as from intentional learning. Keenan, MacWhinney, and Mayhew (1977) measured retention for the exact wording of statements that had occurred spontaneously in an informal luncheon discussion in the Psychology Department at the University of Denver. The participants had not been told to remember the statements that were made. Nevertheless, they recognized the exact wording of over 50 percent of the statements that had conveyed wit, humor, or personal criticism.

Needless to say, we do not always remember information verbatim. As discussed previously, people usually remember the meaning or the theme of prose passages rather than the exact wording and form of the sentences. If, for example, you tried to recall *Great Expectations*, you would probably remember parts of the theme but few of the exact sentences. Further, remembering the theme or the gist of what we have read or heard seems not to be a passive process of activating facts stored in memory. In many instances, we remember by actively reconstructing information, and we sometimes interject new information in the process. For these reasons, many psychologists have redirected their research away from studies concerning verbatim memory for word lists toward memory for the meaning of stories. We now examine reconstructive retrieval and the conditions that lead to the occurrence of errors in recalling stories and pictures.

Reconstructing Stories and Pictures

Sir Frederick Bartlett (1932) proposed that retrieval is a reconstructive process. As you may recall from the first chapter, Bartlett studied how

British adults recalled *The War of the Ghosts*, a folktale of North American Indians that contained mystical elements. To get a feeling for the kinds of results Bartlett obtained, you should take several moments and try to recall the story verbatim and then check your answer against the original story on page 22. Bartlett observed that the subjects often erred by omitting details and by making the story more consistent with their cultural expectations. Because the subjects distorted the stories in accord with their beliefs and expectations, Bartlett argued that they were not simply retrieving stored copies of what they had read. Rather, they were using their general knowledge and their expectations, combined with a few fragmentary details, to reconstruct or to piece together the story. You probably made similar observations concerning your own performance.

Not all subsequent studies have reported the gross distortions in story recall that Bartlett had observed (Spiro, 1977). As a result, some theorists have suggested that retrieval is more a process of reproduction than of reconstruction. But in fact, one need not choose between theories of verbatim memory and theories of reconstructive memory. Human memory is remarkably flexible, so it is unreasonable to claim that people remember in one manner rather than another. Consistent with this view, Spiro (1980) has observed that verbatim and reconstructive memory occur under different conditions.

WHEN RECONSTRUCTION OCCURS

Like Bartlett, Spiro hypothesized that distortions in story recall will occur when the story violates the subjects' expectations. Spiro (1980) manipulated his subjects' expectations by having them read different stories. All of the subjects read a story about an engaged couple, Bob and Margie. Bob and Margie were happily planning their marriage, but Bob had one problem that he was reluctant to discuss: he did not want children. Finally, he told Margie about his feelings about having children. In one version of the story, Margie was elated because she wanted time to pursue a career. In another version of the story, Margie was horrified because she had always wanted to be a mother, and a bitter argument ensued. These two stories, which were read by different groups of subjects, were designed to induce the subjects to expect either future happiness or serious trouble for Bob and Margie. The subjects were told that they would be asked later about their reactions to the story.

About eight minutes after the subjects had read the story, Spiro mentioned that either (1) Bob and Margie did get married and are living together happily or (2) Bob and Margie broke off their engagement. Depending upon which story the subjects had read earlier, this information either confirmed (the confirmatory condition) or violated (the contradictory condition) the subjects' expectations about the long-term prospects of the relationship between Bob and Margie. For example, the statement that Bob and Margie were married and living happily contradicted the expectations of the subjects who had read previously that Bob and Margie had argued bitterly about whether to have children. Spiro predicted that the contradictory information would lead to the formation of new expectations and to the occurrence of systematic errors in recall. In particular, the subjects who had heard that Bob and Margie were happily married would modify their initial expectation of trouble for the couple. In recalling the initial story, they would use their expectation that Bob and Margie were married happily to guide their reconstruction of the initial story. As a result, they would err systematically by downplaying the initial degree of conflict between Bob and Margie or by remembering fictitious events that could have resolved the conflict.

Following a delay of two days, three weeks, or six weeks, Spiro asked the subjects to reproduce the story. As predicted, the subjects in the contradictory condition distorted the story systematically and more frequently than the subjects in the confirmatory condition, particularly following the retention intervals of three and six weeks. Here are some examples of the errors made by the subjects who had read initially that Bob and Margie argued about having children and who heard later that the couple was happily married:

1. They separated but realized after discussing the matter that their love mattered more.
2. They underwent counseling to correct the major discrepancy.
3. They discussed it and decided they could agree on a compromise: adoption.
4. She was only a little upset at the disagreement.

Note that the first three errors introduced events that had not been mentioned in the story and that the fourth error minimized the initial degree of conflict. These distortions were clearly consistent with the subjects' new expectations. Remarkably, the subjects were more confident that these distortions had occurred in the story than they were of statements that had actually occurred. Thus the subjects believed the distortions; they were not consciously fabricating information in order to fill gaps in memory. Strong confidence in one's memory, then, is no guarantee of accuracy.

These observations show that people do use their expectations to guide the reconstruction of a story. In the same set of experiments, however, Spiro showed that retrieval does not always occur via reconstruction. He repeated the experiment, but this time he told the subjects that they would be asked to remember the story. The results were that the subjects made very few systematic errors or distortions in recall. Further, the subjects in the contradictory condition made no more errors than did the subjects in the confirmatory condition. Apparently, the subjects were not actively reconstructing the story. This outcome reminds us that the instructions to remember that pervade studies of memory are not simple requests but powerful determinants of processing.

Collectively, these observations suggest that reconstructive retrieval occurs when the remembered information conflicts with the present expectations of the subject and when the instructions to the subjects do not induce them to encode the exact wording of the story. Reconstructive retrieval may also occur when we have very few details concerning the original story or episode stored in memory but have strong expectations about what must have occurred. As these comments suggest, the dividing line between inference and memory can be exceedingly thin.

RECONSTRUCTING PICTURES

Reconstruction also occurs in remembering pictures. In an early experiment, Carmichael, Hogan, and Walters (1932) showed subjects patterns such as those shown in the center column of Figure 5.10. The top pattern was described as a crescent moon to some subjects and as the letter "C" to others. The bottom pattern was described either as eyeglasses or dumbbells. Later, the subjects were asked to draw the pattern they had seen. The results were that the subjects' reproduction of the patterns tended to correspond to the labels that had been provided. People who had received the *eyeglasses* label tended to draw a pair of eyeglasses, whereas people who had received the *dumbbell* label tended to draw dumbbells. That this effect was due to retrieval processes was shown in subsequent experiments. For example, the groups that received different labels did not differ in their performance on a recognition test (Prentice, 1954), which suggests that the two groups had encoded similar visual information. Moreover, the labels influenced recall when they were provided only at the time of recall (Hanawalt and Demarest, 1939).

These results suggest that the subjects did not recall the figures by retrieving copylike traces of the patterns. Rather, they recalled the verbal labels and used the labels to reconstruct the patterns. In one sense, the labels acted as retrieval cues. We now see, however, that retrieval

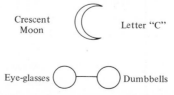

Figure 5.10   The effect of verbal labels that had been provided at the time of encoding upon the reproduction of figures. (After Carmichael, Hogan, and Walters, 1932.)

cues do not always operate by providing direct access to a memory trace, for a cue can also operate by guiding an effort at reconstruction.

Contemporary observations also suggest that people remember pictures by reconstructing them under the guidance of their expectations (Mandler and Ritchey, 1977). In many instances, then, retrieval is unlike activating a replica of remembered items. It is more like piecing fragments together into a pattern, as a biologist might put bone fragments together to reconstruct the skeleton of a dinosaur (Neisser, 1967). These ideas are important not only theoretically but also practically, as shown in the following section.

The Eyewitness Report

In our legal system, decisions about the guilt or innocence of a defendant are frequently based on the testimony of eyewitnesses. Relying upon eyewitness reports is justifiable only to the extent to which those reports are accurate. The fact that remembering often occurs through reconstructing leads us to expect that eyewitness reports, no matter how fervently believed by the eyewitness, will sometimes be quite inaccurate. Unintended distortions can occur in the process of reconstruction, even when the witnesses claim that the original events stand in their minds like clear pictures.

In one early demonstration (Muensterberg, 1908), a psychologist addressed a class in which two students suddenly began shouting at each other:

> STUDENT 1: "I wanted to throw light on the matter from the standpoint of Christian morality!"
> STUDENT 2: "I cannot stand that!"
> STUDENT 1: "You have insulted me!"
> STUDENT 2: "If you say another word . . ."

At this point, the first student pulled a gun from his pocket. The second student charged towards the first, and the professor tried to grab the arm of the first student. The gun fired, and the classroom became chaotic. Actually, this episode had been staged to study how accurately the students recalled the events. When the students had been calmed down, they were asked to write down exactly what they had witnessed. The accounts varied from one witness to another, but the percentage of erroneous statements was consistently high, ranging from 26 percent to 80 percent. Some witnesses included events that had not occurred, and some failed to report the most essential events in the episode. Also, more erroneous statements were made about the second half of the episode than about the first half. This probably resulted from the greater emotionality of the second half. These results, which have been confirmed in many

other studies (Loftus, 1979), are consistent with the view that rec-
ollections are often reconstructions rather than copies of the original
events.

Errors in reconstructing witnessed events may also result from the
questions put to the witness (Loftus, 1979). Loftus and Palmer (1974)
showed subjects a film of an automobile accident and then questioned
the subjects about the speed of the cars. Some subjects were asked
"About how fast were the cars going when they smashed into each
other?" Others were asked "About how fast were the cars going when
they hit each other?" The subjects who had been asked the "smashed"
question gave much higher estimates of speed. In a later study, the same
subjects were asked a week later, "Did you see any broken glass?" In
fact, no broken glass had been shown in the film. But broken glass is typically copious where a high-speed accident has occurred. The results
were that the subjects who had previously heard the "smashed" question
reported seeing broken glass more often than the subjects who had previously heard the "hit" question. This suggests that the subjects who had
heard the "smashed" question and given a high estimate of speed actually remembered having seen a high-speed accident. What eyewitnesses report, then, depends both on what they have seen and on the
questions that have been put to them.

Observations such as these give little comfort to those who would
accept eyewitness testimony at face value. For some fascinating reading
concerning the implications of this type of observation for legal practices, see Loftus (1979) and Yarmey (1979).

• *Summary.* Information that is stored in memory is often inaccessible or
difficult to retrieve. In general, the forgetting of well-learned information results primarily from retrieval failures. Many laboratory studies of
forgetting have concerned interference. In the standard interference
paradigms, the subjects learn two successive word lists and then recall
either the first (the retroactive interference paradigm) or the second (the
proactive interference paradigm).

Initially, retroactive interference was attributed to competition between responses from the two lists and to the unlearning of responses
from the first list during the learning of the second list. Yet studies that
used recognition tests to measure retention showed that the responses
from the first list had not been unlearned or lost from storage but had
become difficult to retrieve. Subsequently, the notion of unlearning was
largely replaced by the hypothesis of response set suppression, which
states that the responses from list one become suppressed as the result of
learning list two. Proactive interference is now believed to result from a
failure to differentiate clearly between the two lists, which impairs re-

trieval. Both retroactive and proactive interference can be overcome by the presentation of retrieval cues. For this reason, interference is an example of cue-dependent forgetting.

Amnesia and emotionally induced forgetting also stem from retrieval failures. Retrograde amnesia, the forgetting of the events that preceded a traumatic incident, usually decreases over time. So the forgotten information had not been lost from storage but had become difficult to retrieve. Similarly, anterograde amnesia, the forgetting of information acquired following a traumatic incident, results from retrieval failures. Supplying retrieval cues enables amnesics to achieve high levels of recall. In at least some instances, emotional factors produce retrieval failures. Clinical studies of repression suggest that retrieval is impaired when the content of memories is aversive or ego-threatening. And in laboratory studies, subjects have failed to retrieve well-learned words that are associates of aversive, shock-paired words.

Because forgetting often results from the lack of effective retrieval cues, it is important to discover what makes cues effective or ineffective. According to the theory of encoding specificity, retrieval cues will be effective if they have been processed at both the time of encoding and the time of retrieval. Effective retrieval cues may be provided by the external context, for example, by the appearance of a room in which a test is taken. Similarly, the internal context that accompanies states such as alcoholic intoxication can facilitate retrieval. Additionally, effective retrieval cues may be self-generated, and this principle may be used to prevent forgetting in everyday situations.

Attempts to construct a broad theory of retrieval have led to inquiries into the relationship between recognition and recall. Recognition and recall seem related since they are affected in similar ways by factors such as context and retroactive interference. Other factors, such as word frequency, have opposite effects on recognition and recall, which suggests that different processes operate in recognition and recall. To account for these observations, many theorists have proposed that recall involves two processes: generating candidate items by searching through memory and recognizing items that had been presented by assessing their familiarity or their contextual associations. According to this generation-recognition model of retrieval, recognizing items requires the recognition but not the generation process. This model accounts for many observations, including the surprising observation that subjects can recall words that they have previously failed to recognize. Numerous observations, however, suggest that the generation-recognition model lacks generality and identifies only one of many strategies adults use to retrieve information. The model also fails to take into account that recall and recognition may be based on different kinds of information. Comprehensive theories of retrieval must be highly flexible. Retrieval may occur by assessing information directly through the aid of retrieval cues, by generating and evaluating items in memory, by evaluating the context in which the target items occurred, and by checking the familiarity of items.

Studies that have examined the retention of prose and of episodes such as traffic accidents have established that retrieval is often a reconstructive process. Adults tend to remember those aspects that are most meaningful and that fit in best with their expectations. If the subjects' expectations have changed since a story was read initially, then they will distort the story in accord with their current expectations. In some cases, the subjects believe that their plausible reconstructions and even their fabrications are accurate. Retrieval, then, can be a highly active process that is guided by plausible inferences. These inferences are based upon our conceptual, semantic knowledge of the world. The following chapters inquire into that knowledge.

Chapter 6
Categorization and
Concept Formation

In every known culture, people divide the world into categories. With nary a reflection, we call some animals *dog*, whereas we call other animals *bird, monkey,* or *human.* The obviousness of this fact should not obscure the importance of our knowledge of categories. People draw on their knowledge of categories to answer everyday questions. For example, is a dolphin a fish or a mammal? You could not answer this simple question unless you had previously formed the categories *dolphin, fish,* and *mammal.* The importance of categories is also apparent in pattern recognition, which occurs by assigning incoming stimuli to existing categories. Similarly, organizing items by categories aids memory. Our categories, then, are a fundamental aspect of our knowledge, and they constitute the cornerstone of many of our cognitive activities.

The process of categorization entails both generalization and discrimination. We categorize different animals as dogs by recognizing features that are common to various dogs. In other words, we generalize from one dog to another, abstracting features shared by different dogs. So important is generalization that we say people have mastered the concept *dog* only if they can respond correctly to novel dogs. At the same time, we discriminate or notice the differences between dogs and other animals. If a boy called monkeys, horses, and dogs *dog*, we would be unwilling to say that he had mastered the concept.

In combination, generalization and discrimination make categories powerful tools of thought. Generalization allows us to reduce Nature's endless diversity to manageable proportions. By noting similarities among stimuli and by grouping stimuli into categories, we avoid the burden that would exist if we treated each and every object as a category unto itself. In a similar vein, discrimination is advantageous because it enables us to make important distinctions between groups of stimuli. After all, if we failed to distinguish between wolves and sheep, between pastors and criminals, or between food preservatives and poisons, we would probably not live to tell about it.

Because our categories are based on both generalization and discrimination, categories convey a large amount of information. For example, if we are told that a particular car is a Honda, we know immediately that the car was made in Japan, has a four-cylinder engine, gets good gas mileage, and so on. We also know that the object is not a Ford, not an animal, and not a tractor. Thus being told what category an object belongs to tells us much about what the object is and what it is not. Overall, then, categorization allows us to apply our existing knowledge to new situations and to avoid being overwhelmed by Nature's endless diversity.

In the first section of this chapter, we inquire into the nature of conceptual categories. As a rough definition, a category is a class of stimuli that are treated in an equivalent manner. For example, in calling various dogs by a common label, *dog*, we treat the animals as if they were equivalent. Technically speaking, however, not all the members or exemplars of a category are equivalent psychologically. As an illustration, think of a bird. You most likely thought of a robin or a sparrow rather than a turkey or an ostrich. Although all of these birds belong to the category *bird*, we view some birds as more typical of the category than others. Similarly both chihuahuas and collies are dogs, but collies seem to many people to be typical dogs, whereas chihuahuas seem atypical. These comments indicate that categories have structure: some items seem to lie near the center of the category, but others lie at the periphery.

In the second and third sections of the chapter, we analyze the manner in which concepts are learned. People use a variety of strategies or plans of attack in learning concepts. For example, you might learn the concept *marmoset* (a soft-furred monkey having claws rather than nails on all but the first toe) by memorizing the appearance of several marmosets you saw at a zoo. You could say whether novel animals were or were not marmosets by comparing the animals to the marmosets that you remember. Alternately, you might learn the concept *marmoset* by examining several marmosets in a zoo and abstracting the physical features or attributes that they have in common. You could then classify a novel animal by checking to see whether the animal had the same features as the marmosets. In using various strategies, people often proceed as if they were forming and testing hypotheses about which features define the category. We shall examine these processes and look into the effects of factors such as attention upon concept learning.

Not all conceptual categories are formed through learning. During the evolution of our species, selective pressures probably favored individuals who categorized important stimuli such as colors in a particular manner. As a result, people from many different cultures categorize colors in a similar manner, despite the fact that different languages name colors in very different ways. We conclude this chapter by exploring the relationship between language and categorization. We shall see that both genetic and experiential factors influence the formation of categories.

THE STRUCTURE OF CATEGORIES

At the outset, we should say what we mean by the structure of a category. The structure of a category refers to its architecture, the manner in which the category is put together. A particular category may be large or small, well-defined or ill-defined, and so on. Of course, a category appears stable only when we examine it at a particular slice of time. Over time, categories are dynamic and subject to change. For example, in using the word *dog*, 3-year-olds sometimes make errors of overextension, calling all four-legged animals *dog* (Clark and Clark, 1977). Through experience, however, children's categories change and come into correspondence with those of adults. Of course, adult categories often change too. For example, your category of cancer-causing substances expands constantly as medical research advances. There is no danger in discussing the structure of categories so long as we remember that the structure changes over time.

Traditionally, most psychologists defined categories in terms of attributes that combined according to rules (Bourne, 1966). For example, the category *water* was defined by the conjunction or the simultaneous presence of the attributes *colorless, odorless, tasteless,* and *liquid.* This view emphasized that categories are structured according to logical rules. It was implied that all members of a category were equally good instances of the category and that the distinction between different categories is clear-cut and logical (Rosch, 1973, 1975). These implicit assumptions were reinforced in laboratory research, which concerned the learning of artificial categories such as *red queen* in a deck of cards.

Subsequently, theorists pointed out that many natural categories defy logical definitions. For example, the categories *plant* and *animal* seem to shade into each other, so it is difficult to make sharp, logical distinctions betw en them. Additionally, natural categories such as *dog* have internal structure, as stated above. Recent conceptions of the structure of natural categories have departed from the traditional view of categories. But because both outlooks have useful elements and have influenced research, both are discussed in this section.

Attributes and Rules

One important property of many cognitive categories is that they can include an infinite number of members. The category *dog*, for example, includes not only the dogs you have seen or read about but also an indefinitely large number of novel dogs. For this reason, categories cannot be described adequately by listing all of the members of the category. Yet many of the members of a category may have attributes in common. For example, most birds have feathers and a beak, and most dogs have teeth and can bark. This consideration has led to the view that attributes are important in the description of our cognitive categories. This view agrees with the idea discussed earlier that recognizing and encoding stimuli involves analyzing their features or attributes.

Our knowledge of categories includes not only attributes but also relationships among the attributes. These relationships may be described by rules, which are logical statements that specify how attributes are combined. Rules are illustrated by considering a set of artificial stimuli of the sort that have been used in much laboratory research. The stimuli, shown in Figure 6.1, include three dimensions or bases for variation:

Rule	□	□	■	■	△	△	▲	▲
1. Affirmative (e.g., + if dark)	−	−	+	+	−	−	+	+
2. Conjunctive (e.g., + if light *and* square)	+	+	−	−	−	−	−	−
3. Inclusive disjunctive (e.g., + if light *and/or* square)	+	+	+	+	+	+	−	−
4. Conditional (e.g., if △, then dark; if □, then light)	+	+	−	−	−	−	+	+
5. Joint denial (e.g., + if not small and not △)	−	+	−	+	−	−	−	−

Figure 6.1   Five rules that may define concepts. The positive instances of each concept are marked by a plus sign, and the negative instances are marked by a minus sign.

brightness, size, and shape. Each dimension has two attributes. Square-ness and triangularity are the attributes for the dimension of shape; light and dark are the attributes for the dimension of brightness; large and small are the attributes for the dimension of size.

An *affirmative* rule specifies a particular attribute that by itself de-fines the category. In Figure 6.1, the affirmative rule specifies darkness as the defining attribute. All of the dark stimuli are said to be positive in-stances of the category, whereas the light stimuli are said to be negative instances. In this example, the dimension of brightness is said to be rele-vant to the category or concept. Because size and shape do not define positive instances, they are irrelevant dimensions. An everyday example of an affirmative concept is *red,* which can be defined by the attribute *redness.*

Most of our concepts are too complex to be described by the affir-mative rule. The concept *father,* for example, includes the attributes *male* and *has children.* A *conjunctive rule* is used to describe concepts defined by the presence of several attributes. The concept *light square* illustrated in Figure 6.1 is described by a conjunctive rule since positive instances must be both light and square.

Figure 6.1 also illustrates the inclusive disjunctive, the conditional, and the joint denial rules. The *inclusive disjunctive* rule specifies that all positive instances include either one attribute or another, or both, as in the concept *light and/or square.* The inclusive disjunctive rule applies to the concept *bad song,* which may include the attribute *bad lyrics* or *bad musicianship,* or both. A *conditional rule* might specify that stimuli are positive instances if they are dark and are triangles or if they are squares. The concept *good citizen* is defined by a conditional rule. A man is a good citizen if he votes wisely, pays taxes, and works to improve society, but only if he does not commit a felony. A variation of the conditional rule is the biconditional rule, which might state, for example, that triangles are instances if and only if they are light. The last rule mentioned here is *joint denial.* It is illustrated by the concept *peace,* which is defined in part by the joint absence of attributes such as fighting and fearful-ness.

The view that conceptual categories can be described adequately by attributes and rules applies to some natural concepts. For example, the concept of *negative number* is defined adequately by the attribute *less than zero.* Because the concept is a logical one, the distinction be-tween members of the category (−1, −283, −1/12) and nonmembers of the category (1/8, 14, 2) is clear and simple. In general, mathematicians, logicians, and scientists have devised many categories that are defined logically. These categories can be defined in terms of attributes and rules. Yet as discussed in the following section, many natural categories defy attempts at strictly logical definitions.

Fuzzy and Variable Boundaries

Many natural concepts have boundaries that are vague and fuzzy (Zadeh, Fu, Tanaka and Shimura, 1975). What exactly is the distinction between life and death, between plant and animal, or between stream and river? The legal, scientific and philosophical controversies sparked by such questions attest to the fact that membership in natural categories is not an all-or-none matter but one of degree. It is the vagueness of category boundaries that leads us to qualify statements with phrases such as "roughly speaking" or "speaking loosely." For example, if we were describing a body of water but were unsure whether it was a stream or a river, we might say "Speaking loosely, this is a river." This type of linguistic qualifying device is called a *hedge* (Lakoff, 1972). Hedges help us to communicate and to circumvent unresolved problems that are not critical at a particular moment.

The boundaries of many categories are not only fuzzy but also variable. For example, Labov (1973) has shown that the boundaries of the category *cup* vary depending upon the context. Labov showed people 20 drawings such as those in Figure 6.2a and asked them to name the pictured objects. This classification task was performed in four different contexts. In the neutral context, the subjects were told to imagine the object in someone's hand. In the coffee context, the subjects were asked to imagine someone holding the object and drinking coffee from it. In the food context, the subjects were told to imagine the object filled with mashed potatoes and sitting on the dinner table. In the flower condition, the subjects were asked to imagine the object on a shelf, filled with cut flowers.

As Figure 6.2b shows, the context influenced how the subjects classified the drawings. In the coffee and the neutral contexts, almost everyone described the second drawing as a cup, whereas this did not occur in the food and the flower contexts. Similarly, the third drawing was often called a cup in the coffee and the neutral contexts. But in the food condition, the subjects tended to call the third drawing *bowl* rather than *cup*. And in the flower condition, the subjects called the third drawing *vase* as often as *cup*. Also notice the lack of discrete boundaries for the *cup* category. As the shape of the object varied, there were gradual, not precipitous, changes in how often objects were called *cup*. This shows that the boundaries of the *cup* category are fuzzy rather than discrete.

The context-dependency of categories is apparent from our everyday experiences. We might call a spider an *insect* when talking with children, but we might use another classification in talking with a naturalist. This ability to classify the same object in different ways depending on the context and the demands of the task is also apparent among physicists, who sometimes conceive of light as waves and at other times as

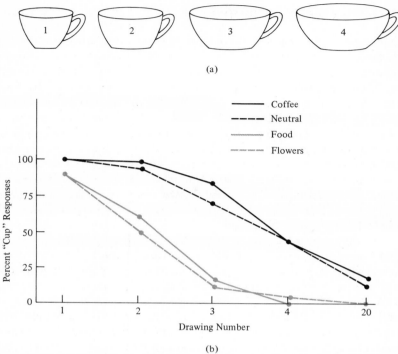

Figure 6.2   The boundaries of the *cup* category. (a) Four of the draw-ings that people classified in various contexts. (b) The percentage of sub-jects who called the various objects *cup*. (From W. Labov, 1973. The boundaries of words and their meanings. In C. J. N. Bailey and R. W. Shuy, Eds., *New ways of analyzing variation in English*. Washington, D.C.: Georgetown University Press. P. 354. Copyright © by Georgetown University.)

particles. No doubt this ability adds to the flexibility of our everyday thinking. For example, if a knife could be assigned to only one category such as *cutting instrument,* we would fail to notice that it can be used as a screwdriver, a paperweight, or a tent stake.

Prototypes and Internal Structure

Categories have been described traditionally in terms of attributes com-mon to all members of a category. This view, despite its intuitive appeal, has been shown not to apply to many natural categories. Ludwig Witt-genstein (1953), a philosopher, argued that a category such as *game* has no attributes that are shared by virtually all its members. Games such as chess involve boards, whereas others, such as squash, do not. Some games involve cards, others involve balls, racquets, bats and so on, while others, such as tag, require no equipment at all. Many games have winners and losers, but others, such as catch or frisbee, do not. The attribute of amusement may seem to be common to all games, but many professional athletes claim they dislike their sport and participate solely for the money.

These observations led Wittgenstein to propose that members of a category bear a relationship of *family resemblance.* If you looked at pictures of your immediate family and other relatives, you would probably not find attributes shared by virtually everyone. But you probably would find common attributes such as tallness or high cheekbones among particular subgroups of the family. Further, two subgroups, call them A and B, might have no attributes common to all the members of both groups. Yet the two subgroups might overlap in that one member of subgroup A might have an attribute in common with a member of subgroup B. In this view, categories have internal structure; they contain subgroups of items sharing common attributes, and there is some overlap between various subgroups. Wittgenstein's proposals were based on logical considerations alone, but Rosch and her colleagues have documented them empirically.

TYPICALITY AND FAMILY RESEMBLANCE

Rosch (1973, 1975, 1978) has shown that many natural categories have internal structure in that some members are seen as more typical category members than others. In one experiment, Rosch (1975) presented names of members of everyday categories, as described in Table 6.1. The subjects' task was simply to rank order the items according to how exemplary they were of the category. The subjects reported that the rating task made sense, and the normative rankings for two of the categories are shown in Table 6.1. When two items, for example, *chair* and *sofa*, tied for a particular rank, both items received a split rank, as in 1.5. As shown by Table 6.1, *carrots* were judged to be a more typical vegetable than *squash*. Similarly, *chair* was judged to be a more typical piece of furniture than *bureau* was. Thus the categories had internal structure. As stated in our previous discussion of pattern recognition (see pages 54–55), the most typical member of a category is called the prototype. Metaphorically, the prototype lies at the center of the category whereas atypical members lie near the periphery of the category.

Rosch and Mervis (1975) examined how attributes are distributed among category members. They gave subjects 20 names of common objects from each of six categories such as *furniture* and asked them to list all of the attributes of the object they could think of. Consistent with Wittgenstein's proposals, the subjects very seldom listed the same attribute for all the members of a category. Rosch et al. also observed that groups of items within a category did have common attributes. On the average, 10 of the attributes listed were common to two members

Table 6.1 RATINGS OF THE DEGREE TO WHICH VARIOUS CATEGORY MEMBERS EXEMPLIFIED CATEGORIES SUCH AS FURNITURE

CATEGORY: FURNITURE		CATEGORY: VEGETABLES	
EXEMPLAR	GOODNESS OF EXAMPLE RANK	EXEMPLAR	GOODNESS OF EXAMPLE RANK
Chair	1.5	Peas	1
Sofa	1.5	Carrots	2
Couch	3.5	Green beans	3
Table	3.5	String beans	4
Easy chair	5	Spinach	5
Dresser	6.5	Broccoli	6
Rocking chair	6.5	Asparagus	7
Coffee table	8	Corn	8
Rocker	9	Cauliflower	9
Love seat	10	Brussels sprouts	10
Chest of drawers	11	Squash	11
Desk	12	Lettuce	12
Bed	13	Celery	13
Bureau	14	Cucumber	14
End table	15.5	Beets	15

SOURCE: After Rosch, 1975. Copyright 1975 by the American Psychological Association. Reprinted by permission.

of the category, and about four of the attributes were common to 10 members of the category. Thus the notion of family resemblance does apply to natural categories.

Rosch and Mervis also found large differences in the extent to which particular category members shared attributes with other category members. As you might expect, the atypical category members had few attributes in common with other members. In contrast, highly typical members shared many attributes in common with other members. For example, the five most typical members of the *furniture* category had 13 attributes in common. But the five least typical members of the *furniture* category had only two attributes in common. Thus, the more attributes an item has in common with other category members, the higher the judged typicality of that item will be. Another way of saying this is that the level of typicality depends on the degree of family resemblance—the extent to which an item shares attributes with other members. Rosch and Mervis also showed that the higher the typicality of an item, the fewer the attributes that item had in common with members of other categories. Highly typical items, then, share many attributes with other members of the same category but share few attributes with members of different categories.

Incidentally, these results suggest why many people think that categories have attributes common to all members. Upon hearing the name of a category, we may tend to think of the prototype or of other highly typical members. These are just the members that share many attributes with other members. The intuition that there are attributes common to all members would undoubtedly weaken if a name such as *bird* made us think of odd instances such as *penguin* and *turkey*.

Overall, the results discussed in this section question whether all categories can be described adequately by clearly defined rules and by attributes common to all category members (Rosch, 1973). Because many natural categories have internal structure and fuzzy boundaries (Rosch, 1978), theorists have developed new conceptions of categories.

PROTOTYPES PLUS TRANSFORMATIONS

Numerous theorists now believe that categories are best described in terms of prototypes (Franks and Bransford, 1971; Posner and Keele, 1968; Rosch, 1978; but see also Osherson and Smith, 1981). The prototype of a category, the most typical member of the category, shares many attributes with other typical members. But no attributes are shared by all members of the category. In this conception, category membership is a matter of degree. Members that have many attributes in common with the prototype are seen as highly typical, whereas members that have few attributes in common with the prototype are seen as atypical. This type of category description has the joint advantages of capturing the internal structure of the category and avoiding the suggestion of attributes common to all category members.

Usually, this conception is formalized by describing both a prototype and a set of transformation rules. These rules define the boundaries of the concept, and they indicate the degree of similarity between a particular category member and the prototype of the category.

The prototype plus transformation view of concepts is illustrated by an experiment by Franks and Bransford (1971). They made up a card containing four figures: a square, a diamond, a heart, and a triangle. This card was designated as the prototypical pattern. Then they made up a set of rules for transforming the prototype, and these were applied to the prototype to construct a set of target cards that showed modifications of the prototype. As shown in Figure 6.3a, one rule simply reversed the left-hand and right-hand figures of the prototype card. Another rule deleted one of the figures from the prototype. The subjects studied the target cards, but they never saw the prototype card. Subsequently, the subjects received a recognition test in which they were shown a series of cards including the prototype. The task was to identify the target cards and to use a five-point scale to rate how confident they were of their decisions.

Surprisingly, the subjects were most confident of having seen the prototype, even though the prototype had not been presented previously. Also, the more similar a target card was to the prototype, the higher was the confidence rating it received. As Figure 6.3b shows, the fewer the transformations that separated a target card and the proto-

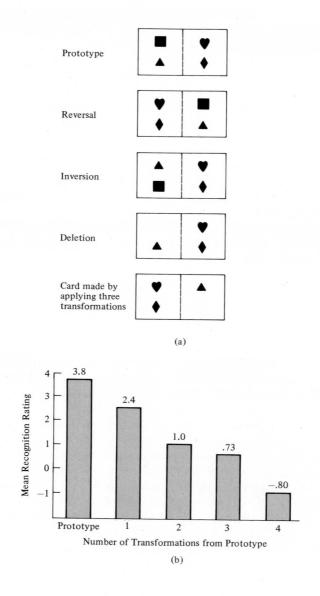

Figure 6.3 The stimuli and the results of the experiment by Franks and Bransford (1971). (a) The prototype pattern and the transformations applied to it. (b) The confidence ratings assigned to various cards. (From Franks and Bransford, 1971. Copyright 1971 by the American Psychological Association. Reprinted by permission.)

type, the greater was the subjects' confidence that they had seen that target card before. These observations support the view that the categories people form can be described by prototypes and transformation rules.

Whether categories are better described by prototypes and transformations than by attributes and rules cannot be decided yet. But the two outlooks are compatible to some degree. As discussed above, a prototype has many attributes in common with other category members. It may be possible to define a prototype as a set of attributes, some of which are more important or heavily weighted than others (cf. Neumann, 1974, 1977; also see Hayes-Roth and Hayes-Roth, 1977; Kellog, 1980). The most heavily weighted attributes would be those that are common to many category members and that occur infrequently in other categories. The less heavily weighted attributes in a category would include the unique attributes of the atypical category members and the attributes that occur often in other categories. Describing categories in terms of both attributes and prototypes may help to bridge the traditional and the contemporary views of categorization. That description might also help clarify how prototypes are represented in the memory system.

Basic-Level Categories

So far, we have examined the internal structure of particular categories but have said little about the relationships between categories. One important type of intercategory relationship is *class inclusion*, illustrated by biological taxonomies. *Animal* is a superordinate category that contains the subordinate categories *vertebrates* and *invertebrates*. *Vertebrates* includes the subcategories *reptiles, fish, birds*, and *mammals*. In turn, these categories can be subdivided further. The result is a hierarchical arrangement of categories in which a category at one level includes all the items and categories directly below it. There are many natural taxonomies of categories bearing the relationship of class inclusion (Rosch, Mervis, Gray, Johnson, and Boyes-Braem, 1976). For example, *fruit* is a superordinate category that includes categories such as *apple* and *peach*, each of which can be broken down into specific types of apples and peaches.

In taxonomies there is a level that has special properties; the categories occurring at this level are called *basic-level categories* (Rosch et al., 1976). These categories occur at the most inclusive level—at the highest point in the hierarchy—at which there are attributes common to many members of a category, and few attributes that occur in other categories. These characteristics are best illustrated by the following experiment. Subjects were given the names of categories of various levels within a taxonomy and were asked to list all the features that applied to the items of each level. One taxonomy was the *furniture* taxonomy, which includes categories such as *chair*. In turn, *chair* includes the categories *kitchen chair* and *living-room chair*. In this taxonomy, *furniture* is the superordinate category, *chair* is the basic-level category, and *kitchen chair* and *living-room chair* are subordinate categories. Nine different taxonomies were included in the study.

As predicted, the subjects listed very few attributes for the superordinate categories. But they listed many attributes for the basic-level and the subordinate categories. Recall that the basic-level categories (*chair*, for example) are more inclusive than the subordinate categories (*kitchen chair*). Thus, the basic-level categories appeared to be the most inclusive categories that had attributes common to many members. In addition, the categories at the basic level were maximally different from other categories, for they had few attributes in common, just as *chair* and *desk* have few common attributes. Subordinate categories, however, had many attributes in common, as *kitchen chair* and *living-room chair* do. For the basic-level categories then, there were attributes common to many members of the same category and few attributes in common with the members from other categories.

In subsequent experiments, Rosch et al. (1976) showed that the basic level of a taxonomy is the most inclusive level at which category members tend to look alike. The implication is that the basic level is the highest level at which there can be an image that applies to many category members. To illustrate, try to form a generalizable image for the category *chair*. This is a relatively simple task, for many chairs have common attributes. Now try forming an image for the superordinate category *furniture*. This task is much harder if not impossible since the different types of furniture do not have many visual attributes in common. Rosch et al. also showed that the basic level is the most inclusive level at which most category members call for similar movements on our part. We respond in similar ways to many different chairs, for example. But we move in very different ways in interacting with lamps, desks, and beds.

Basic-level categories are highly informative because they have many attributes in common. If some friends told us they had recently purchased a chair, for example, we would know many of the attributes of the object they had bought. But if they had told us only that they had bought a piece of furniture, we would know little about the object they had purchased. Because basic-level categories are highly informative, it is useful to divide the world up at the basic level. If we divided the world only into subordinate categories, we would have a very large number of categories, perhaps too many to be used efficiently. Cognitive economy is gained by forming highly inclusive, superordinate categories. But the gain in economy could be offset by the decrease in informativeness.

Basic-level categories strike a balance between the demands for both economy and informativeness.

Further, basic-level categories reflect the structure of our environment (Rosch et al., 1976; Rosch, 1978). In the world we perceive, attributes tend to occur in groups or clusters; they are not distributed randomly. For example, the attributes *has wings, has a beak, can fly,* and *has feathers* tend to occur together, whereas *has gills, photosynthesizes its food,* and *has hair* do not. Our basic-level categories capture important interrelations among attributes that occur in our environment. This consideration will be important in our analysis of how categories are formed.

PROCESSES IN CONCEPT FORMATION

Early studies of how people form concepts used an introspective, nonexperimental method. For reasons discussed previously, that type of method is flawed. It remained for Clark Hull (1920), one of the most influential psychologists of this century, to initiate an experimental analysis of concept formation.

In one of Hull's experiments, adults learned six lists of 12 paired-associates. The stimuli were Chinese letters that contained one of 12 features, some of which are shown in Figure 6.4. The subjects learned to

Figure 6.4   The stimuli used in the experiment by Hull. (From Hull, 1920.)

name each of the 12 patterns and then learned a second list. The second list included 12 different Chinese letters, but the letters contained the same features that had appeared in the first list. As before, the task was to name each pattern. This procedure continued until the subjects had learned six lists. The chief result was that the subjects learned the later lists much faster than the initial ones. In learning the sixth list, for example, the subjects named about 60 percent of the letters correctly on the very first trial. Over trials, then, the subjects learned to classify the stimuli, even novel ones, into the categories defined by the 12 features. Hull concluded that the subjects had learned or abstracted the common features shared by the letters in each category. He believed that the abstraction process occurred outside the scope of conscious awareness, for few of his subjects stated that they had abstracted features during learning.

Hull's view that concept formation involved the discrimination of common features was consistent with the prevailing associationistic outlook. But later research has shown that people form concepts by actively testing hypotheses and using sophisticated, logical strategies. The latter processes are beyond the scope of traditional associationistic theories. In this section, we examine the process of testing hypotheses and using strategies.

Hypothesis Testing

The idea that concept formation involves forming and testing hypotheses seems plausible intuitively. But as Hull's observations suggested, people are sometimes not conscious of the processes through which they form concepts. For this reason, we cannot discover the role of processes such as hypothesis testing by simply asking people to reflect upon and state what they are doing. Special procedures must be devised to externalize subjects' hypotheses and circumvent introspectionist procedures.

One special procedure, designed by Levine (1966, 1975), is called the blank trials procedure. This procedure includes a repetitive cycle of a study trial followed by four blank trials. The stimulus presented on a study trial could be a card showing a large black X on the left and a small white T on the right, as shown in the center of Figure 6.5. The letters can differ in color, identity (X or T), size, and position. The concept devised by the experimenter consisted of a single attribute such as white. On each study trial, the subjects selected either the X or the T, and they were told whether their choices were correct. Presumably, the subjects used this feedback to choose a hypothesis about which attribute defined the concept. In order to determine whether the subjects were testing hypotheses, each study trial was followed by four blank trials. In each blank trial, a stimulus was presented and the subjects chose one of the letters, but no feedback was provided. Which hypothesis the subjects were test-

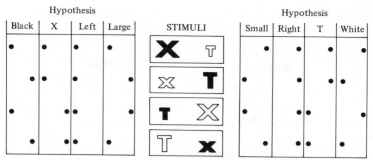

Figure 6.5   The stimuli used in the blank trials procedure. The various hypotheses that might be followed are listed on the left and right of the stimuli. Each column displays a pattern of choices that indicates the hypothesis that the subject had tested. For example, if the subject's hypothesis had been "large," then the pattern of choices was left, right, right, left. (From Levine, 1966. Copyright 1966 by the American Psychological Association. Reprinted by permission.)

ing was revealed by the pattern of responses that occurred over the four blank trials. Assume, for example, that the cards presented in a block of four blank trials were those shown in Figure 6.5. If the subjects had adopted the hypothesis "black is correct," then they would have tracked the black letter, as shown on the far left of Figure 6.5. Likewise, if the hypothesis had been "large is correct," then the subjects would always have chosen the large letter in the blank trials. If the subjects had not tested a particular hypothesis, then the sequence of choices would have deviated from those shown in Figure 6.5. By studying performance over several cycles of study and blank trials, Levine was able to observe how the subjects revised their hypotheses in trying to solve the problem.

The results of these studies have shown that adults engage in hypothesis testing on over 95 percent of the trials. Additionally, adults tend to adopt a win-stay, lose-shift strategy—they stick with a particular hypothesis only as long as it works. When a hypothesis was confirmed on a feedback trial, that hypothesis was retained throughout the following block of no-feedback trials 95 percent of the time. But when a hypothesis was not confirmed on a feedback trial, that hypothesis was not used in the subsequent no-feedback trials.

INCREMENTAL OR ALL-OR-NONE LEARNING?

In many everyday situations, learning seems to occur in a gradual, continuous manner. If you think back on learning to multiply and divide, you will probably remember struggling with problems initially. But as you practiced solving problems, your performance improved steadily. You probably did not fail your math assignments miserably on one day and then move to the head of the class the following day. This type of observation suggests that learning occurs gradually, with steady improvement over time. Perhaps concept learning, too, is a gradual, incremental process.

An alternate possibility, however, is that people learn concepts in a discontinuous, all-or-none manner. Indeed, early models of hypothesis testing had emphasized that concept formation is an all-or-none process (Bower and Trabasso, 1964). In this view, individual subjects do not show gradual improvement while learning a concept. Rather, the learning process is discrete; subjects perform at a chance level on one trial and move immediately to a high, stable level of performance on the next trial.

Using a blank trials procedure, Levine, Miller, and Steinmeyer (1967) obtained evidence in favor of the all-or-none view. They found that the performance of individual subjects did not improve on the trials preceding the solution of the problem. Before the subjects solved the problem, they seldom based their hypothesis on the correct stimulus dimension. For example, in the presolution trials of a problem in which "black" was correct, neither "black" nor "white" tended to occur as hypotheses. The only exception to this rule was the trial that immediately preceded the solution. Once the subjects used the correct hypothesis, they used that hypothesis in the following trials and made no errors. Thus the subjects made the transition from error-ridden to error-free performance in a single trial. These observations suggest that concept formation is an all-or-none process, not a gradual, incremental one.

It should be noted, however, that the experiments done by Levine and many others are studies of concept identification. The subjects' task is to identify a concept such as "white" that they have learned previously. Might gradual learning occur if the subjects were required to learn a novel concept defined by attributes they had never seen before? No one has answered this question satisfactorily, so we should remain open to the possibility that concept learning may occur gradually under some conditions.

TESTING MULTIPLE HYPOTHESES

Levine also used the blank trials procedure to determine whether the subjects were testing one or multiple hypotheses at a time. If the subjects tested only one hypothesis at a time, they would not learn all that was possible from a single trial. When the hypothesis was "white," they would choose the white letter, and if this choice was incorrect, they would then reject only the "white is correct" hypothesis. Note, however, that they could learn much more from an incorrect response by testing several hypotheses. The incorrectness of the small white T invalidates the hypotheses "T," "white," "small," and "right." So each feedback trial could eliminate half of the viable hypotheses.

Using the observations from several experiments, Levine (1966) estimated how many hypotheses the subjects tested on each feedback trial. The top line (labelled "no memory") in Figure 6.6 shows the results that would be expected if the subjects had tested only one hypothesis at a time and did not remember which hypotheses had been tested. The bottom line (labelled "perfect processing") shows the results that would be expected if the subjects had eliminated as many hypotheses as possible on each feedback trial and remembered the previous hypotheses and trial outcomes perfectly. As shown by the middle line in Figure 6.6, the subjects performed with less than maximal efficiency, but they did eliminate more than one hypothesis on the basis of particular feedback trials.

These results contradict some early theories of concept formation that assumed that subjects did not remember previously tested hypotheses (Bower et al., 1964; Restle, 1962). In order to perform as efficiently as they did, Levine's subjects must have remembered which hypotheses had and had not been tested. The results of other experiments agree that subjects do remember particular hypotheses (Chumbley, 1969). And Dyer and Meyer (1976) have shown that concept learning can be facilitated by training subjects to use an imagery mnemonic to remember pos-

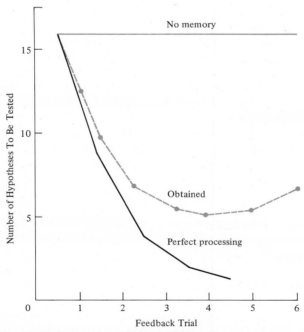

Figure 6.6   The number of hypotheses that subjects tested over successive feedback trials. (From Levine, 1966. Copyright 1966 by the American Psychological Association. Reprinted by permission.)

itive instances. So memory does seem to contribute to concept formation, although the importance of remembering no doubt depends on the
complexity of the task.

Levine's observations also contradict early models that assumed that
subjects learned only on error trials. Indeed, Levine's subjects eliminated
more hypotheses on trials in which correct responses occurred than on
trials in which incorrect responses occurred.

Taken together, these observations demonstrate the futility of depicting humans as learning on only one type of trial or as consistently
forgetting or remembering hypotheses they have tested. Human cognition is so flexible that it resists dichotomous descriptions. Our flexibility is
highlighted by the diversity of strategies we use in learning concepts.

Analytic and Nonanalytic Strategies

Associationistic theories had viewed concept learning as a process of associating stimulus features with responses. Because associationists believed that associations formed automatically via stimulus-response contiguity, they depicted concept learning as a relatively passive process. In
the 1950s, however, Bruner, Goodnow, and Austin (1956) argued that
people learn concepts by actively planning a method or strategy that
guides their performance. These strategies were beyond the scope of associationistic theory and encouraged the development of active, cognitive theories. In this section, we discuss some of the different kinds of
strategies that people use in learning concepts.

There are two general types of strategies: analytic and nonanalytic
(Brooks, 1978). *Analytic strategies* involve the abstraction of attributes,
rules, or prototypes. Levine's subjects followed an analytic strategy since
they abstracted various attributes from the presented stimuli and tested
whether those attributes defined the concept. Similarly, Hull's subjects
followed an analytic strategy since they appeared to have abstracted attributes during learning. And in the experiments on prototypes, the subjects seemed to have abstracted a prototype or best representative of the
category.

In contrast, *nonanalytic strategies* involve remembering particular
positive instances which are then used to decide whether stimuli belong
to the category. A subject who used a nonanalytic strategy to form the
category *Rolls-Royce* would first remember particular Rolls-Royce auto-
mobiles. New stimuli would be categorized by comparing them with the
remembered positive instances. If there were a high degree of overlap
between a novel car and a remembered Rolls-Royce, the novel car would
be assigned to this category. The chief characteristic of nonanalytic strategies is that they involve the use of particular instances, not attributes or
global properties abstracted from these instances. As we shall see, the

usefulness of analytic and nonanalytic strategies depends upon the type of task, and subjects often use a blend of analytic and nonanalytic strategies.

ANALYTIC STRATEGIES

The classic study of concept formation by Bruner, Goodnow, and Austin (1956) illuminated some of the analytic strategies that adults use. Their procedure was to show subjects a large array of cards that contained figures such as squares, crosses, and circles. The cards differed in the type of figure shown, the number and the color of the figures, and the number of borders (drawn along the outer edge of the cards). First the subjects were allowed to choose a card. Then the experimenter said whether the card was an instance of the concept. The experimenter then asked the subjects to identify the concept. If the subjects erred, they were allowed to choose another card, and the cycle was repeated. This method is called the *method of selection* since the subject chooses the stimulus on each trial. The advantage of this method relative to that used in the studies described above is that it allows one to observe sequences of unrestrained choices by the subjects. In turn, these sequences can be used to infer which strategy the subject used.

One analytic strategy inferred by Bruner et al. is called *conservative focusing.* This strategy involves identifying a positive instance, formulating a hypothesis that includes all of the attributes contained in that instance, and systematically testing the relevance of each attribute. Assume that the first correct card the subject chose contained one red cross and three borders. The correctness of this choice allows the subject to rule out attributes such as green, two figures, and one border. A conservative focuser would note which attributes were irrelevant and form a global hypothesis including all of the potentially relevant attributes, namely *one figure, red,* and *three borders.* The subject would then test each of the latter attributes. For example, the subject might test the attribute *red* by choosing a card having one green cross and three borders. If that card were correct, the subject would reject *red* from the class of potentially relevant attributes. The subject might next pick a card containing one red cross and two borders (the original correct card had three). If that choice were incorrect, the attribute of three borders would be retained in the class of relevant attributes. By continuing to test one attribute at a time, the subject would eventually discover the concept.

A related but riskier strategy is called *focus gambling.* Unlike conservative focusing, this strategy involves changing two or more attributes at a time. If, as before, the first correct card contained one red cross and three borders, a focus gambler might next choose a card with one red square and two borders. In this way, the subject would have simultaneously changed two attributes, namely, *cross* and *three borders.* The focus gambling strategy carries both greater potential risks and greater potential payoffs than the conservative focusing strategy. The risk is that errors are not very formative. If one varied two attributes at once and were wrong, one could not determine which attribute was irrelevant. The potential advantage of focus gambling is that if one changed two attributes and were correct, two irrelevant attributes and perhaps all of the correct attributes would have been identified in a single choice. As you might expect, the focus gambling strategy can lead to either very rapid or very slow solutions, but which occurs depends largely on chance.

A third type of analytic strategy is called *scanning.* Scanning strategies differ from the focusing strategies in that the subjects test hypotheses that do not include all of the potentially relevant attributes. If the first correct card contained one red cross and three borders, the subject might select the attribute *red* and test it systematically, without regard to the other relevant attributes. Thus, the subject might next choose a card containing two green circles and one border. But the subject in the example is not yet testing attributes such as form and number of borders; only the color is being attended to. This strategy is called *successive scanning* since the subject tests one hypothesis at a time. This method is relatively inefficient since there are many individual hypotheses to test. More important, the subjects who use the strategy do not use all of the information about which attributes are relevant and irrelevant.

A related strategy is *simultaneous scanning,* in which the subject tests numerous attributes at once. The difference between this strategy and focus gambling is that, as in other scanning strategies, the subject's hypotheses do not include all of the relevant attributes. If the first correct card contained one red cross and three borders, the subject might next test the two hypotheses *red* and *three borders.* The main problem with this strategy is that it places heavy demands on memory, for the subject must remember which attributes have been tested and which were correct or incorrect.

In the Bruner et al. study, many adults used the conservative focusing strategy and often solved the problem faster than subjects who used other strategies. The chief advantage of conservative focusing is that it reduces the demands on memory. Subjects who use the strategy need not remember which cards have been selected and which were positive or negative. Only the current hypothesis, which contains all of the possibly relevant features, must be remembered. Conservative focusing is not, however, an ideal strategy for forming concepts. With complex concepts, in particular, it is helpful to remember which particular cards have been selected, which were positive or negative, and so on. With the aid of paper and pencil, subjects can derive the maximum amount of information from each choice and use that information in all successive choices. The conservative focusing strategy, despite its effectiveness, is at best a compromise between the logical and the memorial demands of the task. And as shown in the following section, analytic strategies are not invariably the most effective routes for forming concepts.

NONANALYTIC STRATEGIES

Nonanalytic strategies do not involve the abstraction of attributes or prototypes from the positive instances of the concept. Subjects who use a nonanalytic strategy remember specific positive instances; then they compare these instances to new stimuli in deciding whether the new stimuli belong to the category.

Experimental evidence concerning the use of nonanalytic strategies has come from studies by Brooks (1978). The stimuli used were two sets (categories A and B) of letter sequences composed of the letters X, V, M, R, and T. Each set was formed by applying particular sequencing rules to the letters. For example, two of the rules in category A were X → X and X → M. These rules indicate that an X may be followed by another X or by an M, respectively. The rules for category B were similar but led to the formation of sequences that could not have been formed by the rules of category A. Two of the sequences that belonged to category A were VVTRXR and XMVRXR. Two sequences from category B were VVTRVV and MRMRTV. As you can see, the letter sequences from categories A and B appeared similar even though they had been generated by different sets of rules.

In the memorization condition, the subjects learned lists of paired-associates in which there were two types of pairs. Half of the pairs had letter sequences from category A as stimuli and names of cities as responses. The other half had letter sequences from category B as stimuli and names of animals as responses. The subjects were not told that there were two separate classes of letter sequences, and the two types of pairs were intermixed in the list. The subjects were told to simply say the appropriate word in the presence of each stimulus. This paired-associate procedure, which was intended to teach the subjects particular letter sequences, continued until the subjects had gone through 30 different pairs errorlessly.

In the concept learning condition, the subjects were shown the same 30 letter sequences, but these subjects were told that the letter sequences had been generated by two different sets of rules. The subjects' task was to classify each letter sequence into either category A or B, and feedback was provided after each response. This task continued until the subjects had classified all of the sequences correctly. This task was intended to encourage subjects to abstract from the sequences and to look for the properties that defined the two categories.

Upon completing their respective tasks, all subjects were asked to classify novel letter sequences as members of category A, category B, or neither. Recall that the subjects in the memorization condition had not been told previously that the sequences learned earlier had belonged to two categories, and they stated that they had not noticed there were two different categories. To help them classify the novel sequences, the experimenter stated that the stimuli they had learned had come from either category A or category B. Understandably, the subjects from the memorization condition were puzzled at their task; they giggled and complained they did not know how to classify the sequences, but they agreed to try.

Surprisingly, the subjects in the concept learning condition correctly classified only 46 percent of the novel sequences. They did little better than a group of subjects who had participated in neither the paired-associate nor the concept learning procedures. In contrast, the subjects in the memorization condition correctly classified 60 percent of the novel sequences. Since they showed no knowledge of the properties of the two categories, they must have used a nonanalytic strategy. Brooks suggested that these subjects classified novel sequences by comparing them to particular sequences that had been memorized in the paired-associate learning procedure. We may conclude that nonanalytic routes to categorization are sometimes more effective than analytic routes are.

In many situations, adults use a mixture of analytic and nonanalytic strategies. Reber and Allen (1978), for example, observed that subjects who have participated in a paired-associate procedure like that described above do show some knowledge of the rules used to produce the sequences. These same subjects also used knowledge concerning particular stimuli. So adults use both types of strategy, sometimes in combination. Which strategy, if either, predominates depends upon numerous situational factors which we consider next.

FACTORS FAVORING THE USE OF ANALYTIC AND NONANALYTIC STRATEGIES

As discussed above, memorial factors can lead people to use analytic strategies. When the task requires the processing of many stimuli, it may be difficult to remember all of the positive instances. By abstracting features of the positive instances, the burden on memory is reduced. The use of analytic strategies is also facilitated by stimulus and procedural factors. When the stimuli have highly salient or noticeable attributes in common, as, for example, red-wing blackbirds do, then people tend to abstract the salient attribute. In a similar vein, people tend to use analytic strategies when the rules that define a category are salient (Reber, Kassin, Lewis, and Cantor, 1980). This and other procedural factors, such as telling the subjects to look for regularities, can lead to the use of analytic strategies (Brooks, 1978).

Prior experience may also lead us to use analytic strategies. Through formal education, we learn to give definitions for many categories. In learning to define categories such as *noun, dinosaur,* and *ocean,* we were taught to state the attributes that define the category. In the author's elementary school, the teachers accepted definitions such as "A noun is the name of a person, place, or thing." But definitions based on examples, as in "Nouns are words like *chair, Don,* and *Colorado,*" elicited only the teacher's wrath. This type of training could lead us to learn new concepts by looking for attributes and other regularities that can be used to define the concept. Incidentally, this type of training can be valuable since abstraction from particulars is a highly useful cognitive activity. By abstracting, we learn that different types of birds have common properties, that birds and mammals have common properties, and so on. In a sense, the abstraction of regularities among objects and events is the goal of scientific inquiry. Because abstracting common properties often helps us to notice and to make use of the regularities in our environment, it is unsurprising that we often use analytic strategies in everyday affairs.

Now consider the use of nonanalytic strategies. Nonanalytic strategies are favored when the relevant attributes are not obvious or when we have seen only one or two instances of a complex category such as *lemur* or *anteater.* These conditions are likely to occur when one is just beginning to learn a new category, as when a child who has seen only one dolphin tries to classify novel animals as dolphins or nondolphins. It then makes sense to classify novel stimuli by comparing them to remembered positive instances. Nonanalytic strategies are also likely to be used in classifying atypical category members. Since natural categories lack attributes common to all members, strategies involving the abstraction of defining attributes do not apply to all category members.

People may tend to use a nonanalytic strategy when they remember particular instances very well and when a speedy classification must be made. Through incidental learning, people remember particular stimuli—their cars, their friends, their pets, and so on—very well. These remembered items can be used to classify novel stimuli. When there is a premium on classifying stimuli quickly, as in recognizing a poisonous snake, people may benefit from comparing the snake to well-remembered snakes rather than to a prototype of a poisonous snake.

These comments indicate that different situations favor the use of analytic and nonanalytic strategies. Yet we should also recognize that the two types of strategy are complementary and can both be used in a particular situation. In classifying a novel animal, we might begin by evaluating the creature's attributes. But if we were uncertain that our classification was correct, we might take a nonanalytic route.

Analytic and nonanalytic strategies are also complementary in that the knowledge derived from one can provide the basis for using the other. For example, through using nonanalytic strategies, one can acquire knowledge about many instances of a category. This knowledge can be used to abstract attributes common to the various instances, thereby enabling one to subsequently use an analytic strategy. Consistent with this view, concept learning occurs most rapidly when subjects learn both rules and particular instances (Reber et al., 1980). It is through our flexibility in using strategies that we satisfy the demands of the diverse categorization tasks that occur in everyday life.

DETERMINANTS OF CONCEPT FORMATION

How we cut the world up into categories depends partly upon the consequences of our activities with regard to particular classes of stimuli. Having eaten two types of berries, one delicious and nourishing and one poisonous, we can come to divide the two types of berries into separate categories. It is not, however, an arbitrary matter as to which categories will be formed. Some categories appear to be universal and biologically determined. Further, the internal structure of some categories influences the rate at which those categories are acquired. In this section, we examine some of the primary determinants of how rapidly we acquire concepts and where we locate their boundaries.

Type of Rule

On an intuitive level, some concepts seem to be more difficult than others. Concepts may differ in complexity partly because of differences in the complexity of the rules that define them. Neisser and Weene (1962) classified conceptual rules according to how many logical operations they involved. The simplest rules specify merely that a particular attribute must be present or absent in all positive instances. More complex rules, such as conjunctive and joint denial rules, specify that positive instances must have or lack two particular attributes. Neisser and Weene identified three levels of difficulty defined by the number of logical operations required in each. They had inexperienced subjects learn concepts at all three levels of classification. In general, the greater the logical complexity of the rule, the longer it took the subjects to learn the concept. Similar results have been obtained in other investigations (Haygood and Bourne, 1965).

Subsequent experiments (Bourne, 1970) have examined whether some conceptual rules are inherently more difficult than others. Different groups of subjects learned concepts defined by one of four rules: the conjunctive, the disjunctive, the conditional, and the biconditional rules. The subjects in each group learned in succession several concepts defined by a particular type of rule. In order to permit the subjects to concentrate on learning the rules rather than on discovering the relevant at-

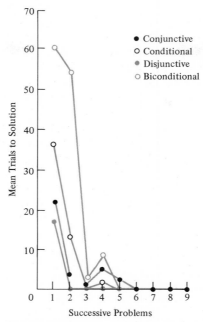

Figure 6.7   The number of trials required to learn various types of conceptual rules. (From Bourne, 1967.)

tributes, the experimenter told the subjects which attributes were relevant for each problem.

The results, shown in Figure 6.7, were that there were significant differences in the number of trials required to solve the first problem of each type. The conjunctive and disjunctive rules were learned fairly quickly. But the conditional and biconditional rules were learned quite slowly. With added practice, however, the differences in the rate of learning disappeared. This practice effect suggests that the initial difference in the rate of learning was not due to differences in the inherent difficulty of the rules. Most people have probably not had much practice in learning biconditional rules. But most people have had experience with conjunctive rules, for everyday concepts ranging from *water* to *bird* to *truck* are conjunctive. So the initial differences in learning the different types of rule may have arisen from prior experience, not from inherent differences in the difficulty of various rules.

Practice in learning concepts defined by one type of rule can also facilitate the learning of concepts defined by other types of rule (Bourne, 1970). For example, practice in learning concepts defined by conjunctive rules can speed the learning of concepts defined by disjunctive rules. This suggests that practice with different kinds of rules gives rise to knowledge of the entire system of logical rules. According to Bourne (1974), it is as if the subjects learn to use a truth table to analyze the attribute relationships defined by various rules. A truth table is a system used by logicians to determine the truth value of arguments. Any concept involving two attributes can be described by the combinations TT, TF, FT, and FF, where T indicates that an attribute is allowed and F indicates that it is not allowed. For example, since the conjunctive concept *red square* is defined by the presence of two attributes, the concept would be described by TT. In one experiment (Dodd, Kinsman, Klipp, and Bourne, 1971), practice in assigning stimuli to the categories of the truth table facilitated performance on a subsequent rule-learning problem. Research has not yet clarified exactly what subjects learn from pretraining with logic and truth tables. To a first approximation, they learn to perform particular logical operations and combinations thereof. Learning the various logical operations makes it easier to learn rules that include those operations.

Attention and Concept Formation

The role of attentional factors has been documented in the context of studies of the development of conceptual ability in children. Piaget (1952; Piaget and Inhelder, 1956) and his coworkers have shown that developmental differences occur in the mastery of the concepts of *conservation*. In one type of quantitative conservation problem, a child is shown two identical glasses (one and two) containing equal amounts of water and asked if both contain the same amount. Most children, even very young ones answer "Yes." Next the contents of glass one are poured into a taller, thinner glass while the child looks on. Naturally, water level in the thin glass is higher than in glasses one or two. Then the child is shown the tall, thin glass beside one of the smaller glasses and is asked whether both contain equal amounts of water. If the child states that both glasses have the same amount of water and can justify her answer adequately, she is said to understand the concept of quantitative conservation. Most preschool children do poorly on this type of conservation problem, but school-aged children do quite well.

On the basis of observations such as these, Piaget proposed that there is a stage of cognitive development marked by the ability to perform concrete operations. In this view, children who have reached the stage of concrete operations show reversibility in their thinking. Simplifying a bit, the idea is that older children recognize that the effects of one operation—the pouring of the water from one container to another—can be reversed by performing the opposite operation. Presumably, young children who have not reached the stage of concrete operations do not comprehend the principle of reversibility. Consequently, they fail to solve or to understand conservation problems, which involve reversing states of affairs.

This account has considerable merit, but nonconservation may also result in part from inattention to irrelevant stimulus attributes (Miller, 1973). For example, young children could have trouble solving the water conservation problem because they attend only to the height of the water in the glasses. In many everyday situations, the height of a liquid in a container is a useful index of the amount of liquid. But in the conservation problem, the height is an irrelevant attribute. If this interpretation is correct, then training young children to seek out relevant attributes and ignore irrelevant ones should improve performance on conservation tasks.

Evidence pertaining to this view comes from a study by Gelman (1969), who first identified 5-year-olds who did not understand conservation in either the water problem or similar ones such as the stick problem. The stick problem is designed to measure the conservation of length. Two sticks of equal length are placed side by side so that their ends are aligned. Then one is moved to the right so that its end is ahead of the other. When the two sticks are aligned, young children often say they are equal in length. But when the edge of one stick leads the edge of the other, young children tend to say that the stick with the leading edge is longer. Gelman divided the children into two groups. The training group was given 16 different oddity problems to solve. Each problem included three sticks, two of which were identical, placed at different angles to each other. The task was to choose the two sticks that were the same. The entire set of problems involved sticks of various sizes and colors. In some of the problems, two of the nonidentical sticks had an irrelevant attribute such as redness in common. Solving the problems required that the children ignore the irrelevant attributes. The second group was a control group that was allowed to play with the sticks presented to the training group but was not asked to solve particular problems. Subsequently, both groups were retested on conservation problems involving water and stick length.

The results were that the children in the training group solved the oddity problems readily. More important, they subsequently solved about 60 percent of the conservation problems, including the water problems on which there had been no training. In contrast, the control group showed no improvement on the conservation problems. It seems unlikely that the training group learned the concept of conservation through the small amount of oddity training. The children probably already had some understanding of conservation and reversibility, but that understanding was masked by the children's tendency to attend to irrelevant attributes. In this account, the oddity training succeeded by teaching the children to ignore irrelevant attributes.

This conclusion does not deny developmental differences in cognitive ability. Rather, it recognizes that developmental differences in concept formation can result from many different factors, including attention. Understanding the causes of differences in attention would no doubt advance our understanding of cognitive development.

Typicality and Exemplar Variability

We saw earlier that many theorists view concept formation as a process of abstracting prototypes and learning transformation rules. If we indeed form categories by organizing them around prototypes, we would expect that highly typical category members are learned faster than atypical members are. This view has been supported in recent research (Rosch, Simpson, and Miller, 1976), which we now examine.

Adults were asked to classify nonsense patterns of dots into four categories. Each category included a prototypical pattern and several distortions of the prototypes. Some distortions were minor, whereas others were extreme. In all, there were five levels of distortions that were intended to produce different levels of typicality. The subjects were shown the prototypes and one pattern from each level of distortion from each category. The stimuli from the four categories were presented in a random order, and the subjects were to assign the stimuli to four categories. The experimenter told the subjects whether their responses were correct. This procedure was continued until the subjects had classified all of the stimuli correctly. Then the subjects used a five-point scale to rate how typical each item was of the category it belonged to.

Despite the fact that all of the stimuli had been presented with equal frequency, the subjects learned more rapidly to categorize the highly typical items than the less typical items. Further, when the subjects were asked to draw as many of the presented items as possible, they drew more of the typical items and they tended to draw the typical items first. They also showed that the rapid learning of typical items is not due to a higher frequency of presentation for those items. The effects of typicality remained even when the atypical items had been presented more often than the typical items. Collectively, these observations suggest that the level of typicality influences the rate of learning category members. As discussed above, learning category members can contribute to concept learning via both analytic and nonanalytic strategies. Regardless of what type of strategy one employs, it is advantageous to learn highly typical category members first.

Learning the boundaries of concepts also appears to be facilitated by processing highly variable or dispersed category members. Posner and Keele (1968) used four prototypical dot patterns to generate other patterns at various degrees of distortion from the prototypes, as shown in

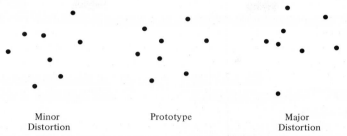

Minor   Prototype   Major

Distortion   Distortion

Figure 6.8   The kinds of stimuli used in the experiment by Posner and Keele (1968).

Figure 6.8. In the low variability condition, the subjects were shown only minor distortions of the prototypes of the categories. In the high variability condition, the subjects studied both minor and extreme distortions of the prototypes. The subjects learned to classify the dot patterns into the four categories. Then they were asked to classify novel but extremely distorted patterns. The results were that the accuracy in classifying the novel patterns was better in the high variability condition than in the low variability condition. This shows that the degree of variability of the presented instances of a category affects how novel instances will be classified (Homa, 1978; Homa and Vosburgh, 1976). Presenting highly similar instances, ones that are low in variability, may enhance the abstraction of prototypes and the recognition of common features. But it is difficult to know what the boundaries of a category are when one has seen only a few highly similar instances. For this reason, presenting highly dispersed instances facilitates the learning of category boundaries.

Information and Concept Formation

We say that an item is informative to the extent that it reduces our uncertainty. For example, the statement that an unknown name begins with *J* and has four letters is more informative than the statement that the name is not *Tom*. Knowing that the name is not *Tom* rules out only one of a tremendous number of names and does little to reduce our uncertainty. But stating that the name begins with *J* and contains four letters eliminates many possibilities and is highly informative.

     Some early experiments on concept formation suggested that people learn concepts more readily from positive than from negative instances since positive instances are more informative (Smoke, 1933; Hovland, 1952). On this account, people should learn concepts equally well on the basis of positive or negative instances if they were equally informative. This idea was tested by exposing people to positive and negative instances that conveyed equal amounts of information. Yet adults still learned more slowly from the negative instances than from the positive ones (Hovland and Weiss, 1953).

Reflection upon how we learn many natural concepts helps reveal why people learn concepts best from positive instances. For natural concepts such as *bird*, negative instances far outnumber the positive instances. Consequently, negative instances are less informative than positive instances. Additionally, we are seldom if ever required to learn natural concepts solely on the basis of negative instances. This analysis leads us to expect that people could learn concepts rapidly by studying negative instances if they received extensive practice in learning from negative instances. In fact, this prediction has been confirmed (Freibergs and Tulving, 1961). Overall, then, it appears that the information value of the stimuli does influence concept formation.

Theorists now believe that informational variables are fundamental determinants of concept formation (Rosch, 1977, 1978). For example, prototypes are believed to be the most informative members of categories. Relative to other members of the category, the prototype has the most attributes in common with other members. Also, the prototype has the fewest attributes in common with the members of other categories. If you knew the prototype of a particular category, you would know a great deal about the category—much more than you would understand if you knew only an atypical member. According to Rosch, the prototypes are informative in that they reflect the structure of the environment. In a sense, then, the effects of typicality reviewed earlier may be accounted for in terms of information value. From this perspective, it is unsurprising that the best or prototypical members of categories are learned fastest during concept learning (Mervis and Pani, 1980; Rosch, 1978).

For similar reasons, informational variables may determine which categories people are likely to form. As stated previously, basic-level categories are the most informative categories in a taxonomy of categories. That is, basic-level categories occur at the highest level at which there are many attributes common to most category members and few attributes characteristic of other categories. Because of these properties, people may be particularly likely to divide up the world at the basic level (Rosch, 1977, 1978). Thus it is not an entirely arbitrary matter as to which conceptual categories we form. This view draws support from research into the universal categories that humans form.

Biological Determinants: Universal Color Categories

One of the most fundamental questions we can ask is whether our categories are determined by biological, genetic factors. If biological factors do influence categorization, then the categories people form should to some degree be universal, that is, found in all cultures. But to the extent that our categories are shaped primarily by our experience and by the particular needs and characteristics of each culture, categories should vary from one culture to another. Much of the contemporary research on this issue has centered around the question whether language determines thinking, so we too shall pursue this issue briefly.

LINGUISTIC RELATIVITY AND DETERMINISM

Upon examining different languages, one cannot help but be impressed by the diversity of linguistic categories across cultures. The English language has numerous color words. But the Dani tribe of New Guinea has only two color words: *mola* for bright, warm hues and *mili* for dark, cold ones (Heider and Olivier, 1972). Whereas English has few words for different kinds of rice, the Hanoo of the Philippines have names for over 90 kinds of rice (Brown, 1965). Similarly, Eskimos have more words for different kinds of snow than speakers of English have. Observations such as these have led some anthropologists and linguists to propose that members of different cultures cut up the world into different categories. On the broadest level, the suggestion is that members of different cultures have different world views.

Whorf (1956) and Sapir (1958) believed that the essential categories and outlook of each culture are embedded within the language shared by the members of a culture. When young members of a culture learn their native language, they learn the categories and take on the world view characteristic of their culture. In other words, learning a language involves learning the implicit metaphysical system accepted by the members of the culture. As Whorf put it, "Every language contains terms that have come to attain cosmic scope of reference, that crystallize in themselves the basic postulates of an unformulated philosophy, in which is couched the thought of a people, a culture, a civilization, even of an era" (1956, p. 66). In support of this view, Whorf (1956) observed that the Hopi Indians have no words or other linguistic devices to refer to past, present, or future. He claimed that the Hopi world view simply did not include the concept of time that is so vital in our outlook. As another example, we distinguish between objects and events. We distinguish birds from the various events in which they participate (flying, eating, etc.), just as we distinguish between objects such as rocks and the events in which they participate (falling, crushing, rolling, etc.). This distinction is reflected in the separate words in our language for objects (nouns) and events (verbs). In contrast, the Hopi speak only of events. Whorf argued that the Hopi simply did not divide the world into objects and events. This account suggests that for the Hopi, events such as rock-falling have a unitary nature; the rock and the action of falling are not separated. According to Whorf, the Hopi would have conceived of objects and events as separate only if the Hopi language had included devices for distinguishing between objects and events.

Whorf's view included two key notions. The first, called *linguistic determinism* was that language determined thought. In his words, "We dissect nature along lines laid down by our native languages" (1956, p. 213). In this view, the categories we form are determined by our language. Once we have learned our language and the categories implicit within it, we interpret the world in terms of those categories. Moreover, we find it difficult or impossible to conceive of the world in any other way. It is as if our language locks us in on a particular world view and set of categories. This idea suggests a corollary, called *linguistic relativity.* Since language determines thought and languages differ, one thinks in ways that are relative to one's language. This position predicts that people in different cultures form different categories. Cross-cultural similarities in categories should occur only in cultures having similar languages.

Whorf's outlook received support from some early experiments. A classic study by Brown and Lenneberg (1954) investigated the effects of language on memory for colors. Adult speakers of English were asked to name a variety of color patches. The subjects agreed on the names of some colors and classified them quickly with a single word such as *blue.* These colors were said to be high in codability since they were easily coded linguistically. Other colors were low in codability—they were not named in the same way by all subjects, they took longer to respond to, and they were described by phrases (for example, *light green*) rather than single words. Then the subjects were shown four different colors. Following a delay, there was a recognition test in which a set of many different colors was presented, and the subjects tried to choose ones that matched the four colors they had seen earlier. The chief result was that the higher the codability of a color was, the better that color was remembered. This result suggested that memory was influenced by the color categories contained in the English language. Because the results showed that a linguistic variable such as codability can determine an aspect of thought, namely, remembering, they supported the Whorfian hypothesis.

Of course, the preceding observations do not advise us to accept Whorf's far-reaching hypothesis. For one thing, the experiment did not test Whorf's broader claim that one's language determines one's world view. Even today, Whorf's broader proposals remain untested (though some experiments of a broader nature have been conducted; see Caroll and Casagrande, 1958). Ironically, the studies of codability that had appeared to confirm Whorf's views led to further research on color categories that contradicted Whorf's ideas.

memorizes instances of a category and compares those instances to novel stimuli in order to decide whether the novel stimuli belong to the category. Adults probably use analytic and nonanalytic strategies in different situations, and the two types of strategy can be viewed as complementary.

There are numerous determinants of concept formation. Attentional factors are important in that attending to irrelevant attributes retards concept formation, whereas attending to relevant attributes facilitates it. The prior experience of the learner influences concept formation in several ways. Subjects who have received special training learn from negative instances as well as from positive instances. Also, people who have learned several different types of conceptual rules learn new rules very quickly. Through practice, subjects may become more efficient in finding and testing relevant attributes and in learning the logical system implicit in conceptual rules. Concept formation is influenced strongly by informational variables. Highly typical category members are highly informative, and they are learned faster than atypical, less informative members of the category are. Within taxonomies, the basic-level categories are the most informative, and they are likely to be learned early in the development of language.

Biological factors also influence category formation. Theorists once believed that people perceive colors in accord with the color categories inherent in their language. In this view, one's perception of color is determined by and relative to one's language. This position has now been shown to be incorrect. People all over the world find the same colors to be highly salient, regardless of the vast differences in how their languages divide up the color spectrum. Additionally, the color names in all languages come from a small, highly constrained set, and linguistic color categories are organized around the colors that are universally salient. So the color categories people form are not arbitrary but are determined by biological factors. Although our language no doubt does influence how we categorize, our nonlinguistic categories can also influence our language. In the following chapters, we take a closer look at our linguistic and nonlinguistic forms of knowledge and their interrelations.

Chapter 7
Knowledge and Representation

Is a trout a vertebrate? Does the Pope favor euthanasia? Most likely, you answered these questions easily even though you have probably never been told explicitly that a trout is a vertebrate or that the Pope opposes euthanasia. In answering these questions, you made inferences based upon your knowledge of language and of the world. In this chapter, we inquire into the semantic knowledge that people use in the everyday activities of making inferences, answering questions, and forming visual images. We begin by examining briefly the distinction between semantic and episodic knowledge (Tulving, 1972).

As you may recall from Chapter 1, semantic knowledge includes our knowledge of rules, facts, and meanings that are not tied to particular contexts. To obtain a better idea of what semantic knowledge is, answer these questions: Does $9 \times 7 = 63$? Is an aardvark a primate? Does the earth have an infinite oil supply? What does *transient* mean? In answering these simple questions, you used your knowledge of the rules of arithmetic, of the relationships between categories of animal, of facts concerning our physical resources, and of the meanings of words. These are all aspects of semantic knowledge, and they are all relatively context-free. For example, you know that $9 \times 7 = 63$ regardless of the situation you are in. And semantic information can be retrieved without the aid of contextual cues. In order to recall the meaning of *car, lamp,* or *frog,* for example, you do not have to remember the contexts in which you had previously encountered these words.

Semantic information contrasts with episodic information, which includes autobiographical information about particular events and the contexts in which they occurred. Episodic information is called for by these questions: What clothes did you wear yesterday? What did you eat for lunch two days ago? What did you do last Saturday night? In answering these questions, you remember information about events in which you participated at a particular time and place. Thus episodic information concerns the context in which personal experiences occurred.

The distinction between semantic and episodic information is important because it has guided ecologically valid research. In traditional laboratory studies of verbal learning and cognition, subjects studied lists of words and then tried to remember them. In these studies, the subjects did not really learn new words. Rather, they learned which words occurred in the context of the experimental setting. For example, if the list contained *horse, truth,* and *bent,* the subjects' task was to learn that those familiar words had occurred in the setting of the experiment. As you can see, studies of memory for lists of words concern episodic information for the most part. Episodic information is important in many daily activities, for example, in remembering whether you had mailed a letter or had finished a job your boss had asked you to do. But consider the tremendous number of tasks that require the use of semantic information. In comprehending a lecture or in talking to a friend, we use our knowledge of language. In balancing a checkbook or in shopping, we use our knowledge of arithmetic. Reflection reveals that many of our most important daily activities require the use of episodic information. Traditional studies of memory for episodic information shed little light on the processes involved in reading, speaking, listening, and problem solving. By distinguishing between semantic and episodic information, Tulving (1972) sounded a call for conducting ecologically valid research. Investigators are now answering this call.

The distinction between semantic and episodic information is useful, but it is not as clear-cut as it appears initially. For one thing, our semantic knowledge can include information concerning particular episodes. As an example, I know that cats hate getting wet. My knowledge of this fact is one piece of semantic knowledge. But this knowledge seems to be based upon my memory of particular episodes, for example, of the time when my fastidiously clean cat, Lorien, suffered the indignity of slipping off a log into the cold, muddy water below. And as noted in the preceding chapter, conceptual knowledge is often based upon one's recollection that particular instances had occurred in the context of the experiment. In at least some cases, then, our knowledge of episodes may be closely related to our semantic knowledge.

The haziness of the distinction between episodic and semantic information is also apparent in regard to the acquisition of knowledge. For example, if you remembered having eaten spaghetti at home last Wednesday, the remembered information is episodic. But if you ate spaghetti at home every Wednesday, you would eventually learn that spaghetti is served every Wednesday. This rule is a bit of semantic knowledge that is acquired as the result of exposure to many episodes. It is as if the episodic knowledge shaded into semantic knowledge. But there need be no discrete point of transition nor even awareness that the transition has occurred.

Since the boundary separating episodic information from semantic information is fuzzy, it is unsurprising that theorists disagree over the relationship between them (Kihlstrom, 1980; McKoon and Ratcliff, 1979; Shoben, Westcourt, and Smith, 1978). Perhaps episodic and semantic information are best seen as lying on a single continuum. At one end of the continuum, information is tied tightly to the context in which it had occurred. At the other end, information is relatively context-free. In this conception, the difference between episodic and semantic information is mainly a matter of degree.

One point on which all theorists agree is that in order to understand semantic knowledge, we must determine the representation of knowledge in the processing system. After all, our knowledge is believed to consist of symbolic representations. And how can we understand how people process information unless we understand what it is that people process? By analogy, how could we understand how people use the information in libraries if we did not know what the information consists of (books, call numbers, and so on) to begin with? If we knew the kinds of symbolic representations that people use in solving problems, constructing images and in reading, we would know a great deal about cognition. For this reason, many theorists see the chief goal of cognitive psychology as that of specifying the manner in which semantic knowledge is represented in the memory system.

In this chapter, we examine the representation of semantic knowledge. We begin by inquiring into relatively simple representations, the representations of word meanings. Then we investigate a complex type of representation called propositional representation. Stated simply, a proposition is a symbolic representation that expresses a relationship between concepts and that can be either true or false. For example, the proposition BELOW (BALL, CHAIR) could represent the meaning of the sentence *The ball was below the chair.* This proposition includes the concepts BALL and CHAIR and the relational concept BELOW. The proposition is true if it corresponds to an actual state of affairs, for example, if a ball was in fact beneath the chair. We shall see that propositions are remarkably versatile devices for representing information. For example, the proposition described above could represent the spatial information given in a picture of a chair with a ball underneath it.

Because propositions can represent the information provided by many different pictures and sentences, some theorists believe that all of our semantic knowledge is represented via propositions. But others argue that our knowledge is represented in two different ways. In particular, they contend that our verbal knowledge is represented by propositions, whereas our visual knowledge, the knowledge we use to construct images and to perceive scenes, is not. Further, some theorists have proposed that the human brain contains two separate processing systems, one specialized for processing language and the other specialized for processing spatial, nonpropositional representations. In the third section, we examine visual imagery and the evidence concerning brain processes with an eye toward determining whether all of our knowledge is propositional.

MODELS OF SEMANTIC MEMORY

Analyzing semantic knowledge is an enormously complex task. In order to reduce this task to manageable proportions, some investigators have decided to study relatively simple aspects of our knowledge (Smith, 1978). Their hope is that the discovery of basic representations and processes will set the stage for analyzing more complex aspects of semantic knowledge. In this section, we discuss our knowledge of word meanings in the context of three models: the hierarchical network model, the spreading activation model, and the feature-comparison model.

The Hierarchical Network Model

Collins and Quillian (1969, 1972) reasoned that a good way to begin the study of knowledge is to analyze the manner in which people comprehend simple sentences and make simple inferences. Accordingly, they presented sentences such as *A canary has skin* and *A canary can sing* one at a time. They asked the subjects to indicate quickly whether the sentence was true or false by pushing one of two buttons. This is a speeded verification task. They assumed that the amount of time it took the subjects to respond might reveal the manner in which the subjects represented the semantic information used in the verification task. For example, if it took longer to verify *A canary has skin* than *A canary can sing,* that might indicate differences in the structuring of the semantic information used to process the two sentences. In order to see this, we need to examine some assumptions regarding the representation and the processing of semantic knowledge.

Collins and Quillian proposed that semantic knowledge can be represented as a network of interconnected concepts, as illustrated in Figure 7.1. The circles are nodes that stand for concepts, for example, the concepts *canary* and *bird.* The concepts are arranged in a hierarchy. The more inclusive a concept is, the higher it is located within the hierarchy. Thus *animal* is located above *bird,* for *bird* is a subset of *animal.* Similarly, *fish* is superordinate to *shark,* so *fish* is placed higher in the hierarchy. The pointers emanating from the concept nodes designate three types of relations. The pointers that move toward superordinate concepts designate subset relations. For example, the upward pointer from *bird* to *animal* indicates that *bird* is a subset of *animal.* Because a bird is an animal, the link connecting *bird* and *animal* is labelled *isa.* The smaller pointers designate attribute relations. For example, birds have wings, so *bird* and *wings* are connected by a link labelled *has.* Of course, birds can fly, and this is indicated by the link labelled *can* that connects *bird* and *fly.*

One of the chief characteristics of the hierarchical representation is that properties are stored in a very economical way. Each property is represented only once—at the highest level. Even though canaries, ostriches, and salmon all breathe, the *breathes* attribute is stored at the most inclusive level possible, namely, the level *animal.* This approach eliminates the need to represent the attribute *breathes* many times, once for every animal. This approach was crucial for Collins and Quillian, who embodied their model in a computer program designed to comprehend simple statements. Because their computer had a limited storage capacity, they tried to conserve space by representing each property in

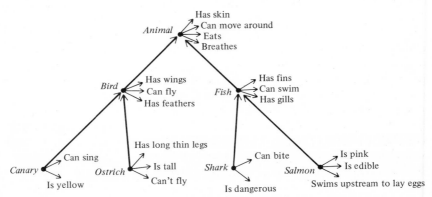

Figure 7.1   A hierarchical network representation for semantic knowledge pertaining to animals. (From Collins and Quillian, 1969.)

the network only once. The assumption that each property is stored only at the highest possible level is called the *cognitive economy* assumption.

Another important characteristic of this network representation is that it depicts our knowledge as highly organized and interrelated. This is reasonable since we can discern clear relations and connections between various concepts. For example, we know that all birds are animals, and this knowledge is embodied directly in the network. The interconnections in the network provide pathways through which memory may be searched. In the absence of organized associative pathways, it would be difficult to conduct directed memory searches as we often do.

Collins and Quillian proposed that information is retrieved from semantic memory by searching the pathways in the knowledge structure. As an illustration, consider how one might verify sentences. To determine the truth of *A canary can sing*, one needs to simply find the *canary* node and to retrieve the properties stored at that node. But comprehending *A canary has skin* requires finding the *canary* node, moving up two levels to the *animal* node, and retrieving the properties stored at the *animal* node. Collins and Quillian assumed that it takes a constant amount of time to move one level in the hierarchy. Thus, more time should be required to comprehend that *A canary is an animal* than *A canary is a bird*, because *animal* is two levels away from *canary*, whereas *bird* is only one level away. For similar reasons, *A canary can sing* should be comprehended faster than *A canary has skin*.

To test these predictions, Collins and Quillian presented a series of sentences such as *A canary can fly*, *Tennis is a game*, and *A pine is barley*. Consistent with the predictions, the greater the number of levels the subjects had to search through, the longer it took to verify the statement. These results support the idea, implicit in the model, that verifying statements is often an inferential process. For example, the proposed memory network does not contain the fact *A canary is an animal*. But the network does contain the information required to infer that a canary is an animal. One reason why the model was so attractive was that it provided a plausible mechanism, the search of interconnected pathways, for making simple inferences.

PROBLEMS WITH THE HIERARCHICAL NETWORK MODEL

The network model just described stimulated a large amount of research, some of which contradicted the model. The model predicts that it will take longer to verify *A bear is an animal* than *A bear is a mammal* since *animal* is more levels above *bear* than *mammal* is. But in fact, just the opposite occurs: It takes longer to verify *A bear is a mammal* (Rips, Shoben, and Smith, 1973; Smith, Shoben, and Rips, 1974). One interpretation of this effect is that *bear* and *animal* are perceived as being more closely related than are *bear* and *mammal*. Indeed, experiments have shown that the more closely related two categories within a statement are judged to be, the faster that statement will be verified (Smith et al., 1974).

A second troublesome observation, related to the first, is that some instances of a category can be verified faster than others, even though the instances are equidistant from the superordinate category in the network (Smith et al., 1974; Wilkins, 1971). For example, *robin* and *chicken* both belong to the category *bird*, but people verify *A robin is a bird* faster than *A chicken is a bird*. This observation can be interpreted via the concept of typicality that was discussed in the preceding chapter. Most people judge robins to be highly typical birds, whereas chickens are judged to be atypical birds. In general, the degree of typicality strongly influences reaction times; typical instance-category pairs are analyzed faster than atypical pairs. The hierarchical network model fails to accommodate the effects of typicality. More important, the typicality effects show that semantic concepts have internal structure, just as nonlinguistic concepts do. Semantic concepts also have fuzzy boundaries (McCloskey and Glucksberg, 1978). These observations argue against the hierarchical network model, which defines concepts and conceptual hierarchies in a logical, precise manner.

A third problem concerns the notion of cognitive economy. In its strong form, this assumption is that each property is represented only once in a hierarchy and at the highest possible level. The evidence that supported this assumption was that subjects took longer to verify statements such as *A canary has skin* than *A canary can sing*. Collins and Quillian had explained this by proposing that subjects must search through several levels in the hierarchy to verify *A canary has skin*, and the more levels are searched, the longer the reaction times are. Conrad (1972) challenged this interpretation by suggesting that the concept *canary* is more strongly associated with the property *can sing* than with *has skin*. To test this idea, she had subjects describe nouns such as *canary*, *bird*, and *animal*. She found large differences in the frequency with which particular properties were used to describe a particular noun. For example, *canary* was often described by *is yellow* but not by *has skin*. Having collected normative data concerning the strength of association (or production frequency, as she called it) for various noun-property pairs, she examined performance in a verification task much like that used by Collins and Quillian. The results were that the verification times depended more on the strength of the noun-property relation than on how many levels separated the noun and the property in the hierarchy. When the noun and the property were strongly associated, the subjects verified the statements quickly. This was true even of statements such as *An orange is edible*, despite the fact that *orange* and *is edible* are separated by at least two levels in a hierarchy. And as predicted, the reaction times were slow when the noun and the property were weakly associated, regardless of the proximity of the noun and the property in the hierarchy. These results contradict the hierarchical network model and argue against the cognitive economy assumption.

The assumption of cognitive economy, in its strongest form, can also be faulted on logical grounds. Our knowledge of general properties must to some extent be abstracted from our knowledge of particular instances and subordinate categories. For example, we may learn that animals can move by virtue of having seen many different types of animal move. Initially, we might know that dogs move, cats move, people move, and so on; the property *can move* might initially be stored with many different subordinate categories. Subsequently, the property *can move* might be elevated to the highest level possible. But while knowledge about animals is being acquired, particular properties may be represented more than once in the network. Even after knowledge has been acquired, some redundancy may remain in the memory network. Which properties are represented more than once probably depends upon one's experiences. For example, to me, the eyes of owls are highly salient, and *has eyes* is the first property that comes to mind when I hear the word *owl.* The property *has eyes* could be stored with a more inclusive category such as *animal.* But it is unnecessary to assume that it is stored only at a superordinate level. When representing information in a computer, it may be logical and economical to represent each property only at the highest level possible in order to conserve the limited storage capacity. But it is not at all clear that the knowledge of people is actually represented in a perfectly logical and efficient manner. For these reasons, it is best to reject the strong form of the cognitive economy assumption.

In fairness, however, it should be pointed out that the model did not claim that all information is stored in an economical, nonredundant manner, and the model may provide a valid account of some of our semantic knowledge. Nevertheless, theorists want the most general model possible, so they revised the model.

The Spreading Activation Model

In the revised model proposed by Collins and Loftus (1975), the memory network is no longer structured hierarchically. Instead, it is structured around the principle of semantic relatedness or semantic distance. A small fragment of the memory network is shown in Figure 7.2. As before, many of the concepts are interconnected, as indicated by the lines running between the ovals. The shorter the line connecting two concepts is, the more closely related the two concepts are. Thus, *bus* is more closely related to *school* and to *student* than to *accident* or *fire engine.* The clusters of related concepts shown in the figure capture our intuition that concepts such as *flower* belong to a group of concepts that differs from the group of vehicle-related concepts.

The extent to which various concepts are related is determined empirically. One method is to simply give subjects pairs of words and ask them to rate on a scale how closely related the concepts are. Of course, one could also use many other measures such as ratings of typicality and norms for production frequency. Unfortunately, there is no consensus about how to measure semantic relatedness, for theorists disagree over whether there is a single underlying dimension that is assessed by ratings of typicality, strength of association, production frequency, and so on. The discovery of a single underlying dimension would simplify and add power to theories of semantic memory. Such a discovery would also solidify the base of the spreading activation model.

Like its predecessor, the spreading activation model includes labelled *isa* links that indicate which categories are superordinate to

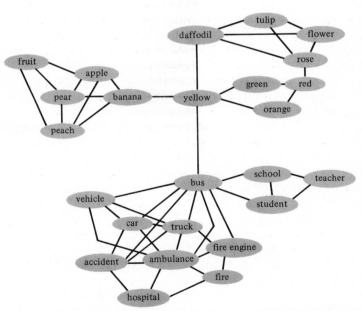

Figure 7.2   A portion of the semantic memory network proposed by the spreading activation model. (From Collins and Loftus, 1975. Copyright 1975 by the American Psychological Association. Reprinted by permission.)

others. For example, *canary* and *bird* are connected by an *isa* link. The model also includes *isnota* links, which indicate, for example, that a bat is not a bird. In order to see why these links were included, consider the sentence *A bat is a bird*. According to the hierarchical model, people decide this sentence is false by conducting a search of the memory network. Specifically, they search along the paths emanating from the *bat* and the *bird* nodes, looking for an *isa* relation. This search process takes time, so subjects should be relatively slow to indicate that the sentence is false. In fact, however, people decide very quickly that *A bat is a bird* is false, suggesting the decision is not based upon a memory search (Holyoak and Glass, 1975). This observation can be accommodated by the inclusion of an *isnota* link connecting *bat* and *bird*. People can access this link quickly, so they respond "False" quickly. Because the knowledge that a bat is not a bird is stored directly in the network, this bit of knowledge is said to be *prestored knowledge*. In general, network models assume that much of our knowledge is prestored (Smith, 1978). Later on, we will discuss a model that does not make this assumption.

The spreading activation model includes a number of assumptions concerning processing. One is that the links differ in accessibility or strength, and it takes less time to traverse a strong path than a weak one. How accessible or strong a link is depends on variables such as how frequently that link has been used. Since the concepts teacher and school have often occurred together in our experience, the link between the two concepts will be strong and readily accessible. In contrast, tennis and fires have seldom occurred together in our experience, so the link between *tennis* and *fire* will be weak and inaccessible. The second processing assumption is that when a concept is processed, activation spreads from that concept to neighboring ones. This spread of activation resembles what happens when one drops a rock into a pool of still water: the disturbance spreads out in all directions from the point of entry. The magnitude of the disturbance depends on the weight of the rock, on the proximity to where the rock had been dropped, and on the amount of time that passed since the rock had entered the water. In much the same way, the spread of activation in the memory network depends on the strength of the initial activation, the proximity to the point of activation, and the amount of time that has passed since the activation began. Additionally, when the links emanating from an activated node are strong, the activation will spread far and fast. But when the links are weak, the spread of activation will be restricted and slow.

The model also includes a complicated set of decision processes that will only be outlined here. If the sentence *A car is a vehicle* were read, the *car* and *vehicle* nodes would be activated, and the activation would spread out from both nodes. The paths of activation will intersect at numerous points in the network. The job of the decision process is to evaluate the evidence from various intersections. Some of the evidence is provided by the labels of the links connecting the nodes. The link between *car* and *vehicle* (an *isa* link) would indicate that *vehicle* is superordinate to *car*, and this label would provide strong evidence in favor of verifying the sentence. Similarly, in evaluating the sentence *A bat is a bird*, the decision process would discover an *isnota* link between *bat* and *bird*. This information would allow the decision process to determine rapidly that *A bat is a bird* is false. In addition to assessing the label of the links connecting two concepts, the decision process evaluates the total strength of activation at a particular point. Making a decision requires the achievement of a criterion level of activation. As we shall see, the criterion level of activation at a point can be reached through the summation of activation spreading from adjacent points in the network.

To see how the model operates, consider an experiment by Meyer and Schvaneveldt (1971). They presented a list of items, for example, *spoon* and *fork*, one at a time and asked subjects to indicate as quickly as possible whether each item was a legal word. This is called a lexical decision task (*lexical* means "pertaining to words"). In this task, the time required to decide if an item is a word or a nonword is influenced by the items that have been processed recently. For example, people classified *butter* as a word faster if they had just classified *bread* than if they had just classified *nurse*. This outcome is called the *semantic priming effect* because the processing of one word prepares or primes the system for processing a semantically related word.

The model accounts for this priming effect in the following manner. The decision as to whether *bread* was a word activated the *bread* concept in the memory network, and the activation spread to closely related concepts, including *butter*. Thus the concept *butter* had already been activated when the word *butter* was actually presented. Consequently, the threshold level of activation required for a decision about *butter* was reached sooner. On the other hand, *nurse* and *butter* are unrelated. As a result, no activation spread between those concepts, and the reaction time to *butter* was not reduced by the prior classification of *nurse*. As this example illustrates, the spreading activation process is important in that it provides a mechanism for the effects of semantic context, which, as we have seen, contribute to daily activities such as reading.

REPRESENTATION AND PROCESSING

So far, we have examined semantic knowledge in the context of models of processing. You may be wondering at this point why so much attention is devoted to processing in a chapter concerning representation. The reason is quite simple: we cannot observe representations directly, so we infer the properties of representations from performance. Because performance depends upon both representations and processing, for example, on retrieval operations, our studies of representation are actually studies of representation and processing. By studying representation in the context of models of processing, we can test different conceptions of semantic knowledge and make specific predictions about performance.

In a particular model of processing, an intimate relationship exists between assumptions regarding representation and processing. As an illustration, consider how the spreading activation model explains the observation that people take less time to verify *A robin is a bird* than *A chicken is a bird.* According to the model, the path between *robin* and *bird* is more accessible or stronger than that between *chicken* and *bird.* The plausible reason is that people often use the *robin-bird* link, but they seldom use the *chicken-bird* link. Consequently, activation will spread faster between *robin* and *bird,* thereby allowing the rapid verification of *A robin is a bird.* The model also provided other mechanisms that contribute to typicality effects, but these need not concern us. For now, the chief point is that the model accounts for typicality effects in terms of processing. Alternative accounts could, however, be based upon representational properties. For example, one could assume that all links are equally accessible but that closely related concepts are joined by shorter links than unrelated concepts are. In this account, activation emanates at the same rate along all of the paths leading from a node, and the activation reaches the closely related concepts before reaching the unrelated concepts. Since *robin* and *bird* are closely related, the activation of one concept results in the activation of the other. This proposal is not intended to replace the mechanism suggested by Collins and Loftus. It simply demonstrates that a particular model can accommodate particular observations via concepts pertaining either to representation or to processing.

On a deeper level, what one assumes about representations influences what one assumes about processing. If the relatedness of two concepts is reflected by the distance between them in the network, then there is less need to assume that the links connecting the concepts differ in strength and that activation spreads faster along some paths than others. Because notions concerning representation and processing are inextricably interwoven in our theories, it is probably best to avoid talking of either representations or processes in isolation. Instead, we should speak of representation-process pairs (Anderson, 1976, 1978).

CONCLUDING REMARKS
Overall, the spreading activation model is an advance over the hierarchical network model. The spreading activation model avoids the assumption that knowledge is structured hierarchically and in the most economical manner. It is consistent with the effects of typicality and many other variables (cf. Collins and Loftus, 1975). Additionally, the concept

of spreading activation has proven to be highly useful in accounting for the effects of context (Anderson, 1976).

In general, network models have provided useful frameworks for conceptualizing human knowledge. We often think of words as being separate psychological entities whose meanings are independent of other words. As network models suggest, however, the meaning of a word depends in large part on the relationships between that word and the myriad concepts in memory with which it is associated. We tend to define words in terms of other words and concepts, much as a dictionary does. We might single out one or a few attributes that define a particular word. But as we have seen, not all members of a category have attributes in common. Furthermore, we know much more about a word than the attributes that we often use to define it. Network models readily accommodate these aspects of meaning. The meaning of a word is given by the many concepts that the word relates to, including the concepts that constitute our general knowledge of the world.

Network models are also useful because of their potential scope and power (Anderson, 1976). Some network models (Glass and Holyoak, 1975) have helped to clarify complex activities such as the processing of semantic contradictions (for example, *All canaries are crows*) and semantic anomalies (for example, *All tractors are sailors*). These models have also been extended to activities such as the comprehension and memory of complex sentences and prose passages (Anderson and Bower, 1973; Anderson, 1976). However, these are not strong arguments in favor of accepting the spreading activation model, which currently includes only simple relations such as the *isa* relation. The generality of the spreading activation model has not yet been evaluated fully. Moreover, the model faces some influential rivals, one of which is examined next.

The Feature-Comparison Model

The network models assumed that much of our knowledge is prestored in memory. In contrast, the feature-comparison model assumes that much of our knowledge is *computed* from the information stored in memory (Smith, 1978). To clarify the distinction between prestored and computed knowledge, consider the knowledge that a robin is a bird. According to the network models, this knowledge is stored directly in the network via an *isa* link connecting *robin* and *bird*. On the other hand, the knowledge that a robin is a bird could be computed or inferred from other knowledge. Assume, for example, that memory contains these two lists of features:

Robin: living, animate, feathered, red-breasted . . .
Bird: living, animate, feathered, two-legged . . .

Perhaps we verify *A robin is a bird* by comparing these two lists of features and deciding upon the degree of overlap. In this scenario, the relation between *robin* and *bird* is computed at the time of verification; it is not prestored in a memory network (Smith, 1978). Unlike the network models, the feature-comparison model assumes that most of our knowledge of word meanings is computed rather than prestored.

The feature-comparison model, proposed by Smith, Shoben, and Rips (1974), represents words as sets of features or attributes. The semantic features are assumed to vary along a continuum of definingness (Smith, 1978). At one end of this dimension are the features, called **defining features**, that are essential for defining a word. At the other end of the dimension are *characteristic features* that are characteristic of the concept but not essential to it. For example, the word *bird* has the defining features *animate* and *has feathers*. These features are essential for defining the concept. *Bird* also has characteristic features such as *can sing* or *can be eaten by dogs*. The latter features are characteristic of many birds, but they are not essential for defining the word. After all, many birds cannot sing, and a bird is a bird regardless of what preys on it.

The view that word concepts are represented by features is consistent with the idea that stimuli are encoded as ensembles of features or attributes. Rips, Shoben, and Smith (1973) presented evidence in support of this featural representation. They had subjects rate how closely related various instances (such as *robin, canary,* and *chicken*) of a category were to a superordinate category (*bird*) and to each other. By using sophisticated methods for analyzing the degree of relatedness of the concepts, a semantic space was constructed. The semantic space resembled a map containing concepts rather than cities. The more closely related two concepts had been judged to be, the shorter was the distance between them. In the semantic maps that were constructed for birds and mammals, the concepts tended to form clusters, as shown in Figure 7.3. In both semantic spaces, the smaller animals tended to fall on the right-hand side, whereas the larger animals fell on the left-hand side. For this reason, the horizontal axis represents the dimension of size. The vertical axis seems to represent a quite different dimension. The upper halves of both spaces include tame, domesticated animals such as *duck, goat,* and *cow.* The lower halves contain animals that tend to prey on other animals for food. For this reason, the vertical dimension was said to indicate the degree of predacity. These results suggest that the semantic features pertaining to size and predacity were the basis for the subjects' judgments about the relatedness of various concepts.

MAKING FEATURE COMPARISONS

The model asserts that verifying statements such as *A robin is a bird* occurs by comparing the features of *robin* and *bird*. The model includes

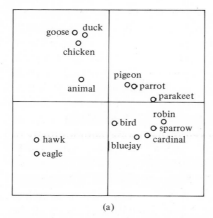

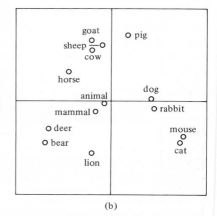

(a)   (b)

Figure 7.3   Semantic space for animals, as determined from ratings of the degree of relatedness among the various animals. (a) The space for birds. (b) The space for mammals. The horizontal axis represents the dimension of size, and the vertical axis represents the degree of predacity. (From Rips, Shoben, and Smith, 1973.)

two stages. In the first stage, the overall featural similarity of the two nouns is compared. This comparison includes both the defining and the characteristic features. If the featural similarity is very high, as it is in the comparison of *robin* and *bird*, then the subject rapidly responds *true*. Similarly, if the featural similarity is very low, as in the comparison of *robin* and *car*, then the subject rapidly responds *false*. The model includes decision processes that set the criteria that define high and low featural similarity and that determine whether the overall level of similarity is very high or very low.

In many instances, two nouns will be neither very high nor very low in featural similarity. If the first stage had determined that there is an intermediate level of similarity between the two nouns, then the second stage is begun. In this stage, only the defining features of the two nouns are compared. If all of the defining features match exactly, then the subject responds *true*. But if any of the defining features of one noun do not match those of the other noun, the subject responds *false*.

Examining how the model accounts for typicality effects clarifies the operations of the model. In verifying sentences such as *A robin is a bird*, people presumably compare the features of *robin* and *bird* in a holistic manner. *Robin* and *bird* have many features in common, for robins are highly typical birds. During the first stage, the subjects notice the high degree of similarity and make a rapid *true* response without executing the second stage. But when the sentence is *A chicken is a bird*, the overall comparison at the first stage will determine that *chicken* and *bird* are neither highly similar nor highly dissimilar. Accordingly, the subjects must execute the second stage, which requires additional time. The end result is that it takes longer to verify *A chicken is a bird* than *A robin is a bird.*

Note that it is the characteristic features that are essential for the occurrence of typicality effects. The model proposes that all or most members of a category have the same defining features. So the differences between category members must be due to differences in the extent to which they have features that are characteristic of the category. The difference between *robin* and *chicken* is that *robin* includes many of the features that are characteristic of *bird,* whereas *chicken* does not. In this account, *A robin is a bird* is verified quickly because of the extensive overlap in the characteristic features of *robin* and *bird.*

The model is consistent with the way people use linguistic hedges in everyday situations (Lakoff, 1972). Porpoises have many of the features that are characteristic of fish. As a result, most of us would agree with this statement: *Loosely speaking, a porpoise is a fish.* But *porpoise* and *fish* do not have the same defining features, so we tend to reject the hedgeless statement *A porpoise is a fish.* In a similar way, the model clarifies how we use hedges such as *technically speaking,* as in *Technically speaking, a whale is a mammal.* A whale is a mammal in that *whale* has the defining features of *mammal* (for example, whales nourish their offspring by milk secreted by mammary glands). But whales are atypical mammals in that they lack characteristic features such as *has hair* and *lives on land.* It is the presence of defining features and the absence of the characteristic features that leads to the use of the hedge *technically speaking.*

The model also clarifies how people make errors in verifying sentences. Errors are infrequent but do occur sometimes in processing sentences such as *A bat is a bird.* This type of sentence may be classified incorrectly as *true* because *bat* and *bird* have many common features, for example, *has wings* and *can fly.* These common features are presumably detected in the stage one comparison; this leads to a rapid *true* response. That comparison process does not evaluate the defining and the characteristic features separately, so there is no way of knowing in stage one that bats and birds have different defining features. If, on the other hand, stage two had been executed, the difference between the defining features of *bat* and *bird* would have been detected, and the subject would have made a correct *false* response. One reason for the low error rate in the sentence verification task is that in most cases, two nouns (for example, *robin* and *bird*) that share many characteristic features tend to have common defining features.

PROBLEMS WITH THE MODEL

One of the chief problems facing the feature-comparison model concerns the distinction between defining and characteristic features. This distinction is crucial since the model uses characteristic features to account for typicality effects. And it states that the defining features provide the basis for comparisons during stage two. Unfortunately, the model does not include rules that stipulate which features are defining and which are characteristic. This limits our ability to specify exactly how people make semantic comparisons.

Attempts have been made to distinguish empirically between defining and characteristic features, but the results have not been encouraging. For example, Hampton (1979) observed that people judge categories as having features that are common to most members of the category. For example, the members of the *vegetable* category had features such as *is edible, is a plant,* and *is cultivated.* These common features might be considered as defining features of the *vegetable* category. Unfortunately, there were numerous vegetables such as *avocado* and *olive* that had all the defining features yet were not rated as definitely belonging to the category *vegetable.* In other words, the defining features did not really define category membership. This observation could be explained away by saying that the experiment simply failed to identify the defining features of the categories. But that gets us back to the original problem: Just how do we determine which features are defining features? Furthermore, it is possible, as Wittgenstein (1953), Rosch (1978) and others have argued, that natural categories may not have defining features that are common to all or most members of the category.

Another problem for the model is that some evidence contradicts it. The model states that false statements such as *All collies are birds* will be disconfirmed faster than statements such as *All collies are shepherds.* The reason is that *collie* and *bird* are very low in overall featural similarity, so *All collies are birds* could be rejected on the basis of the comparison at stage one. But since *collie* and *shepherd* have common features, *All collies are shepherds* cannot be disconfirmed at the first stage, and executing the second stage takes time. Contrary to this prediction, people disconfirm *All collies are shepherds* more quickly than *All collies are birds* (Holyoak and Glass, 1975; Lorch, 1978). People probably have a variety of strategies for disconfirming sentences, and comparing features may be only one useful strategy. One could disconfirm *All collies are shepherds* by thinking of a counterexample, say, a collie that does not look like a shepherd. This strategy and others are beyond the scope of the feature-comparison model.

Another contradictory observation concerns the effects of semantic relatedness. For example, subjects verify *All robins are birds* faster than *All penguins are birds.* The featural similarity of *robin* and *bird* exceeds the subjects' criterion for high relatedness, so only the first stage is executed. But the featural similarity of *penguin* and *bird* is low, so subjects must execute both stages, which requires additional time. According to the model, this relatedness effect should disappear or be reduced if the subjects were induced to set their criterion defining relatedness at a very high level. When the criterion is set very high, the relatedness of the nouns in most sentences will not be sufficiently high to allow the rapid decision at stage one. As a result, most sentences must be processed through both stages, thereby reducing differences in the time required to verify different sentences. McCloskey and Glucksberg (1979) tried to induce subjects to set a very high criterion for relatedness by presenting false sentences containing highly related nouns (as in *All birds are sparrows*). These highly related, false sentences were interspersed among true sentences that were either high or low in relatedness. This arrangement should have led subjects to adopt a very high criterion so that they could avoid finding a high level of relatedness in sentences such as *All birds are sparrows* and responding *true* (incorrectly). In fact, the subjects made few errors in verifying the true sentences and disconfirming the false ones. But a large effect of semantic relatedness remained for the verification of the true sentences. This observation goes against the model for the reasons given above.

Perhaps the most serious question is whether meanings can be described adequately by semantic features. Whereas some linguists believe that features can capture a rich array of word meanings (Katz, 1972), others express doubt (Bar-Hillel, 1969, 1970). Even if most words can be decomposed logically into a set of features, that does not mean that people actually use those features in performing semantic tasks. For example, *robin* can be decomposed logically into numerous features. But do people really decompose that word in order to understand its meaning? As discussed previously, in processing a concept such as *robin* people may not break the prototype down into its component features.

CONCLUDING REMARKS

Research concerning our knowledge of word meanings is of recent origin, and it is too early to decide the extent to which our knowledge is prestored, as posited by the network models, or computed, as posited by the feature-comparison model. Most likely, a particular piece of knowledge can be both prestored and computed. For example, if you were asked whether an orangutan is a monkey or an ape, your decision could follow several routes. You might recall having read in a biology text that orangutans are apes. On the other hand, you might fail to retrieve that prestored knowledge. Yet you could still answer the question by comparing the features of orangutans with those of gorillas or chimps. Thus your knowledge that an orangutan is an ape could be both prestored and computed. Human knowledge is too diverse and flexible to be categorized as strictly prestored or computed. Future research, then, should take this flexibility into account.

Future research should also extend beyond the simple verification paradigm. It is reasonable to restrict the scope of one's inquiries in the initial stages of research. But in the long run, theories of semantic knowledge must clarify how people understand complex sentences and stories, remember prose passages, and so on. In the following section, we inquire into more complex aspects of knowledge.

PROPOSITIONAL KNOWLEDGE

A proposition is a symbolic representation that expresses a relationship between two or more concepts and that can be either true or false. The proposition HIT (CAR, TRUCK), which could represent the meaning of the sentence *The car hit the truck*, includes the concepts HIT, CAR, and TRUCK. HIT is called the relational term of the proposition because it designates the relationship between CAR and TRUCK. By convention, the relational term is written as the first term of the proposition and is placed outside of the parentheses, which enclose the two concepts (called arguments) that are related by the relational term. This type of layout is called a propositional format. As additional examples of a propositional format, the meaning of the sentence *The girl ate the salad* can be represented as EAT (GIRL, SALAD), and the meaning of *The man rode on the motorcycle* can be represented as RIDE (MAN, MOTORCYCLE).

Theorists are interested in propositional representations because propositions are thought to be capable of embodying the complex knowledge that is used to comprehend prose, carry on conversations, form images, and so on (Pylyshyn, 1973). Needless to say, the knowledge of word meanings that was discussed above is too simple to enable us to perform many everyday tasks. For example, the meaning of the paragraph you are now reading cannot be decomposed into semantic features. Nor can it be represented in a network containing simple semantic relations, for example, the *isa* relation.

In this section, we examine the evidence that people represent complex information in a propositional format. Then we inquire into a global model of processing that uses propositional representations. We shall see that many investigators believe that propositional representations can embody most if not all of our semantic and world knowledge.

Propositions and Paragraph Processing

Evidence that people use propositional representations in processing sentences and stories comes from various sources (Anderson, 1976; Anderson and Bower, 1973; Buschke and Schaier, 1979; Kintsch, 1974;

Kintsch and Keenan, 1973). For the sake of clarity and thoroughness, we shall consider in detail a single experiment concerning the processing of simple paragraphs (McKoon and Ratcliff, 1980).

The meaning of a paragraph can be expressed in a series of propositions, as indicated in Table 7.1. The paragraph includes six sentences, and the meaning of each sentence is embodied in a single proposition: P1 expresses the meaning of the first sentence, P2 expresses the meaning of the second sentence, and so on. The propositions are interconnected in that a single concept can occur in two propositions. For example, both P1 and P2 contain the concept INSECTS, and P5 and P6 contain the concept CROWS. Because the propositions connect into a straight line or linear sequence, the paragraph is said to have a linear meaning structure. Adjacent propositions are relatively close in the meaning structure, whereas nonadjacent propositions are relatively far apart. For example, P1 and P2 are more closely related than P1 and P3 or P2 and P6.

McKoon and Ratcliff hypothesized that people who read the paragraph discern the propositions and the meaning structure shown in Table 7.1. In order to test this hypothesis, they made use of the observation that semantically related words can prime each other, as in the semantic priming effect. Recall, for example, that people decide that *butter* is a word faster if they have just processed *bread* rather than an unrelated word, *nurse*. McKoon and Ratcliff predicted that words from propositions that were close in the meaning structure of the paragraph would prime each other more than words from propositions that were distant in the meaning structure. This prediction agrees with the idea that the closer two propositions are in the meaning structure, the more closely related psychologically the nouns in those propositions will be.

Table 7.1 A SIMPLE PARAGRAPH, ITS PROPOSITIONS, AND ITS LINEAR MEANING STRUCTURE

SENTENCES	PROPOSITIONS
The crops drew insects.	P1 DRAW, CROPS, INSECTS
The insects troubled the farmer.	P2 TROUBLE, INSECTS, FARMER
The farmer surveyed the fields.	P3 SURVEY, FARMER, FIELDS
The fields needed pesticides.	P4 NEED, FIELDS, PESTICIDES
The pesticides poisoned crows.	P5 POISON, PESTICIDES, CROWS
The crows fouled the countryside.	P6 FOUL, CROWS, COUNTRYSIDE

Propositional connections:
  P1 —— P2 —— P3 —— P4 —— P5 —— P6

Connections between nouns:
  N1——— N2 ———N3———N4——————— N5———————N6———————N7
  CROPS INSECTS FARMER FIELDS PESTICIDES CROWS COUNTRY-
                                                                                SIDE

SOURCE: From McKoon and Ratcliff, 1980.

In each trial of the experiment, the subjects read two unrelated paragraphs and then took a test of word recognition. In the test, individual words were presented, and the subjects' task was to press quickly one of two keys, thereby indicating whether the word had been in either of the paragraphs. There were a total of 72 trials, so the subjects read a total of 144 different paragraphs. Some of the test words were preceded in the test list by words that were closely related in the meaning structure of the paragraphs. For example, COUNTRYSIDE might have been preceded by CROWS. Other test words were preceded by unrelated words (for example, CROPS might have been preceded by CAR) or by words that were relatively distant in the meaning structure (for example, FIELDS might have been preceded by INSECTS). The prediction was that recognition would occur most rapidly when the test word was preceded by a word that was closely related in the meaning structure of the paragraph.

In fact, this prediction was confirmed. Additionally, the closer two nouns were in the meaning structure of a paragraph, the larger the priming effect was. For example, the subjects recognized COUNTRYSIDE faster when the preceding word was CROWS than when the preceding word was PESTICIDES. These results suggest that the proximity of the words in the meaning structure determines the magnitude of the priming effect.

Before accepting this conclusion, however, two alternate accounts must be ruled out. Perhaps CROWS primed the recognition of COUNTRYSIDE because COUNTRYSIDE and CROWS had been associated before the experiment more strongly than COUNTRYSIDE and PESTICIDES. This possibility was assessed by interchanging the words INSECTS and CROWS in the paragraph shown in Table 7.1 and repeating the procedure with new subjects. Under these conditions, CROWS primed COUNTRYSIDE less than PESTICIDES did. Thus the amount of priming depended on the closeness of the priming and the target words in the meaning structure, not on the strength of the preexperimental associations.

A second possibility was that the amount of priming depended upon the physical proximity of the words in the paragraph. Perhaps CROWS had facilitated the recognition of COUNTRYSIDE because those two words had occurred close together in the paragraph, not because they were close in the meaning structure. To evaluate this possibility, McKoon and Ratcliff followed the procedure described above, but they presented paragraphs like that shown in Table 7.2. In this type of paragraph, two words or concepts may be close together in the meaning structure even though they are separated by many words in the paragraph. For example, the sentences *The businessman gestured to a waiter* and *The businessman flourished documents* were separated by three sen-

Table 7.2 A SIMPLE PARAGRAPH AND ITS PROPOSITIONAL
STRUCTURE

SENTENCES	PROPOSITIONS
The businessman gestured to a waiter.	P1 GESTURE TO, BUSINESSMAN, WAITER
The waiter brought coffee.	P2 BRING, WAITER, COFFEE
The coffee stained the napkins.	P3 STAIN, COFFEE, NAPKINS
The napkins protected the table-cloth.	P4 PROTECT, NAPKINS, TABLE-CLOTH
The businessman flourished documents.	P5 FLOURISH, BUSINESSMAN, DOCUMENTS
The documents explained a contract.	P6 EXPLAIN, DOCUMENTS, CONTRACT
The contract satisfied the client.	P7 SATISFY, CONTRACT, CLI-ENT

Propositional connections:

```
                 ┌── P2 ──── P3 ──── P4
        P1 ──────┤
                 └── P5 ──── P6 ──── P7
```

Connections between nouns:

```
            N2 ──────────── N3 ──────────── N4 ──────────── N5
            WAITER          COFFEE      NAPKINS    TABLECLOTH
     N1
BUSINESSMAN
            N6 ──────────── N7 ──────────── N8
            DOCU-
            MENTS          CONTRACT       CLIENT
```

SOURCE: From McKoon and Ratcliff, 1980.

tences. As shown by the connections between nouns, WAITER is relatively close in the meaning structure to DOCUMENTS even though WAITER and DOCUMENTS had been far apart physically. Further, WAITER primed the recognition of DOCUMENTS more than NAPKINS primed the recognition of CLIENT. These two pairs of words were equally distant physically, but WAITER and DOCUMENTS were closer in the meaning structure. So it is closeness in the meaning structure that determines the amount of priming. These priming effects seem to occur rapidly and automatically (Ratcliff and McKoon, 1981), and this probably facilitates the reading process.

Overall, these observations suggest that in reading paragraphs, the subjects had represented the meaning of the passage in a propositional form. In deciding whether a concept had occurred in the text, they accessed the propositional representations. Other research, too complex to review here, has shown that people form and use propositional representations in reading paragraphs and longer passages of the type that we encounter in everyday situations (Kintsch and Vipond, 1979). For these reasons, some theorists are now constructing large-scale or global models of comprehension and memory using the proposition as a basic unit of knowledge (Anderson, 1976; Kintsch, 1974; Norman and Rumelhart, 1975). The nature of the global models can be illustrated by examining HAM, one of the first and most influential of the global models.

HAM

HAM is the acronym for Human Associative Memory, the model constructed by Anderson and Bower (1973). Before discussing the details of the model, it is important to point out the aims of HAM and of global models in general. The first aim is to specify the knowledge that people use in performing tasks ranging from reading to remembering to forming images. Unlike the simple models of semantic memory, the global models are concerned with the knowledge that underlies all of our cognitive activities, even the most complex ones. The second aim is to specify the mechanisms whereby people use their knowledge to perform everyday activities. These two aims are complementary because hypotheses about representations must be evaluated in the context of a processing model. And the performance of a processing model that uses stored representations is determined by the kinds of representations it has.

The magnitude of these aims should be appreciated. Together, they call for nothing less than a model of the entire cognitive system. Why would anyone aspire to such lofty aims at a time when psychology is so young? One reason is that everyday activities are so complex that they require complex models. On a deeper level, the cognitive system is a unified, integrated system in which the various parts work together. For this reason, it is important to identify various parts of the system and to study how they work in unison. An understanding of the entire system cannot be achieved by analyzing particular parts in isolation, just as an understanding of the human body cannot be achieved by analyzing an arm or a brain in isolation. Of course, an analysis of the parts of a system may contribute to our understanding of the whole system. In the long run, then, simple and global models of semantic knowledge and processing may be complementary.

REPRESENTATION IN HAM

The proposition is the basic unit of representation in HAM. The propositions are composed of five kinds of associations, as summarized in Figure 7.4a. The first association consists of a context and a fact. The fact indicates what happened and the context indicates the time and the place of the event. The second association is between a location and a time. This association is a breakdown of the context from the first association. The third association consists of a subject and a predicate. The subject indicates the topic of the fact, and the predicate indicates a property of the subject or tells what happened to the subject. The fourth association

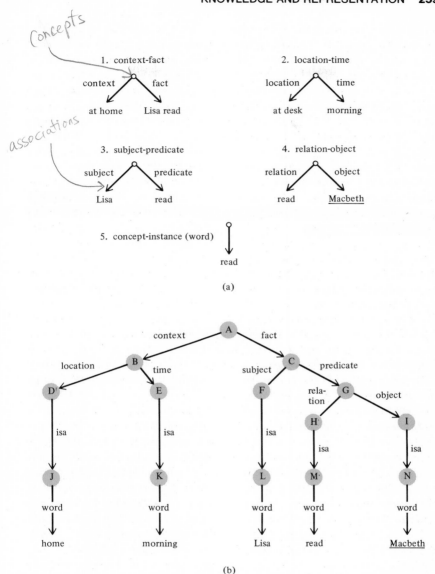

Figure 7.4   Propositional representation in HAM. (a) Five kinds of associations occur in the propositions. (b) The propositional structure of the sentence *At home, Lisa read* MACBETH.

consists of a relation and an object. This association breaks down the predicate from the third association. The fifth association is between a concept and an instance of that concept, for example, between the concept *house* and an individual house or word referring to the house.

These five associations combine to form a treelike structure, as shown in Figure 7.4b. This structure consists of nodes that stand for concepts and pointers that stand for associations. Point A is the proposition node of the tree, and it divides into a context node (B) and a fact node (C). In turn, the context node divides into a location node (D) and a time node (E). Similarly, the fact node divides into a subject node (F) and a predicate node (G). The predicate node breaks down into a relation node (H) and an object node (I). Attached to each of these nodes is a general concept node and a particular word or instance of the concept. Thus node D is attached to node J, the concept of home; in turn, node J is attached to the word *home*. This entire tree diagram represents the proposition expressed by the sentence *At home, Lisa read* MACBETH. As you may have noticed, HAM represents both episodic and semantic information via propositions.

HAM AND ASSOCIATIONISM

You may have been surprised to find propositions described as a set of associations. After all, cognitive psychology evolved in part as a reaction against associationism. In fact, HAM retains some valuable associationistic notions, but it departs radically from traditional associationistic models. For one thing, the associations in HAM are not all of the same kind. Rather, there are several different kinds of association, each of which indicates how two ideas are related. The use of different kinds of association makes HAM much more powerful than traditional associationistic models.

HAM differs from conventional models also because it represents sentences as having hierarchical structure. For this reason, HAM accounts for the internal structure of sentences, and it avoids the traditional view that a sentence is a chain of associated ideas. Equally important, this hierarchical representation allows propositions to be embedded within one another. For example, the sentence *That Lisa had read* MAC-BETH *pleased the teacher* contains two propositions. In sentence form, the two propositions are *Lisa read* MACBETH and *It pleased the teacher*. Both propositions can be combined into a single propositional tree as shown in Figure 7.5. In this tree, the subject is the proposition diagrammed in Figure 7.4b. This manner of combining propositions allows for the construction of sophisticated representations that combine many propositions. This feature adds power to the model because it enables the model to represent very complex ideas.

A third difference is that HAM includes a *type-token distinction*. A type is a general concept and a token is an instance of the category. As shown in Figure 7.4b, each word is an instance or token of a general concept. For example, the word *home* is a token of the general concept of *home* (the node labelled D). This is indicated by the pointer connect-

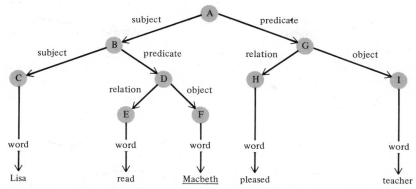

Figure 7.5 The embedding of propositions in HAM. In this diagram, the proposition *Lisa read* MACBETH is the subject of another proposition. The diagram has been simplified by the omission of the type nodes and the context nodes.

ing the D node and the word *home*. The importance of the type-token distinction is illustrated by the sentence *In the park yesterday, I dodged one attacker and chased the other*. The representation of this sentence is shown in Figure 7.6. The sentence includes two facts which can be stated as *I dodged one attacker* and *I chased the other*. The subject of these two facts is the same, as indicated by the arrows connecting nodes J and F in the network. There were two attackers, as indicated by the type nodes M and I. Since both attackers are instances of the general concept *attacker*, nodes M and I are both connected to node R, which designates the concept *attacker*.

This type of representation embodies information about particular instances or tokens, and it also indicates the general categories or types to which the instances belong. Connecting types and tokens in memory is advantageous because it allows us to apply our knowledge of general concepts to instances of the concept. By attaching an instance of *attacker* to the general concept *attacker*, we can apply our general knowledge of attackers (they often want money, they carry dangerous weapons, and so on) to the particular instance. Conversely, we can use our knowledge of particular instances to make judgments about general categories. As discussed above, people often use their knowledge of instances to make decisions about general categories. If, for example, you remembered having seen a lemur's tail, you might agree that *Lemurs have tails* is true. But the distinction between types and tokens also recognizes that our knowledge of general categories and of particular instances is different. Having seen one attacker wearing a red shirt, we do not acquire the general knowledge that attackers wear red shirts. To some extent, we keep our

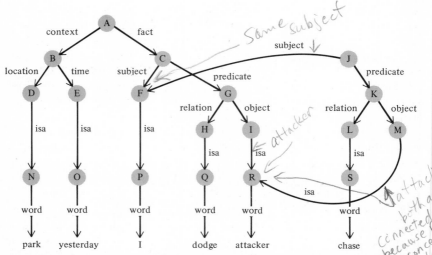

Figure 7.6 The type-token distinction in HAM. The diagram represents the meaning of the sentence *In the park yesterday, I dodged one attacker and chased the other.*

knowledge of particular instances separate from our knowledge of general categories, and this fact is reflected in the type-token distinction.

Overall, then, HAM does include some features of traditional associationistic models. But HAM differs from those models in that it uses different kinds of associations, it represents sentences in a hierarchical form, and it includes a type-token distinction. These features make HAM a sophisticated and powerful model.

POWER AND EFFICIENCY

The type of representation used in HAM is attractive because it combines power and efficiency. According to the model, our long-term memory is a vast network of propositional trees. Indeed, the model makes the sweeping assumption that all of our knowledge is represented in propositional trees such as the ones shown above. For example, the proposition shown in Figure 7.4b could represent the knowledge used to generate an image of Lisa studying MACBETH or to interpret a picture of Lisa reading. In their book, *Human Associative Memory,* Anderson and Bower gave formal arguments showing that their propositional representation can embody many different kinds of knowledge. Because propositions can represent much of our knowledge, they are viewed as a very powerful form of representation.

The capacity for representing diverse kinds of information is important because in daily activities, people use diverse aspects of knowledge.

If, for example, a loved one were sitting in your home and said *It's cold in here,* you would probably interpret that statement as a polite request to turn up the heat or to close the windows. In order to make that interpretation, you had to know the meanings of your friend's words and the rules of conversation that led you to infer that the statement was an indirect request. Also, you had to use your knowledge of what makes people feel cold and of how to warm up a room. If a global model could not represent these diverse aspects of knowledge, it could not explain how we interpret and respond to everyday sentences.

Propositional representations also are useful because they are efficient. For one thing, a single proposition can represent the meaning of several different sentences. For example, the propositional tree shown in Figure 7.4b could represent the meaning of either *Lisa read* MACBETH *at home* or MACBETH *was read by Lisa at home.* It is not always necessary to store a unique proposition for every sentence that has been processed, and this conserves storage space.

The representation used in HAM also allows for the efficient retrieval of information. The labelled links that connect various nodes provide the information required to conduct a directed search of memory. Consider, for example, how the system would respond to the question *What did Lisa read?* HAM would first form a propositional tree for this sentence, as shown on the left side of Figure 7.7. Through a process called "Match," HAM attempts to find a matching propositional tree in memory. It starts by locating the words *Lisa* and *read* in memory. *Read* no doubt has many associations in memory, but not all of these are searched. Instead, the Match process notes that *read* is linked in the input tree (the tree shown on the left of Figure 7.7) to a general concept (f) via an *isa* relation. The Match process then searches only those links in memory that connect *read* to the general concept node for *read.* In this manner, the Match process uses the labelled associations to direct the search process and to restrict the number of nodes to be searched, thereby improving the efficiency of the retrieval process.

The Match process continues the search until it finds a propositional tree in memory that matches the input tree, as shown in Figure 7.7. Having found the matching propositional tree, HAM can answer the question by searching the predicate and the object links and finding the MACBETH node (E). Of course, if HAM found no MACBETH node, or if it failed to access the correct propositional tree in memory, then it could not answer the question. As a result, it would reply "Don't know."

TESTING THE MODEL

Global models may be tested in various ways. One way is to embody the model in a computer program and to then determine whether the model can do all the things it was intended to do. For example, Anderson and

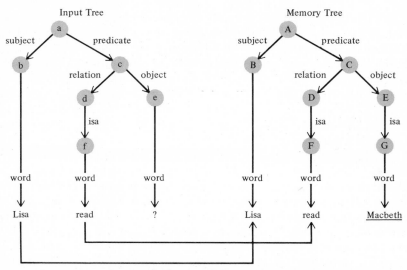

Figure 7.7   The Match process in HAM as applied to the question *What did Lisa read?* HAM constructs an input tree and determines the labels of the links leading to the words *Lisa* and *read* in the input tree. Then it accesses the concepts *Lisa* and *read* in memory and uses the labeled links to construct a propositional tree that matches the input tree and supplies the missing information.

Bower had designed HAM to represent sentences in propositional form and to answer questions. They tested HAM by embodying the model in a computer program and by presenting new sentences to the computer. The results were that the computer succeeded in representing many English sentences in the format described above. It also answered correctly many of the questions that were put to it.

This outcome is important for two reasons. First, it shows that HAM could do what Anderson and Bower had intended. If the program had failed to answer the questions, that would have indicated a flaw in the model and would have necessitated a revision of the model. Second, it shows that the model can be made very explicit. Computers can process only those programs that are logical and explicit. Because the program worked as it should have, we know that the model is explicit and logical. Needless to say, explicitness and logical consistency are desirable characteristics of any model.

But a computer model that represents sentences and answers questions is not necessarily a psychological model. A global model is a psychological model only if it processes information in the same way that people do and if it makes testable predictions about how people will perform in a particular task. To their credit, Anderson and Bower relied heavily on experimental data in constructing and evaluating HAM.

One prediction made by HAM was that the repetition of a proposition would improve the retention of the elements in that proposition. This prediction followed from the idea that the proposition is the basic unit of processing (for example, the Match process works with only one proposition at a time). The prediction was tested by presenting pairs of sentences such as 1 and 2 or 3 and 4.

1. The hippie who was tall touched the debutante.
2. The hippie who was tall kissed the prostitute.
3. The hippie who was tall touched the debutante.
4. The captain who was tall kissed the debutante.

In Sentences 1 and 2, the proposition *The hippie was tall* was repeated, so the words *hippie* and *tall* were repeated within a single proposition. In Sentences 3 and 4, *tall* was repeated, but the repetition occurred in two different propositions, *The hippie was tall* and *The captain was tall*. If the proposition is the unit of processing, then performance should be influenced more by the repetition of words within a single proposition than by the repetition of words in different propositions.

The subjects studied a list of 16 sentences that were presented one at a time in a scrambled order. Then they took a cued-recall test in which they tried to fill in the blanks in this type of sentence: The _____ who was tall touched the _____. After this, another list was presented for study. This list contained some new sentences, but it also contained some of the words that had occurred in the first list. The repeated words occurred either in the same proposition that had occurred in the first list (as in Sentences 1 and 2) or in different propositions (as in Sentences 3 and 4). Thus the repetitions occurred in different lists. Following the presentation of the second list, a cued-recall test was given. The subjects studied and tried to recall eight lists in all.

The results were that the repetition of a word within a single proposition increased the level of recall of those words. The more times a word was repeated, the higher the level of recall was. In contrast, the repetition of a word in different propositions had no effect on the level of recall. Thus the repetition of particular items per se did not influence memory; what mattered was whether a particular word was repeated in the same proposition. These observations and many others supported HAM.

Not all experimental data have supported HAM (Anderson, 1976; Foss and Harwood, 1975), and Anderson (1976) has revised the initial model extensively. But this state of affairs is unsurprising, since global models are in the early stage of development. At present, it is unrealistic to expect any one model to provide a complete account of cognition. Nevertheless, the present generation of global models suggests that many cognitive activities are based upon propositional representations.

In the next section, we examine whether propositional representations provide an adequate conceptualization of our nonverbal, spatial knowledge.

SPATIAL KNOWLEDGE AND IMAGERY

This chapter has concentrated on the representation and the processing of verbal information. The question that arises now is whether our nonverbal knowledge is represented in the same manner as our verbal knowledge. This question has been raised primarily in connection with studies of visual information processing. For example, Shepard (1967) showed college students a series of 612 pictures from magazines. After the subjects had examined each picture at their own pace, they took a test of recognition. In the test, pairs of pictures were presented, and the subjects indicated which one they had seen earlier. When the test followed the presentation of the pictures immediately, the subjects identified 98 percent of the pictures correctly. Even more impressive results came from a study of Standing (1973) in which several stalwart subjects studied 10,000 pictures. On a test of recognition, they identified 75 percent of the pictures correctly.

Do people represent the information in pictures in a propositional format, as they represent verbal information? Perhaps, but some observations indicate that they represent pictures and words differently. For example, Bahrick, Bahrick, and Wittlinger (1975) compared the level of retention for the names and the faces of high-school classmates following various periods of time after graduation. They presented sets of five graduation pictures and asked people to choose the picture that had come from their own yearbook. Similarly, they presented sets of five names and asked people to choose which one had been a former classmate. Within 14 years of graduation, the subjects recognized both the faces and the names at a very high level, about 90 percent correct. Impressively, the subjects recognized 90 percent of the faces of former classmates 35 years following graduation. And after 47 years, the level of recognition fell to 73%, far above the level of recognition that would have been achieved by guessing (20 percent correct). In contrast, the level of recognition for names dropped to the 78 percent level after 25 years. So people remember faces better than names over long periods of time.

Superior retention for pictures relative to words has occurred in many experiments (Erdelyi and Becker, 1974; Paivio and Csapo, 1973). This suggests that the subjects may have represented the pictures and the words in different formats. It is only a short leap to the position that words and sentences are represented propositionally, whereas pictures are not.

Yet the observations concerning memory for pictures and words are not conclusive. First of all, people sometimes integrate the information from pictures and words, suggesting that verbal and pictorial information is represented in a common format (Pezdek, 1977). Secondly, the level of picture recognition is not always high. When the target and the test pictures are very similar, the level of picture recognition is low (Goldstein and Chance, 1970). Third, it is difficult to compare memory for pictures and words because the target and the test pictures may be more or less similar to each other than the target and the test words. Since this methodological problem has never been resolved, many theorists have looked to studies of hemisphere specialization and visual imagery to evaluate whether verbal and visual information are represented in different ways. We now examine these studies.

Hemisphere Specialization

The human brain is divided into two roughly symmetrical halves called hemispheres. Figure 7.8a shows the left and the right hemispheres as they would appear if you looked down on a person's brain.

The two hemispheres look similar, but they appear to be specialized for particular types of processing. For example, in right-handed people, damage to the left hemisphere can produce a variety of language disorders, collectively called *aphasias*. Damage to Broca's area in the left hemisphere (see Figure 7.8b) produces *Broca's aphasia*, a disorder of ex-

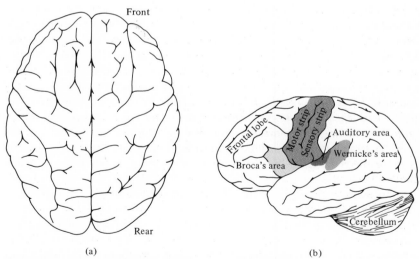

Figure 7.8   The human brain. (a) An overhead view showing that the cerebrum is divided into two hemispheres. (After Gray, 1901.) (b) The left hemisphere, which contains Broca's area and Wernicke's area. (After Zurif, 1980. Reprinted by permission of *American Scientist,* journal of Sigma Xi, The Scientific Research Society.)

pression marked by hesitation, distorted pronunciation and effortful speech, but comprehension is relatively normal. In contrast, damage to Wernicke's areas produces *Wernicke's aphasia,* a receptive disorder in which comprehension of spoken words is impaired but the patient remains fluent orally. In Wernicke's aphasia, the patients have difficulty finding the right words, and their speech seems relatively meaningless and stereotyped (Goodglass and Geschwind, 1976; Zurif, 1980).

Damage to the right hemisphere, by contrast, produces disorders not of language but of spatial organization (Gardner, 1974; Gazzaniga, 1970). For example, the patients often have difficulty orienting themselves, and they become lost easily (Benton, 1969). The patients also show deficits in copying drawings or assembling colored blocks to match presented patterns. Overall, then, for the right-handed person, the left hemisphere is specialized for processing language, and the right hemisphere is specialized for processing spatial information.

This picture gains support from studies of split-brain patients, who have had their two hemispheres disconnected surgically in order to control severe epilepsy. This is accomplished by severing the *corpus callosum,* a large mass of fibers that normally connect the hemispheres (Sperry, 1968). In order to understand the behavior of split-brain patients, we must first understand the sensory and motor connections to each hemisphere.

As shown in Figure 7.9, the connections between the cerebral hemispheres and the other parts of the body are contralateral, or opposite-sided. The left hemisphere connects with the right side of the body. For example, the left hemisphere controls and receives input from the right arm, hand, and leg. Conversely, the right hemisphere connects with the left side of the body and controls and receives input from the left arm, hand, and leg. The connections between the eye and brain also follow the contralateral pattern (see Figure 7.9). If you stare at a particular point, the light from the left side of the visual field stimulates the right half of the retinas of both eyes. Optic fibers from the right half of the retina eventually connect to the right hemisphere. So information from the left visual field will be transmitted to the right hemisphere. Just the reverse is true for the right visual field, the information from which is passed on to the left hemisphere.

In one experiment on the abilities of split-brain patients (Sperry, 1968), the patient stared at a point on a screen, and an object or the name of an object was flashed briefly on the left or the right side. When a common object such as a nut was flashed on the right side, so that the information was transmitted to the left hemisphere, the patients said they had seen a nut. But when the nut was flashed on the left, so that it was seen by only the right hemisphere, the patients said they had seen nothing. Yet they were able to retrieve the object by touch. In particular, they reached behind a screen with the left hand (which connects with the

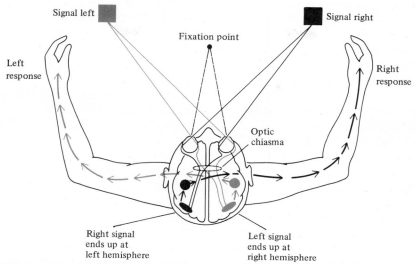

Figure 7.9   The organization of the pathways to and from the brain. The left hemisphere controls the right arm and receives input from the right side of the visual field. The right hemisphere controls the left arm and receives input from the left side of the visual field. (From Lindsay and Norman, 1972.)

right hemisphere) and chose the nut by touch from a group of objects. Thus the right hemisphere was neither blind nor dumb, but it lacked the ability to control speech as the left hemisphere did.

The most intriguing result from the object retrieval test was that neither hemisphere knew what the other was doing. For example, when the patients retrieved the unseen objects using the left hand, they could not say what they had retrieved. In fact, they denied being able to use the left hand at all. Apparently, the left hemisphere lacked access to the actions and the abilities of the right hemisphere. When the experimenter pointed out to the patients that they had retrieved objects with the left hand even though they had said they could not use it, the patients replied "Well, I was just guessing," or "Well, I must have done it unconsciously" (Sperry, 1968). It was as if two independent persons inhabited the same skull!

Tests of the ability of the right hemisphere in split-brain patients have shown that the right hemisphere processes spatial information very well. In one experiment (Zaidel and Sperry, 1973), patients viewed a pattern that had a piece missing. They reached behind a screen and touched three plates, each of which contained a pattern that could be felt. The patients' task was to choose the design that would complete the visual pattern. The results were that the patients performed this task much better with the left hand than with the right hand. Therefore, the right hemisphere outperformed the left hemisphere on this task. Along similar lines, the patients reproduced three-dimensional drawings as well after the operation as before it, so long as they used the left hand. The operation impaired the ability to draw the figures right-handed, even though the patients continued to write well right-handed (Gazzaniga, 1967).

Collectively, these observations suggest that the right hemisphere is specialized for processing spatial information and spatial relations, whereas the left hemisphere is specialized for processing language and verbal information (Nebes, 1974). Yet the picture is more complicated than these observations imply. For one thing, the patients can spell words presented to only the right hemisphere, so the right hemisphere does have some capacity for language (Searleman, 1977; Sperry, 1968). Because hemisphere specialization is not complete but is a matter of degree, it may be more appropriate to think of the split-brain results in terms of cerebral dominance (Kinsbourne, 1978). Another complication is that the split-brain patients had a history of severe epilepsy, and it is not known whether the epilepsy had altered the normal brain function. For our purposes, however, the key point is that there may be two processing systems that use different kinds of representations, though much more research is required to resolve the issue. In the following section, we examine studies of visual imagery, which have had the greatest bearing on the question whether people form and use different kinds of representations.

Images and Analog Representation

In performing everyday tasks, many people form visual images. For example, if a student asked you how to get to the student union or campus center, you might construct an image or mental map of your college campus and use that image to give the correct verbal instructions. Introspectively, our images seem to resemble or mirror the objects they represent. For example, the two-storied student union building on a campus might be located 50 meters from a lake on the left and 20 meters from a four-storied administration building on the right. Your image of this scene could preserve much of the spatial, visual information present in the actual physical layout. In your image, the student union building might appear half as large as and to the left of the administration building. Similarly, the student union might appear to be farther from the lake than from the administration building. Thus the image preserves the spatial relations that are present in the external scene.

Because our images resemble the objects they represent, many theorists believe that images are analog representations (Kosslyn, 1975;

Kosslyn and Pomerantz, 1977; Paivio, 1978). An *analog representation* is one that mirrors or is analogous to the things that are represented. The difference between analog and propositional representations can be illustrated by a simple example. If a letter was sitting on top of a box, the scene could be represented partially by the proposition ABOVE (LETTER, BOX). Needless to say, this propositional representation does not resemble the physical scene. In contrast, an analog representation, for example, a photograph of the scene, does resemble the physical scene.

Does this mean that visual images are pictures in the head? Not necessarily. When we imagine a yellow tennis ball, we do not have a yellow image or picture inside the brain. Similarly, when we say we have an image of a large ball on the left of a small ball, we do not mean that we have corresponding large and small pictures of balls inside our heads. What we mean is that our internal representations of the balls are like those we construct when we perceive the corresponding physical scene (Kosslyn and Pomerantz, 1977). On this view, images are analogous to perceptions, and both involve analog representations.

This position has two testable implications. First, our images should have many of the properties that perceived objects have—shape, size, detail, and so on. It may seem obvious that images have these properties. But because introspections can be misleading and unreliable, the properties of images must be determined through experimentation. Second, people should process and manipulate imagined and perceived objects in a similar manner. We now examine some studies pertaining to both points.

SPATIAL AND VISUAL INFORMATION IN IMAGES

Shepard and Chipman (1970) asked people to judge the similarity of 15 states of the United States. In one condition, the subjects viewed outlines of the states, so they could perform the task by making perceptual comparisons. In another condition, only the names of the states were presented, so the subjects should have made the comparisons via imagery. Interestingly, performance in the two conditions was highly similar. Sophisticated scaling procedures showed that in both conditions, the subjects based their judgments on features such as horizontal versus vertical elongation and rectangular versus irregular borders. Further, the subjects who had heard only the names of the states said they had performed the task by forming visual images of the states and comparing them. Taken together, these observations suggest that perceiving and imagining are similar activities and that the representations underlying both contain spatial information.

The idea that images contain visual information gains support from an experiment by Brooks (1967, 1968). As mentioned previously, people are better at dividing their attention between an auditory and a visual

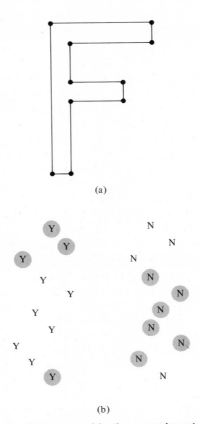

(a)

(b)

Figure 7.10 The stimuli presented in the experiment by Brooks. (a) The letter which the subjects imagined and scanned. (b) The Ys and Ns that the subjects pointed to in the visual condition. The circles indicate the correct sequence of responses. (From Brooks, 1968. Copyright 1968 Canadian Psychological Association, reprinted by permission.)

task than between two visual tasks. It is as if two visual tasks compete for limited visual resources. If visual images include visual information, then it should be difficult to process the image while performing another visual task simultaneously. Brooks tested this hypothesis by showing people a picture of the letter *F* (see Figure 7.10a) and asking them to form a visual image of it. Then the letter was withdrawn and the subjects were asked to scan the imagined letter from the lower lefthand corner in a clockwise direction. The task was to respond "Yes" if the corner was on either the top or the bottom of the figure and to respond "No" otherwise. In the verbal condition, the subjects responded verbally by saying "Yes" or "No." In the visual condition, the subjects responded by pointing to either a Y ("Yes") or an N ("No"), as shown in Figure 7.10b. If the first response were "Yes," then the subject pointed to a Y in the first row; if the second response were "Yes," the subject pointed to a Y in the second row, and so on.

The results were that the subjects in the visual condition took over twice as long to perform this task as subjects in the verbal condition. So it appears to be more difficult to scan a visual image while performing another visual task (pointing) than to scan a visual image while performing a verbal task.

Brooks obtained further support for this view by performing a second experiment in which the subjects memorized a sentence, for example, *A bird in the hand is not in the bush.* The subjects' task was to go through the sentence mentally and respond "Yes" if a word were a noun and "No" if it were not a noun. Because this is a verbal task, performance should have been disrupted more by the simultaneous performance of another verbal task than by the execution of a visual task. As in the first experiment, the subjects in the verbal conditions responded by saying "Yes" or "No," and the subjects in the visual condition responded by pointing to Ys or Ns. The results of this experiment were exactly the opposite of the first experiment: performance was faster in the visual condition than in the verbal condition. Thus, maximum interference occurred when both tasks required verbal processing (the second experiment) or when both required visual processing (the first experiment). For this reason, the interference is said to be modality-specific.

We may conclude that the greater disruption of the image-scanning task by the pointing response did not reflect the greater difficulty of the pointing response. The pointing task disrupted performance on the image-scanning task because both tasks required visual processing. In particular, the pointing task required the perception of visual information from the external environment, whereas the image-scanning task required the processing of stored visual information. The spatial and visual information used in both tasks must have been similar, suggesting that the mental representations used in imagining are analogous to those used in perceiving.

MENTAL ROTATION
External objects can be rotated in a smooth, continuous manner, without discrete jumps. For example, the second hand on a clock revolves around a shaft in a slow, continuous manner. And on a particular revolution, the second hand sweeps past all of the points on the face of the clock. If images resemble the external objects they represent, then it should be possible to rotate mental images continuously so that the image passes through the intermediate positions in a rotation.

Evidence on this point comes from an experiment by Shepard and Metzler (1971). In order to illustrate the procedure they used, decide as

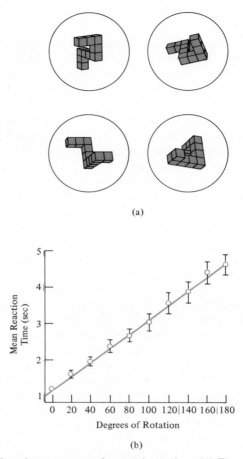

(a)

(b)

Figure 7.11   The phenomenon of mental rotation. (a) The drawings that subjects were asked to compare. (b) The effects of the degree of rotation on the reaction times. (From Shepard and Metzler, 1971. Copyright 1971 by the American Association for the Advancement of Science.)

quickly as possible whether the top pair of drawings in Figure 7.11a show the same figure. Then do the same with respect to the bottom pair. Shepard and Metzler presented many different pairs of drawings that showed objects rotated in various planes from 0° to 180°. As shown in Figure 7.11b, the greater the degree of rotation separating the two objects, the longer the reaction times were. The subjects stated that they performed the task by forming an image of one drawing and then rotating it mentally to the same position as the other. Then they compared the two objects mentally to determine whether they matched. You probably did much the same as you performed the task.

Note that there was a linear relation between the reaction times and the angular difference between the two objects in the drawings. This outcome, which has occurred in many experiments, indicates that the subjects rotated their images in a continuous manner and at a constant pace. The farther the image had to be rotated, the more time was required to make the decision. Apparently, as the subjects rotated their images between two points, for example, between 0° and 180°, the internal representations passed through the intermediate positions of 10°, 30°, and so on. Thus mental images can be rotated in the same way that physical objects can be rotated, and this applies to nonvisual images as well as to visual images (Marmor and Zaback, 1976). In this respect, images resemble the things they represent.

Overall, these and other observations suggest that images are analog representations. (Finke, 1980; Kosslyn, 1978, 1980, 1981; Kosslyn and Pomerantz, 1977; Paivio, 1978). But this does not mean that images are based entirely upon nonpropositional knowledge. In the next section, we see that images consist of both propositional and analog representations.

Images and Propositions

Pylyshyn (1973, 1978, 1980) has argued persuasively that images are based upon propositional knowledge. He pointed out that images are analyzed entities that are unlike pictures or the objects they represent. As an illustration, try forming an exact image of a particular room. Later on, visit the room and check the accuracy of your image. Chances are that your image omitted some of the items in the room. Curiously, when we forget an item, for example, a chair, we delete it from our images entirely. We do not include the top part of the item in the image and delete the bottom part. In this respect, the image is unlike a picture, for a picture can be torn in such a manner as to delete half of an item. Additionally, we sometimes remember that a particular part of the room is occupied by an item even though we cannot visualize the exact item. Some people even report that they can "see" an outline of a chair or sofa but cannot tell anything about its color or its texture.

These observations suggest that your image of the room is based upon an abstract description, not upon a picture-like representation of the room. The description can be represented by propositions such as BESIDE (CHAIR, TABLE) and ON (BOOK, SHELF). Of course, it would take many propositions to describe an entire room and its contents, and we need not dwell on the exact form of the representation. But the idea that images are based on propositional representations makes sense in light of the nonpictorial characteristics of images. For example, one or several missing propositions could lead to the deletion of an entire object from an image. And propositions could indicate that a location was occupied by an item even if we were unable to picture the item.

Thus images may be based upon abstract, propositional descriptions that bear little resemblance to the objects they represent. For this reason, it is probably incorrect to assume that images are stored in memory as little pictures or as raw sensory data that must be interpreted. Most likely, memory contains already analyzed propositions.

A related point is that in forming images, we use our world knowledge, which many theorists believe is represented in propositional form. As an illustration, imagine a bear wearing running shoes sprinting two-legged up Heartbreak Hill during the Boston Marathon. This image could not have been stored as a picture in memory since you have never witnessed such a ludicrous event. Rather, you have to construct the image by using your knowledge of how a bear is built, of how one runs up a hill, of where runners wear their running shoes, and so on. This is just the kind of knowledge that Pylyshyn and Anderson and Bower argue is represented propositionally.

Pylyshyn also contended that the properties of the images that we introspect on do not influence performance. Because images are constructed from underlying propositions, the effects of forming images must be explained in terms of the mechanisms that generate the propositions and construct the images. On this account, we cannot explain the effects of forming interactive images on memory by saying "Because the subjects visualized the two items interacting, memory of the items was facilitated." Rather, we must specify the propositions and the processing mechanisms that were used to construct the interactive image in the first place. Essentially, this view asserts that our mental images are epiphenomena, surface manifestations of underlying processes. An image may be like the whistle of a train: we hear the whistle as the train passes, but the whistle does not cause the train to move. Similarly, we may "see" an image when we remember items well, but that image may not cause us to remember the items well.

Using arguments such as these, Pylyshyn contended that images are based upon propositional representations. He supplemented his position by pointing out the power and the efficiency of propositional representations and by noting that computer models of images have used propositional representations successfully. He concluded that there is one fundamental form of representation, propositional in form.

A RAPPROCHEMENT

Understandably, Pylyshyn's position ignited a controversy about whether all knowledge is propositional or whether we use both propositional and analog representations. This controversy is unresolved at present, partly because too little is known about the exact differences between the two kinds of representations (Kolers and Smythe, 1979). But the controversy may be unnecessary since analog and propositional representations may complement each other. For example, one computer model (Kosslyn and Schwartz, 1977; also see Kosslyn, 1980) has incorporated both analog and propositional representations. In this model, propositional knowledge is combined with perceptual and spatial information to generate a two-dimensional image like that which appears on a television screen. The image is constructed from propositional knowledge, but it has analog properties since it resembles the objects it represents.

The model asserts that images are not mere epiphenomena, for they have emergent properties that are not readily apparent in the underlying propositions. As an example, two different sets of propositions could be used to generate images of two different houses. Consider what might occur if someone asked "Which house is prettier?" Answering this question requires a holistic comparison of the houses; a proposition-by-proposition evaluation of the sizes of the windows, the designs of the doors, and the colors of the walls will not do. The best way to answer the question is to imagine the two houses side by side and to evaluate the overall appearances of the two. The overall appearance of a house is an emergent property that is not conveyed by the propositions that were used to form the image of the house. The model assumes that images are functional since it performs operations such as scanning and rotating directly on the images, just as we seem to do introspectively. Thus the model can perform some activities by processing analog representations, though the analog representations are constructed from underlying propositional representations. Overall, the model shows that propositional and analog representations may be used in a complementary manner and that images are the basis of some holistic processing.

ARE IMAGES FUNCTIONAL?

If images are functional, then performance should be influenced by the perceptible features of images. This view has been tested in many experiments (Kosslyn, 1980; Kosslyn and Pomerantz, 1977; Paivio, 1978; Pinker, 1980). Kosslyn (1975) had people imagine animals in various sizes. For example, a large image of a cat was induced by telling the subjects to imagine the cat next to a fly. A small image of a cat was induced by having the subjects imagine the cat beside an elephant. The subjects formed a large or small image and then heard the name of a feature, for example, *claws*. Their task was to indicate quickly whether the feature was appropriate to the cat. If the task were performed solely by accessing abstract propositions such as HAS (CAT, CLAWS), then the size of the imagined cat should not have influenced performance.

The results were that the smaller the image was, the more time was required to imagine the named features of the animal. Apparently, it took longer to scan the details of a small image than those of a large image. The subjects stated that they examined the small images by zooming in on the relevant part of the animal. This operation seemed to have provided the detail needed to make the decision, but it also used up time. According to this account, the subjects made their decisions by examining the perceptible parts of the image.

Other investigators have reported similar observations. For example, Keenan and Moore (1979) had subjects imagine scenes that described an object as either concealed or unconcealed. In Sentence 1, the coin is concealed, whereas in Sentence 2, the coin is unconcealed.

1. Deep inside the pitch-dark barrel of the cannon, there is a rare coin.
2. On top of the cannon, glittering in the sunlight, there is a rare coin.

The subjects imagined scenes such as these after receiving instructions to imagine the scenes exactly as described and to avoid seeing the coin through the cannon. In an unannounced test of memory, the subjects recalled the unconcealed objects, which they could see in their images, better than the concealed objects. Thus seeing objects in an image has effects that cannot be attributed entirely to the processing of abstract propositions.

We may conclude that people use both propositional and analog representations and that analog representations may be constructed from propositional representations. Instead of asking which representation is more fundamental, perhaps we should ask which conditions favor the use of which kind of representation.

• *Summary.* Our cognitive activities are based upon both episodic and semantic knowledge. Episodic knowledge is autobiographical and includes memories of events and episodes that occurred at a particular time and place. For example, the memory of what was served at dinner last night is episodic in nature. Semantic or world knowledge includes factual, conceptual, and linguistic information that is not tied to a particular context. Semantic knowledge includes, among other things, the definition of words and our knowledge of concepts such as causation and gravity. The distinction between episodic and semantic information has stimulated research into everyday activities of reading, talking, and using conceptual knowledge to solve problems. Yet the distinction is not a sharp one. Our world knowledge is based on and evolves out of our knowledge of episodes, and there is no discrete point at which information loses its ties with contextual information. Episodic and semantic knowledge differ mainly in the degree to which they include contextual information.

Some relatively simple models of semantic memory have been put forth to explain how people make simple inferences and verify sentences such as *A canary is a bird.* In the spreading activation model, knowledge is represented in a network containing concepts and links that interconnect different concepts. The links are labelled and indicate the relationship between two connected concepts. The more closely related two concepts are, the closer together they are in the semantic network. Verification of sentences such as *A bear is an animal* occurs through a process of spreading activation. Reading the words *bear* and *animal* activates the corresponding concepts in the network, and activation spreads out from the two concepts. At some point, the paths of activation intersect, and decision processes then judge whether the sentence is true. This model accounts for the fact that people verify sentences more quickly if they contain two highly related nouns (for example, *bear* and *animal*) rather than two less closely related nouns (*bear* and *mammal*, as in *A bear is a mammal*).

A rival model, the feature-comparison model, proposes that sentences can be verified in either one or two stages. Upon reading a sentence such as *A bear is an animal,* the subject quickly compares the features of *bear* and *animal.* If the features are either highly similar or highly dissimilar, the subject makes a rapid judgment; otherwise, a second stage is executed. In the second stage, the subject compares the defining features of the two nouns. The defining features are necessary for the definition of the word, whereas characteristic features are properties that occur often but are nonessential. For the category *bird, has feathers* is a defining feature, whereas *perches in trees* is a characteristic feature since not all birds perch. The chief problem with this model is that it is unclear how to distinguish between defining and characteristic features, and little evidence supports the distinction.

One important difference between the two models is that the spreading-activation model represents relationships between concepts directly in the network, whereas the feature-comparison model computes those relationships from information about features. It is difficult to judge the extent to which knowledge is prestored or computed. Most likely, a particular bit of knowledge can be both prestored and computed, and models must take this flexibility into account.

Many theorists believe that the simple models of semantic memory are too narrow in scope and too closely tied to the sentence verification paradigm. These theorists have devised broad, global models of cognition that are expressed in the form of a computer program and are designed to comprehend complex utterances, remember prose, and so on. Many global models represent knowledge in a propositional format. A proposition is a symbolic expression that can be true or false and that designates a relationship between two or more concepts, as in BITE (DOG, BOY), which represents the meaning of the sentence *The dog bit the boy.* People seem to represent sentences and paragraphs in propositional form.

For example, the presentation of a word from a paragraph facilitates the recognition of another word if the two words are related closely in the propositional structure of the paragraph. Global models such as HAM (Human Associative Memory) use propositional representations because they are powerful enough to embody much of our knowledge and they allow for efficient processing. Additionally, propositional representations can be used to state the model in a computer program. By testing the program, theorists can decide whether the model can do what it was designed to do.

Many theorists believe that all of our knowledge is represented in a propositional form. But others contend that our knowledge of visual objects and of spatial relationships—the knowledge we use in recognizing pictures and forming visual images—is not represented propositionally. Physiological evidence indicates that the two cerebral hemispheres of the brain act as two separate processing systems. For example, damage to the left hemisphere produces language disorders, called aphasias, in a high percentage of right-handed people. Yet that damage seldom impairs spatial abilities. In contrast, damage to the right hemisphere of right-handers produces deficits in the ability to draw items, to judge spatial relationships, or to move about without getting lost. These observations, which are backed by observations concerning the behavior of split-brain patients, suggest that the two hemispheres may process different kinds of representations. In turn, this idea has fuelled the notion that propositional representation is not the only kind of representation people use.

The most convincing evidence that people use nonpropositional representations comes from studies of visual imagery. Visual images are analogous to our visual perceptions of objects: both contain visual and spatial information that can be quite detailed. Furthermore, mental images can be scanned and rotated, just as external objects can. Overall, images seem to resemble the objects that they represent. For this reason, images are believed to be based upon analog representations, which resemble the represented objects. Images are also based upon propositional representations, for we use our abstract, propositional knowledge of concepts and of spatial relations to construct images. In conclusion, then, our semantic or world knowledge consists of both propositional and analog representations.

Chapter 8
Comprehension

In talking and reading each day, we comprehend a large number of sentences. Successful comprehension is a prerequisite for effective communication, the foundation of our social interactions. For these reasons, it is important to inquire into the knowledge and the processing that enable us to comprehend.

Comprehending language requires the use of many kinds of knowledge, including syntactic, semantic, pragmatic, and world knowledge. In this chapter, we will examine the processing of these aspects of knowledge. But it is best to begin with a brief overview. Syntactic knowledge includes our knowledge of how the words and phrases within a sentence relate to one another, for example, which word is subject and which is predicate. As an illustration of the importance of our knowledge of syntax, children under 5 years of age usually fail to understand the difference between Sentences 1 and 2:

1. The wolf is happy to bite.
2. The duck is fun to bite.

Apparently, they do not understand that *wolf* is the subject in Sentence 1, whereas *duck* is the object in Sentence 2 (Cromer, 1970). Adults do understand grammatical relations such as subject and object, and they use this syntactic knowledge in reading and talking.

Semantic knowledge consists of our familiarity with the meanings of particular words and with the relationships between them. Obviously, one cannot understand a sentence containing the words *fibrillation* and *infarction* unless one knows their meaning. Further, our knowledge of the relations between words is the basis of the conceptually driven processing that occurs in talking and reading. As discussed earlier, in comprehending the sentence *The name of our planet is 'earth,'* the concept *earth* can be accessed before we actually read the word *earth*. The reason is that *name of our planet* and *earth* are closely related in meaning, and we use this knowledge of semantic relations to guide the processing of incoming information. In general, semantic knowledge is important because comprehending a sentence is a process of determining the meaning of the sentence.

Pragmatic knowledge consists of understanding how to communicate effectively. For example, we know that the sentence "Do you know what time it is?" has two meanings, literal and intended. The literal meaning concerns whether the listener knows the time. But the intended meaning is "Will you please tell me the time?" In order to comprehend the original question, we must use our knowledge that the question is really a polite request. In other words, we must infer the intention of the speaker. Our knowledge of what speakers and writers really mean, of how to ask questions politely, and of how to communicate clearly are all aspects of pragmatic knowledge, and they all influence the process of comprehension.

World knowledge also plays an important role in the comprehension of language. Consider what would happen if someone shouted from your kitchen "Jimmy has a chicken bone stuck in his throat!" You would understand not only that Jimmy had a bone lodged in his throat but also that he was in danger of choking to death and that immediate action was necessary. This understanding is based upon the world knowledge that objects lodged in the throat prevent breathing, that people can survive only a short time without breathing, that there are ways to dislodge the object, and so on. As this example illustrates, we can understand statements on many different levels (Mistler-Lachman, 1972). Achieving the deeper levels of comprehension often involves making inferences on the basis of our world knowledge.

Earlier, we used the terms semantic knowledge and world knowledge interchangeably. We abandon that practice here because the term semantic knowledge has a specialized meaning in the study of language, referring to our knowledge of the meanings of words and sentences but not to our nonlinguistic, conceptual knowledge. Therefore, our nonlinguistic, conceptual knowledge will be called world knowledge. Keeping this in mind, we begin our inquiry by examining the role of syntactic knowledge.

THE ROLE OF SYNTACTIC KNOWLEDGE

Research in the discipline of linguistics, the study of language, has clarified the nature of syntactic knowledge and has influenced the direction of psychological research into comprehension. In order to show the historical context from which contemporary theories of comprehension have emerged, we start with a discussion of the linguistic theory proposed by Noam Chomsky.

Competence and Generative Grammar

Chomsky (1957, 1965) was impressed by the fact that language speakers know much more than they can ever reveal in words. In particular, people can produce and understand a virtually infinite number of utterances in their native language. Although we are bombarded by repetitive cliches and idioms, most of the sentences we speak and hear are novel. If you were to observe carefully what you read, say, and hear for an entire day, you would find that few sentences are repeated; most have probably never been said before in identical words. Furthermore, it is easy to compose and to comprehend odd sentences that have probably never been said before. Because we can say and understand an infinite number of sentences, we are said to exhibit *linguistic creativity*. The capacity for linguistic creativity is very important. It allows us to communicate about novel events, thereby helping us to adapt to diverse and changing environments.

Linguistic creativity is important theoretically because it shows that our knowledge of language is inexhaustible. No matter how many sentences we actually say or read, we could always say or read many other sentences that we have never encountered before. Thus, our knowledge of language outstrips our use of language. As linguists put it (Chomsky, 1957), our knowledge or *linguistic competence* is greater than what can actually be revealed in our *linguistic performance*, that is, in speaking, writing or comprehending sentences. Chomsky's view, which is now widely accepted in linguistics, is that linguistic theory is concerned with linguistic knowledge or competence, not with performance. Since comprehending sentences is based partly on linguistic knowledge, some of the concepts from linguistic theory may be useful in a theory of comprehension.

The phenomenon of linguistic creativity drew attention to a significant theoretical puzzle: How is it that human beings of finite mental capacity can understand an infinite number of sentences? Chomsky's answer was that our linguistic competence includes a finite number of rules that can generate all the well–formed sentences of a language. More specifically, Chomsky proposed that a theory of linguistic competence should consist of a *generative grammar,* a set of rules for generating an infinite number of grammatical sentences. Thus, his theory of competence centered around syntactic rules for combining words to form grammatical sentences. Some important aspects of syntax are illustrated by considering phrase-structure grammar.

Phrase-Structure Grammar

Linguistic theories are based largely upon linguistic intuitions, the judgments that language users make about their language. For example, most people agree that Sentence 3 is an acceptable, well-formed English sentence, whereas 4 is not.

3. The ambiguous lecture confused the bright students.
4. The students the ambiguous confused lecture bright.

A second type of intuition concerns the groupings of words within sentences (Levelt, 1970). For example, if native speakers were asked to divide Sentence 3 into two clusters or groups that seem natural, most would probably do so as follows:

The ambiguous lecture confused the bright students.

The ambiguous lecture   confused the bright students.

Because sentences contain natural groups or constituents, they are said to have internal structure. A third type of intuition concerns ambiguous sentences. The sentence *They are visiting parents* is ambiguous in that it can be interpreted in either of two ways: *They are visiting their parents* or *They are parents who are visiting.* These intuitions about which sentences are acceptable, which are ambiguous, and about the internal structure of sentences constitute the observations that linguistic theory seeks to explain.

One model that accounts for these intuitions is called a *phrase-structure grammar.* Examining this grammar briefly will provide the foundation for discussing a more powerful type of grammar called transformational grammar. As shown in Figure 8.1, a phrase-structure grammar consists of a set of rules, and the arrow in each rule indicates that the symbol on the left can be rewritten as the symbols on the right. For example, Rule 1 stipulates that *sentence* may be rewritten as a noun phrase (*NP*) and a verb phrase (*VP*). Rule 2 specifies that the element *NP* can be rewritten as an article (*Art*), an adjective (*Adj*) and a noun (*N*). The brackets around the *Adj* element indicate that it is optional. The braces

Phrase-structure rules.

(1) Sentence (S) → Noun Phrase (NP) + Verb Phrase (VP)
(2) NP → Article (Art) + [Adjective (Adj)] + Noun (N)
(3) VP → Verb (V) + NP
(4) N → (person, man, woman . . .)
(5) V → (greeted, saw, hit . . .)
(6) Adj → (cheerful, bright, dangerous, angry . . .)
(7) Art → (the, a, that . . .)

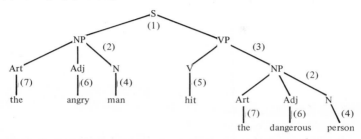

Figure 8.1   A simple phrase-structure grammar and the constituent structure of one of the sentences that it can generate. The numbers in parentheses indicate the operation of particular rules. (From Donahoe and Wessells, 1980.)

around the words in Rule 4 indicate that any of the nouns listed may be selected.

The lower portion of Figure 8.1 shows diagrammatically how the rules may be used to derive or generate an acceptable English sentence, *The angry man hit the dangerous person.* Beginning with Rule 1, S is rewritten as *NP + VP.* Applying Rule 2, the *NP* is rewritten as *Art + Adj + N.* The generation of the noun phrase is completed when Rule 7 rewrites *Art* as *the,* Rule 6 rewrites *Adj* as *angry,* and Rule 4 rewrites *N* as *man.* The derivation of the verb phrase follows a similar course. Rule 3 rewrites *VP* as *V + NP. V* is written as *hit* by Rule 5. Then the *NP* is derived in the same way described above. These same rules could be used to generate a number of other sentences. But the list of rules would have to be expanded considerably in order to generate an impressive variety of English sentences.

The rules listed in Figure 8.1 are called *phrase-structure rules* which always rewrite one element (for example, *NP* or *Adj*) as one or more different elements. By applying the appropriate rules, we derive or generate a grammatical sentence. Equally important, we describe the internal structure of the sentence, also called its *constituent structure.* The tree diagram in Figure 8.1 shows the constituent structure of one sentence. The diagram captures the observation that the sentence can be divided intuitively into two constituents: *The angry man* and *hit the dangerous person.* The grammar accounts for this intuition chiefly by assigning sentences a hierarchical structure in which the sentence is first divided or parsed into an *NP* and a *VP,* each of which is then divided further. In summary, then, this type of grammar can account for some of our intuitions about which sentences are grammatical and about the internal structure of sentences.

Phrase-structure grammars can also account for some of our intuitions regarding ambiguity. For example, we know that Sentence 5 has two different meanings, as restated in 6 and 7.

5. They are cutting boards.
6. Those boards are for cutting.
7. Those people are cutting boards.

The ambiguity arises because Sentence 5 has two different internal structures, shown in Figure 8.2. Phrase-structure grammars are useful because they can clarify ambiguities that arise from a sentence having different constituent structures.

The realization that the syntactic structure determines the meaning

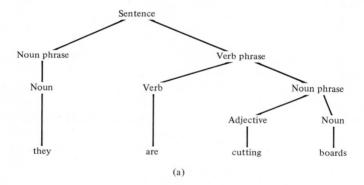

(a)

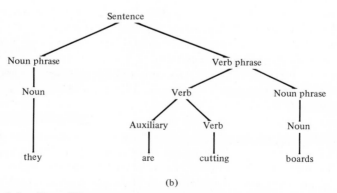

(b)

Figure 8.2   Two different constituent structures of *They are cutting boards*, an ambiguous sentence.

of a sentence has strongly influenced the study of language. For one thing, it suggests that the derivation of the sentence meaning occurs only after the syntactic structure has been analyzed. Additionally, it led Chomsky and others to believe that a viable theory of syntactic knowledge would have to be devised before an effective semantic theory could be achieved. Chomsky did not disparage the importance of semantic analyses, but he focused attention squarely on the syntactic aspects of knowledge. Another implication was that theories of linguistic knowledge that fail to describe the internal structure of sentences are seriously limited. Chomsky pointed out that associationistic theories of language which then (in the late 1950s) dominated psychology were inadequate in principle. These theories described sentences as linear sequences of associated words. For example, in Sentence 5, *They* and *are* are associated, as are *are* and *cutting,* and *cutting* and *boards.* This conception failed to describe our intuitions about the internal structure of the sentence. Presumably, knowledge of the internal structure was crucial for determining the meaning of the sentence. Chomsky's rebuttal of associationistic theories, together with his new theory of language, led many psychologists to inquire into linguistics, thereby paving the way for the evolution of psycholinguistics.

Phrase-structure grammars, despite their advantages, were thought not to provide a comprehensive theory of syntax (Chomsky, 1957). There are many linguistic intuitions that cannot be explained by phrase-structure grammars. For example, Sentences 8 through 11 are closely related.

8. The militants questioned the hostages.
9. The hostages were questioned by the militants.
10. The militants did not question the hostages.
11. Were the hostages questioned by the militants?

But sentences such as 8 and 9 have very different constituent structures, so the relations between the sentences cannot be accounted for by phrase-structure grammars. Accordingly, Chomsky (1957, 1965) proposed a more comprehensive and powerful model of syntax called *transformational grammar.* In the following section, we examine the early version of Chomsky's transformational theory because it had a strong impact on psychology.

Transformational Grammar

Chomsky proposed that sentences have two levels of structure: surface structure and deep structure. The *surface structure* corresponds to the constituent structure described above. The *deep structure* consists of the underlying grammatical relations that determine the meaning of the sentence. For example, the meaning of a sentence depends upon which word is the subject and which is the object. This information is provided by the deep structure, not by the surface structure.

The value of distinguishing between deep and surface structure can be seen by looking at Sentences 12 and 13.

12. The professor is easy to understand.
13. The professor is anxious to understand.

These sentences have similar surface or constituent structures, but they have different meanings. In Sentence 12, *professor* is the object, for it is implied that someone is trying to understand the professor. But in Sentence 13, *professor* is the subject since it is the professor who is trying to understand something. These differences are not revealed by the surface structure of the sentences, but they are revealed in the deep structures, as shown in Figure 8.3. By postulating a level of deep structure, then, it is possible to specify the differences between sentences such as 12 and 13.

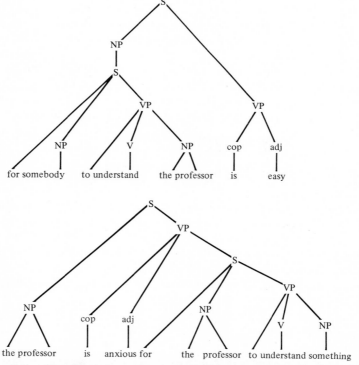

Figure 8.3 Simplified deep structures for the sentences *The professor is easy to understand* and *The professor is anxious to understand*. (From Helen S. Cairns and Charles E. Cairns, *Psycholinguistics: A cognitive view of language.* Copyright © 1976 by Holt, Rinehart and Winston. Reprinted by permission of Holt, Rinehart and Winston.)

It is at the level of deep structure that many linguistic ambiguities are resolved. For example, Sentences 14 and 15 are ambiguous.

14. Wrestling gorillas can be dangerous.
15. Changing theories can be difficult.

This type of ambiguity cannot be resolved by phrase-structure grammars since each sentence has only one constituent structure but it can be accounted for by a transformational grammar. A transformational grammar can assign sentences such as 14 two different deep structures even though the sentence has only one surface structure.

The distinction between deep and surface structure also helps to account for our intuitions about which sentences are related. Sentences 8 through 11 have different constituent or surface structures, so their similarity is not indicated by a phrase-structure grammar. But in a transformational grammar, groups of related sentences have similar deep structures, whereas unrelated sentences have different deep structures.

The notion that sentences can have similar deep structures but different surface structures implies that deep structures can be transformed and manipulated in various ways to form surface structures. In a transformational grammar, the deep structures are generated by rules like the phrase-structure rules discussed previously. Then the deep structure is transformed into one or more surface structures by *transformation rules.* Transformation rules cannot be described in detail here (see Akmajian and Heny, 1975), but a few general properties will be noted. Unlike phrase-structure rules, transformation rules rewrite strings of elements, not just single elements. Further, transformation rules perform powerful operations such as adding, deleting, and rearranging constituents.

To illustrate the features of transformation rules, consider the sentence *The playful cat broke the vase.* The deep structure that underlies this sentence includes two noun phrases and a verb:

$$\text{NP1} \quad + \quad \text{V} \quad + \quad \text{NP2}$$
$$\text{(The playful cat)} \quad \text{(broke)} \quad \text{(the vase)}$$

A similar deep structure underlies the passive version of the sentence, *The vase was broken by the playful cat.* The surface differences in the sentences occur because the deep structures are operated on by different transformation rules. For example, the passive transformation is applied in the generation of the passive sentence, not the active sentence. The passive transformation inverts the two noun phrases so that the noun phrase containing *vase* precedes the noun phrase containing *cat* in the surface structure. It also adds the preposition *by* and a form of the auxiliary verb *be* (which appears in the surface structure as *was*). Last, it adds a participial affix *en* to the verb, converting *broke* to *broken.* The passive transformation rule may be summarized as follows:

$$\text{NP1} \quad + \quad \text{V} \quad + \quad \text{NP2}$$
(the playful cat)   (broke)   (the vase)

$$\rightarrow \quad \text{NP2} \quad + \quad \text{be} \quad + \quad \text{V} \quad + \text{en} + \quad \text{by} \quad + \quad \text{NP1}$$
(the vase)   (was)   (broken)   (by)   (the playful cat)

Other transformation rules can convert the same deep structure into other surface structures, for example, *The playful cat did not break the vase* and *Did the playful cat break the vase?* Through the application of transformation rules, then, deep structures are converted into surface structures.

The theory of transformational grammar caught on in linguistics for several reasons. Chomsky showed that the theory can generate an infinite number of grammatical sentences (and no ungrammatical ones), thereby accounting for linguistic creativity. He also showed that the theory can account for our intuitions about ambiguities and the relations between groups of sentences. Perhaps most importantly, he showed that his transformational grammar applies to many different languages, not just to English. He showed that the sentences of all natural languages have both a deep and a surface structure, that all languages have transformation rules, and that the transformation rules of all languages perform the same operations (for example, deleting and rearranging elements). Thus Chomsky (1968, 1975) argued that there are universal properties of human language that reflect the innate knowledge of the human mind.

Overall, the theory of transformational grammar had much greater power, generality, and promise than its competitors had. Psychologists, recognizing that the theory might be used to construct psychological models of how people use language, soon constructed models of syntactic processing.

Syntactic Processing During Comprehension

The theory of transformational grammar had pointed out that the meaning of a sentence can be derived only after the syntactic structure of the sentence has been specified. This conception led investigators to hypothesize that during comprehension, people determine the syntactic structure of a sentence before analyzing the meaning of the sentence. This idea was implicit in the derivational theory of complexity and its offshoots, which we now consider.

THE DERIVATIONAL THEORY OF COMPLEXITY
This theory proposed a correspondence between psychological processes and the linguistic derivation or generation of a sentence. As discussed

above, it takes more rules to generate some sentences than others. The more rules it takes to generate a sentence, the greater is the derivational complexity of the sentence. According to the derivational theory of complexity, the greater the derivational complexity of a sentence, the more difficult comprehension will be. In this view, each rule involved in the derivation of a sentence by a grammar maps onto a psychological operation that occurs in processing the sentence.

In the initial theory of transformational grammar, active, affirmative, declarative sentences were converted into passive form by the passive transformation. Similarly, active sentences were converted into passive, negative form by the application of two transformations: the passive transformation and the negative transformation. According to the derivational theory of complexity, it should take longer to perform two transformations than only one. Miller, McKean, and Slobin (cited in Miller, 1962) tested this theory by presenting lists of sentences, as shown in Table 8.1. The subjects' task was to match the sentences in the left-hand column with a particular transformation of the sentences in the right-hand column. Some subjects matched passive sentences (for example, *The child was chased by the dog*) to corresponding sentences that were both passive and negative (for example, *The child was not chased by the dog*). Other subjects matched active, affirmative sentences (for example, *The dog chased the child*) with the corresponding passives, negatives, or passive negatives.

The matching task required that the subjects read the sentence on the left, transform the sentence, and find the appropriate sentence on the right. Because Miller et al. were interested mainly in the amount of time required to transform the sentences, they included a control group. The subjects in the control group read a particular sentence in the left-hand column and searched for the identical sentence in the right-hand column. Thus control subjects did everything that the other subjects did except transform the sentences. By subtracting the time required to perform the task by the control group from the time required to perform the task by the groups that transformed the sentences, Miller et al. estimated the amount of time required to perform the various transformations. The prediction was that it would take longer to perform two transformations (for example, active to passive negative) than only one (for example, passive to passive negative).

As predicted, the subjects did take longer to perform two transformations than only one. Further, a particular transformation, for example, the negative transformation, required the same amount of time, regardless of whether the transformation was from active to active negative or from passive to passive negative. These observations supported the derivational theory of complexity, as did other observations (Clifton, Kurcz, and Jenkins, 1965; McMahon, 1963; Mehler, 1963). And they raised the hope that linguistic theory would provide the base for viable psychological models.

Before long, however, the derivational theory of complexity encountered serious problems. Some predictions of the theory were disconfirmed (Fodor and Garrett, 1966). Moreover, the effects of syntax were overshadowed by the effects of semantic factors. For example, the theory predicted that it takes longer to comprehend passive sentences than active sentences. Slobin (1966) showed that this prediction holds up under some semantic conditions but not under others.

Table 8.1 SAMPLE LISTS THAT WERE USED IN THE EXPERIMENT BY MILLER, MCKEAN, AND SLOBIN

____The old woman was warned by Joe	1. The small boy wasn't warned by John
____The small boy wasn't liked by Joe	2. The old woman wasn't warned by Jane
____The young man was liked by John	3. The young man was warned by Jane
____The old woman wasn't liked by Joe	4. The old woman wasn't warned by Joe
____The young man wasn't warned by Jane	5. The old woman was liked by John
____The small boy was liked by Jane	6. The small boy wasn't liked by John
____The young man wasn't liked by Jane	7. The young man wasn't warned by John
____The old woman was warned by Jane	8. The old woman was warned by John
____The small boy wasn't warned by Joe	9. The young man wasn't warned by Joe
____The small boy was warned by John	10. The small boy was warned by Jane
____The young man was warned by John	11. The small boy was warned by Joe
____The small boy wasn't warned by Jane	12. The small boy wasn't liked by Jane
____The small boy was liked by John	13. The young man wasn't liked by John
____The young man wasn't liked by Joe	14. The young man was liked by Jane
____The young man was warned by Joe	15. The old woman was liked by Joe
____The old woman was liked by Jane	16. The old woman wasn't liked by Jane
____The old woman wasn't liked by John	17. The small boy was liked by Joe
____The old woman wasn't warned by John	18. The young man was liked by Joe

SOURCE: From Miller, 1962. Copyright 1962 by the American Psychological Association. Reprinted by permission.

In Slobin's experiment, adults heard sentences such as 16 through 19 one at a time.

16. The dog chased the cat.
17. The cat was chased by the dog.
18. The boy washed the car.
19. The car was washed by the boy.

After a sentence had been presented, a picture was shown. The subjects' task was to indicate as quickly as possible whether the sentence was true or false with regard to the picture. The results were that the subjects verified active sentences such as 16 faster than passive sentences such as 17. But in sentence pairs such as 18 and 19, the subjects verified the passive sentences as fast as the active sentences.

This outcome can be understood in terms of the semantic constraint called *irreversibility*. Sentence 17 is a reversible passive since the subject and the object could be reversed to produce an acceptable sentence, namely, Sentence 20.

20. The dog was chased by the cat.

In contrast, Sentence 18 is an irreversible passive, for reversing the subject and the object produces Sentence 21, which is unacceptable semantically.

21. The boy was washed by the car.

Sentence 21 violates the constraint that states that the subject that does the washing must be animate. The fact that the syntactic complexity of a sentence had an effect only for reversible sentences indicated the importance of semantic factors in sentence comprehension. This type of observation led many psychologists to emphasize and to examine the influence of semantic variables and drew attention away from the syntactic factors that were highlighted in the derivational theory of complexity.

Another blow to the derivational theory occurred when Chomsky revised his initial theory of transformational grammar. In the revised theory, passive sentences were no more complex than active sentences, thereby undermining the conceptual base for the derivational theory of complexity. For these and other reasons, psycholinguists have abandoned the derivational theory. But theories of competence may yet prove to be relevant to models of performance. In particular, the surface and the deep structures identified by competence theories may be useful in performance models, as shown in the following section.

CONSTITUENTS AND COMPREHENSION

In linguistic theory, the meaning of a sentence depends upon its syntactic structure. In keeping with this idea, some theorists have suggested that in order to comprehend a sentence, listeners must first determine its syntactic structure. Fodor and Bever (1965) proposed that people listening to a sentence segment it into its major surface structure constituents (for example, a noun phrase and a verb phrase). In one experiment (Garrett, Bever, and Fodor, 1966), this idea was tested by using a dichotic listening procedure. Sentences such as 22 and 23 were presented to one ear.

22. As a direct result of their new invention's influence/the company was given an award.
23. The retiring chairman whose methods still greatly influence the company/was given an award.

The slash marks indicate the principal breaks in the surface structure. As the subjects listened to a sentence with one ear, a click was presented to the other ear. The click was presented at the same time the subjects heard "the company" in the other ear and this was true for both sentences. Objectively, the click was located at the midpoint of "the company." After the subjects had listened to each sentence and click, they recalled the sentence and indicated the exact point at which they had heard the click.

The subjects sometimes identified the actual click location correctly, but when they erred, they did so in the direction of the constituent boundary. Subjects tended to locate the click in Sentence 22 between *influence* and *the*, right at the boundary of the major constituents. Having heard Sentence 23, the subjects tended to locate the click between *company* and *was*, at the major constituent boundary. The difference in click placement for 22 and 23 did not result from differences in the rhythm and the pronunciation of the two sentences. By means of tape splicing, the two sentences had been made acoustically identical from the word *influence* on. So the errors of displacement depended upon the surface structure of the sentence. In a related experiment, Fodor and Bever (1965) showed that the subjects located the clicks more accurately when they occurred at the major syntactic boundary than when they occurred just before or after the boundary.

These results were explained in terms of constituent segmentation. Fodor and Bever suggested that the subjects processed the sentences in large units that corresponded to the surface constituents of the sentences. These units have a gestalt-like, unitary character and resist interruption from external sources. In this view, each major syntactic clause was processed as a whole. When a click came just before the constituent boundary, the subjects did not attend to it immediately. Rather, they postponed the processing of the click until the end of the constituent had been reached. Consequently, they reported (erroneously) having heard the click at the break between the constituents. When the click occurred at the constituent boundary, it did not disrupt a syntactic unit and was therefore placed accurately.

It is uncertain whether the click displacement effect described above depends upon the deep structure segmentation of the sentence. In one experiment (Bever, Lackner, and Kirk, 1969), clicks were presented at or near the boundary between the clauses in the deep structure of sentences. When the break between the surface constituents coincided with the break at the level of deep structure subjects tended to locate the clicks at the boundary even when the clicks had actually occurred only near the boundary. When the deep structure did not correspond to the surface structure, the subjects misplaced the clicks toward the deep structure boundaries. This suggests that the subjects had been processing units that corresponded to deep structure clauses, not surface structure clauses. However, this view has been challenged on the grounds that the deep structure breaks proposed by Bever et al. were in fact surface structure breaks (Chapin, Smith, and Abrahamson, 1972). This controversy cannot be resolved until linguists have agreed on the exact locations of boundaries in the deep structures of sentences.

The click displacement studies are difficult to interpret for several reasons. The studies discussed so far were designed to identify the units of processing that people use in perceiving and comprehending sentences, but they measured what happened after the sentence had been comprehended. The subjects first recalled the sentence and then located the point at which they had heard the click. Thus, the processing of clauses as units may have occurred at the time of recall, not during initial comprehension. This possibility has been tested by leading subjects to expect to hear a click and then not presenting it. The result was that the subjects tended to say they had heard clicks at the constituent boundaries (Ladefoged, 1967; Reber, 1973). Apparently, they were biased towards reporting that the clicks had occurred at the constituent boundary. So the fact that the subjects had located the clicks at the boundaries in the studies described above may say little about how comprehension occurs. Similar problems of determining which effects occur strictly at the time of comprehension pervade many of the procedures that have been used to study syntactic processing (cf. Levelt, 1978).

What is needed is a method of measuring what happens as the subjects are actually listening to the sentences. Fortunately, such methods are available. For example, Holmes and Forster (1970) had subjects push a button as quickly as possible when they heard a click while listening to a sentence. They observed that the subjects responded faster when the clicks occurred at the break in the surface structure than when the clicks occurred at other points. Similar results have been obtained in studies that used very different procedures (Flores d'Arcais, 1978). Despite the methodological problems, then, the available evidence suggests that under some conditions people do analyze syntactic constituents during comprehension.

SYNTACTIC CUES AND STRATEGIES

People probably use a variety of cues to identify the syntactic constituents of sentences (Bever, 1970; Fodor, Garrett, and Bever, 1968; Kimball, 1973). In English, words such as *to* signal the beginning of a prepositional phrase, and *who* and *that* mark the beginning of a new clause. One comprehension strategy is to begin processing a new constituent whenever one of these signal words is encountered. If people use this strategy, then preventing its use should impair comprehension. Following this logic, Fodor and Garrett (1967) presented sentences such as 24 and 25.

24. The car which the man whom the lady liked owned was new.
25. The car the man the lady liked owned was new.

In Sentence 24, *which* and *whom* signal the beginning of new constituents. But Sentence 25 does not include those signal words, so it is difficult to know where one constituent ends and the next one begins. For example, *the man* in 25 could belong to the same constituent as *the car*, as in Sentence 26.

26. The car, the man, and the captive were never seen again.

Because 24 contains better cues to the constituent structure than 25, Sentence 24 should be comprehended more readily. This prediction was confirmed.

It is important to note that the inclusion of signal words does not always facilitate comprehension. As an illustration, read Sentences 27 and 28 and decide which is easier to comprehend.

27. The story he told was true.
28. The story that he told was true.

Many people find 27 easier to understand, even though in 28 the new constituent is signalled by *that.* As good writers and editors know, the word *that* sometimes increases sentence length unnecessarily and separates related phrases without simplifying comprehension.

In processing sentences, people use various strategies which are task dependent. For example, Aaronson and Scarborough (1976) had subjects read sentences word by word at a rapid pace. In the memory condition, they were told to remember the sentences verbatim. In the comprehension condition, they were told to understand the sentences. The results were that in the memory condition, the reading time per word varied according to the surface structure of the sentence: The longest reading times occurred at the constituent breaks within the sentences. But the phrase structure did not influence the reading times in the comprehension condition. Thus, the manner in which the subjects processed the sentence depended upon the type of task.

These considerations advise us to be cautious in interpreting the results of studies using only one or two types of tasks and sentences. It is all too easy to observe that people process, say, the constituent structure of sentences in one or two conditions and to conclude that processing the constituent structure is an essential aspect of the comprehension process. There is no denying that comprehension sometimes requires the analysis of syntactic structure. But it does not follow that syntactic processing is always required or that syntactic analyses invariably precede semantic analyses. As we move on, we shall see that comprehension in everyday settings is often guided by our semantic knowledge.

SEMANTICS AND PRAGMATICS

Comprehension is a process of determining meanings. By definition, someone has comprehended a sentence only if he or she can follow instructions provided by the sentence, ask an appropriate question, and so on. We often think of the meaning of a sentence as what the sentence says or conveys. This notion applies reasonably well to Sentences 29 and 30 which make a straightforward assertion that can be represented propositionally as ANNOY (SALESMAN, WOMAN).

29. The woman was annoyed by the salesman.
30. The salesman annoyed the woman.
31. It's sweltering in here.

Yet sentences can do much more than simply make assertions. For example, Sentence 31 asserts that it is very hot. But if a friend uttered this sentence upon entering your home, you would probably interpret it as a polite, indirect request to turn on a fan or to move to cooler quarters. Sentence 31 obviously has both a literal meaning and an intended meaning (Clark, 1978; Grice, 1975). The *literal meaning* is what the sentence asserts. The *intended meaning* is what the speaker intends to convey. In the preceding example, the speaker had intended to make an undemanding request that could have been worded directly in any of the following ways.

32. I'm hot; can we go out on the porch?
33. Let's go someplace cooler.
34. Could we move outside where it's not so warm?
35. Would you mind turning the fan on?

In order to understand a sentence fully, one must apprehend both the literal and the intended meaning of the sentence. Failures of understanding occur when we grasp the literal meaning but miss the intended meaning, as occurs when we misinterpret a statement intended to be a joke as serious. As mentioned earlier, we infer the intended meaning of sentences by using our pragmatic knowledge, our knowledge of how to communicate effectively. In this section, we examine the manner in which people use their semantic and pragmatic knowledge to determine the meanings of sentences.

The Role of Semantic Constraints

Language users know implicitly that there are many constraints on how words may be combined to form legal, semantically acceptable sentences. For example, you know that Sentence 36 is gibberish, that Sentence 37 contains a contradiction since infants are, by definition, very young and that Sentence 38 is anomalous because chairs cannot move of their own accord.

36. Purple road vice am light gets.
37. The infant was 80 years old.
38. The chair raced up the stairs.

Our knowledge of semantic constraints is important because it provides part of the basis for conceptually driven processing. As an illustration, read Sentences 39 and 40.

39. The doctor performed the operation.
40. The banker deposited the newspaper.

In reading 39, you probably expected to see the word *operation* or a related word before you actually read the word. This expectation, which is based on your knowledge that doctors often perform operations, guided your analysis of the sentence and probably enabled you to comprehend it quickly and easily. But in Sentence 40, the first three words lead us to expect to see the word *money*. Because that expectation was violated, you probably found Sentence 40 somewhat more difficult to comprehend. These illustrations indicate that semantic analysis is an ongoing process during comprehension.

The view that people can analyze meaning and take advantage of semantic constraints at all points within a sentence is appealing intuitively. Having heard a friend say one or two words, we often know what the friend is about to say. Nevertheless, this view conflicts with one prominent hypothesis that had originated in the early research concerning the theory of transformational grammar. The hypothesis was called the *clausal hypothesis* because it asserted that semantic processing occurred only at the breaks between the major syntactic constituents in the deep structure of the sentence (cf. Fodor, Bever, and Garrett, 1974). This hypothesis followed from the notion that a sentence or a clause could be interpreted only after its deep structure had been determined. On the clausal hypothesis, listeners analyze the syntactic structure of sentences before they process the meaning of the sentence. Further, the listeners are assumed to perform the syntactic analyses independently of the semantic analyses (cf. Forster, 1979).

Recent evidence has discredited the clausal hypothesis and supported the view that semantic constraints influence processing at all points in sentences, not just at the boundary between clauses (Marslen-Wilson, Tyler, and Seidenberg, 1978). In one experiment (Marslen-Wilson and Tyler, 1975), adults listened to sentences and simultaneously performed a semantic detection task. Each trial began with the presentation of an instruction such as CATEGORY: FISH. This indicated that the subjects were to search for a target word, in this case, the name of a fish. Then a sentence was presented aurally, and the subjects' task was to press a button as quickly as possible when they heard a target word. In the normal prose condition, the sentences were meaningful and syntactically well-formed, as in *The fisherman reeled in the struggling perch.* In the syntactic prose condition, the sentences had the appropriate syntactic form, but they were uninterpretable (as in *Fruitless climbers built perch yesterday*). The latter type of sentence lacks the semantic constraints that are inherent in normal sentences. If the subjects analyzed semantic constraints in sentences, they should have detected the semantic targets faster in the normal prose than in the syntactic prose.

This prediction was confirmed. In Figure 8.4, this effect is shown by

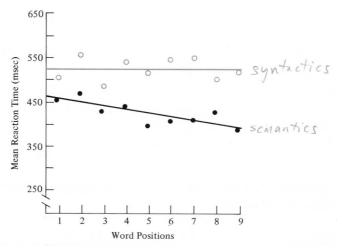

Figure 8.4   The reaction times for monitoring the semantic targets in the normal prose condition (closed circles) and the syntactic prose condition (open circles). (From Marslen-Wilson and Tyler, 1975.)

the fact that the line labelled "normal prose" lies below that labelled "syntactic prose." This outcome was not too surprising since only the normal prose sentences contained the semantic constraints that made the location of the target word predictable. What was more interesting was that the detection times in the normal prose condition were less than those in the syntactic prose condition, regardless of where the target word occurred. Even when the target word occurred as the second or third word in the sentence, performance was better in the normal prose condition. This means that performance in the normal prose condition was influenced by semantic constraints throughout the sentence, not just at major clause boundaries. Another interesting result was that the reaction times in the normal prose condition decreased as the prose passage continued. For example, the reaction times were lower when the target word occurred in position nine than when it occurred in position three. This decrease is probably due to the fact that as normal sentences continue, the degree of semantic constraint increases; there is more semantic context available at the end of a sentence than at the beginning. Consistent with this interpretation, the reaction times in the syntactic prose condition remained constant across the target positions, presumably because there was no increase in the strength of the semantic constraint.

These observations have been confirmed by the results of studies that used very different methods than that described above (cf. Marslen-Wilson et al., 1978). Collectively, these observations speak against the clausal hypothesis. Semantic processing can occur continuously during sentence comprehension. As a result, comprehension at any point in a sentence can be influenced by the prior semantic constraints, and this probably increases our speed of reading. But the semantic constraints are not always completely effective, as shown by studies of the processing of ambiguous sentences.

Resolving Ambiguity

Linguistic ambiguities arise in many everyday situations, thereby impeding effective communications. Suppose you are driving a car and you ask the passenger "Do we turn left here?" and the passenger says "Right." The word *right* is ambiguous because it could mean either that you should turn right or that left is the correct direction. This is an example of a lexical ambiguity since the ambiguity concerns the meaning of a particular word.

A second kind of ambiguity concerns entire sentences. For example, assume a novice cook had just prepared a meal for a group and was setting the food on the table. A jesting member of the group, impressed by the large quantity of food, says in a serious tone, "I doubt there's enough to go around here." The chef hesitates and blushes, realizing that the statement could have been intended either as a joke or as a reprimand. The literal meaning of the statement was clear enough, but the intended meaning was ambiguous. Accordingly, the sentence is an example of pragmatic ambiguity. In this section, we examine the manner in which people process ambiguous statements, focusing on the role of semantic context.

In our daily interactions with others, potentially ambiguous statements occur often, but we seldom notice the ambiguities. Why is this? One possibility is that most potentially ambiguous statements are in fact not ambiguous at all, owing to the context in which they occur. As a simple example, if you and a friend were watching a tennis match and your friend said "Boy, my serving has a long way to go," you would undoubtedly interpret *serving* as a part of playing tennis, not as part of providing dinner. Similarly, if someone asked "Where is the jam" during lunch, you would probably notice only the food interpretation of jam. Thus, people might access only the contextually appropriate meaning of a potentially ambiguous word or sentence. Another possibility, however, is that people momentarily access both meanings of an ambiguous word and then select the appropriate meaning by using the contextual information that is available. According to this *multiple access hypothesis*, accessing the different meanings and choosing one occur without conscious attention. Under this view, ambiguities are genuine, but they are resolved rapidly and nonconsciously.

LEXICAL AMBIGUITY AND MULTIPLE ACCESS

Evidence from several experiments has supported the multiple access hypothesis (Lackner and Garrett, 1972; Mackay, 1966, 1973). In one experiment (Swinney, 1979), subjects listened to passages that contained a potentially ambiguous word such as *bugs* (the kind that crawl or that detectives use for surveillance). In the no-context condition, illustrated in Passage 41, the semantic context of the passage did not bias the selection of either meaning of the ambiguous word. But in the biased-context condition, there were semantic constraints favoring one meaning over the other, as in Passage 42.

41. Rumor had it that, for years, the government building had been plagued with problems. The man was not surprised when he found several bugs* in the corner of his room.
42. Rumor had it that, for years, the government building had been plagued with problems. The man was not surprised when he found several spiders, roaches, and other bugs* in the corner of his room.

The question of interest was whether hearing *bug* activated both meanings of the word. The experimenters had the subjects listen to the passages and simultaneously decide quickly whether a group of letters (the target word) flashed on a screen was a legal word. This lexical decision task was designed so that one of the target words was presented just after the ambiguous word. In Passages 41 and 42, target words were presented immediately following *bugs,* as indicated by the asterisks. Some target words, for example, *sew,* were semantically unrelated to the ambiguous word in the sentence. Others were related to one meaning of the ambiguous word. For example, the target word *ant* was related to the *insect* meaning of *bug,* whereas the target word *spy* was related to the *surveillance* interpretation. If the subjects had accessed both meanings of *bug* upon hearing it, their decision as to whether *ant* or *spy* are words should have been speeded up relative to semantically unrelated words such as *sew.*

In the no-context condition, the subjects accessed both meanings of the ambiguous word, for the reaction times to both target words that were semantically related to the ambiguous word were faster than those to the semantically unrelated target word. Surprisingly, similar results occurred in the biased-context condition, even though the context of the sentence strongly favored one interpretation of the ambiguous word. This effect could have occurred because the subjects noticed that target words often followed the ambiguous word in the sentence. But this was unlikely since few noticed the time-locked relationship between the words in the sentence and the visual target words. Apparently then, the subjects accessed both meanings of the ambiguous words, regardless of the presence of a biasing semantic context.

These observations suggest that lexical access occurs automatically, without being influenced by semantic constraints. Eventually, of course, the semantic context does have an effect, and the listener chooses one interpretation of the ambiguous word. Swinney (1979) measured how long it takes listeners to resolve lexical ambiguities. Using a procedure like that of the preceding experiment, he varied the time lag between the ambiguous word in the sentence and the visual target word. When the target word followed the ambiguous word by three-quarters of a second, the listeners had already selected a single meaning of the ambiguous word. Having heard the ambiguous word facilitated the lexical decision regarding target words that were related to a particular meaning of the ambiguous word, but not to both meanings. A more detailed analysis has shown that people consider both meanings of ambiguous words for less than one-fifth second in contextually biased settings (Tanenhaus, Leiman, and Seidenberg, 1979).

As a whole, these observations suggest that people resolve lexical ambiguities in two stages. First, they momentarily access both meanings of the ambiguous word, although they are not aware of having done so.

Under this view, lexical access is an automatic process not guided by the surrounding context. In the second stage, people use the contextual information to select the appropriate meaning. This selection process occurs rapidly and consciously. Thus, the ambiguity is resolved quickly, without conscious attention, and sentence processing can then continue under the guidance of the selected semantic interpretation. If the interpretation turns out to be incorrect, the listeners must backtrack and reinterpret the ambiguous segment.

Ambiguity resolution may not always occur in the two-stage manner outlined above. In some instances, the contextual constraints may be so strong that the listener accesses only a single meaning of the potentially ambiguous word. For example, it seems highly unlikely that someone watching a baseball game computes both meanings of *bat* when she hears a nearby spectator say *This hitter has a hot bat.* In fact there is some evidence that the strength of the contextual bias determines whether one or both meanings are accessed (Foss and Jenkins, 1973; but see Mehler, Segui, and Carey, 1978). Contextual bias can be thought of as a continuum that ranges from very strong, as in the baseball example, to very weak, as in an isolated sentence fragment. Multiple access may occur chiefly in the middle and lower (weak bias) portions of the continuum.

Similarly, people might access only one meaning of a potentially ambiguous word when the other meaning is rare or unlikely from the listener's viewpoint. For example, *roast* can be interpreted either as a type of meat or as a gathering at which a group of friends lightheartedly criticize and poke fun at one member of the group. For most people, however, the latter meaning is so unlikely that they would probably not access it upon hearing *They had a roast last night,* even if the sentence were presented outside of a biased context.

Another reason for questioning the multiple access hypothesis concerns the methodology of the experiments discussed earlier. In those studies, investigators used performance on a subsidiary task (for example, the lexical decision task) to measure whether the subjects had accessed both meanings of an ambiguous word. It is possible that the subsidiary task actually induced the subjects to process both meanings. After all, the subjects sometimes had to make judgments concerning *ant* or *spy* after they had heard the word *bug.* This type of procedure could have induced the subjects to access both meanings of *bug,* whereas under everyday reading conditions, the subjects might have accessed only one meaning of *bug.* In conclusion, then, multiple access occurs under some conditions, but single access may occur under other conditions. The single access view has received some support from studies involving syntactic ambiguity.

SYNTACTIC AMBIGUITY

Logically, there are several ways of processing syntactically ambiguous sentences such as *Challenging teachers can be threatening.* One way is to use the available contextual information to select one syntactic structure without accessing the other possible structure. Another way is to compute both structures and then select that which is most appropriate to the context. This route involves multiple access. The multiple access view, like the clausal hypothesis, asserts that the listener first analyzes the syntactic structure of a clause or a sentence and then processes its meaning. Thus the multiple access hypothesis asssumes that syntactic processing proceeds independently of semantic processing. In an experiment designed to test the multiple access view (Tyler and Marslen-Wilson, 1977), subjects listened to sentences such as 43 and 44 that contained a potentially ambiguous phrase.

43. If you walk too near the runway, landing planes . . .
44. If you've been trained as a pilot, landing planes . . .

The phrase *landing planes* could mean either *planes that are landing* or *the landing of planes.* The former interpretation is favored by the context of Sentence 43, whereas the latter is favored by Sentence 44. According to the multiple access hypothesis, people who hear ambiguous sentences access both possible syntactic structures. This hypothesis was tested by presenting visually either an appropriate or an inappropriate verb following the final word in the ambiguous phrase (*planes*). *Are* is an appropriate verb for Sentence 43 since it could be used to continue the sentence. The verb *is* is inappropriate for Sentence 43 since it could not be used to continue the sentence. The subjects' task was to comprehend the sentences they heard and to repeat as quickly as possible the verb that was presented visually at the end of the ambiguous phrase. The multiple access hypothesis predicts that the subjects will compute both syntactic structures and be equally prepared to hear *is* or *are.* As a result, they should respond equally fast to both verbs.

Contrary to the multiple access hypothesis, the subjects who listened to sentences such as 43 responded faster to *are* than to *is.* And for sentences such as 44, the subjects responded faster to *is* than to *are.* So the subjects had been prepared to hear only the verb that fit in with the context provided by the first clause in the sentence. Apparently, the semantic constraints stipulated in the first clause led the subjects to compute one syntactic structure rather than another.

This single access interpretation was supported by other observations from the same experiment. With sentences containing unambiguous phrases such as *flattering remarks,* the subjects should have computed only one meaning of the phrases. In fact, they appeared to have done just that, for there was a large difference in their reaction times to appropriate and inappropriate verbs. But that difference was no greater than that which had occurred in processing the ambiguous phrases such as *landing planes*. Put simply, the subjects responded to ambiguous and unambiguous sentences in the same way. This suggests that they had computed only one syntactic structure for both kinds of sentences.

Overall, these observations agree with the view that listeners process semantic information continuously, not just at major syntactic breaks. More important, they show that the semantic context can guide syntactic processing. In the preceding experiment, the semantic constraints from one clause led the listeners to assign only one syntactic structure to the following clause, even when two structures were possible. Syntactic analyses are not always independent of semantic analyses; ongoing semantic analyses may direct syntactic analyses (Tyler et al., 1977).

This is not to say that semantic processing always guides syntactic processing. When there is little contextual information available, syntactic processing may precede and guide semantic analyses. In this view, comprehension does not invariably follow a particular path. As the syntactic, contextual, and semantic properties of the input vary, so do the activities of the listener. Ultimately, our theories must reflect the flexibility inherent in the processing that leads to comprehension.

Integration, Inference, and the Given-New Contract

When people read a book or listen to others, they determine the meaning of individual sentences by analyzing the syntactic structure and the meanings of words, phrases, and clauses. Yet this is only a small part of the overall process of comprehension. Readers must also determine how the sentences relate to one another to form a coherent message or theme. In other words, the listener must integrate the information from different but topically related sentences.

The difficulty of integrating information across sentences is all too apparent in some everyday situations. Few have been spared the frustration of listening to a speaker and understanding the individual sentences but failing utterly to understand what the speaker had been talking about. When listeners do not integrate information across sentences in the appropriate manner, they fail to discern the gist or "catch the drift" of what was said.

Discovering how listeners combine information from different sentences requires that investigators in linguistics and psychology go beyond the analysis of single sentences. This realization has stimulated inquiry into connected discourse and into the processing of prose passages. From this point onward, we shall be concerned increasingly with the comprehension of interconnected sentences and the pragmatic and world knowledge on which comprehension is based.

ARGUMENT REPETITION

The difficulty of integrating information across sentences depends partly on the structure of the message sent by the speaker. For example, comprehension occurs faster when different sentences repeat the same concept or propositional arguments than when they do not. In one study (Kintsch, Kozminsky, Streby, McKoon, and Keenan, 1975), subjects read brief passages such as 45 and 46.

> 45. The Greeks love beautiful art. When the Romans conquered the Greeks, they copied them, and thus learned to create beautiful art.
> 46. The Babylonians built a beautiful garden on a hill. They planted lovely flowers, constructed fountains, designed a pavilion for the queen's pleasure.

Passage 45 contains repeated concepts such as *the Greeks* and *the Romans;* it also includes the pronouns *they* and *them,* which refer back to *the Romans* and *the Greeks,* respectively. On the other hand, Passage 46 repeats few concepts (*they* refers back to *the Babylonians*). It took subjects less time to read and comprehend passages such as 45 than passages of equal length such as 46. Similar effects of argument repetition have been observed even when the two passages contained equal numbers of propositions and arguments (Manelis and Yekovich, 1976; Manelis, 1980).

Repeating concepts probably facilitates comprehension by decreasing the number of new concepts that must be integrated into memory. If concepts are repeated in separate sentences, it is relatively easy to integrate the information from the sentences.

These effects of structural factors arise from the listener's use of pragmatic knowledge, as is shown by this example:

> 47. The angry gardener chased the playful dogs off his plot. Waving a large stick and yelling loudly, he pursued them down to the end of the street.

In comprehending Passage 47, we integrate the information from the two sentences. The process of integrating is facilitated by the implicit repetition of the concept *gardener* in the words *his* and *he.* But how do we know that *gardener, his,* and *he* all refer to the same person? Perhaps the speaker had intended to refer to different people in the two sentences. We infer that both sentences are about the same person because we are following standard rules of communication. In most of our communicative interactions with others, we obey unstated social rules or conventions: be truthful, be informative, be relevant, be clear (Grice, 1975). Our tacit knowledge of these rules is an important part of our pragmatic knowledge. If the speaker of Passage 47 had intended to refer to different people in the two sentences, she would have violated the pragmatic rule that calls for clarity. Knowing this, and assuming that the speaker knows how to communicate clearly, we assume that *gardener, his,* and *he* all refer to the same person.

In this section, we inquire into the pragmatic knowledge that people use in communicating. We will be concerned primarily with a tacit social contract called the given-new contract (Clark and Haviland, 1977).

THE GIVEN-NEW CONTRACT

One of the chief functions of communication is to transmit new information from one person to another. In order to communicate effectively, speakers must somehow make contact with the information that the listener already knows. That already known or old information is called *given information*. Speakers must also present new information in a manner that allows the listener to recognize that the information is new. These rules of communication are summarized in the given-new contract.

> Given-New Contract: The speaker agrees (a) to use given information to refer to information she thinks the listener can uniquely identify from what he already knows and (b) to use new information to refer to information she believes to be true but is not already known to the listener. (Clark and Clark, 1977, p. 92)

Under this contract, it is the speaker's job to help the listener identify what is given and what is new in every sentence.

There are numerous devices that speakers can use to help the listeners to distinguish between the given and the new information in a sentence (Halliday, 1967). For example, in the sentence *It was Leah who was upset,* the given information is *someone was upset.* Because this information was given or implicitly assumed, it is said to be a *presupposition* of the sentence. The new information is *that someone is Leah.* The phrase *it was* marks the new information for the listener. New information can also be marked by phrases such as *the one who* as in *The one who was upset was Leah* and *what X* as in *What happened was that Leah became upset.* Quite often, however, speakers introduce new information without using obvious syntactic devices. Similarly, they do not mark the given information explicitly but assume that the reader will identify the given information by using contextual information and prior knowledge.

Looking back at Passage 47, we can see why readers interpret *he* as referring to *the gardener. He* usually refers to a previously mentioned, uniquely identifiable male. Because many gardeners are male and because *he* and *the gardener* are not far apart in the passage, the speaker assumes that the listener will infer that *he* refers to *the gardener.* If the speaker had assumed differently or had intended to refer to someone other than the gardener, then her use of the pronoun *he* would have been misleading, thereby violating the given-new contract. The key point is that the listener knows or assumes all of this, for he or she is also party to the given-new contract. Since the speaker did not do anything to identify *he* as someone other than *the gardener,* the listener infers that *he* in fact referred to *the gardener.* This simple inference allows the listener to integrate the information from the two sentences.

THE GIVEN-NEW STRATEGY

Recent research has helped clarify how listeners use their pragmatic knowledge of the given-new contract to integrate information from different sentences (cf. Clark, 1977, 1978). Listeners appear to use the procedure called the *given-new strategy* (Haviland and Clark, 1974), which includes three steps:

Step 1: Identify the given and the new information.
Step 2: Search memory for a proposition that matches the given information; call it the antecedent proposition.
Step 3: Integrate the new information into memory by adding it to the antecedent proposition.

To illustrate how this strategy works, assume that the listener has just heard these two sentences: *Someone chased Lisa. It was John who chased Lisa.* In comprehending the first sentence, the listener forms the proposition E_6 *chased Lisa*, where E_6 means "an unidentified entity." In comprehending the second sentence, the listener applies the given-new strategy. Through the first step, he divides the sentence into given and new information. The given information here is *someone (X) chased Lisa,* and the new information is $X = John.$ At Step 2, the listener searches memory for an antecedent proposition that matches the given information. He finds the antecedent proposition E_6 *chased Lisa.* At Step 3, the listener integrates the new information into the antecedent proposition by substituting *John* for E_6. As a result, he has comprehended the second sentence and has integrated the information from the two sentences into the proposition *John chased Lisa.*

The best way to understand how the given-new strategy works is to apply it to other sentences for yourself. Try applying it to the second sentence of this passage: *Someone robbed the bank. It was Tom who robbed the bank.* How the strategy applies to the second sentence is outlined in Table 8.2.

The given-new strategy may seem more like an arcane device for

Table 8.2 THE APPLICATION OF THE GIVEN-NEW STRATEGY TO *IT WAS TOM WHO ROBBED THE BANK*

Step 1: Identify the given and the new information.

Given: X robbed the bank
New: X = Tom

Step 2: Search memory for antecedent proposition containing the given information.

Antecedent: E_9 robbed the bank

Step 3: Integrate the new information by setting E_9 = Tom.

Outcome: Memory now contains the proposition *Tom robbed the bank.*

---

solving mathematical problems than a method that people use to integrate across sentences. But theorists do not assume that listeners use the strategy consciously and deliberately as in the examples above. Rather, listeners are believed to use the strategy rapidly, automatically, and without conscious attention, at least in simple situations.

Several lines of evidence show that listeners use the given-new strategy in comprehension tasks. One is that comprehension is impaired if not impossible when the strategy cannot be applied effectively. For example, if you walked up to a friend and said *The man got away,* your friend might understandably give you a puzzled look and ask *What man?* The problem is that your friend has no antecedent proposition to relate *the man* to, so he or she cannot understand what you are talking about. There would have been no problem if you had specified an antecedent, as in *A man and woman robbed our office. The man got away.* Thus, the given-new strategy allows listeners to determine the referents of the speaker's statement. When the strategy breaks down, comprehension fails, for the listener cannot determine who or what the speaker is talking about.

The view that listeners use the given-new strategy also has implications for how long it will take to comprehend a sentence. Comprehension should occur more quickly when the listener does not have to engage in an extended memory search in order to find the antecedent proposition. In one experiment (Clark and Sengul, cited in Clark, 1978), subjects read passages such as 48 and 49.

48. In one corner of the room was an upholstered chair. A broadloom rug in rose and purple colors covered the floor. Dim light from a small brass lamp cast shadows on the walls. The chair appeared to be antique.
49. A broadloom rug in rose and purple colors covered the floor.

Dim light from a small brass lamp cast shadows on the wall. In one corner of the room was an upholstered chair. The chair appeared to be an antique.

The experimenters measured how long it took subjects to read and understand the last sentence, which was the same in both passages. The passages differed in that the referent of *the chair* occurred in the first sentence of Passage 48, whereas it occurred in the penultimate sentence in 49. Since there was more distance between *the chair* and its referent in 48 than in 49, the readers should have taken more time to identify the referent of *the chair* in 48 than in 49. In fact, the subjects read and comprehended the last sentence in 49 faster than in 48.

How long it takes listeners to identify the antecedent proposition also depends on the clarity and the appropriateness of the marking of the given and the new information. An an illustration, read the following passages.

50. The ballerina captivated a musician in the orchestra during her performance. The one who the ballerina captivated was the trombonist.
51. The ballerina captivated a musician in the orchestra during her performance. The one who captivated the trombonist was the ballerina.

Passage 50 seems easy to understand; in the second sentence, the given information (the ballerina captivated a musician) is marked clearly by the phrase *the one who*. But in Passage 51, the given information is not clearly marked. In fact, the second sentence marks inappropriately the fact that the trombonist was captivated by someone as old information, but that information is actually new. As a result, Passage 51 seems difficult, and it takes people longer to comprehend than Passage 50 (Carpenter and Just, 1977). This observation is consistent with the view that listeners use the given-new strategy.

BRIDGING INFERENCES

In the examples discussed above, the application of the given-new strategy is relatively straightforward since there was an antecedent proposition in memory. Yet comprehension often occurs in situations in which there is no explicit antecedent proposition, as in Passages 52 and 53.

52. Jim accepted the award eagerly. It was the money he wanted most.
53. The robbery was most unusual. The victims laughed as they looked on.

In Passage 52, the money is marked as the given information in the second sentence. If the listeners were using the given-new strategy, they would search memory for an antecedent proposition concerning the money. But their search would fail since the money had not been mentioned previously.

Haviland and Clark proposed that in this type of situation, listeners form bridging assumptions or *implicatures* to help make the passage comprehensible. Bridging assumptions are inferred antecedent propositions that the listener can use in integrating the information from the two sentences. For example, listeners could comprehend Passage 52 by constructing the bridging assumption *the prize included money.* Using this proposition as a bridge, they can integrate the information from the two sentences. Similarly, Passage 53 lacks an explicit antecedent for *the victims,* but listeners could comprehend the passage by forming the bridging assumption *There were victims of the robbery.* The given-new strategy can be used to integrate information across sentences even when there is no explicit antecedent proposition.

Evidence on this view comes from several sources. In one experiment (Haviland et al., 1974; also see Keenan and Kintsch, 1974), subjects read one of two brief passages such as 54 and 55.

54. Esther got some beer out of the car. The beer was warm.
55. Esther got some picnic supplies out of the car. The beer was warm.

Since beer is mentioned in both sentences in Passage 54, the readers could integrate the information from the two sentences without forming bridging assumptions. On the other hand, comprehending Passage 55 requires the formation of a bridging assumption such as *the picnic supplies included beer.* Forming this bridging assumption should take time. Indeed, it took people longer to read and comprehend the second sentence of Passage 55 than of Passage 54 even though the sentence was the same in both passages. This observation suggests that the readers of 55 constructed a bridging assumption, which required extra time.

These observations indicate that comprehension is based largely on inferences. In turn, the inferences derive in part from world knowledge, for example, the knowledge that people often take beer on picnics and that robberies have victims. In the next section, we probe further into the role of world knowledge and inferences.

SCHEMA THEORY AND PROSE PROCESSING

In the daily use of language, there is a premium on being concise and stating the informative, not the obvious. As a result, much of a speaker's message is nestled between the lines and must be inferred by the listener. This indirect manner of communicating is effective in many circumstances, as is illustrated by the following paragraph.

Bill and Sheila ate lunch at a new restaurant today. They said that the lobster was superb and the prices were reasonable. The only drawback was that they had to wait over an hour to get a table.

Did either Bill or Sheila eat lobster? Examine a menu? Pay for lunch? Leave a tip? None of these events had been stated explicitly. Yet in reading the paragraph, we infer automatically that either Bill or Sheila did all of these. The inferences are based upon our world knowledge about what happens when eating at a restaurant.

Inferences often guide the process of comprehension. For example, as soon as you read the opening sentence that mentions the restaurant, you can begin using your knowledge about what happens at restaurants to look for information concerning the quality of the food, the fairness of the prices, and so on. Thus world knowledge underlies the expectations that lead to conceptually driven processing.

In order to understand comprehension, we must identify the knowledge that allows people to make inferences and to form expectations. Many investigators believe that world knowledge can be described in terms of a *schema* (pronounced skee-ma; pluralized as schemata), an organized framework of knowledge. Schema theory was advocated by Bartlett, whose work on reconstructive retrieval we have already considered. When we read a passage concerning a restaurant, we may try to fit the incoming information into our existing framework of knowledge pertaining to restaurants—our restaurant schema. Bartlett never defined clearly what a schema is, and he worried about the vagueness of the concept. But recent research in computer science has defined the schema concept explicitly, though the concept goes by many names, including scripts (Schank and Abelson, 1977), frames (Minsky, 1975), and descriptions (Norman and Bobrow, 1979). As a tribute to Bartlett, the term *schema* will be used here.

The Restaurant Schema

The nature and the use of schemata can be illustrated with the restaurant schema. This schema has been studied extensively (Schank et al., 1977) because it is relatively simple and it concerns a frequently occurring episode. Also, it embodies knowledge common to many members of our society, so it provides part of the knowledge that underlies our communications about eating out.

The restaurant schema, shown in Figure 8.5, consists of four main components: entering, ordering, eating, and leaving. Each of these components is subdivided into several other components. Each subcomponent could be broken down further. For example, leaving a tip could be broken down into the activities of reaching for one's wallet and taking

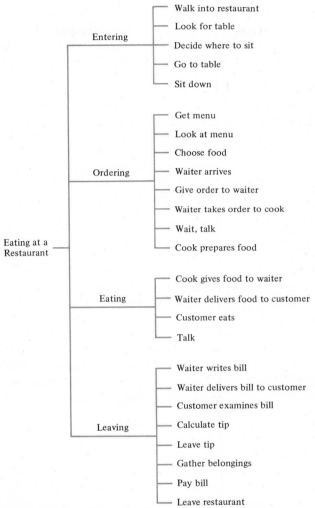

Figure 8.5 A hypothetical schema for eating at a restaurant.

out the appropriate amount of money. Thus the components in the schema can be thought of as subschemata that can be embedded within each other.

Bower, Black, and Turner (1979) have tested whether people have a common restaurant schema. If they do, then their descriptions about what happens when eating at a restaurant should agree closely. The subjects were told to list in order about 20 actions or events that occur commonly in eating at a restaurant. Eating at a restaurant could be described in many ways. Yet there was extensive agreement in the language people used to describe the event. For example, out of 730 actions mentioned by all of the subjects, only four were completely unique, and they were given by a single person. Further, particular actions, for example, *look at menu, order food,* and *pay bill* were mentioned by almost all of the subjects.

Bower et al. also tested whether people divide the restaurant schema into similar components. The subjects read a paragraph that described in detail an episode in which a person got hungry and went out to eat. The subjects were asked to divide the paragraph into units that seemed natural. Overall, the subjects showed extensive agreement about the components of the story, suggesting that they had similar schemata for eating at a restaurant.

USING THE SCHEMA

Now consider how people might use the restaurant schema in comprehending a story about someone eating out. If someone said to you "I ate at a new restaurant today," the word *restaurant* would activate your restaurant schema, thereby preparing you to hear about the quality of the food, fairness of the prices, and so on. It is as if your restaurant schema contains a number of open slots (also called variables) that correspond to the atmosphere of the restaurant, the foods that were eaten, the quality of the service, and so forth. As you listen, you fill in the open slots, incorporating the details of the particular episode into your representation of what happened at the restaurant. The result is a representation that includes both your world knowledge about what happens while eating at restaurants and episodic information about the particular event.

What happens if the speaker does not provide all of the information required to fill every slot in the listener's schema? Most likely, the listener fills these slots by assigning them typical values, which depend upon the history of the listener. If the listener lived in a society in which meals involving lobster typically cost about $15, then $15 would be used to fill the price slot. By assigning a typical value to the open slot, the listener achieves a sort of "knowledge by default." This *default knowledge* provides the basis for many inferences (Brewer and Treyens, 1981). For example, the previous description of the lunch eaten by Bill and Sheila stated that the price was reasonable, but the exact price was not specified. Under these conditions, the listener might fill the price slot with the default value of $15, thereby inferring tacitly that the meal cost approximately $15. When all of the slots have been filled, the schema is said to have been instantiated, and the comprehension process has been completed. On this account, inference plays a significant role in comprehension, and inferences are made in accord with our schemata.

ADVANTAGES OF SCHEMATA

One way to think of a schema is as a portion of a propositional network. For example, a schema for *face* can be thought of as a network of propositions concerning a face (for example, *has two eyes, has a mouth*) and their typical spatial relationships. Schemata are advantageous because they have the power of propositional representations (Rumelhart and Ortony, 1977; Schank et al. 1977). They are powerful also because they can represent global, multifaceted objects or events in a unitary manner.

A related advantage is that schemata are useful in a wide range of activities. They help, for example, to account for global analyses and conceptually driven processing in perception (Friedman, 1979; Minsky, 1975; Neisser, 1976). If you looked through some trees and saw the roof of a house, you would automatically expect to see walls, windows, and doors in a global configuration that conforms to the schema for house. Once activated, this schema can guide the processing of new information. In a sense, the house schema constitutes a tacit model that guides observations and makes predictions about what should happen next.

An important point is that as a schema is used to pick up new information, it can be modified by the incoming information. Assume, for example, that when you were 8 years old, your schema for eating at a restaurant did not include the step *leaving a tip*. As you grew older and paid a tip on numerous occasions, this step would be incorporated into your schema. Similarly, if your default value for the price of a French dinner were $10 at one time but the cost of all of your most recent French meals was $15, the default value might increase to $15. Thus schemata are dynamic and subject to change. If they were inflexible, it would be difficult to form new schemata and to modify existing ones on the basis of our experience. The ability to construct and to modify schemata contributes greatly to our ability to learn.

The Processing of Prose

This section examines the evidence concerning the importance of schemata in processing prose. In order to demonstrate the role that schemata play in comprehension, read the following paragraph.

> The procedure is actually quite simple. First you arrange things into different groups. Of course, one pile may be sufficient depending on how much there is to do. If you have to go somewhere else due to lack of facilities that is the next step, otherwise you are pretty well set. It is important not to overdo things. That is, it is better to do too few things at once than too many. In the short run, this may not seem important but complications can easily arise. A mistake can be expensive as well. At first the whole procedure will seem complicated. Soon, however, it will become just another facet of life. It is difficult to foresee any end to the necessity for this task in the immediate future, but then one can never tell. After

the procedure is completed one arranges the materials into different groups again. Then they can be put in their appropriate places. Eventually they will be used once more and the whole cycle will then have to be repeated. However, that is part of life. (Bransford and Johnson, 1973, p. 400)

You no doubt found this passage difficult to comprehend. The main problem is that the central theme is obscure. Consequently, it is difficult to activate and to apply an appropriate schema in reading the passage. The passage becomes easy to understand when you know that the topic is washing clothes. Knowing this, you can relate each statement in the passage to your existing framework of knowledge. You can verify this by rereading the passage now.

This demonstration establishes two points. First, we comprehend passages by relating incoming information to our existing frameworks of knowledge, our schemata. Comprehension is an active process of interpretation in which you use the concepts and schemata that you know already. Second, schemata are activated by particular words or by other contextual information. As you read the passage initially, your schema for washing clothes was probably not activated. But if the passage had occurred in an article about washing clothes, the schema for washing clothes would have been activated, and comprehension would have been relatively easy. So the difficulty of comprehension depends on the structure of the passage and on the availability of contextual information that activates the pertinent knowledge.

Evidence that schemata influence comprehension has come from studies involving simple stories (Rumelhart, 1977; Thorndyke, 1977). Stories ranging from novels to murder mysteries have a conventional structure. For example, consider the following story entitled *Circle Island* (Thorndyke, 1977, pp. 80–82).

(1) Circle Island is located in the middle of the Atlantic Ocean, (2) north of Ronald Island. (3) The main occupations on the island are farming and ranching. (4) Circle Island has good soil, (5) but few rivers and (6) hence a shortage of water. (7) The island is run democratically. (8) All issues are decided by a majority vote of the islanders. (9) The governing body is a senate, (10) whose job is to carry out the will of the majority. (11) Recently, an island scientist discovered a cheap method (12) of converting salt water into fresh water. (13) As a result, the island farmers wanted (14) to build a canal across the island, (15) so that they could use water from the canal (16) to cultivate the island's central region. (17) Therefore, the farmers formed a pro-canal association (18) and persuaded a few senators (19) to join. (20) The pro-canal association brought the construction idea to a vote. (21) All the islanders voted. (22) The majority voted in favor of construction. (23) The senate, however, decided that (24) the farmers' proposed canal was ecologically unsound. (25) The senators agreed (26) to build a smaller canal (27) that was two feet wide and one foot deep. (28)

After starting construction on the smaller canal, (29) the islanders discovered that (30) no water would flow into it. (31) Thus the project was abandoned. (32) The farmers were angry (33) because of the failure of the canal project. (34) Civil war appeared inevitable.

This type of story can be divided into a hierarchy of levels, as illustrated in Figure 8.6. At the broadest level, the story consists of a setting (where and when the event occurred), a theme (the main idea), a plot (what happened) and a resolution (the outcome of the story). The plot is decomposed further into a set of episodes, each of which is divided in turn into a subgoal, an attempt, and an outcome. The numbers at the bottom of the hierarchy refer to particular propositions from the story.

Thorndyke hypothesized that in reading *Circle Island*, people try to interpret the passage in terms of a schema that includes categories such as those shown in Figure 8.6. He tested this hypothesis by arranging three conditions that varied in the degree to which the structure of the passage corresponded to the schema describing the conventional story structure. In the normal story condition, the subjects read the full story, which conformed to the conventional story structure. In the late theme condition, the theme of the passage was moved from the beginning of the passage to the end. This was accomplished by moving to the end of

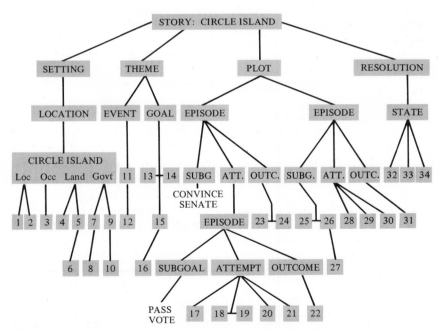

Figure 8.6   The hypothetical story structure for the Circle Island story. (From Thorndyke, 1977.)

the story the sentences explaining that the farmers were angry because they had wanted the canal in order to cultivate the central region. These sentences stated the highest level goal of the story (propositions 13 and 14 in Figure 8.6). Moving these sentences to the end of the story disrupted the normal organization that readers expect to find. In the no theme condition, those sentences were omitted from the story, thereby removing one of the chief structural elements that readers presumably look for in trying to comprehend the story. After the subjects had read a particular story, they were asked to rate how comprehensible the story was on a scale of one to ten and to recall the story verbatim.

As predicted, the passages used in the normal story condition were rated as highly comprehensible. The passages from the late theme condition received lower ratings, and the passages from the no theme condition received the lowest ratings of all. Thus the comprehensibility of a story depends on the extent to which the story conforms to the typical story organization that readers expect. This conclusion supports the view that readers use a story schema to guide comprehension.

RECALLING PROSE

Schema theories of comprehension are also supported, though indirectly, by studies of recall for prose. We saw previously that people often remember stories by reconstructing them. If people use a schema to comprehend a story, they may well use the schema to recall the story. This view is backed by several lines of evidence. For the subjects who had read the normal Circle Island story described above, the level of recall for a proposition depended upon how high that proposition was in the story hierarchy. The higher the propositions were in the hierarchy, the better recall was. This observation, called the *levels effect,* has been made in many studies (Dooling and Christiaansen, 1977; Kintsch and van Dijk, 1975; Rumelhart, 1977). According to a schema theory of retrieval, the levels effect occurs because people start retrieving at the top of the schema hierarchy and move downward in a probabilistic manner. On this account, access to the lower-level propositions depends on prior access to the higher-level propositions, so a lower-level proposition cannot be recalled better than a higher-level one. And since the retrieval of a proposition at one level does not guarantee the retrieval of the propositions beneath it, the propositions at one level are recalled better than the ones below.

If this account is valid, then no levels effect should occur when the subjects have no schema available. Recall that in the no theme condition used by Thorndyke, the story violated the conventional story schema. Consequently, the readers should not have had a schema that they could use in retrieving the story. As predicted, no levels effect occurred in the no theme condition.

Overall, the evidence from studies of comprehension and recall indicates that people use schemata in processing prose. Schema theories are interesting because they explicate the daily activities of reading and comprehending. But by the same token, schema theories face numerous challenges. How exactly are new schemata learned? Some suggestions about schema learning have been made (Anderson, Kline, and Beasley, 1979; Rumelhart et al., 1977), but the details of the learning process have not been determined. Another challenge is that schemata have not been defined clearly on an empirical level. Most of the current definitions are based ultimately on the intuition of the experimenter. This is undesirable since different investigators may have different intuitions and since schemata may include tacit knowledge that is beyond the scope of human intuition. We also need to know more about the conditions that activate particular schemata. These challenges invite further inquiries.

• *Summary.* In comprehending sentences and passages of prose, adults use their syntactic, semantic, pragmatic, and world knowledge in an interactive manner. The study of syntactic knowledge was stimulated by Chomsky's linguistic theory, the theory of transformational grammar, which concerns linguistic knowledge or competence, not performance. Chomsky proposed that linguistic knowledge consists largely of rules that can generate an infinite number of grammatical sentences. In his view, syntactic knowledge consists of phrase-structure rules and transformation rules. The phrase-structure rules produce the deep structure of a sentence, which specifies important grammatical information such as what is the subject and what is the object. The transformation rules transform the deep structure into a surface structure which corresponds roughly to what we hear. The theory of transformational grammar was important because it alerted psychologists to the importance of linguistic structures and knowledge, thereby spurring the development of the field of psycholinguistics.

Early psycholinguistic theories stressed the role of syntactic processing during comprehension. The influential clausal hypothesis stated that listeners decompose sentences into the syntactic units or clauses that had been specified by the theory of transformational grammar. This hypothesis also proposed that listeners process meaning only at the major syntactic breaks in the sentence and that they process meaning and syntax independently. Some evidence has supported the view that listeners decompose sentences into major syntactic clauses. But semantic processing can occur throughout the entire sentence, not just at the clausal boundaries. Additionally, semantic analyses can guide syntactic analyses, so those two kinds of analysis are not independent. Contemporary theories recognize that people process syntactic information in diverse ways through the use of strategies tailored to fit the task, the type of sentence, and the listener's memory capacity.

Comprehension is largely an effort after meaning, so semantic processing is of central importance. As people hear sentences, semantic knowledge and expectations can guide both syntactic and semantic processing. Knowledge of semantic constraints is essential in interpreting ambiguous words. When the semantic context is weak or moderately strong, both meanings of the ambiguous word are accessed automatically, but only for a short time and without the listener's awareness. Then a single interpretation is selected by using the available contextual information and the knowledge of semantic constraints. But lexical access may not always occur automatically, for an unequivocal context may lead to the activation of only the contextually appropriate meaning of the word. Having determined the meaning of the words and phrases in a sentence, the listener presumably constructs a propositional representation of the sentence. But the processes whereby this is achieved are unclear.

In order to comprehend a sentence, listeners must determine not only its literal meaning but also its intended meaning. Determining the speaker's intention is essential for integrating topically related information from different sentences in passages. Readers integrate information partly on the basis of their communicative or pragmatic knowledge, for example, the knowledge that the word *she* refers to an entity that had just been mentioned. Using the given-new strategy, the listener searches memory for a proposition containing the given information and then adds the new information to the memory representation. When the reader is unable to find in memory a proposition that contains the given information, he or she makes an inference that bridges the given and the new information.

The importance of world knowledge and inferences is highlighted in schema theories of comprehension. A schema is an organized framework of knowledge that describes objects, places, or episodes. A schema for eating at a restaurant, for example, describes the sequence of events that occurs in eating at a restaurant—getting a table, ordering, eating, and so on. Using the world knowledge embodied in the restaurant schema, listeners can make inferences about the events that probably occurred at a dinner that someone is talking about. For example, the schema can be used to infer that the speaker examined a menu, even though the speaker never mentioned having done so. Further, listeners use schemata to form expectations about what the speaker is about to say. Thus, schemata contribute to the conceptually driven processing thought to be fundamental for comprehension. The evidence indicates that the comprehension and the recall of prose are facilitated when the listener uses an appropriate schema.

At present, schema theory is new and has been tested more extensively in computer science than in psychology. Yet as this chapter shows, the study of comprehension has benefitted from a cross-fertilization of ideas from computer science, linguistics, and cognitive psychology—the components of an emerging discipline called cognitive science.

Chapter 9
Problem Solving and Reasoning

Each day we face many problems ranging from the simple problem of fixing flat tires to the challenging problems of science and foreign affairs. Understanding how we solve problems is crucial for two reasons. First, it is our skill in solving problems that gives human activity the flexible, intelligent quality that we esteem so highly. In order to understand human intelligence, we must probe into the process of problem solving. Second, if we understood the process of problem solving, we would be in a better position to teach people how to solve problems quickly and intelligently. The results would be improved education, job training, psychotherapy, and so on.

Broadly speaking, problems can be classified as well-defined or ill-defined. In well-defined problems, the starting point or the initial state of the problem is clear, as is the end point or the goal state of the problem. For example, the problem of preparing all of the items in a meal so that they are ready at the same time has a clear starting point—all of the items are present but unprepared. The goal state is also unambiguous—the aim is to finish preparing all of the items at about the same time. On the other hand, ill-defined problems lack clear starting points and end points. For example, the problems of writing a good novel or of creating a new form of art are ill-defined. How do we decide whether a novel is good or whether a new form of art is creative? No standard yardstick exists for measuring creativity, so it is difficult to tell whether one has succeeded in the task of creating.

Whether the problem one is working on is well-defined or ill-defined, the process of problem solving includes four steps. The first step is to define the problem, and it requires the identification of both the initial state and the goal state of the problem. In working on an ill-defined problem, this step can be of extraordinary difficulty. Scientists, inventors, and scholars from all disciplines spend many agonizing hours trying to formulate questions or problems that are important. And they will tell you that half the cognitive battle is won when the good question has been proposed.

The second step is to devise a strategy, a method or plan of attack. People use many different kinds of strategies, ranging from simplistic trial-and-error approaches to the sophisticated approaches of the scientific method and reasoning by analogy. Planning an effective strategy requires the use of knowledge about the type and the difficulty of the problem, the likelihood that particular strategies will succeed, and the characteristics of the problem solver. As a simple example, in deciding which move to make in a game of chess, you would probably not consider all of the possible moves. For the number of possible moves is usually very large, and many of them are weak. Knowing that, a reasonable strategy is to consider moving the powerful pieces first. The use of this type of strategy is based upon your knowledge of the game and on your history of successes and failures in moving chess pieces.

The third step, executing the strategy, is often a straightforward, even trivial, matter when working on simple, well-defined problems. For example, the strategy of studying for a test by reviewing class notes can be executed simply, barring trivial factors such as fatigue and momentary lapses of attention. But in working on many everyday problems, the execution of a strategy is by no means straightforward. For example, problems of foreign policy are inherently dynamic. What seems to be a reasonable execution of a policy at one moment may seem unacceptable a short time later, before earlier decisions have been carried out. Before November 4, 1979, the United States had agreed to sell weapons and military supplies to Iran in order to preserve the balance of power in the Middle East. But that policy could not be executed when the Iranians took 52 United States personnel hostage. Many ill-defined problems are inherently dynamic, and this complicates the use of even the best planned strategy.

The fourth step is to evaluate one's progress toward the goal. This requires making decisions about whether the problem has been solved, whether progress toward the goal has occurred, and whether the current strategy should be executed further or should be abandoned. These decisions are no doubt tied closely to the type of strategy that has been chosen. For example, if the solver were using a strategy of doing whatever brought her closer to the goal, then actions that led away from the goal would receive a negative evaluation and be avoided in the future. Other strategies, however, might allow taking one step backward so that two forward steps could eventually be taken. Following the latter type of strategy, actions leading away from the goal would not automatically receive a negative evaluation. But if the solver has decided that the present strategy is unworkable, then additional planning must be initiated and the early stages of the problem-solving process must be repeated. As these comments suggest, the four steps of defining the problem, planning a strategy, executing the strategy, and evaluating progress can interact extensively as problem solving occurs.

In order to understand the manner in which people execute these four steps, we must inquire into the representations used in problem solving. Our internal representations embody our semantic and world knowledge, and it is this knowledge that enables us to solve problems. The first section of this chapter examines the role of representation in solving problems ranging from anagrams to logical syllogisms.

In the second section, we analyze the strategies used to solve problems. Some of the strategies that people use are general in that they apply to many different kinds of problems. Other strategies, for example, those used to play tic-tac-toe, are task-specific since they work on only one type of problem. We shall concentrate primarily upon the general strategies that people use. Then we shall inquire into attempts to simulate human problem solving using computer programs. Computer models carry the view that people are information processors to its logical extremity. Analyzing these models will bring the assumptions of cognitive psychology into sharper focus.

THE ROLE OF REPRESENTATION

An essential part of the problem-solving process is the formation of an internal representation of the problem. As an example, consider the nine-dot problem shown in Figure 9.1. The problem is to draw exactly

Figure 9.1 The nine-dot problem is to connect all of the dots using four straight lines without lifting your pen from the page.

four straight lines so that a line passes through each point. The hard part is that the lines must be drawn without lifting the pencil off the paper; the end of one line must begin the next one. One way to solve this problem is to look at the dots and imagine drawing the four lines so as to connect all of the dots. This imaginal strategy involves constructing visual representations of the dots and the lines.

The importance of visual representations is attested to by the reports of famous scientists. Albert Einstein claimed that his discovery of space-time relativity owed partly to the insights he had while he imagined himself journeying through the universe riding on a beam of light. Similarly, Friedrich Kekulé, the discoverer of the benzene ring, reported having many spontaneous images in which atoms united to form molecules and chains thereof. In a dream one night, Kekulé saw long chains of atoms writhing in a snakelike manner. Then, "One of the snakes got hold of its own tail and the whole structure was mockingly twisting in front of my eyes." (MacKenzie, 1965, p. 135) Kekulé claimed it was this snakelike apparition which grabbed its own tail that revealed the long-sought benzene ring, one of the most fundamental molecular structures in organic chemistry.

Of course, people use representations other than imaginal ones in order to solve problems. For example, solve this simple verbal analogy: daughter : mother :: cousin : _____. In solving this analogy, you probably formed a nonvisual representation that indicated the semantic relationship between *daughter* and *mother*. So there are many ways of representing problems, and skilled problem solvers no doubt tailor their representations to fit the problem. This ability to adjust the representation to fit the task at hand arises through experience. We now examine some of the classical studies showing the effects of experience on the use of internal representations.

Functional Fixedness, Organization, and Insight

In representing objects and events, we use the world knowledge that is based largely on our prior experiences. When, for example, a pair of pliers is presented, we tend to encode the pliers as a tool used for gripping. Having represented the pliers in terms of their usual function, we may readily solve problems that require that something be gripped. But we may have trouble using the pliers in novel ways that do not involve the function of gripping.

This idea was developed in experiments by the Gestalt psychologists (Maier, 1931). In one study (Dunker, 1945), people were asked to solve the candle problem. The subjects sat at a table, on top of which were tacks, small boxes, matches, and candles. Their problem was to use the materials to mount a candle on a door in such a way that the wax would

Problem   Solution

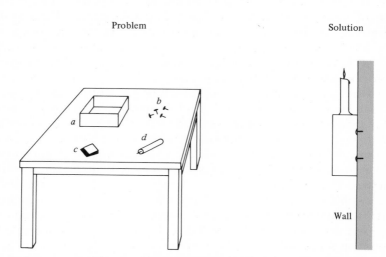

Wall

Figure 9.2   The candle problem as presented in the control condition and the solution to the problem. (From Wingfield, 1979.)

not drip onto the floor. As shown in Figure 9.2, the solution was to use the box as a platform by tacking the box to the door and mounting the candle on the box with wax. The subjects were divided into two conditions designed either to emphasize or to deemphasize the usual containing function of the boxes. In the experimental condition, the boxes were presented as containers, for they held either the candles, the matches, or the tacks. In the control condition, the boxes were presented empty alongside of the other materials.

The results were that all of the subjects in the control condition solved the problem, but less than half of the subjects in the experimental condition solved it. According to Dunker, the experimental subjects had fixated on the container function of the boxes, and they therefore failed to think of using the box as a platform for holding the candle. Stated differently, the experimental subjects formed representations that specified only the usual function of the box. These representations might enhance performance on problems that can be solved by using items in the usual way, but they can impede performance on tasks that require the use of the objects in novel ways.

REDUCING FIXEDNESS

Fortunately, *functional fixedness,* the fixation on a single function of an object, can be reduced in several ways, one of which is labelling. In an experiment similar to the preceding one, Glucksburg and Weisburg (1966) presented the box with the candles, tacks, and matches inside, and they also provided labels such as *box* and *tacks*. Labelling the box clearly facilitated the solution of the problem. The labels may have led the subjects to encode the box independently of its contents, thereby disrupting the tendency to represent the box as a container for the other materials.

Labelling, however, does not always reduce functional fixedness. Glucksburg and Danks (1968), for example, asked subjects to complete an electrical circuit for turning on a light. The subjects were given a bulb, batteries, a switch, and a screwdriver, but they were given too little wire to complete the circuit. The problem could be solved by using the metal shaft of the screwdriver instead of the missing wire as a conductor. For one group, the screwdriver was labelled as *screwdriver*, whereas for another group, the handle and the blade of the screwdriver were labelled separately. In a control condition, the screwdriver was presented without a label. The results were that labelling the handle and the blade separately facilitated performance on the problem, probably by leading the subjects to think about the handle and the blade separately, as they had to do in order to solve the problem. In contrast, labelling the entire screwdriver did not facilitate performance. The label *screwdriver* could have led the subject to encode the item as a unitary tool used to drive screws.

A follow-up experiment involved the same problem except that a wrench was substituted for the screwdriver. Here, the label *wrench* actually impaired performance. More subjects solved the problem when they referred to the wrench using a nonsense name than when they referred to it using the usual name. Overall, these observations suggest that labels influence the manner in which subjects represent the materials that can be used to solve problems. When the labels suggest only the standard function of the item, functional fixedness tends to occur. When the labels suggest novel functions or help the subjects to reorganize the materials in novel ways, functional fixedness may be reduced or even prevented.

Functional fixedness can also be reduced through nonverbal pretraining, as shown by studies of the two-string problem. In this problem, subjects are asked to tie together two strings that hang from the ceiling but are too far apart to grab simultaneously. One solution is to tie an object to one string and swing the object in the direction of the other string so that the object can be reached while holding onto the stationary string. Solving this problem requires using ordinary objects such as switches and pliers in a novel way, namely, as pendulums. Failure to solve this problem will occur if the subjects fixate on the typical function of the object. Flavell, Cooper, and Loiselle (1958; but also see Yonge, 1966) had subjects use such ordinary objects in numerous different ways before asking them to solve the two-string problem. The results were that if the subjects had used an object such as a switch in several different ways before working on the two-string problem, then they tended to use that object to solve the two-string problem. But if they had used an object in only the conventional way, then they seldom used that object to solve the two-string problem. These results show both that functional fixedness arises from prior experience and that training in novel uses can reduce functional fixedness.

ORGANIZATION, INSIGHT AND FLEXIBILITY

The early Gestalt theorists interpreted the preceding observations in terms of organization. Recall that the Gestaltists emphasized that perception is a process of actively organizing objects or elements into a coherent overall pattern. In this view, people fail to solve problems when they organize the elements of the problem in an inappropriate manner. For the subjects who tried to solve the candle problem, organizing the materials as a box plus contents probably impaired the solution of the problem, for that organization centered around the container function of the new box. This inappropriate organization tended to occur when the matches, candles, and tacks had been presented inside the box and the box had not been labelled. Thus, the manner of presenting the materials of a problem is a critical determinant of the organization achieved by the subjects. Ultimately, the Gestaltists tried to explain the effects of the mode of presentation by appealing to organizing principles, for example, the laws of proximity and similarity. Unfortunately, these laws remain too vague to have a high degree of predictive and explanatory power.

Nevertheless, the organizational view helped psychologists to go beyond relatively simple conceptions of how problem solving occurs. In the early part of the twentieth century, associationists had described problem solving as a process of trial-and-error. Wolfgang Köhler (1925), one of the foremost Gestaltists, took a more cognitive approach and emphasized the role of *insight*, a process of structuring the elements of a problem into a holistic configuration that reveals the solution to the problem. In a classic demonstration, Köhler placed a banana outside the cage of a chimp named Sultan, out of Sultan's reach. Inside the cage were two sticks, each of which was too short to reach the banana. The two sticks could, however, be fit together to make a single long stick that could be used to reach the banana. Köhler observed that Sultan initially reached outside the cage with one stick and failed to reach the banana. Later, Sultan sat holding one stick in each hand. While manipulating the two sticks, he happened to hold them in such a way that they formed a straight line. Suddenly he inserted the thin stick inside the thick one, ran to the edge of the cage, and reached the banana. Elements of trial-and-error did occur in this episode, particularly when Sultan had manipulated the two sticks initially. But when the chimp had held the sticks in a partially aligned manner, he seemed to have realized instantly how to solve the problem. It was as if he had had a flash of insight in which he had organized the sticks into a new cognitive pattern that he recognized as the solution to the problem. Virtually everyone has had the similar, pleasant experience of being rescued from endless slaving over a problem by suddenly seeing the problem in a new light and thinking "Aha! Now I've got it."

Both insight and functional fixedness point to the importance of flexible encoding processes in problem solving. If one is locked into a single representation of a problem, it is difficult to generate the alternative, perhaps novel, representations needed to solve the problem. A useful first step toward improving one's own problem-solving skills is to generate and explore several different representations of a problem in the early stages of trying to solve it. This procedure should help to prevent fixation early on and should also increase the chances that insight will occur. If you find yourself fixating on a particular representation, you might try thinking about the problem in different contexts. As we saw previously, people tend to encode a particular object in different ways in different contexts. By changing the context, then, you may devise new ways of representing the problem.

These comments, however, have greater practical than theoretical utility. At present, functional fixedness and insight describe but do not explain the observations discussed above. In order to achieve a deeper understanding of problem solving, we must identify more precisely the external conditions and the internal processes that lead to appropriate or inappropriate representations.

Syllogistic Reasoning

Deductive reasoning and problem solving are closely related topics. For one thing, people often solve problems by stating their assumptions and then reasoning out the conclusions that follow logically. In many instances, doctors observe their patients' symptoms and then deduce the probable causes of the illness from their knowledge of the origins of disease. Likewise, scientists evaluate their formal models by deducing testable propositions from their assumptions and then testing the propositions experimentally. Deduction, however, is not only a logical process but also a type of problem, the problem of reasoning correctly so that one's conclusions follow necessarily from one's premises. Solving this problem is the goal of logic, the branch of philosophy concerned with the principles for correct reasoning.

Historically, logic and psychology belonged to a single discipline aimed at determining how people think. The underlying assumption was that the laws of logic describe the principles whereby thinking occurs (cf. Henle, 1962). But this approach did not sit well with the work of Darwin and Freud, which lowered humans from the pedestal of rationality and stressed the biological determinants of thought. From this viewpoint, the laws of logic say more about how people should reason than about how they actually do reason. By analogy, the laws of logic resemble the rules for playing chess—they prescribe what is legal but do not clarify how people make legal moves and deductions. Further, the laws of logic could explain neither why people err as they do nor why people appear to be alogical at times. For these reasons, investigators began to work toward a psychological theory of reasoning. In this section, we examine some of the research on reasoning with an eye toward discerning the role of representation.

Deductive reasoning has been studied extensively in the prototypical logical task: the completion and evaluation of syllogisms. A syllogism is a simple form of argument that contains two premises and a conclusion. One example of a syllogism is as follows:

Premise 1:   All chairs are furniture.
Premise 2:   Some furniture is wooden.
Conclusion: Some chairs are wooden.

In logic and in studies of syllogistic reasoning, the two premises are assumed to be true. The problem is to decide whether the stated conclusion must be true given the premises. According to logical criteria, the conclusion of the syllogism stated above is invalid. If no conclusion is stated, the problem is to state or to identify the logical conclusion. In many experiments, the syllogisms are stated abstractly:

Premise 1:   All A are B.
Premise 2:   Some B are C.
Conclusion: Some A are C.

Note that this syllogism has the same form as that stated above, though the content of this syllogism does not include the everyday categories of *chairs* and *furniture*. Presumably, studying performance on abstract syllogisms allows researchers to examine the deductive process apart from the effects of content-induced biases. Of course, errors occur in both types of task. Analyzing these errors has helped to reveal the psychological processes involved in deduction.

ERRORS IN SYLLOGISTIC REASONING
People often err in reasoning tasks by responding on the basis of their prior knowledge and attitudes rather than on the basis of logic. As Henle (1962) put it, they fail to accept the logical task. For example, Janis and Frick (1943) asked people to evaluate syllogisms involving familiar terms such as the following:

No Bolsheviks are idealists and all Bolsheviks are Russian.
Therefore, some Russians are not idealists.

They also asked the subjects whether they personally agreed with the conclusions. The results were that the subjects misjudged approximately one-fourth of the syllogisms. More important, the subjects tended to agree with the syllogisms they had erroneously marked as valid. And they tended to disagree with the syllogisms they had erroneously marked as invalid. Apparently, then, the subjects' attitudes toward the conclusions biased their decisions.

Similar experiments (for example, Frase, 1968) have established that errors occur frequently when the content of the premises contradicts the semantic and world knowledge that people have. In everyday situations, we probably base many decisions on our prior knowledge and attitudes rather than on logic. But this is not to disparage human decision making. After all, correct decisions can often be reached without reasoning by following educated advice, our own prior experiences, and our intuitions.

Failure to accept the logical task also occurs in tasks involving abstract syllogisms. For example, people who are untrained in formal logic tend to agree with the following conclusions:

All A are B.
All B are C.
Therefore all C are A.

This conclusion does not follow necessarily, as Figure 9.3 illustrates. Each circle represents a set of items such as set A or set B. This type of representation is called a Venn diagram. The premise "All A are B" can mean either that A and B overlap entirely or that A is a subset of B. Similarly, the premise "All B are C" can mean either that B and C overlap entirely or that B is a subset of C. The two premises can be combined in four different ways, as shown at the bottom of the figure. Since A and C are identical in only one of those representations (the one on the far left), the conclusion that "All C are A" cannot be accepted.

One influential account of the preceding type of error is called the *atmosphere hypothesis* (Woodworth and Sells, 1935). This hypothesis states that the premises of a syllogism establish a context—an atmosphere—favorable for the acceptance of a particular conclusion. For example, the occurrence of the word *All* in both premises creates a favorable context or atmosphere for accepting or generating a conclusion containing *All*. In a similar manner, the occurrence of *Some* in the two premises creates an atmosphere that favors the acceptance of a conclusion containing *Some*. Indeed, many people accept the following erroneous conclusion:

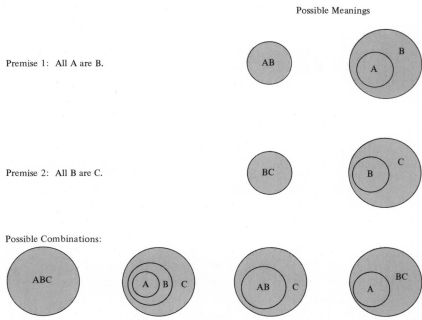

Figure 9.3   Venn diagrams in which the meanings of each statement are represented by classes symbolized by circles. Each of the first two premises has two possible representations, which may be combined in four possible ways.

Some A are B.
Some B are C.
Therefore, some A are C.

Begg and Denny (1969) summarized the atmosphere hypothesis via two principles. First, subjects tend to choose a negative conclusion when at least one premise is negative. Second, when one or both of the premises contain *Some,* the subjects tend to choose a conclusion containing *Some.* Otherwise, the subjects tend to choose a universal conclusion, one that contains *All.* This hypothesis is hardly flattering, for it proposes that people base their decisions on the overall atmosphere of the syllogism rather than the logical relations contained therein.

Luckily for us, the atmosphere hypothesis is only partially correct (Begg et al., 1969). People can be swayed by the atmosphere of an argument, but they can also evaluate the logical relations within arguments (Revlis, 1975). For example, subjects sometimes state that no valid conclusion can be drawn from a particular set of premises (Johnson-Laird and Steedman, 1978). Accordingly, they respond (correctly) "Can't say."

Because the premises cannot establish an atmosphere for "Can't say" responses, these responses must be based upon the evaluation of logical relations. Overall, then, people are neither strictly logical nor consistently alogical in making their decisions. For this reason, contemporary theories accommodate subjects' logical successes and their failures in the syllogistic task through a mixture of representational strategies and purely logical processes.

ANALYTIC REPRESENTATIONS AND SELECTIVE ENCODING

As an alternative to the atmosphere hypothesis, Chapman and Chapman (1959) proposed that errors in syllogistic reasoning stem from invalid *premise conversions.* They observed that some people converted the premise "All A are B" to "All B are A." This conversion is erroneous. For example, the fact that all cats are animals does not imply the converse, that all animals are cats. Conversion can lead to errors, as shown by subjects' decisions regarding the syllogism:

All A are B.
All B are C.
Therefore, all C are A.

This invalid conclusion will be accepted if "All A are B" is taken as implying "All B are A" and if "All B are C" is taken as implying "All C are B." Chapman and Chapman pointed out that although people sometimes err by converting the premises illicitly, they may reason correctly from their interpretations of the premises.

The essential idea in theories of premise conversion is that people err by representing and combining premises in inappropriate ways. Erikson (1974) formalized this idea in a model emphasizing analytic representations, representations that include abstracted properties and classes rather than specific class members. The model states that people represent the premises in a manner analogous to forming Venn diagrams. This representational process is selective in that the subjects do not form all of the possible representations for a particular premise. For example, the premise "Some A are B" ha~ four valid representations, illustrated in Figure 9.4. Without training in logic, however, people tend to represent "Some A are B" as the partially overlapping circles in the upper left corner of Figure 9.4. The model does not specify why people choose this particular representation, but knowledge of everyday language and of nonartificial conceptual classes probably plays a role. In ordinary conversation, the construction "Some X are Y" (for example, in "Some dogs are mongrels") is used to imply that some X are not Y (some dogs are not mongrels). When speakers want to say clearly that all X are Y, they use the universal quantifier *all* rather than the particular quantifier *some.* So it could be the prior experience in the use of ordinary language that leads

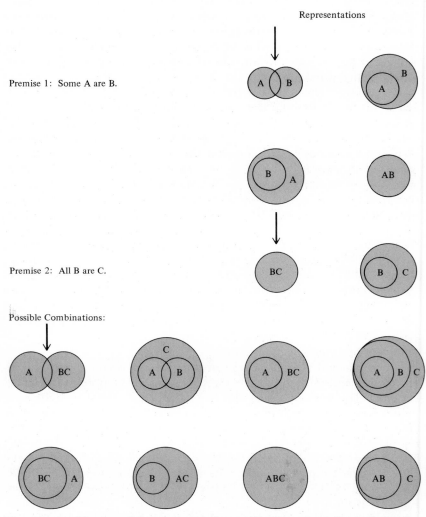

Figure 9.4 The possible representations of the premises *Some A are B* and *All B are C,* and the possible combinations of those representations. The arrows indicate the representations that people tend to construct.

subjects to represent a premise such as "Some A are B" in only one way. The important point is that selective representation does occur, and it sets the stage for the occurrence of errors.

Having represented each of the premises, the next step is to combine the premises by combining the Venn diagrams. Logically, there are eight ways of combining the different representations of the two premises. But since the subjects encoded the premises in a selective manner, they did not construct all eight of the possible combined representations listed in Figure 9.4. Assume, for example, that the subjects had represented each premise by forming only the diagrams marked by the arrows. Combining these two diagrams leads to the first diagram at the bottom of Figure 9.4. That combined representation leads to the acceptance of the conclusion "Some A are not C." Of course, the conclusion is invalid since it is inconsistent with combined representations such as the fourth one.

The model has numerous virtues. It allows for the occurrence of logical decisions following the combination of the premises. Additionally, it identifies the selective formation and combination of representations as the primary source of errors. In line with this view, the frequency of errors is reduced by presenting the premises in a manner that leads to complete representations (Ceraso and Provitera, 1971). The model has also helped to call attention to the importance of encoding processes and to identify one type of representation that people may construct. But the model is incomplete in that people do not always form analytic representations. As shown in the discussion of categorization, people also construct nonanalytic representations. Moreover, the model does not spell out how people make decisions after combining the premises. We next examine a more complete model that emphasizes the construction of nonanalytic representations.

NONANALYTIC REPRESENTATION
Traditionally, investigators examined performance on a limited number of syllogisms, many of which were invalid and were stated in terms of abstract classes such as A and B. But in everyday situations, people judge both valid and invalid arguments that include concrete, well-known categories. Additionally, research has established that people evaluate concrete syllogisms differently than abstract syllogisms (Wason and Johnson-Laird, 1972). Thus the observations made in the traditional procedures may be inadequate for developing a general theory of deductive reasoning.

Johnson-Laird and Steedman (1978) broke from the traditional procedure by presenting many different kinds of syllogisms that contained concrete, familiar categories. For example, they asked people to supply the conclusion to the following kind of syllogism.

Some musicians are professors.
All professors are intellectuals.

Therefore, some musicians are intellectuals.   (15 subjects)
Therefore, some intellectuals are musicians.   (2 subjects)

Note that both conclusions are valid but that the subjects preferred the first one overwhelmingly. This outcome was reversed when a syllogism having a different arrangement of terms was presented.

All professors are musicians.
Some intellectuals are professors.

Therefore, some intellectuals are musicians. (16 subjects)
Therefore, some musicians are intellectuals. (1 subject)

Thus the arrangement of the terms within the syllogism—the figure of the syllogism—determined the conclusions that the subjects made. This observation is called the *figural effect.*

Figural effects are important because the figure of the syllogism influenced whether the subjects generated valid conclusions. The subjects seldom erred when the valid deductions were compatible with the figure. But they made erroneous deductions as often as 80 percent of the time when the valid conclusion was incompatible with the figure.

In order to account for the figural effect, as well as for other observations concerning deduction, Johnson-Laird and Steedman put forth a four-stage model. In the first stage, the subjects form nonanalytic representations of the premises. For example, they might represent the premise *All chemists are professors* by thinking of an arbitrary number of chemists and tagging each one as a professor. This representation can be diagrammed as follows:

chemist   chemist   chemist
↓   ↓   ↓
professor   professor   professor   (professor)

The arrow stands for the *isa* relation and signifies that the imagined chemists are marked as professors. The direction of the arrows indicates that the retrieval path from *chemist* to *professor* is easy to follow, whereas going from *professor* to *chemist* is more difficult. The parenthetical item not pointed to by an arrow allows for the possibility that some professors are not chemists. This type of representation is nonanalytic since it contains individual items rather than abstracted classes or properties.

The second stage involves combining the representations of the premises. The model assumes that subjects do this by using the strategy of linking up the beginning and end items via the middle items, as shown in Figure 9.5a. The premise *All chemists are professors* is represented as before. Similarly, the premise *Some professors are geniuses* is represented by arrows leading from at least one *professor* to at least one *genius*. In the combined representation, a *chemist* is linked up with a *genius* by way of a common *professor*.

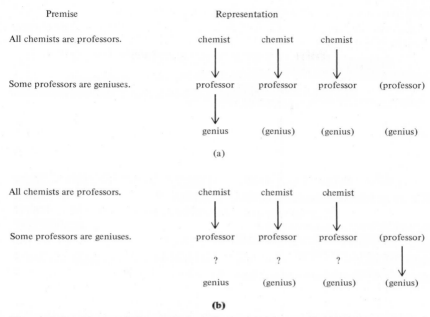

Figure 9.5   Nonanalytic representations used in a syllogistic reasoning task. (a) The initial representation of the premises at the end of stage two. (b) The revised representation constructed by applying the logical tests.

The third stage involves using the combined representations to generate a conclusion. This is accomplished by searching the paths between the top and the bottom items and marking whether those items connect. Searching the representation in Figure 9.5a indicates that a path connects from a *chemist* to a *professor* to a *genius*. Thus this representation leads to the erroneous conclusion that *Some chemists are geniuses.* In fact, 12 out of 20 subjects actually made this type of invalid conclusion. This representation also influences the form of the conclusion. Since the paths all lead in the direction of *chemist* to *genius,* the subjects tend to state the conclusion as *Some chemists are geniuses* rather than *Some geniuses are chemists.* So the form of the combined representation is responsible for the figural effects described earlier.

Genuine logic enters in the fourth stage, at which the subjects attempt to falsify the conclusion made at stage three. They do so by evaluating possible pathways they had not formed earlier. For example, the subjects might examine the representation in Figure 9.5a and notice that the *geniuses* could be linked with the *professors* that are not connected to the *chemists.* If so, they would modify the representation, as shown in Figure 9.5b. The question marks indicate uncertainty about the existence of a particular path. The new representation reveals that the conclusion based on the initial representation is false and that no valid conclusion can be reached.

This model is advantageous because it specifies some of the strategies used to represent premises and to test their representations. Equally important, the model does a better job than its rivals of accounting for the existing data on syllogistic reasoning. Yet the model is best seen as a working conceptualization, not as a finished theory, for it does not specify the exact conditions under which the logical tests are made and evaluated. Nevertheless, the model recognizes the importance of nonanalytic representation in reasoning.

Overall, the data from studies of reasoning indicate that deductions can be based on several kinds of representation. As was true in the case of categorization, people may use both analytical and nonanalytical strategies in complementary ways. Specifically, they may use analytic representations in processing abstract statements such as *All A are B*. But when the statements refer to easily imagined entities such as professors, people may tend to use nonanalytic representations. Because people can and do use different representations under different conditions, theories that single out any particular representation as fundamental are ill-conceived. It remains for future research to identify which conditions lead to the use of which representations. Encouragingly, this type of research is already being conducted in the attempt to understand how people process linear orderings.

Integration in Linear Orderings

A linear ordering is a series of items arranged in rank order along a single dimension. An example of a problem in linear ordering is the three-term series problem:

> Bill is taller than Joe.
> Joe is taller than Tom.
> Is Bill taller than Tom?

The people named in this problem can be ordered as Bill > Joe > Tom.

Conceivably, people could solve this problem logically by making the transitive inference that since Bill > Joe, and since Joe > Tom, therefore Bill > Tom. In fact, however, people seem to solve the problem in other ways. Many people say that they form an image in which the names are ordered Bill - Joe - Tom in either a vertical or horizontal dimension (Desoto, London, and Handel, 1965; Hunter, 1957). In order to determine whether Bill is taller than Tom, the subjects scan their images and see whether Bill is above Tom (or to his left, depending on the representation). Consistent with this view, people respond similarly to questions about imagined arrays of items as to questions about actually presented arrays of items (Huttenlocher, 1968).

People also use linguistic representations in the three-term series problem. Clark (1969) proposed that subjects represent the presented sentences in a deep structural form. He argued that sentences such as *Joe is better than Tom* are represented differently than sentences such as *Tom is worse than Joe*. The reason was that words such as *good, tall,* and *more* can be used in a neutral sense. For example, the question *How tall was Napoleon?* does not imply that Napoleon was a tall man. But the question *How short was Napoleon?* does imply that Napoleon was short. Words such as *bad, short,* and *less* cannot be used neutrally. Because they always have evaluative connotations, they are said to be *marked.* In contrast, the neutral adjectives *good, tall,* and *more* are *unmarked.* Clark argued that sentences containing unmarked adjectives are easier to represent and to retrieve than are sentences containing marked adjectives. Consequently, the theory predicts that subjects will answer questions such as *Is Joe better than Tom?* faster than questions such as *Is Tom worse than Joe?* This prediction has been confirmed. The theory also accounts for many other observations that cannot be explained readily by the imagery models.

These observations do not necessarily indicate that people use linguistic rather than imaginal representations in solving problems of linear ordering. For one thing, people probably use a combination of linguistic and imaginal representations. For example, in order to construct a useful image, one must comprehend the linguistic statement of the problem; this requires the formation of a linguistic representation. In general, people can use many kinds of representation. Some of these, for example, integrated representations, are not strictly linguistic.

Evidence concerning the formation of integrated representations comes from studies of linear orderings consisting of as many as six items (Potts, 1972, 1974; Scholz and Potts, 1974). In these experiments, people read the following kind of paragraph.

Mary is smarter than Jim, and Jim is smarter than Betty.
Betty is smarter than Tom. Tom is smarter than Alice, and Alice is smarter than Bob.

The people named in this paragraph can be arranged according to how smart they are into this linear ordering:

Mary > Jim > Betty > Tom > Alice > Bob

Following the presentation of the paragraphs, a series of test statements was presented and the subjects indicated quickly whether the statements were true. Some of the test statements included adjacent pairs, as in *Betty is smarter than Tom.* Other statements included nonadjacent or remote pairs, as in *Jim is smarter than Alice.* The results were that the subjects verified the statements containing the remote pairs faster and more accurately than the statements containing the adjacent pairs. In fact, the greater the distance between the items in the ordering, the faster the reaction times were. This outcome is called the *distance effect.*

What is surprising about this effect is that the subjects responded faster to novel test statements than to the statements that had been presented during training. The distance effect indicates that the subjects had not encoded the adjacent pairs presented during training separately and then used that information to draw inferences about the remote pairs. If the subjects had done that, they would have verified the statements containing remote pairs more slowly than the ones presented during training. After all, it takes time to make inferences. Most likely, the subjects constructed a unified representation of all of the items in the ordering during training. That holistic representation could have been an image of the entire ordering. In imagining, as in perceiving, it is easier to discriminate between distant points than between nearby points. So the distance effect arises in part from the construction of an integrated, possibly analog representation and from the comparison processes involving that representation.

Whether people construct an integrated representation of a linear ordering hinges on numerous factors. Integration tends to occur when the items are presented in the context of a paragraph but not when they are presented in a paired-associate learning procedure, in which it is not obvious that the pairs can be integrated into a common ordering (Mayer, 1979). Furthermore, subjects tend to construct an integrated ordering when the relationships between items are easily imagined but not when the relationships are abstract (Mynatt and Smith, 1977). Thus, the type of representation people form depends upon both the learning procedure and the properties of the items used in the experiment.

The type of test given also influences how subjects represent the items in the ordering. In a study by Griggs, Townes, and Keen (1979), subjects learned orderings that contained information not only about the ordinal rank of the items but also about the quantitative differences between them. For example, the subjects studied a paragraph stating that city A was 25 miles north of city B, that city B was 75 miles north of city C, and that city C was 200 miles north of city D. Then the subjects verified test statements concerning both ordinal relationships (for example, *City B is north of city C*) and quantitative relationships (for example, *City A is 100 miles north of city C*). The results were that no distance effect occurred: the subjects responded equally fast to statements about adjacent and remote cities. Apparently they had encoded individual propositions and had not constructed a single linear ordering. Very different results occurred when the test statements concerned only the ordinal relationships between the cities. Specifically, the subjects responded faster in the first two trials to the statements about adjacent cities than to those about remote cities. On the third trial, however, they did just the opposite, and a reliable distance effect occurred. It appeared, then, that the subjects learned over trials that the test statements concerned ordinal, not quantitative information. Accordingly, they began constructing integrated representations that helped them to judge ordinal relationships.

These observations leave little doubt that adults adjust their representations to meet the demands of the task. If the use of a particular representation either fails or imposes excessive demands on the available processing resources, then the subjects construct and try out alternative representations. In this sense, the process of constructing representations is guided by the outcome of activities based upon those representations. The next section probes into the activities that follow the formation of the representation.

STRATEGIES FOR SOLVING PROBLEMS

Adults use an impressive number and variety of strategies which fall into several fuzzy, overlapping categories. On a broad level, strategies can be divided into algorithms and heuristics. An *algorithm* is a solution method that always solves a particular type of problem, even if the solver does not understand how the method works. For example, the formula $A = l \times w$ is an algorithm for computing the area of a rectangle; using the formula correctly guarantees the correct result. In contrast, a *heuristic* is a solution method that, like a rule of thumb, can be used to solve a problem but is not guaranteed to do so. For example, a useful heuristic in playing chess is to gain control of the center of the board. This heuristic is not a recipe for winning, but using it does increase one's chances of winning. As another example, some students prepare for a test by using the heuristic of studying class notes while ignoring the reading material. This strategy is neither foolproof nor advisable, yet it does work on some occasions.

The type of strategy that one uses is one of the chief determinants of problem solving. We often describe problems as being inherently easy or difficult, but, in fact, the difficulty of the problem depends upon the type of strategy used by the problem solver. As a simple example, try to solve this addition problem by hand in less than 30 seconds.

```
  85515
  14485
   3555
   6445
  85515
  14485
   3555
+ 6445
```

If you used the standard procedure of adding up all of the numbers in each column, you probably failed to satisfy the time requirement. You undoubtedly would have fared better if you had noticed that each number appears twice, that the first two numbers sum to 100,000 and that the next two numbers sum to 10,000. People who use the strategy of searching for relationships between the numbers find this type of problem easy, whereas those who use the simple addition strategy find the problem difficult. So the difficulty of a problem and the likelihood of achieving a solution depend on the appropriateness of the strategy used by the solver.

In turn, whether a particular strategy is appropriate depends upon the capacities and skills of the solver. Someone who is unusually skilled in performing simple addition could have solved the math problem above by following the standard adding procedure. But most people lack the skills and perhaps the genetic ability to perform such rapid mathematical operations. If a strategy is to be effective, then, it must be tailored to fit the characteristics of both the problem and the solver. Keeping this in mind, we now examine some of the general strategies that people use.

Means-End Analysis

Many problems, called problems of transformation (Greeno, 1978), consist of an initial situation, a goal, and a set of operations that can be used to move from the initial situation to the goal. In resolving these problems, people frequently use the heuristic of *means-end analysis.* This strategy consists of identifying the principal differences between the initial situation and the goal and then taking actions that reduce those differences. Essentially, then, this is a difference-reduction strategy.

This strategy is useful in solving commonplace problems such as how to keep warm outside in winter. The initial state is the feeling of coldness, and the goal state is the sensation of warmth. Using the strategy of means-end analysis, the solver takes whatever steps are available for producing warmth, such as adding clothing, building a fire, or finding shelter from the wind. Of course, these actions may also occur without strategic planning and awareness of the goal. Nevertheless, people do in many instances deliberately strive for goals by using means-end analysis.

The advantages of the strategy of means-end analysis are illustrated by examining performance on the Tower of Hanoi problem. The initial state of a simple version of this problem is shown in Figure 9.6. The task is to move the three disks from peg A to peg C in the fewest moves without violating two constraints: move only one disk at a time from the top of a stack and never put a larger disk on top of a smaller disk. The solver succeeds when the disks are arranged on peg C in order one-two-three. Incidentally, this is called the Tower of Hanoi puzzle because of a legend

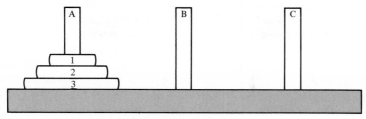

Figure 9.6   The Tower of Hanoi problem.

that monks in Hanoi are trying to solve a more exacting version of the puzzle—one that includes 64 disks. According to the legend, the world will end when the monks complete the puzzle. But this is no cause for alarm. Even if the monks make one correct move each second, they will need about a trillion years to solve the problem (Raphael, 1976).

This problem has a clearly definable goal structure in that it can be divided into several subgoals (Egan and Greeno, 1974; Simon, 1979). One conspicuous subgoal is to move disk three onto peg C. This subgoal is it-self divisible into subgoals such as moving disk one to peg C, moving disk two to peg B, and then moving disk one back to peg B, leaving peg C open to receive disk three. Having moved disk three onto peg C, the solver then works on the next subgoal of moving disk two onto peg C, and so on.

In solving the Tower of Hanoi problem using the strategy of means-end analysis, people apparently do formulate and achieve subgoals. For example, Egan and Greeno (1974) observed that the number of errors decreased as the subjects moved closer to the main subgoals of the prob-lem. When the main subgoal being worked on was distant, the solver had to keep track of numerous moves and of how those moves were related to the subgoal. But when the main subgoal was only one or two moves away, less planning was required. As a result, the subjects allocated their resources chiefly to the next move, thereby avoiding errors. The view that the subjects had divided the problem into subgoals was also sup-ported by the results of a recognition test in which the subjects examined various arrangements of disks and stated whether those arrangements had occurred while working on the problem. The results were that they seldom erred in judging arrangements that were inconsistent with the subgoals (for example, an arrangement in which the largest disk was on peg B). The subjects erred more frequently in judging arrangements that were consistent with the subgoals regardless of whether they had ac-tually produced those exact arrangements earlier. This observation sug-gests that the subjects had indeed formulated subgoals in solving the problem.

As hinted above, means-end analysis is useful partly because it places relatively light demands on processing capacity, particularly when the solver formulates subgoals and works on one at a time (Simon, 1975). If people tried to keep track of all the steps required to solve a problem rather than only the steps in a particular subproblem, their processing capacity would almost certainly be strained. Thus, means-end analysis confers the benefits of planning while avoiding the excess freight of overplanning.

Means-end analysis is also useful in solving problems that have no obvious subgoals. To see this for yourself, take several minutes and try to solve this problem, alternately called the hobbits-and-orcs problem or the missionaries-and-cannibals problem:

> Three hobbits and three orcs stand on one bank of a river. They must cross to the other side by means of a rowboat that holds up to two (but no more than two) creatures. However, if the orcs ever outnumber the hobbits on either bank, the orcs will eat the hobbits. Construct a sequence of crossings that will move all six creatures to the other side without losing any hobbits.

In working on this problem, many people initially adopted a balance strategy in which they attempted to equalize the numbers of hobbits and orcs on each side of the river. They probably used the balance strategy because of the instructions to keep the hobbits from being eaten. This strategy was unnecessary since it is legal to have all of the hobbits on one side while all of the orcs are on the other. As Figure 9.7 shows, just this arrangement must occur in order to solve the problem. After making several moves, most subjects abandoned the balance strategy in favor of means-end analysis (Jeffries, Polson, Razran, and Atwood, 1977; Simon and Reed, 1976). This strategy led subjects to prefer moves that take the greatest number of creatures across the river and bring the smallest number back to the starting side. In this way, the subjects made the greatest reductions between the initial state and the goal state. More important, they made the required moves that led to unequal numbers of hobbits and orcs on the sides of the river. Subsequent studies have shown that the use of means-end analysis can be facilitated by telling the subjects that unbalanced states must occur (Simon and Reed, 1976), for that hint leads away from the use of the balance strategy.

Means-end analysis, however, can be misleading. Using means-end analysis, the subjects included only one creature in each of the first few return trips. Having made several such returns, the subjects may tend to fixate and include only one creature in all of the return trips. But this approach is doomed to failure since both a hobbit and an orc must make the return trip between states six and seven. Understandably, subjects often err on the return move between states six and seven, and they make long pauses before proposing the correct move (Thomas, 1974). As this example shows, it is sometimes necessary to increase the difference between

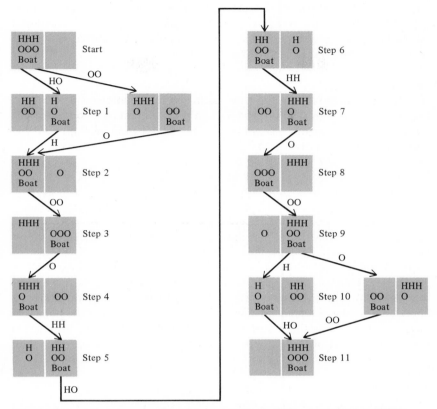

Figure 9.7   The steps required to solve the hobbits-and-orcs problem. The two halves of each box show the positions of the hobbits (H), the orcs (O), and the boat with respect to the two banks of the river. The arrows indicate crossings and the labels above the arrows indicate the passengers at each crossing.

the current state and the goal state in order to solve a problem. This poses problems for a strict means-end analysis, which is inherently a difference-reduction strategy. Fortunately, people seldom adhere rigidly to only one pure strategy. More often, they work with multiple strategies, adapting their methods to the requirements of the task.

Search Strategies

Searching is a pervasive aspect of problem-solving activities. For example, executing the strategy of means-end analysis involves searching for the optimal procedure for reducing the discrepancy between the current state and the goal state. Similarly, solving an anagram problem, such as the problem of forming a legal word from the letters RBETYHE,[1] requires searching through various sequences of letters and finding a permissible word. Whether one is trying to locate an obscure document in a large library or to isolate the cause of an engine malfunction, search activities are essential for achieving a solution.

More important, searching and planning usually go hand in hand, as shown by the following example. Suppose that you were in the first semester of your third year and were taking an introductory course in psychology in order to satisfy a graduation requirement. To your surprise, you found the topic of personality fascinating, far more so than your declared major, chemistry. Having discussed your interests with your psychology instructor, you decide to major in psychology. The immediate problem is to decide which psychology courses to take next in order to rapidly fulfill the prerequisites for seminars in personality and social psychology. In order to solve this problem, you must search among the various alternatives and weigh the consequences of each. The search is best conducted systematically, perhaps by considering each of the possibilities diagrammed in Figure 9.8. Following the paths of this search tree reveals that your next course should be either developmental psychology or social psychology. Looking ahead to your final year, you decide to take the developmental course next since that course is a prerequisite for a greater number of advanced seminars, one of which concerns personality. As this example illustrates, searching through the range of options is an essential part of the planning process. A good way to improve your

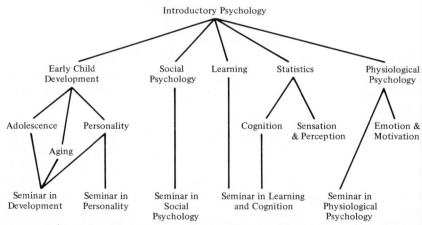

Figure 9.8 A search tree enumerating the possible courses that could be taken following introductory psychology.

[1] The answer is *thereby.*

own planning and problem-solving skills is to learn to search explicitly and thoroughly.

A search may be conducted in many different ways. For example, a tree of options such as that described above can be searched in either a breadth-first or a depth-first manner. Breadth-first searches proceed horizontally before vertically. In a breadth-first search of the tree of course options, the solver initially examines all of the options at one level before considering the options at the lower levels. A depth-first search does just the opposite. The solver examines an option at one level and then considers all of the options beneath the initial one. These two types of search are useful for different purposes. If you wanted to know which psychology courses you could take immediately following the introductory course, or if you wanted to find all of the moves that could get your king out of a check in a game of chess, then a breadth-first search would be useful. On the other hand, a depth-first search would be useful if you had already decided upon either of two courses but you wanted to look farther ahead and determine the consequences of taking each. Of course, these search strategies need not be used single-mindedly. In playing games of strategy, people probably pursue both types of search.

THE GENERATE-TEST STRATEGY

Not all search strategies are so directed and systematic as are breadth-first and depth-first searches. People often use a simple *generate-test strategy* for searching (Newell and Simon, 1973). This strategy involves generating possible solutions to a problem in a relatively unsystematic manner and testing each candidate to see whether it constitutes a solution. For example, the problem of making a word from the letters NADL can be solved by generating all of the possible combinations of the letters and deciding whether each combination is a word. Similarly, the problem of naming the capital of New York could be solved by generating the names of cities in the state of New York and evaluating whether each is sufficiently familiar to be the capital. You probably recognize this as an instance of the generation-recognition strategy that people use to recall lists of items in a free recall procedure.

The generate-test strategy is enticingly simple, for it boils down to suggesting and testing the first items in a category that come to mind. Unfortunately, this strategy is in many instances inefficient or unworkable, sometimes both. First of all, it involves a relatively undiscriminating search; one simply generates candidates and tests each. This undirected approach works when there are only a few possible solutions to be considered. But many problems have a large number of possible solutions, too many to be searched efficiently by a generate-test procedure. Imagine trying to design an experiment or do a crossword puzzle by generating items in an undirected manner. The possible solutions are so numerous that the actual solution may not be generated in a reasonable amount of time. The set of all possible solutions that the solver is willing to consider is called the *search space*. Generally speaking, when the search space is large, the generate-test strategy is inefficient, for the good and the bad candidates for a solution receive equal consideration. What is needed is a way of narrowing the realm of options—of reducing the size of the search space—so that only the better candidates receive consideration.

Another limitation of the generate-test strategy is that it involves generating complete candidate solutions. This approach can succeed on well-defined problems such as anagram problems that have readily recognizable solutions. But on ill-defined problems, the properties of the solution are unknown. An effective approach toward solving ill-defined problems is to identify partial solutions that help to guide subsequent searches. In essence, the generate-test method fails to limit the search space to a manageable size. Once again, what is needed is a method for reducing the size of the search space so that only the closest approximations to a solution are considered.

STRATEGIES FOR LIMITING THE SEARCH SPACE

The search space may be kept limited by means of a variety of memory strategies. The simplest one involves remembering and searching for only the courses of action that have worked in the past. For example, if the problem were to form a word beginning with the letter Q, you might begin by searching through the list of words beginning with a Q that you had previously seen or produced. This strategy, although not very thoughtful, can be useful in solving recurring problems, for example, flat tires, leaking roofs, and broken engines. Indeed, people often solve such recurring problems by remembering how they alleviated the problem the last time it arose.

A more sophisticated memorial strategy consists of reasoning by analogy. In reasoning by analogy, we draw a parallel between a poorly understood state of affairs and one we have experienced or studied previously or know more about. This strategy is advantageous because it allows us to apply our knowledge of the old state of affairs to the new one, thereby reducing the amount of searching that we have to do in order to solve the current problem. Consider, for example, the problem of finding a strong yet lightweight material that could be used to make an artificial hip. The search space for this problem is potentially very large, so an undirected search would probably take too long and might never unearth an appropriate material. The search space can be reduced substantially by noticing that this problem resembles the problem of constructing an airplane that is sufficiently strong and light enough to fly.

Having made this realization, scientists can concentrate their search on the materials used to construct airplanes.

As this example shows, reasoning by analogy involves the discrimination of similarities in form between two things. Scientists and inventors often use such a strategy in order to bring what is already known to bear on unsolved problems. Further, they sometimes define ill-defined, poorly understood problems by way of analogy with well-defined, better understood problems. It is in this way that some of the most perplexing problems are rendered intelligible. If you wish to learn more about how analogical reasoning occurs, see Sternberg (1977).

Another type of strategy for limiting the search space and searching in a highly directed manner is to perform a *constructive search* (Greeno, 1978). In this type of search, the solver uses his or her semantic and world knowledge to produce a partial solution that reduces the number of options remaining to be searched. In order to understand what a constructive search is, try to solve this cryptarithmetic problem:

$$
\begin{array}{r}
D\ O\ N\ A\ L\ D \\
+\ G\ E\ R\ A\ L\ D \\
\hline
R\ O\ B\ E\ R\ T
\end{array}
\qquad \text{(Hint: D = 5)}
$$

Try to substitute the numbers 0 through 9 for letters in a way that leads to a correct addition. In solving this problem, people usually work on the letters in one column in an attempt to identify the value of a particular letter (Newell et al., 1972). For example, most people begin by using their knowledge of arithmetic to reason that $T = 0$ since $D = 5$ and $5 + 5 = 10$. Then the subjects use that partial solution to guide their search. Knowing that the sum of $L + L$ must be an even number but that column two has a carry of 1 (from the addition of $D + D$), the subjects reason that R must be odd. And since $D + G = R$, it follows that R must be greater than 5. Continuing in this manner, many subjects solve the problem. Trying to solve this problem through an undirected search, for example, by substituting a number for a letter at random and trying it out, would surely fail, for there are several hundred thousand possible substitutions of digits for letters in this problem.

The constructive search strategy is used frequently in attempts to solve everyday problems. For example, typists who must decipher an illegible word may use their knowledge of the context and of the rules of language to determine the probable meaning and grammatical class of the illegible word. Then they undertake a search of semantic memory for words that have the specified properties. In this manner, they avoid the inefficient strategy of generating words at random and testing the appropriateness of each. The constructive search strategy is fundamental in almost all types of investigation. If, for example, police investigators were looking for a murderer who had killed someone by using a rare poison, they would undoubtedly use their knowledge of who would be most likely to have access to that poison to guide their search.

This example illustrates that using the constructive search strategy leads to the formulation of subgoals, such as that of finding the source of the problem. In this respect, the constructive search strategy complements the heuristic of means-end analysis, which often involves the pursuit of subgoals. The benefits of both strategies can be achieved by uniting the two heuristics into a higher-order strategy. It is possible that the skill of efficient problem solvers derives in part from the adeptness with which they combine strategies in novel and powerful ways.

THE CONFIRMATION STRATEGY

We next consider how people search for evidence bearing on the validity of hypotheses. This type of search is highly important, for we often search for evidence to evaluate hypotheses about the mechanical problems of a car, the effectiveness of a particular method of reading, and so on. The question of how people search for evidence has obvious relevance to the scientific enterprise, in which the collection of evidence is of the utmost importance.

One of the chief strategies that people use in evaluating hypotheses has been documented in the following type of tasks (Wason, 1960). The experimenter presented a triad of numbers, 2–4–6, and stated that the triad had been generated by a rule. The subjects' task was to discover the rule by producing other triads of numbers, which the experimenter immediately identified as either conforming to or as violating the rule. The subjects were allowed to generate as many triads as they wished, and they were told to state their hypothesis about the identity of the rule only when they were certain that it was correct. The rule that had actually been used to generate the 2–4–6 triad was "any three numbers in ascending order."

Surprisingly, about 80 percent of the subjects announced incorrect hypotheses in this task, although most subjects eventually solved the problem. Why did they do so poorly on an apparently simple task? In part, the answer is that they used a *confirmation strategy* in evaluating their hypotheses. This strategy, which is used in many different tasks (Schustack and Sternberg, 1981), involved searching for evidence that confirmed the hypothesis, but not for evidence that could have falsified it. For example, one subject formulated the incorrect rule that the numbers increased by twos from the initial number. In testing this rule, she generated triads such as 8–10–12 20–22–24 and 1–3–5, all of which were consistent with the correct rule. Consequently, she assumed that her hypothesis was correct, when in fact, it was not. The problem is that triads such as 2–4–6 and 1–3–5 can be generated by many different rules. The only way to eliminate the incorrect rules is to try to falsify them by obtaining disconfirmatory evidence. In order to test her rule of "increasing by twos," the subject described above should have looked for disconfirmatory evidence such as the triad 1–2–3. The consistency of this triad with the experimenter's rule proved that the "increasing by twos" hypothesis is incorrect. Thus, attempts at falsification are essential in critically evaluating a hypothesis. This idea forms the core of some widely respected philosophies of science (cf. Popper, 1972).

At worst, the confirmation strategy is a narrow-minded approach that dogmatists can use to obtain support for their preconceived biases. Yet the positive side of the confirmation strategy should also be recognized. For one thing, the correct hypothesis can sometimes be identified by using the confirmation strategy (Bowers, 1977). For example, the hypothesis that a new drug can control cancer can be tested by seeking only confirmatory evidence, perhaps by administering a particular dosage of the drug to many different cancer patients in many different institutions and looking for reductions in cancerous growth. Moreover, the use of the confirmation strategy makes good sense in the initial stages of inquiry in an area. In the initial stages of inquiry, scientists often have multiple hypotheses about the causes of a particular phenomenon such as cancer. It is probably not worth trying to falsify each one unless some confirmatory evidence already exists in favor of each. After all, it is pointless to try to falsify hypotheses that no one believes in and that are not backed by any positive evidence. Additionally, confirmatory evidence provides valuable clues about where to look in future investigations, whereas disconfirmatory evidence shows only where not to look. Thus, searching for confirmatory evidence can help to guide research. You should be aware, however, that scientists disagree on these issues (for example, compare Bowers, 1977, and Weimer, 1977).

Ideally, scientists evaluate hypotheses by using the method of strong inference (Platt, 1964), in which they perform experiments designed to simultaneously confirm one hypothesis or class of hypotheses and falsify others. In the advanced stages of research, this method is much more powerful than the confirmation strategy, which fails to isolate the correct hypothesis from other interpretations. It may seem that scientific training should bestow some degree of immunity from the tendency to rely too heavily on the confirmation strategy. Contrary to this view, scientists and nonscientists performed at an equally low, unflattering level on the 2–4–6 problem described above (Mahoney and DeMonbreun, 1977). Whether scientists tend to rely too heavily on the confirmation strategy in their professional experimentation remains to be determined. Research on this issue will have fundamental implications for our conceptions about the nature of scientific inquiry.

Strategies for Making Probabilistic Inferences

In everyday situations, people make many predictions and judgments in the face of uncertainty. Beforehand, we never know with absolute certainty which candidate will be the best national leader or which acquaintance will be the best friend. Similarly, we are seldom able to say with absolute certainty that a defendant committed a particular crime or that a decision made in the past was the wisest one possible. In these kinds of situations, we must forgo certainty, assess the odds, and hazard a probabilistic prediction or decision. Probabilistic inferences are important in problem solving because people seldom know certainly which strategy will work best. So in selecting a strategy, people are often forced to judge the probability that a particular strategy will succeed.

Probabilistic inferences can be made in several ways. Applying formal theories of probability and statistics, as psychological researchers do, is no doubt the most accurate method. Yet it is not the method that people ordinarily use. People who have not received formal training in probability theory (and also some who have!) tend to make probabilistic inferences by using the representativeness strategy and the availability strategy (Tversky and Kahneman, 1973; but also see Cohen, 1980), to which we now turn.

REPRESENTATIVENESS

The representativeness strategy involves judging whether an item is a member of a particular class by evaluating how representative that item is of the class. An item is representative of a class to the extent that it is a typical class member. Thus, representativeness and typicality are closely related concepts, and the prototype of a class is the most representative member.

The use of the representativeness strategy is illustrated by an experiment by Kahneman and Tversky (1972, 1973). They gave subjects a list of nine disciplines and asked them to estimate the percentage of all students enrolled in each. The subjects estimated that there were three times as many students in humanities and education than in computer science. Then two groups of naive subjects read this personality sketch:

> Tom W. is of high intelligence, although lacking in true creativity. He has a need for order and clarity, and for neat and tidy systems in which every detail finds its appropriate place. His writing is rather dull and mechanical, occasionally enlivened by somewhat corny puns and flashes of imagination of the sci-fi type. He has a strong drive for competence. He seems to have little feel and little sympathy for other people and does not enjoy interacting with others. Self-centered, he nonetheless has a deep moral sense.

The subjects in the similarity condition rated how similar Tom W. seemed to be to the typical graduate student in each of the nine disciplines. As you might expect, they rated Tom W. as much more similar to the typical student of computer science than to the typical student of humanities and education. The subjects in the prediction group read the sketch about Tom W., along with this information:

> The preceding personality sketch of Tom W. was written during Tom's senior year in high school by a psychologist, on the basis of projective tests. Tom W. is currently a graduate student.

The subjects predicted which field Tom W. was likely to be studying, and they then evaluated the predictive accuracy of projective tests.

The results were that over 95 percent of the subjects in the prediction group judged that Tom W. was more likely to study computer science than humanities and education. Furthermore, these predictions correlated highly with the ratings of the subjects in the similarity condition. This suggests that the subjects made their predictions by judging the similarity of the personality sketch to their conception of the typical graduate student in each field. Presumably, the sketch of Tom W. was highly similar to the subjects' conception of the prototypical graduate student to computer science. Using the representativeness strategy, the subjects predicted overwhelmingly that Tom W. would major in computer science.

The predictions made by the subjects may seem to have been logical, but in fact they were quite the opposite. For one thing, the subjects expressed little faith in the reliability of projective tests, which provided the basis for the personality sketch of Tom W. Since the sketch was invalid, they should have used their knowledge of the likelihood of students majoring in computer science. By applying the rule of probability called Bayes' theorem, it can be shown that the prior odds were much higher that a student will major in humanities and education rather than computer science. In predicting that Tom. W. will major in computer science, the subjects erroneously ignored the prior odds. They also overlooked the obvious point that people change rapidly following high school, so there was little reason to have trusted the stated description. Unfortunately, these considerations do not enter into the use of the representativeness strategy. Consequently, the subjects made unreasonable predictions.

The subjects' disregard of the prior odds probably did not stem from total ignorance of statistics, for subjects do sometimes make use of information concerning prior odds. For example, Kahneman and Tversky told subjects that out of a set of 100 descriptions, 70 were of lawyers, while 30 were of engineers. An unknown individual was selected from the set, and the subjects were asked to predict whether that individual was a lawyer or an engineer. Under these conditions in which the subjects had no information about the individual, the subjects judged that the probability was 0.7 that the individual was a lawyer and 0.3 that the individual was an engineer. So people do know that the prior odds are relevant when making predictions. Yet very different results occurred when the selected individual was described in this way:

> Dick is a 30-year-old man. He is married with no children. A man of high ability and high motivation, he promises to be quite successful in his field. He is well-liked by his colleagues.

This description is uninformative since it could apply equally well to either a lawyer or an engineer. The subjects should have disregarded the description and based their predictions solely on the prior odds. But they did not do so. Instead, they judged the probability that Dick was an engineer to be 0.5. Presumably, the subjects ignored the prior odds because the description was equally representative of lawyers and engineers. It appears, then, that people know how to use information about prior odds but that they disregard those odds when any information is available that permits the use of the representativeness strategy.

If the representativeness strategy does lead to errors, why do people use it? Part of the answer is that the strategy often works. Assume, for example, that you managed a store and had previously been robbed at gunpoint several times. A person enters the store alone late at night, and you have to decide quickly whether the person is dangerous. In making this decision, it would be useful to evaluate the similarity of the customer's appearance and behavior to that of the previously encountered thieves. If the person seemed shifty and anxious, as the previous thieves had been, you would do well to generalize, inferring that this person is probably a thief. As discussed previously, the tendency to generalize from one similar item to another is an important part of the process of categorization. And grouping similar items into a category is advantageous because we can apply our knowledge of an entire category to a particular stimulus that seems representative of the category. Thus, the representativeness strategy is an extension of our natural inclination to divide the world into categories and to apply our knowledge of categories to particular stimuli. Ironically, people may rely on the strategy excessively, as they did in the example concerning Tom W., precisely because the strategy had succeeded in many other situations. Additionally, evaluating similarity may be a fundamental and biologically favored process, for animals ranging from lowly cockroaches to thoughtful primates often respond on the basis of the degree of similarity between stimuli.

THE AVAILABILITY STRATEGY

The availability strategy involves judging the probability of an event by the ease with which instances of the event can be retrieved. In order to demonstrate this strategy, try answering the following questions. Suppose you selected at random a word containing at least three letters from a novel. Is it more likely that the first letter is an *r* or that the third letter is an *r*? Most people state that *r* is more likely to occur in the first position (Tversky et al., 1973). But in fact, *r* occurs more often as the third letter than as the first letter in English words. The reason people err in this task is that they use the availability strategy of retrieving words containing an *r*. It is much easier to retrieve words by their first letter (for example, *rake, raspberry,* and *raft*) than by their third letter (for example, *tar, fort,* and *nurse*). In this sense, words beginning with *r* will appear to be more numerous.

The availability strategy helps to account for striking everyday phenomena such as temporary shifts in subjective probability. If you have just witnessed an automobile accident, your estimate of the probability of an accident rises temporarily. Of if you have just read about a terrible plane crash, your estimate of the probability of a plane crash rises sharply, although temporarily. The reason is that recently experienced events are easily retrievable and are highly available. Also, those events establish a context in which we tend to retrieve information about events of a similar nature. Consequently, we tend to think that they have a high frequency of occurrence when, in fact, they do not. This process seems to occur automatically, so it is best not to think of strategies strictly as consciously applied plans.

In general, we have much to learn about the role of automatic, non-conscious processing in using strategies to solve problems. Many people believe that nonconscious processing contributes substantially to the solution of ill-defined problems. Creative thinkers, for example, often claim that they first gather information about a problem and work on it intensely. Then they set the problem aside in order to allow their ideas to incubate over time. The incubation period sometimes ends unexpectedly when the solution to the problem suddenly pops into awareness, perhaps while the solver is engaged in an unrelated activity such as taking a bath. Of course, the solution may crop up because the solver is in a new context that is conducive to a novel representation of the problem. Or the solver may simply have recovered from fatigue or have forgotten ineffective approaches. Yet it remains possible that well-practiced strategies are executed on a nonconscious level. Identifying these private activities and other processes involved in creative problem solving is a task worth pursuing in future research.

COMPUTER SIMULATION

The guiding idea behind much of the research and theorizing discussed in this text can be stated simply: The human cognitive system is best viewed as an information-processing system. This idea, which constitutes the foundation for cognitive science, has been developed most fully in the field of *computer simulation.* The chief aim of this area of research is to construct computer systems that mimic or simulate both overt human behavior and the cognitive processes that underlie it. An adequate simulation of problem solving, for example, would not only solve all of the problems that people solve but would also solve the problems using the same kinds of representations and strategies that people use.

Cognitive scientists try to devise computer simulations for several reasons. First, they want to test the sufficiency of their theories. As mentioned in the discussion of global, propositional models of cognition, a theory that is embodied in a computer program can be tested by seeing whether the theory can do what it is intended to do, for example, read text and answer questions correctly. Second, theorists want to define terms such as *understanding* and *representation* as explicitly as possible. Theoretical explicitness is no small advantage, for theories are testable only if they are explicit.

Third and most important, a computer simulation is a genuine psychological theory that helps to guide research and unearth useful concepts. Computers and people obviously differ in their physical composition yet they both manipulate symbols, and they may perform a particular act by following logically similar steps and procedures. So to the extent that a simulation models human performance accurately, then to that extent the simulation is an adequate psychological theory. In devising computer models, theorists often break new ground, using information from other disciplines such as computer science. If, for example, cognitive psychologists have not clarified the types of representations people use, then they may turn to computer scientists to pick up ideas about representations. In practice, these ideas often turn out to be useful in psychological theories. Indeed, psychological theories emphasizing schemata and propositional representations owe a large debt to research in computer science. Because successful computer simulations do introduce powerful new concepts, they are genuine theoretical advances, not just noteworthy technological achievements. We now examine briefly one of the most prominent efforts at simulation.

The General Problem Solver

The General Problem Solver or GPS was designed to simulate human problem solving in a broad range of tasks (Newell and Simon, 1972). It includes a long-term memory that stores semantic and world knowledge as well as operations for using that knowledge. GPS also includes a short-term memory of limited capacity that necessitates serial rather than parallel processing. The short-term memory is a work space in which objects are compared and decisions are made about how to act next. The GPS system works by examining a *problem space*. The problem space is the internal representation of the problem, and it consists of all of the legal states that the system could enter while working on a problem. Using the heuristic of means-end analysis, the GPS compares the initial state in a problem to the goal state. Then it selects a move that will reduce the difference between the current state and the goal state.

Most of the knowledge included in GPS is in the form of *production rules*, which instruct the system to take a particular action if a particular condition has been satisfied (Newell, 1973; Simon, 1978). Here are some examples of production rules:

If the light is red, then stop.
If hungry, then eat some food.
If tired, then rest.

Each rule consists of a situation-action pair, and each rule incorporates a tiny bit of knowledge about how to act under particular conditions, either inside of or outside of the system. Of course, a powerful system must have many thousands of production rules.

In order to evaluate whether GPS solves problems in the same way that humans do, researchers must have a good idea of the steps that people go through in solving problems. For this reason, investigators use the method of *protocol analysis*, in which subjects solve a problem while thinking aloud. The verbal protocols of the subjects often reveal the problem space the solver is using, the state of knowledge the solver is currently in, and the operations the solver is using to advance toward the goal state. Having collected this information, the investigator can then evaluate the degree of similarity between the problem spaces, the knowledge states, and the operations used by humans and those used by GPS. This evaluation is difficult to make since there are no accepted rules for deciding the degree of similarity. And the intuition of the investigator plays a key role in all stages of the method of protocol analysis. Nevertheless, the method has proven to be useful.

In several well-defined tasks, such as cryptarithmetic problems and the hobbits-and-orcs problem, the performance of the GPS system resembles that of adults (Atwood and Poulson, 1976; Newell et al., 1972). The performance of GPS deviates somewhat from that of people in being too single-minded, processing in a strictly serial manner, and relying more heavily on means-end analysis than people do (Greeno, 1974). But overall, its achievements are noteworthy, particularly because it performs such diverse tasks using a small number of general elementary processes such as comparing items in short-term memory. Unfortunately, we do not yet know whether the system can be extended in ways that allow it to simulate human performance in more complex tasks, for example, tasks that call for intuition and creativity. At the very least, GPS must be supplemented by programs that form representations for problems, since GPS lacks this ability (cf. Hayes and Simon, 1976).

For our purposes, however, the potential limitations of the GPS system are of less interest than are those of the computer simulation approach in general. We next consider these limitations, not to detract from efforts at simulation, but to identify significant challenges to the entire information processing outlook.

The Limits of Simulation

Attempts to simulate cognition via computer face serious methodological and theoretical obstacles. A severe methodological problem, stemming from the privacy of cognitive processes, is that it is unclear how to assess whether the performance of a computer simulates in detail the performance of people. Protocol analysis can reveal some of the conscious steps that people take in solving problems (Ericsson and Simon, 1980). Using protocol analyses, we can assess the similarity between the steps taken by a computer and the conscious steps taken by people. But nonconscious processing may contribute to human problem solving, and the conscious thoughts that people have may be products of underlying processing that lies outside the scope of protocol analysis. So comparisons of protocol data with data concerning the performance of a computer cannot possibly tell us whether people and computers used similar underlying processes in performing a particular task. Even if we knew that a person and a computer had gone through the same global, macroscopic steps in solving a problem, we could not be sure that they took those steps using similar underlying processes. Until this problem has been resolved, we cannot determine exactly how well computer performance simulates human performance.

A second problem, related to the first, is that human cognition is guided by an immense amount of background knowledge. For example, skilled chess players do not decide how to move by consciously pondering every possible move in a serial manner. Rather, they automatically "zero in" on the strongest moves by using their background knowledge of chess. This knowledge lies on the fringes of consciousness and is applied before logical, conscious planning begins. Further, this knowledge does not enter directly into the representation, yet it shapes the properties of the representation. By analogy to the figure-ground relationship in perception, the background knowledge is the ground in which the representation is formed. Since this background knowledge guides the formation of representations, and since the form of the representations influences problem solving, a comprehensive theory must specify what the background knowledge is and how people use it. Dreyfus (1979) has argued that our background knowledge is holistic in nature and cannot be embodied in the discrete, formal rules used in present computers. Additionally, background knowledge includes our knowledge of bodily skills such as sitting, walking, or eating. This knowledge contributes to our understanding of what it means to sit or to walk. But computers lack human bodies, so they may be unable to have the background knowledge that people have (Dreyfus, 1979). Furthermore, background knowledge is learned and subject to change in people. Computers have been programmed to simulate some aspects of human learning (Anderson, Kline, and Beasley, 1979; Feigenbaum, 1963). But research into learning is in its infancy, and it remains to be determined whether computers can learn background knowledge in the same ways in which humans do.

Another problem is that computer programs tend to become so complex that they are difficult to understand (Weizenbaum, 1976). The best of programmers is seldom so lucky as to have a carefully written program work correctly on its first run. Usually, programmers discover flaws or "bugs" in the program. In debugging an intricate program, the programmer may introduce a large number of minor steps into the system. The ironic result is that the program may work, but the programmer may not fully understand why it works. And when a program is loaded with minor details, it becomes difficult to discern the main theoretical assertions of the system (cf. Smith, 1978).

The last problem we shall consider is that computers lack emotions. The absence of emotions appears to pose no problems in that cognitive and affective processes may be independent, or so they are assumed to be. But even if cognitive and affective processes are independent, they may influence each other extensively (Bower, 1981). A large amount of evidence indicates that human decisions depend upon both emotional and cognitive factors and that the emotional factors operate more quickly than the cognitive factors (Zajonc, 1980). For example, in meeting people, we often experience an immediate gut reaction of like or dislike, whereas our logical, cognitive evaluation of the person tends to be delayed. Because the emotional factors operate first, they can influence, perhaps even guide, cognitive processing. If you had a favorable initial reaction to someone, you might be more likely to evaluate cognitively that person's positive characteristics. But if your initial reaction had been unfavorable, you might tend to look for that person's negative characteristics. In this way, emotional factors could guide our cognitive activities. Computer systems cannot model such a scenario because they have no emotions. Further, an emotion cannot be reduced to a symbol structure of the sort that guides the activities of a computer. Emotions have a bodily component that computers simply do not have. For this reason, it is difficult to see how computers could understand romantic poetry and works of art in the same way in which humans do. A significant challenge for the future, then, is to construct computers having bodies and to determine whether the interplay between human emotion and cognition can be simulated by a machine.

These comments remind us that although the information-processing outlook has been useful, it may not accommodate all of the important facets of human cognition. People may always have abilities that outstrip those of machines, so it is important not to cast human cognition entirely in the image of the computer. But by the same token, cognitive psychology has advanced by uniting ideas from diverse disciplines, and we may expect the field to advance further by building upon the insights from computer science.

• *Summary.* One of the hallmarks of human intelligence is our skill in solving problems ranging from well-defined game problems to the ill-defined problems that defy exact description and require creative solutions. In general, problem solving involves four stages: understanding the problem, planning a strategy, executing the strategy, and evaluating progress toward the goal. These stages interact extensively. For example, in planning a strategy, one often achieves a deeper understanding of the problem.

Understanding a problem involves constructing a representation that specifies the initial state, the goal state or states, and the set of operations or moves that may help one to reach the goal. Forming a representation is a critical step in solving a problem, for the type of representation limits the kinds of strategies that can be used and determines the types of moves the solver will try. As the phenomenon of functional fixedness shows, fixating on an inappropriate representation is one of the chief causes of failures to solve problems. Insight and sudden solutions often occur when the solver breaks away from one representation and restructures the components of the problem into a new organizational pattern.

The role of representation is particularly evident in problems of reasoning. Errors in deductive reasoning often stem from the failure to construct all of the logically possible representations of a statement. For example, people tend to represent the statement *Some A are B* in a manner that indicates that some As are Bs, whereas other As are not Bs. But in fact, *Some A are B* can be represented in several logically acceptable ways, each of which must be considered in order to derive the correct conclusion to a syllogism. In solving problems of deduction, people may use either analytical or nonanalytical representations to which they apply logical tests. People also use a variety of imaginal and linguistic representations in solving problems of linear ordering. Under some conditions, they construct an integrated representation containing all of the items in the ordering, as indicated by the occurrence of distance effects. Whether subjects form a holistic or a piecemeal representation, however, depends upon the materials, the procedure used to present the items, and the test that is administered.

Of the strategies used to solve problems, some are general-purpose, whereas others are task-specific. Means-end analysis is a general heuristic in which the solver discerns the differences between a present state and the goal state and then takes actions that reduce those differences. This strategy is particularly effective in solving tasks that can be divided into subtasks. Although means-end analysis is the central strategy in some theories of problem solving, it is but one of many strategies, and people seldom use it in a highly rigid manner. The efficiency of the problem solving depends largely on the extent to which the subject limits the size of the search space, the set of moves the solver might consider, so that only the strongest moves are examined. People limit the size of the search space by using strategies such as remembering moves that have worked in the past, reasoning by analogy, and engaging in a constructive search. People also use search strategies to collect evidence that can be used to evaluate hypotheses, as in scientific inquiry. One search method that is widely used is the confirmation strategy, in which the solver looks for evidence that could confirm a hypothesis but not for evidence that could falsify it. Although attempts at falsification are required for evaluating a hypothesis fully, the confirmation strategy is useful in the early stages of inquiry.

Strategies are also used to make probabilistic inferences. For example, people predict whether a person is likely to study computer science by evaluating how similar that person is to the prototypical students of computer science. This representativeness strategy often leads to the occurrence of errors and illusions concerning the validity of the prediction. Errors also result from the use of the availability strategy, in which people use the retrievability of an event to judge how frequently that event occurs. Overall, however, the use of strategies helps people to solve problems, particularly those that cannot be solved algorithmically.

Cognitive psychology has drawn some of its most useful theoretical constructs from theories attempting to simulate human cognition via computer. So far, investigators have constructed computer systems that perform like people do in a moderate range of problem-solving tasks and learning tasks. These successes speak well for the view that the human cognitive system is a type of information-processing system. This view has proven to be useful in cognitive psychology and will no doubt continue to be so. Yet much more research needs to be directed at whether computer models can simulate the background knowledge that people have or the affective-cognitive interactions that pervade our lives.

References

Aaronson, D., and Scarborough, H. S. 1976. Performance theories for sentence coding: Some quantitative evidence. *Journal of Experimental Psychology: Human Perception and Performance, 2:* 56–70.

Abramson, A. S., and Lisker, L. 1970. Discriminability along the voicing continuum: Cross-language tests. In *Proceedings of the Sixth International Congress of Phonetic Science.* Prague: Academia. Pp. 569–573.

Acredelo, L. P.; Pick, H. L., Jr.; and Olsen, M. G. 1975. Environmental differentiation and familiarity as determinants of children's memory for spatial location. *Developmental Psychology, 11:* 495–501.

Ades, A. E. 1977. Vowels, consonants, speech and nonspeech. *Psychological Review, 84:* 524–530.

Akmajian, A, and Heny, F. 1975. *An introduction to the principles of transformational syntax.* Cambridge, Mass.: M.I.T. Press.

Anderson, J. R. 1976. *Language, memory and thought.* Hillsdale, N.J.: Erlbaum.

Anderson, J. R. 1978. Arguments concerning representations for mental imagery. *Psychological Review, 85:* 249–277.

Anderson, J. R., and Bower, G. H. 1972. Recognition and retrieval processes in free recall. *Psychological Review, 79:* 97–123.

Anderson J. R., and Bower, G. H. 1973. *Human associative memory.* Washington D.C.: Winston.

Anderson, J. R., and Bower, G. H. 1974. A propositional theory of recognition memory. *Memory and Cognition, 2:* 406–412.

Anderson, J. R.; Kline, P. J.; and Beasley, C. M., Jr. 1979. A general learning theory and its application to schema abstraction. In G. H. Bower (Ed.), *The psychology of learning and motivation* Vol. 13. New York: Academic Press. Pp. 277–318.

Anderson, J. R., and Reder, L. M. 1979. An elaborative processing explanation of depth of processing. In L. S. Cermak and F. I. M. Craik (Eds.), *Levels of processing and human memory.* Hillsdale, N.J.: Erlbaum. Pp. 385–403.

Appel, L. F.; Cooper, R. G.; McCarrell, N.; Sims-Knight, J.; Yussen, S. R.; and Flavell, J. H. 1972. The development of the distinction between perceiving and memorizing. *Child Development, 43:* 1365–1381.

Archer, E. J. 1960. A re-evaluation of the meaningfulness of all possible CVC trigrams. *Psychological Monographs, 74:* No. 497.

Atkinson, R. C. 1975. Mnemotechnics in second-language learning. *American Psychologist, 30:* 821–828.

Atkinson, R. C., and Juola, J. F. 1973. Factors influencing speed and accuracy of word recognition. In S. Kornblum (Ed.), *Attention and Performance IV.* New York: Academic Press. Pp. 583–612.

Atkinson, R. C., and Juola, J. F. 1974. Search and decision processes in recognition memory. In D. H. Krantz, R. C. Atkinson, R. D. Luce and P. Suppes (Eds.), *Contemporary developments in mathematical psychology* Vol. 1. San Francisco: Freeman. Pp. 242–293.

Atkinson, R. C., and Shiffrin, R. M. 1968. Human memory: A proposed system and its control processes. In K. W. Spence and J. T. Spence (Eds.), *The psychology of learning and motivation,* Vol. 2. New York: Academic Press. Pp. 89–195.

Atwood, M. E., and Poulson, P. G. 1976. A process model for water jug problems. *Cognitive Psychology, 8:* 191–216.

Averbach, E., and Coriell, A. S. 1961. Short-term memory in vision. *Bell System Technical Journal, 40:* 309–328.

Baddeley, A. D. 1974. Working memory. In G. H. Bower (Ed.), *The psychology of learning and motivation* Vol. 8. New York: Academic Press. Pp. 47–90.

Baddeley, A. D. 1976. *The psychology of memory.* New York: Basic Books.

Baddeley, A. D. 1978. The trouble with levels: A reexamination of Craik and Lockhart's framework for memory research. *Psychological Review, 85:* 139–152.

Baddeley, A. D., and Ecob, J. R. 1973. Reaction time and short-term memory: Implications of repetition for the high-speed exhaustive scan hypothesis. *Quarterly Journal of Experimental Psychology, 25:* 229–240.

Baddeley, A. D., and Hitch, G. J. 1977. Recency reexamined. In S. Dornic (Ed.), *Attention and Performance* VI. Hillsdale, N.J.: Erlbaum. Pp. 647–667.

Baddeley, A. D., and Patterson, K. 1971. The relationship between long-term and short-term memory. *British Medical Bulletin, 27:* 237–242.

Baddeley, A., and Scott, D. 1971. Short-term forgetting in the absence of proactive inhibition. *Quarterly Journal of Experimental Psychology, 23:* 275–283.

Baddeley, A. D.; Thomson, N.; and Buchanon, M. 1975. Word length and the structure of short-term memory. *Journal of Verbal Learning and Verbal Behavior, 14:* 575–589.

Bahrick, H. P.; Bahrick, P. O.; and Wittlinger, R. P. 1975. Fifty years of memory for names and faces: A cross-sectional approach. *Journal of Experimental Psychology: General, 104:* 54–75.

Balota, D. A., and Neely, J. H. 1980. Test-expectancy and word-frequency effects in recall and recognition. *Journal of Experimental Psychology: Human Learning and Memory, 6:* 576–587.

Banks, W. P., and Atkinson, R. C. 1974. Accuracy and speed strategies in scanning active memory. *Memory and Cognition, 2:* 629–636.

Banks, W. P., and Barber, G. 1977. Color information in iconic memory. *Psychological Review, 84:* 536–546.

Banks, W. P., and Barber, G. 1980. Normal iconic memory for stimuli invisible to the rods. *Perception and Psychophysics, 27:* 581–584.

Bar-Hillel, Y. 1969. Universal semantics and philosophy of language: Quandaries and prospects. In J. Puhvel (Ed.), *Substance and structure of language.* Berkeley: University of California Press.

Bar-Hillel, Y. 1970. *Aspects of language.* Jerusalem: The Magnes Press.

Barnes, J. M., and Underwood, B. J. 1959. "Fate" of first-list associations in transfer theory. *Journal of Experimental Psychology, 58:* 97–105.

Baron, J. 1978. The word-superiority effect: Perceptual learning from reading. In W. K. Estes (Ed.), *Handbook of learning and cognitive processes* Vol. 6. Hillsdale, N.J.: Erlbaum. Pp. 131–166.

Bartlett, F. C. 1932. *Remembering.* Cambridge, England: Cambridge University Press.

Bartling, C. A., and Thompson, C. P. 1977. Encoding specificity: Retrieval asymmetry in the recognition failure paradigm. *Journal of Experimental Psychology: Human Learning and Memory, 3:* 690–700.

Battig, W. F. 1979. The flexibility of human memory. In L. S. Cermak and F. I. M. Craik (Eds.), *Levels of processing in human memory.* Hillsdale, N.J.: Erlbaum. Pp. 23–44.

Battig, W. F., and Belleza, F. S. 1980. Organization and levels of processing. In C. R. Puff (Ed.), *Memory, organization and structure.* New York: Academic Press. Pp. 321–346.

Battig, W. F., and Einstein, G. O. 1977. Evidence that broader processing facilitates delayed retention. *Bulletin of the Psychonomic Society, 10:* 28–30.

Begg I., and Denny, J. P. 1969. Empirical reconciliation of atmosphere and conversion interpretations of syllogistic reasoning errors. *Journal of Experimental Psychology, 81:* 351–354.

Belleza, F. S.; Richards, D. L.; and Geiselman, R. E. 1976. Semantic processing and organization in free recall. *Memory and Cognition, 4:* 415–421.

Benton, A. L. 1969. Disorders of spatial orientation. In P. J. Vinken and C. W. Brayn (Eds.), *Handbook of clinical neurology* Vol. 3. Amsterdam: North Holland Publishing Company.

Berlin, B., and Kay, P. 1969. *Basic color terms: Their universality and evolution.* Berkeley: University of California Press.

Berlin, C. I. 1977. Hemispheric asymmetry in auditory tasks. In S. Harnard, R. W. Doty, J. Jaynes, L. Goldstein and G. Krauthamer (Eds.), *Lateralization in the nervous system.* New York: Academic Press.

Bever, T. G. 1970. The cognitive basis for linguistic structures. In J. R. Hayes (Ed.), *Cognition and the development of language.* New York: Wiley. Pp. 279–352.

Bever, T. G.; Fodor, J. A.; and Garrett, M. 1968. A formal limitation of associationism. In T. R. Dixon and D. L. Horton (Eds.), *Verbal behavior and general behavior theory.* Englewood Cliffs, N.J.: Prentice-Hall. Pp. 421–450.

Bever, T. G.; Lackner, J. R.; and Kirk, R. 1969. The underlying structures of sentences are the primary units of immediate speech processing. *Perception and Psychophysics, 5:* 225–234.

Bjork, R. A., and Whitten, W. B. 1974. Recency-sensitive retrieval processes. *Cognitive Psychology, 6:* 173–189.

Boring, E. G. 1950. *A history of experimental psychology.* Englewood Cliffs, N.J.: Prentice-Hall.

Bouma, H. 1971. Visual recognition of isolated lower-case letters. *Vision Research, 11:* 459–474.

Bourne, L. E., Jr. 1966. *Human conceptual behavior.* Boston: Allyn & Bacon.

Bourne, L. E., Jr. 1967. Learning and utilization of conceptual rules. In B. Kleinmuntz, (Ed.), *Concepts and the structure of memory.* New York: Wiley.

Bourne, L. E., Jr. 1970. Knowing and using concepts. *Psychological Review, 77:* 546–556.

Bourne, L. E., Jr. 1974. An inference model of conceptual rule learning. In R. Solso (Ed.), *Theories in cognitive psychology.* Washington, D.C.: Erlbaum.

Bousfield, W. A. 1953. The occurrence of clustering in recall of randomly arranged associates. *Journal of General Psychology, 49:* 229–240.

Bower, G. H. 1967. A multicomponent theory of the memory trace. In K. W. Spence and J. T. Spence (Eds.), *The psychology of learning and motivation: Advances in research and theory* Vol. 1. New York: Academic Press. Pp. 299–325.

Bower, G. H. 1972a. A selective review of organizational factors in memory. In E. Tulving and W. Donaldson (Eds.), *Organization of memory.* New York: Academic Press. Pp. 93–137.

Bower, G. H. 1972b. Mental imagery and associative learning. In L. W. Gregg (Ed.), *Cognition in learning and memory.* New York: Wiley. Pp. 51–88.

Bower, G. H. 1981. Mood and memory. *American Psychologist, 36:* 129–148.

Bower, G. H.; Black, J. B.; and Turner, T. J. 1979. Scripts in memory for text. *Cognitive Psychology, 11:* 177–190.

Bower, G. H., and Clark, M. C. 1969. Narrative stories as mediators for serial learning. *Psychonomic Science, 14:* 181–182.

Bower, G. H.; Clark, M. C.; Lesgold, A. M.; and Winzenz, D. 1969. Hierarchical retrieval schemes in recall of categorized word lists. *Journal of Verbal Learning and Verbal Behavior, 8:* 323–343.

Bower, G. H., and Karlin, M. B. 1974. Depth of processing pictures of faces and recognition memory. *Journal of Experimental Psychology, 103:* 751–757.

Bower, G. H., and Reitman, J. S. 1972. Mnemonic elaboration in multilist learning. *Journal of Verbal Learning and Verbal Behavior, 11:* 478–485.

Bower, G. H., and Trabasso, T. R. 1964. Concept identification. In R. C. Atkinson (Ed.), *Studies in mathematical psychology.* Stanford: Stanford University Press. Pp. 32–94.

Bowers, K. S. 1977. Science and the limits of logic: A response to the Mahoney-DeMonbreun paper. *Cognitive Therapy and Research, 1:* 239–246.

Bowyer, P. A., and Humphreys, M. S. 1979. Effect of a recognition test on a subsequent cued-recall test. *Journal of Experimental Psychology: Human Learning and Memory, 5:* 348–359.

Bransford, J. D.; Franks, J. J.; Morris, C. D.; and Stein, B. S. 1979. Some general constraints on learning and memory research. In L. S. Cermak and F. I. M. Craik (Eds.), *Levels of processing in human memory.* Hillsdale, N.J.: Erlbaum. Pp. 331–354.

Bransford, J. D., and Johnson, M. K. 1973. Consideration of some problems of comprehension. In W. G. Chase (Ed.), *Visual information processing.* New York: Academic Press.

Bransford, J. D.; Nitsch, K. E.; and Franks, J. J. 1977. Schooling and the facilitation of knowing. In R. C. Anderson, R. J. Spiro, and W. Montague (Eds.), *Schooling and the acquisition of knowledge.* Hillsdale, N.J.: Erlbaum. Pp. 31–55.

Breitmeyer, B. G. 1980. Unmasking visual masking: A look at the "Why" behind the veil of the "How." *Psychological Review, 87:* 52–69.

Brenner, C. 1957. The nature and development of the concept of repression in Freud's writings. *Psychoanalytic study of the child, 12:* 19–46.

Brewer, W. F., and Treyens, J. C. 1981. Role of schemata in memory for places. *Cognitive Psychology, 13:* 207–230.

Broadbent, D. E. 1958. *Perception and communication.* London: Pergamon Press.

Broadbent, D. E. 1977. The hidden preattentive processes. *American Psychologist, 32:* 109–118.

Brooks, L. R. 1967. The suppression of visualization by reading. *Quarterly Journal of Experimental Psychology, 19:* 289–299.

Brooks, L. R. 1968. Spatial and verbal components in the act of recall. *Canadian Journal of Psychology, 22:* 349–368.

Brooks, L. R. 1978. Nonanalytic concept formation and memory for instances. In E. Rosch and B. B. Lloyd (Eds.), *Cognition and categorization.* Hillsdale, N.J.: Erlbaum. Pp. 169–211.

Brown, A. L., and DeLoache, J. S. 1978. Skills, plans, and self-regulation. In R. S. Siegler (Ed.), *Children's thinking: What develops?* Hillsdale, N.J.: Erlbaum. Pp. 3–36.

Brown, A. S. 1976. Spontaneous recovery in human learning. *Psychological Bulletin, 83:* 321–338.

Brown, J. 1976. An analysis of recognition and recall and of problems in their comparison. In J. Brown (Ed.), *Recall and recognition.* New York: Wiley. Pp. 1–35.

Brown, J. A. 1958. Some tests of the decay theory of immediate memory. *Quarterly Journal of Experimental Psychology, 10:* 12–21.

Brown, R. 1965. *Social psychology.* New York: Free Press.

Brown, R., and Lenneberg, E. 1954. A study in language and cognition. *Journal of Abnormal and Social Psychology, 49:* 454–462.

Brown, R., and McNeill, D. 1966. The "tip of the tongue" phenomenon. *Journal of Verbal Learning and Verbal Behavior, 5:* 325–337.

Bruner, J. S.; Goodnow, J. J.; and Austin, G. A. 1956. *A study of thinking.* New York: Wiley.

Burrows, D., and Okada, R. 1971. Serial position effects in high-speed memory search. *Perception and Psychophysics, 10:* 305–308.

Buschke, H., and Schaier, A. 1979. Memory units, ideas, and propositions in semantic remembering. *Journal of Verbal Learning and Verbal Behavior, 18:* 549–563.

Cairns, H. S., and Cairns, C. E. 1976. *Psycholinguistics: A cognitive view of language.* New York: Holt, Rinehart and Winston.

Campbell, F. W., and Maffei, L. 1970. Electrophysiological evidence for the existence of orientation and size detectors in the human visual system. *Journal of Physiology, 207:* 635–652.

Carey, S. T., and Lockhart, R. S. 1973. Encoding differences in recognition and recall. *Memory and Cognition, 1:* 297–300.

Carmichael, L.; Hogan, H. P.; and Walters, A. A. 1932. An experimental study of the effect of language on the reproduction of visually perceived form. *Journal of Experimental Psychology, 15:* 73–86.

Carney, A. E.; Widin, G. P.; and Viemeister, N. F. 1977. Noncategorical perception of stop consonants differing in VOT. *Journal of the Acoustical Society of America, 62:* 961–970.

Carpenter, P. A., and Just, M. A. 1977. Integrative processes in comprehension. In D. LaBerge and S. Jay Samuels (Eds.), *Basic processes in reading: perception and comprehension.* Hillsdale, N.J.: Erlbaum. Pp. 217–242.

Carroll, J. B., and Casagrande, J. B. 1958. The function of language classification. In E. E. Maccoby, T. M. Newcomb, and E. L. Hartley (Eds.), *Readings in social psychology* (third edition). New York: Holt, Rinehart and Winston. Pp. 18–31.

Ceraso, J., and Provitera, A. 1971. Sources of error in syllogistic reasoning. *Cognitive Psychology, 2:* 400–410.

Cermak, L. S., and Craik, F. I. M. (Eds.) 1979. *Levels of processing in human memory.* Hillsdale, N.J.: Erlbaum.

Cermak, L. S., and Reale, L. 1978. Depth of processing and retention of words by alcoholic Korsakoff patients. *Journal of Experimental Psychology: Human Learning and Memory, 4:* 165–174.

Cermak, L. S.; Reale, L.; and Baker, E. 1978. Alcoholic Korsakoff patients' retrieval from semantic memory. *Brain and language, 5:* 215–216.

Chapin, P. G.; Smith, T. S.; and Abrahamson, A. A. 1972. Two factors in perceptual segmentation in speech. *Journal of Verbal Learning and Verbal Behavior, 11:* 164–173.

Chapman, I. J., and Chapman, J. P. 1959. Atmosphere effect reconsidered. *Journal of Experimental Psychology, 58:* 220–226.

Chase, W. G. 1978. Elementary information processes. In W. K. Estes (Ed.), *Handbook of learning and cognitive processes* Vol. 5. Hillsdale, N.J.: Erlbaum. Pp. 19–90.

Chase, W. G., and Simon, H. A. 1973. The mind's eye in chess. In W. G. Chase (Ed.), *Visual information processing.* New York: Academic Press.

Cherry, E. C. 1953. Some experiments on the recognition of speech with one and with two ears. *Journal of the Acoustical Society of America, 25:* 975–979.

Chomsky, N. 1957. *Syntactic structures.* The Hague: Mouton.

Chomsky, N. 1959. A review of B. F. Skinner's *Verbal Behavior. Language, 35:* 26–58.

Chomsky, N. 1965. *Aspects of the theory of syntax.* Cambridge Mass.: M.I.T. Press.

Chomsky, N. 1972. *Language and mind.* New York: Harcourt Brace Jovanovich.

Chomsky, N. 1975. *Reflections on language.* New York: Pantheon Books.

Chumbley, J. 1969. Hypothesis memory in concept learning. *Journal of Mathematical Psychology, 6:* 528–540.

Clark, H. H. 1969. Linguistic processes in deductive reasoning. *Psychological Review, 76:* 387–404.

Clark, H. H. 1977. Inferences in comprehension. In D. LaBerge and S. J. Samuels (Eds.), *Basic Processes in reading: perception and comprehension.* Hillsdale, N.J.: Erlbaum. Pp. 243–263.

Clark, H. H. 1978. On inferring what is meant. In W. J. M. Levelt and G. B. Flores d'Arcais (Eds.), *Studies in the perception of language.* New York: Wiley, Pp. 295–322.

Clark, H. H., and Clark, E. V. 1977. *Psychology and language.* New York: Harcourt Brace Jovanovich.

Clark, H. H., and Haviland, S. E. 1977. Comprehension and the given-new contract. In R. Freedle (Ed.), *Discourse comprehension and production.* Norwood, N.J.: Ablex Publishing.

Clifton, C., Jr., and Birenbaum, S. 1970. Effects of serial position and delay of probe in a memory scan task. *Journal of Experimental Psychology, 86:* 69–76.

Clifton C., Jr.; Kurcz, I.; and Jenkins, J. J. 1965. Grammatical relations as determinants of sentence similarity. *Journal of Verbal Learning and Verbal Behavior, 4:* 112–117.

Cohen, L. J. 1980. Whose is the fallacy? A rejoinder to Daniel Kahneman and Amos Tversky. *Cognition, 8:* 89–92.

Cole, M., and Scribner, S. 1977. Cross-cultural studies of memory and cognition. In Robert V. Kail, Jr. and J. W. Hagen (Eds.), *Perspectives on the development of memory and cognition.* Hillsdale, N.J.: Erlbaum. Pp. 239–272.

Cole, R. A. 1973. Listening for mispronunciations: a measure of what we hear during speech. *Perception and Psychophysics, 11:* 153–156.

Collins, A. M., and Loftus, E. R. 1975. A spreading-activation theory of semantic processing. *Psychological Review, 82:* 407–428.

Collins, A. M., and Quillian, M. R. 1969. Retrieval time from semantic memory. *Journal of Verbal Learning and Verbal Behavior, 8:* 240–247.

Collins, A. M., and Quillian, M. R. 1972. How to make a language user. In E. Tulving and W. Donaldson (Eds.), *Organization of memory*. New York: Academic Press. Pp. 309–351.

Coltheart, M. 1980. Iconic memory and visible persistence. *Perception and Psychophysics, 27:* 183–228.

Conrad, C. 1972. Cognitive economy in semantic memory. *Journal of Experimental Psychology, 92:* 149–154.

Conrad, R. 1964. Acoustic confusions in immediate memory. *British Journal of Psychology, 55:* 75–84.

Corcoran, D. W. J. 1971. *Pattern recognition*. Baltimore: Penguin Books.

Corteen, R. S., and Dunn, D. 1974. Shock-associated words in a non-attended message: A test for momentary awareness. *Journal of Experimental Psychology, 102:* 1143–1144.

Craik, F. I. M. 1979. Human memory. *Annual Review of Psychology, 30:* 63–102.

Craik, F. I. M., and Jacoby, L. L. 1979. Elaboration and distinctiveness in episodic memory. In L. Nilsson (Ed.), *Perspectives on memory research: Essays in honor of Uppsala University's 500th anniversary*. Hillsdale, N.J.: Erlbaum. Pp. 145–165.

Craik, F. I. M., and Lockhart, R. S. 1972. Levels of processing: a framework for memory research. *Journal of Verbal Learning and Verbal Behavior, 11:* 671–684.

Craik, F. I. M., and Tulving, E. 1975. Depth of processing and the retention of words in episodic memory. *Journal of Experimental Psychology: General, 104:* 268–294.

Craik, F. I. M., and Watkins, M. J. 1973. The role of rehearsal in short-term memory. *Journal of Verbal Learning and Verbal Behavior, 12:* 599–607.

Cromer, R. F. 1970. Children are nice to understand; Surface structure clues for the recovery of a deep structure. *British Journal of Psychology, 61:* 397–408.

Cronholm, B. 1969. Post-ECT amnesias. In G. A. Talland and N. C. Waugh (Eds.), *The pathology of memory*. New York: Academic Press.

Crowder, R. G. 1967. Short-term memory for words with a perceptual-motor interpolated activity. *Journal of Verbal Learning and Verbal Behavior, 6:* 753–761.

Crowder, R. G. 1978. Sensory memory systems. In E. C. Carterette and M. P. Friedman (Eds.), *Handbook of Perception*, Vol. VIII. New York: Academic Press. Pp. 344–373.

Crowder, R. G., and Morton, J. 1969. Precategorical acoustic storage (PAS). *Perception and Psychophysics, 5:* 365–373.

Cutting, J. E., and Rosner, B. S. 1974. Categories and boundaries in speech and music. *Perception and Psychophysics, 16:* 564–570.

Darwin, C. T.; Turvey, M. T.; and Crowder, R. G. 1972. An auditory analogue of the Sperling partial report procedure: Evidence for brief auditory storage. *Cognitive Psychology, 3:* 255–267.

De Groot, A. D. 1965. *Thought and choice in chess*. New York: Basic Books.

De Groot, A. D. 1966. Perception and memory versus thought: some old ideas and recent findings. In B. Kleinmuntz (Ed.), *Problem solving*. New York: Wiley.

De Soto, C. B.; London, M.; and Handel, S. 1965. Social reasoning and spatial paralogic. *Journal of Personality and Social Psychology, 2:* 513–521.

Deutsch, J. A., and Deutsch, D. 1963. Attention: some theoretical considerations. *Psychological Review, 70:* 80–90.

Dick, A. O. 1974. Iconic memory and its relation to perceptual processing and other memory mechanisms. *Perception and Psychophysics, 16:* 575–594.

DiLollo, V. 1980. Temporal integration in visual memory. *Journal of Experimental Psychology: General, 109:* 75–97.

Dodd, D. H.; Kinsman, R.; Klipp, R.; and Bourne, L. E., Jr. 1971. Effects of logic pretraining on conceptual rule learning. *Journal of Experimental Psychology, 88:* 119–122.

Dooling, D. J., and Christiaansen, R. E. 1977. Levels of encoding and retention of prose. In G. H. Bower (Ed.), *The psychology of learning and motivation,* Vol. 11. New York: Academic Press. Pp. 1–39.

Dornbush, R. L., and Williams, M. 1974. Memory and ECT. In M. Fink, S. Kety, J. McGaugh, and T. A. Williams (Eds.), *Psychobiology of convulsive therapy.* New York: Wiley. Pp. 199–208.

Drachman, D. A., and Arbit, J. 1966. Memory and the hippocampal complex, II. *Archives of Neurology, 15:* 52–61.

Dreyfus, H. L. 1979. *What computers can't do.* New York: Harper & Row.

Dyer, F. N. 1973. The Stroop phenomenon and its use in the study of perceptual, cognitive and response processes. *Memory and Cognition, 1:* 106–120.

Dyer, J. C., and Meyer, P. A. 1976. Facilitation of simple concept identification through mnemonic instruction. *Journal of Experimental Psychology: Human Learning and Memory, 2:* 767–773.

Dunker, K. 1945. On problem solving. *Psychological Monographs, 58:* No. 270.

Ebbinghaus, H. 1885. *Memory: A contribution to experimental psychology.* Translated by H. A. Ruger and C. E. Bussenius. New York: Dover.

Egan, D. E., and Greeno, J. G. 1974. Theory of rule induction: knowledge acquired in concept learning, serial pattern learning and problem solving. In L. W. Gregg (Ed.), *Knowledge and cognition.* Potomac, Md.: Erlbaum. Pp. 43–103.

Egstrom, G. H., and Bachrach, A. J. 1971. Diver panic. *Skin Diver,* November: 36–39.

Eich, J. E. 1977. State-dependent retrieval of information in human episodic memory. In I. M. Birnbaum and E. S. Parker (Eds.), *Alcohol and human memory.* Hillsdale, N.J.: Erlbaum.

Eimas, P. D. 1978. Developmental aspects of speech perception. In R. Held, H. Leibowitz and H. L. Teuber (Eds.), *Handbook of sensory physiology: Perception.* New York: Springer-Verlag. Pp. 365–382.

Eimas, P. D., and Miller, J. L. 1978. Effects of selective adaptation on the perception of speech and visual patterns: Evidence for feature detectors. In R. D. Walk and H. L. Pick, Jr. (Eds.), *Perception and experience.* New York: Plenum. Pp. 307–345.

Ekstrand, B. R. 1972. To sleep, perchance to dream (about why we forget). In C. P. Duncan, L. Sechrest, and A. W. Helton (Eds.), *Human memory:*

Festschrift in honor of Benton J. Underwood. New York: Prentice-Hall. Pp. 59–82.

Erdelyi, M. H., and Becker, J. 1974. Hyperamnesia for pictures: Incremental memory for pictures but not words in multiple recall trials. *Cognitive Psychology, 6:* 159–171.

Erdelyi, M. H., and Goldberg, B. 1979. Let's not sweep repression under the rug: Toward a cognitive psychology of repression. In J. F. Kihlstrom and F. J. Evans (Eds.), *Functional disorders of memory.* Hillsdale, N.J.: Erlbaum. Pp. 355–402.

Ericsson, K. A.; Chase, W. G.; and Faloon, S. 1980. Acquisition of a memory skill. *Science, 208:* 1181–1182.

Ericsson, K. A., and Simon, H. A. 1980. Verbal reports as data. *Psychological Review, 87:* 215–251.

Erikson, J. R. 1974. A set analysis theory of behavior in formal syllogistic reasoning tasks. In R. Solso (Ed.), *Theories in cognitive psychology: The Loyola symposium.* Potomac, Md.: Erlbaum.

Eyesenck, M. W. 1978. Levels of processing: A critique. *British Journal of Psychology, 68:* 157–169.

Eyesenck, M. W. 1979. Depth, elaboration and distinctiveness. In L. S. Cermak and F. I. Craik. (Eds.), *Levels of processing in human memory.* Hillsdale, N.J.: Erlbaum. Pp. 89–118.

Eyesenck, M. W., and Eyesenck, K. C. 1979. Processing depth, elaboration of encoding, memory stores, and expanded processing capacity. *Journal of Experimental Psychology: Human Learning and Memory, 5:* 472–484.

Feigenbaum, E. A. 1963. Simulation of verbal learning behavior. In E. A. Feigenbaum and J. Feldman (Eds.), *Computers and thought.* New York: McGraw-Hill.

Finke, R. A. 1980. Levels of equivalence in imagery and perception. *Psychological Review, 87:* 113–132.

Fisher, R. P., and Craik, F. I. M. 1977. The interaction between encoding and retrieval operations in cued recall. *Journal of Experimental Psychology: Human Learning and Memory, 3:* 701–711.

Flavell, J. H.; Beach, D. R.; and Chinsky, J. M. 1966. Spontaneous verbal rehearsal in a memory task as a function of age. *Child Development, 37:* 283–299.

Flavell, J. H.; Cooper, A.; and Loiselle, R. H. 1958. Effect of the number of pre-utilization functions on functional fixedness in problem solving. *Psychological Reports, 4:* 343–350.

Flavell, J. H., and Wellman, H. M. 1977. Metamemory. In R. V. Kail, Jr. and J. W. Hagen (Eds.), *Perspectives on the development of memory and cognition.* Hillsdale, N.J.: Erlbaum. Pp. 3–34.

Flexser, A. J., and Tulving, E. 1978. Retrieval independence in recognition and recall. *Psychological Review, 85:* 153–171.

Flores d'Arcais, G. B. 1978. The perception of complex sentences. In W. Levelt and G. Flores d'Arcais (Eds.), *Studies in the perception of language.* New York: Wiley. Pp. 155–185.

Fodor, J. A., and Bever, T. G. 1965. The psychological reality of linguistic segments. *Journal of Verbal Learning and Verbal Behavior, 4:* 414–420.

Fodor, J. A.; Bever, T. G.; and Garrett, M. F. 1974. *The psychology of language: An introduction to psycholinguistics and generative grammar.* New York: McGraw-Hill.

Fodor, J. A., and Garrett, M. 1966. Some reflections on competence and performance. In J. Lyons and R. J. Wales (Eds.), *Psycholinguistics papers.* Edinburgh: University of Edinburgh Press.

Fodor, J. A., and Garrett, M. F. 1967. Some syntactic determinants of sentential complexity. *Perception and Psychophysics, 2:* 289–296.

Fodor, J. A.; Garrett, M. F.; and Bever, T. G. 1968. Some syntactic determinants of sentential complexity II: Verb structure. *Perception and Psychophysics, 3:* 453–461.

Forster, K. I. 1979. Levels of processing and the structure of the language processor. In W. E. Cooper and T. Walker (Eds.), *Sentence processing.* Hillsdale, N.J.: Erlbaum. Pp. 27–85.

Foss, D. J., and Harwood, D. A. 1975. Memory for sentences: implications for human associative memory. *Journal of Verbal Learning and Verbal Behavior, 14:* 1–16.

Foss, D. J., and Jenkins, C. M. 1973. Some effects of context on the comprehension of ambiguous sentences. *Journal of Verbal Learning and Verbal Behavior, 12:* 577–589.

Franken, R. E., and Rowland, G. L. 1979. Nature of the representation for picture-recognition memory. *Perceptual and Motor Skills, 49:* 619–629.

Franks, J. J., and Bransford, J. D. 1971. Abstraction of visual patterns. *Journal of Experimental Psychology, 90:* 65–74.

Frase, L. T. 1968. Associative factors in syllogistic reasoning. *Journal of Experimental Psychology, 76:* 407–412.

Freibergs, V., and Tulving, E. 1961. The effect of practice on utilization of information from positive and negative instances in concept identification. *Canadian Journal of Psychology, 15:* 101–106.

Freud. S. 1957. Repression. *The complete psychological works of Sigmund Freud* Vol. 14. London: Hogarth.

Friedman, A. 1979. Framing pictures: The role of knowledge in automatized encoding and memory for gist. *Journal of Experimental Psychology: General, 108:* 316–355.

Gardiner, J. H.; Craik, F. I. M.; and Birtwistle, J. 1972. Retrieval cues and release from proactive inhibition. *Journal of Verbal Learning and Verbal Behavior, 11:* 778–783.

Gardner, H. 1974. *The shattered mind.* New York: Random House (Vintage Books).

Garner, W. R. 1974. *The processing of information and structure.* Potomac, Md.: Erlbaum.

Garner, W. R.; Hake, H. W.; and Eriksen, C. W. 1956. Operationism and the concept of perception. *Psychological Review, 63:* 149–159.

Garrett, M. F.; Bever, T. G.; and Fodor, J. A. 1966. The active use of grammar in speech perception. *Perception and Psychophysics, 1:* 30–32.

Gazzaniga, M. S. 1967. The split brain in man. *Scientific American, 217:* 24–29.

Gazzaniga, M. S. 1970. *The bisected brain.* New York: Prentice-Hall.

Gelman, P. 1969. Conservation acquisition: A problem of learning to attend to relevant attributes. *Journal of Experimental Child Psychology, 7:* 67–87.

Geiselman, R. E., and Bjork, R. A. 1980. Primary versus secondary rehearsal in imagined voices: Differential effects on recognition. *Cognitive Psychology, 12:* 188–205.

Geyer, L. H., and DeWald, C. G. 1973. Feature lists and confusion matrices. *Perception and Psychophysics, 14:* 471–482.

Gibson, E. 1969. *Principles of perceptual learning and development.* New York: Prentice-Hall.

Gibson, E. J., and Levin, H. 1975. *The psychology of reading.* Cambridge, Mass.: M.I.T. Press.

Glanzer, M., and Cunitz, A. R. 1966. Two storage mechanisms in free recall. *Journal of Verbal Learning and Verbal Behavior, 5:* 351–360.

Glass, A. L., and Holyoak, K. J. 1975. Alternative conceptions of semantic memory. *Cognition, 3:* 313–339.

Glaze, A. J. 1928. The association value of nonsense syllables. *Journal of Genetic Psychology, 35:* 255–269.

Glenberg, A., and Adams, F. 1978. Type I rehearsal and recognition. *Journal of Verbal Learning and Verbal Behavior, 17:* 455–463.

Glenberg, A. M.; Bradley, M. M.; Stevenson, J. A.; Kraus, T. A.; Tkachuk, M. J.; Gretz, A. L.; Fish, J. H.; and Turpin, B. A. M. 1980. A two-process account of long-term serial position effects. *Journal of Experimental Psychology: Human Learning and Memory, 6:* 355–369.

Glucksberg, S., and Danks, J. 1968. Effects of discriminative labels and of nonsense labels upon availability of novel function. *Journal of Verbal Learning and Verbal Behavior, 7:* 72–76.

Glucksberg, S., and King, L. J. 1967. Motivated forgetting mediated by implicit verbal chaining. *Science, 158:* 517–519.

Glucksberg, S., and Weisberg, R. W. 1966. Verbal behavior and problem solving: Some effects of labeling in a functional fixedness problem. *Journal of Experimental Psychology, 71:* 659–664.

Goldstein, A. G., and Chance, J. 1970. Visual recognition memory for complex configurations. *Perception and Psychophysics, 9:* 237–241.

Goodglass, H., and Geschwind, N. 1976. Language disorders (aphasia). In E. C. Carterette and M. P. Friedman (Eds.), *Handbook of perception* Vol. VII. New York: Academic Press. Pp. 389–428.

Greeno, J. G. 1974. Hobbits and Orcs: Acquisition of a sequential concept. *Cognitive Psychology, 6:* 270–292.

Greeno, J. G. 1978. Nature of problem solving abilities. In W. K. Estes (Ed.), *Handbook of learning and cognitive processes* Vol. 5. Hillsdale, N.J.: Erlbaum. Pp. 239–270.

Grice, H. P. 1975. William James Lectures, Harvard University, 1967. In P. Cole and J. L. Morgan (Eds.), *Syntax and semantics.* Vol. 3. New York: Seminar Press.

Griggs, R. A.; Townes, K. J.; and Keen, D. M. 1979. Processing numerical quantitative information in artificial linear orderings. *Journal of Experimental Psychology: Human Learning and Memory, 5:* 282–291.

Hall, J. F. 1954. Learning as a function of word frequency. *American Journal of Psychology, 67:* 138–140.

Halliday, M. A. K. 1967. Notes on transitivity and theme in English: II. *Journal of Linguistics, 3:* 199–244.

Hampton, J. A. 1979. Polymorphous concepts in semantic memory. *Journal of Verbal Learning and Verbal Behavior, 18:* 441–462.

Hanawalt, N. G., Demarest, I. H. 1939. The effect of verbal suggestion in the recall period upon the reproduction of visually perceived forms. *Journal of Experimental Psychology, 25:* 159–174.

Haviland, S. E., and Clark, H. H. 1974. What's new? Acquiring new information as a process in comprehension. *Journal of Verbal Learning and Verbal Behavior, 13:* 512–521.

Hayes, J. R., and Simon, H. A. 1976. Understanding complex task instructions. In D. Klahr (Ed.), *Cognition and instruction.* Hillsdale, N.J.: Erlbaum. Pp. 269–286.

Hayes-Roth, B., and Hayes-Roth, F. 1977. Concept learning and the recognition and classification of exemplars. *Journal of Verbal Learning and Verbal Behavior, 16:* 321–338.

Haygood, R. C., and Bourne, L. E., Jr. 1965. Attributes and rule-learning concepts of conceptual behavior. *Psychological Review, 72:* 175–195.

Heider, E. R., and Oliver, D. 1972. The structure of the color space in naming and memory for two languages. *Cognitive Psychology, 3:* 337–354.

Henle, M. 1962. On the relation between logic and thinking. *Psychological Review, 69:* 366–378.

Hilgard, E. R. 1977. *Divided consciousness: Multiple controls in human thought and action.* New York: Wiley.

Hirst, W.; Spelke, E. S.; Reaves, C. C.; Caharack, G.; and Neisser, U. 1980. Dividing attention without alternation or automaticity. *Journal of Experimental Psychology: General, 109:* 98–117.

Hoffman, J. E. 1980. Interaction between global and local levels of a form. *Journal of Experimental Psychology: Human Perception and Performance, 6:* 222–234.

Holmes, D. S. 1974. Investigations of repression: Differential recall of material experimentally or naturally associated with ego threat. *Psychological Bulletin, 81:* 632–653.

Holmes, V. M., and Forster, K. I. 1970. Detection of extraneous signals during sentence recognition. *Perception and Psychophysics, 7:* 297–301.

Holyoak, K. J., and Glass, A. L. 1975. The role of contradictions and counterexamples in the rejection of false sentences. *Journal of Verbal Learning and Verbal Behavior, 14:* 215–239.

Homa, D. 1978. Abstraction of ill-defined form. *Journal of Experimental Psychology: Human Learning and Memory, 4:* 407–416.

Homa, D., and Vosburgh, R. 1976. Category breadth and the abstraction of prototypical information. *Journal of Experimental Psychology: Human Learning and Memory, 2:* 322–330.

Hovland, C. I. 1952. A "communication analysis" of concept learning. *Psychological Review, 59:* 461–472.

Hovland, C. I., and Weiss, W. 1953. Transmission of information concerning concepts through positive and negative instances. *Journal of Experimental Psychology, 45:* 165–182.

Hubel, D. H., and Wiesel, T. N. 1962. Receptive fields, binocular interaction and functional architecture in the cat's visual cortex. *Journal of Physiology, 160:* 106–154.

Hubel, D. H., and Wiesel, T. N. 1968. Receptive fields and functional architecture of monkey striate cortex. *Journal of Physiology, 195:* 215–243.

Hull, C. L. 1920. Quantitative aspects of the evolution of concepts: An experimental study. *Psychological Monographs, 28:* No. 123.

Hunter, I. M. L. 1957. The solving of three-term series problems. *British Journal of Psychology, 48:* 280–298.

Huttenlocher, J. 1968. Constructing spatial images: A strategy in reasoning. *Psychological Review, 75:* 550–560.

Hyde, T. S., and Jenkins, J. J. 1969. Differential effects of incidental tasks on the organization of recall of a list of highly associated words. *Journal of Experimental Psychology, 82:* 472–481.

Hyde, T. S., and Jenkins, J. J. 1973. Recall of words as a function of semantic, graphic and syntactic orienting tasks. *Journal of Verbal Learning and Verbal Behavior, 12:* 471–480.

Hyman, R. 1953. Stimulus information as a determinant of reaction time. *Journal of Experimental Psychology, 45:* 188–196.

Jacoby, L. L., and Bartz, W. H. 1972. Encoding processes and the negative recency effect. *Journal of Verbal Learning and Verbal Behavior, 11:* 561–565.

Jacoby, L. L.; Bartz, W. H.; and Evans, J. D. 1978. A functional approach to levels of processing. *Journal of Experimental Psychology: Human Learning and Memory, 4:* 331–346.

Jacoby, L. L., and Craik, F. I. M. 1979. Effects of elaboration of processing at encoding and retrieval: Trace distinctiveness and recovery of initial context. In L. S. Cermak and F. I. M. Craik (Eds.), *Levels of processing in human memory.* Hillsdale, N.J.: Erlbaum. Pp. 1–21.

James, W. 1890. *Principles of psychology.* New York: Holt, Rinehart and Winston.

Janis, I. L., and Frick, F. 1943. The relationship between attitudes toward conclusions and errors in judging logical validity of syllogisms. *Journal of Experimental Psychology, 33:* 73–77.

Jeffries, R.; Polson, P. G.; Razran, L.; and Atwood M. E. 1977. A process model for missionaries-cannibals and other river-crossing problems. *Cognitive Psychology, 9:* 412–440.

Jenkins, J. G., and Dallenbach, K. M. 1924. Oblivescence during sleep and waking. *American Journal of Psychology, 35:* 605–612.

Jenkins, J. J. 1974. Remember that old theory of memory? Well forget it! *American Psychologist, 29:* 785–795.

Johnson-Laird, P. N., and Steedman, M. 1978. The psychology of syllogisms. *Cognitive Psychology, 10:* 64–99.

Johnston, W. A., and Heinz, S. P. 1978. Flexibility and capacity demands of attention. *Journal of Experimental Psychology: General, 107:* 420–435.

Kahneman, D. 1973. *Attention and effort.* Englewood Cliffs, N.J.: Prentice-Hall.

Kahneman, D., and Tversky, A. 1972. Subjective probability: a judgment of representativeness. *Cognitive Psychology, 3:* 430–454.

Kahneman, D., and Tversky, A. 1973. On the psychology of prediction. *Psychological Review, 80:* 237–251.

Katz, J. J. 1972. *Semantic theory.* New York: Harper & Row.

Keenan, J. M., and Kintsch, W. 1974. The identification of explicitly and implicitly presented information. In W. Kintsch (Ed.), *The representation of meaning in memory.* Hillsdale, N.J.: Erlbaum.

Keenan, J. M.; MacWhinney, B.; and Mayhew, D. 1977. Pragmatics in memory: A study of natural conversation. *Journal of Verbal Learning and Verbal Behavior, 16:* 549–560.

Keenan, J. M., and Moore, R. E. 1979. Memory for images of concealed objects: A reexamination of Neisser and Kerr. *Journal of Experimental Psychology: Human Learning and Memory, 5:* 374–385.

Keeney, T. J.; Cannizo, S. R.; and Flavell, J. H. 1967. Spontaneous and induced verbal rehearsal in a recall task. *Child Development, 38:* 953–966.

Kellog, R. T. 1980. Feature frequency and hypothesis testing in the acquisition of rule-governed concepts. *Memory and Cognition, 8:* 297–303.

Keppel, G. 1968. Retroactive and proactive inhibition. In T. R. Dixon and D. L. Horton (Eds.), *Verbal behavior and general behavior theory.* Englewood Cliffs, N.J.: Prentice-Hall.

Keppel, G., and Underwood, B. J. 1962. Proactive inhibition in short-term retention of single items. *Journal of Verbal Learning and Verbal Behavior, 1:* 153–161.

Kihlstrom, J. F. 1980. Posthypnotic amnesia for recently learned material: Interactions with "Episodic" and "Semantic" memory. *Cognitive Psychology, 12:* 227–251.

Kimball, J. P. 1973. Seven principles of surface structure parsing in natural language. *Cognition, 2:* 15–47.

Kinchla, R. A., and Wolfe, J. M. 1979. The order of visual processing: "Top-down," "bottom-up," or "middle-out." *Perception and Psychophysics, 25:* 225–231.

Kinney, G. C.; Marsetta, M.; and Showman D. J. 1966. Studies in display symbol legibility, Part XII. The legibility of alpha-numeric symbols for digitalized television. Bedford, Mass.: The Mitre Corporation, ESD-TR-66-117.

Kinsbourne, M., and George, J. 1974. The mechanism of the word-frequency effect on recognition memory. *Journal of Verbal Learning and Verbal Behavior, 13:* 63–69.

Kinsbourne, M., and Hicks, R. E. 1978. Functional cerebral space: A model for overflow, transfer and interference effects in human performance: A tutorial review. In J. Requin (Ed.), *Attention and performance VII.* Hillsdale, N.J.: Erlbaum. Pp. 345–362.

Kintsch, W. 1968. Recognition and free recall of organized lists. *Journal of Experimental Psychology, 78:* 481–487.

Kintsch, W. 1970. *Learning, memory and conceptual processes.* New York: Wiley.

Kintsch, W. 1974. *The representation of meaning in memory.* Hillsdale, N.J.: Erlbaum.

Kintsch, W., and Keenan, J. 1973. Reading rate and retention as a function of the number of propositions in the base structure of sentences. *Cognitive Psychology, 5:* 257–274.

Kintsch, W.; Kozminsky, E.; Streby, W. J.; McKoon, G.; and Keenan, J. M. 1975. Comprehension and recall of text as a function of content variables. *Journal of Verbal Learning and Verbal Behavior, 14:* 196–214.

Kintsch, W., and van Dijk, T. A. 1975. Comment on se rappelle et on résume des histoires. *Langages, 40:* 98–116.

Kintsch, W., and Vipond, D. 1979. Reading comprehension and readability in educational practice and psychological theory. In Lars-Goran Nilsson (Ed.), *Perspectives on memory research.* Hillsdale, N.J.: Erlbaum. Pp. 329–365.

Köhler, W. 1925. *The mentality of apes.* London: Routledge & Kegan Paul.

Köhler, W. 1947. *Gestalt psychology.* New York: Liveright.

Kolers, P. A. 1979. A pattern-analyzing basis of recognition. In L. S. Cermak and F. I. M. Craik (Eds.), *Levels of processing in human memory.* Hillsdale, N.J.: Erlbaum. Pp. 363–384.

Kolers, P. A., and Ostry, D. J. 1974. Time course of loss of information regarding pattern analyzing operations. *Journal of Verbal Learning and Verbal Behavior, 13:* 599–612.

Kolers, P. A., and Smythe, W. E. 1979. Images, symbols and skills. *Canadian Journal of Psychology, 33:* 151–184.

Kosslyn, S. M. 1975. Information representation in visual images. *Cognitive Psychology, 7:* 341–370.

Kosslyn, S. M. 1978. Imagery and internal representation. In E. Rosch and B. B. Lloyd (Eds.), *Cognition and categorization.* Hillsdale, N.J.: Erlbaum. Pp. 217–257.

Kosslyn, S. M. 1980. *Image and mind.* Cambridge: Harvard University Press.

Kosslyn, S. M. 1981. The medium and the message in mental imagery: A theory. *Psychological Review, 88:* 46–66.

Kosslyn, S. M., and Pomerantz, J. R. 1977. Imagery, propositions, and the form of internal representations. *Cognitive Psychology, 8:* 52–76.

Kosslyn, S. M., and Shwartz, S. P. 1977. A simulation of visual imagery. *Cognitive Science, 1:* 265–296.

Kreutzer, M. A.; Leonard, C.; and Flavell, J. H. 1975. An interview study of children's knowledge about memory. *Monographs of the society for research in child development, 40:* No. 159.

Kroll, N. E. A.; Parks, T.; Parkinson, S. R.; Bieber, S. L.; and Johnson, A. L. 1970. Short-term memory while shadowing: recall of visually and aurally presented letters. *Journal of Experimental Psychology, 85:* 220–224.

Kucera, H., and Francis, W. N. 1967. *Computational analysis of present-day American English.* Providence: Brown University Press.

Kuhl, P. K., and Miller, J. D. 1975. Speech perception by the chinchilla:

Voiced-voiceless distinction in alveolar plosive consonants. *Science, 190:* 69–72.

Kuhn, T. S. 1970. *The structure of scientific revolutions* (second edition). Chicago: University of Chicago Press.

Kunen, G.; Green, D.; and Waterman, D. 1979. Spread of encoding effects within the nonverbal visual domain. *Journal of Experimental Psychology: Human Learning and Memory, 5:* 574–584.

LaBerge, D. 1973. Attention and the measurement of perceptual learning. *Memory and Cognition, 1:* 268–276.

LaBerge, D. 1976. Perceptual learning and attention. In W. K. Estes (Ed.), *Handbook of learning and cognitive processes* Vol. 4. Hillsdale, N.J.: Erlbaum. Pp. 177–236.

LaBerge, D., and Samuels, S. J. 1974. Toward a theory of automatic information processing in reading. *Cognitive Psychology, 6:* 292–323.

Labov, W. 1973. The boundaries of words and their meanings. In C. J. N. Bailey and R. W. Shuy (Eds.), *New ways of analyzing variation in English.* Washington, D.C.: Georgetown University Press.

Lachman, R.; Lachman, J. L.; and Butterfield, E. C. 1979. *Cognitive psychology and information processing: An introduction.* Hillsdale, N.J.: Erlbaum.

Lackner, J. R., and Garrett, M. F. 1972. Resolving ambiguity: Effects of biasing contexts in the unattended ear. *Cognition, 1:* 359–372.

Ladefoged, P. 1967. *Three areas of experimental phonetics.* London: Oxford University Press.

Lakoff, G. 1972. Hedges: A study in meaning criteria and the logic of fuzzy concepts. *Papers from the eighth regional meeting, Chicago Linguistics Society.* Chicago: University of Chicago Linguistics Department.

Lasky, R. E.; Syrdal-Lasky, A.; and Klein, R. E. 1975. VOT discrimination by four to six and a half month old infants from Spanish environments. *Journal of Experimental Child Psychology, 20:* 215–225.

Lenneberg, E. H. 1967. *Biological foundations of language.* New York: Wiley.

Leonard, J. A. 1958. Partial advance information in a choice reaction task. *British Journal of Psychology, 49:* 89–96.

Levelt, W. J. M. 1970. Hierarchical clustering algorithm in the psychology of grammar. In G. B. Flores and W. J. M. Levelt (Eds.), *Advances in psycholinguistics.* Amsterdam: North Holland Publishing. Pp. 101–140.

Levelt, W. J. M. 1978. A survey of studies in sentence perception: 1970–1976. In W. J. M. Levelt and G. B. Flores d'Arcais (Eds.), *Studies in the perception of language.* New York: Wiley. Pp. 1–74.

Levine, M. 1966. Hypothesis behavior by humans during discrimination learning. *Journal of Experimental Psychology, 71:* 331–338.

Levine, M. 1975. *A cognitive theory of learning.* Hillsdale, N.J.: Erlbaum.

Levine, M.; Miller, P. I.; and Steinmeyer, H. 1967. The none-to-all theorem of human discrimination learning. *Journal of Experimental Psychology, 73:* 568–573.

Lewis, D. J.; Miller, R. R.; and Misanin, J. R. 1968. Recovery of memory following amnesia. *Nature, 220:* 704–705.

Lewis, J. L. 1970. Semantic processing of unattended messages using dichotic listening. *Journal of Experimental Psychology, 85:* 225–228.

Liberman, A. M.; Harris, K. S.; Hoffman, H. S.; and Griffith, B. C. 1957. The discrimination of speech sounds within and across phoneme boundaries. *Journal of Experimental Psychology, 54:* 358–368.

Light, L. L., and Carter-Sobell, L. 1970. Effects of changed semantic context on recognition memory. *Journal of Verbal Learning and Verbal Behavior, 9:* 1–11.

Light, L. L.; Kimble, G. A.; and Pellegrino, J. W. 1975. Comments on "Episodic memory: When recognition fails" by Watkins and Tulving. *Journal of Experimental Psychology: General, 1:* 30–36.

Lindsay, P. H., and Norman, D. A. 1972. *Human information processing.* New York: Academic Press.

Lisker, L., and Abramson, A. S. 1964. A cross-language study of voicing in initial stops: Acoustical measurements. *Word, 20:* 384–422.

Lockhart, R. S.; Craik, F. I. M.; and Jacoby, L. 1976. Depth of processing, recognition and recall. In J. Brown (Ed.), *Recognition and recall.* New York: Wiley. Pp. 75–102.

Loftus, E. F. 1979. *Eyewitness testimony.* Cambridge, Mass.: Harvard University Press.

Loftus, E. F., and Palmer, J. C. 1974. Reconstruction of automobile destruction: An example of the interaction between language and memory. *Journal of Verbal Learning and Verbal Behavior, 13:* 585–589.

Loftus, G. R., and Patterson, K. K. 1975. Components of short-term proactive interference. *Journal of Verbal Learning and Verbal Behavior, 14:* 105–121.

Lorch, R. F., Jr. 1978. The role of two types of semantic information in the processing of false sentences. *Journal of Verbal Learning and Verbal Behavior, 17:* 523–538.

Lupker, S. J. 1979. On the nature of perceptual information during letter perception. *Perception and Psychophysics, 25:* 303–312.

Luria, A. R. 1968. *The mind of a mnemonist.* New York: Basic Books.

MacKay, D. G. 1966. To end ambiguous sentences. *Perception and Psychophysics, 3:* 426–436.

Mackay, D. G. 1973. Aspects of the theory of comprehension, memory and attention. *Quarterly Journal of Experimental Psychology, 25:* 22–40.

MacKenzie, N. 1965. *Dreams and dreaming.* London: Aldus Books.

Mahoney, M. J., and DeMonbreun, B. G. 1977. Psychology of the scientist: An analysis of problem-solving bias. *Cognitive Therapy and Research, 1:* 229–238.

Maier, N. R. F. 1931. Reasoning in humans. II. The solution of a problem and its appearance in consciousness. *Journal of Comparative Psychology, 12:* 181–194.

Maki, R. H., and Schuler, J. 1980. Effects of rehearsal duration and level of processing on memory for words. *Journal of Verbal Learning and Verbal Behavior, 19:* 36–45.

Mandler, G. 1979. Organization and repetition: Organizational principles with special reference to rote learning. In L. Nilsson (Ed.), *Perspectives on memory research: Essays in honor of Uppsala University's 500th anniversary.* Hillsdale, N.J.: Erlbaum. Pp. 293–327.

Mandler, G., and Boeck, W. 1974. Retrieval processes in recognition. *Memory and Cognition, 2:* 613–615.

Mandler, J. M., and Ritchey, G. H. 1977. Long-term memory for pictures. *Journal of Experimental Psychology: Human Learning and Memory, 3:* 386–396.

Manelis, L. 1980. Determinants of processing for a propositional structure. *Memory and Cognition, 8:* 49–57.

Manelis, L., and Yekovich, F. R. 1976. Repetitions of propositional arguments in sentences. *Journal of Verbal Learning and Verbal Behavior, 15:* 301–312.

Marmor, G. S., and Zaback, L. A. 1976. Mental rotation by the blind: Does mental rotation depend on visual imagery? *Journal of Experimental Psychology: Human Perception and Performance, 2:* 515–521.

Marslen-Wilson, W. D., and Teuber, H. L. 1975. Memory for remote events in anterograde amnesia: recognition of public figures from newsphotographs. *Neuropsychologia, 13:* 353–364.

Marslen-Wilson, W. D., and Tyler, L. K. 1975. Processing structure of sentence perception. *Nature, 257:* 784–786.

Marslen-Wilson, W.; Tyler, L. K.; and Seidenberg, M. 1978. Sentence processing and the clause boundary. In W. J. M. Levelt and G. B. Flores d'Arcais (Eds.), *Studies in the perception of language.* New York: Wiley. Pp. 219–246.

Marslen-Wilson, W. D., and Welsh, A. 1978. Processing interactions and lexical access during word recognition in continuous speech. *Cognitive Psychology, 10:* 29–63.

Martin, E. 1975. Generation-recognition theory and the encoding specificity principle. *Psychological Review, 82:* 150–153.

Mason, M. 1975. Reading ability and letter search time: Effects of orthographic structure defined by single-letter positional frequency. *Journal of Experimental Psychology: General, 104:* 146–166.

Massaro, D. 1975. Acoustic features in speech perception. In D. W. Massaro (Ed.), *Understanding language.* New York: Academic Press. Pp. 129–150.

Mayer, R. E. 1979. Qualitatively different encoding strategies for linear reasoning premises: Evidence for single association and distance theories. *Journal of Experimental Psychology: Human Learning and Memory, 5:* 1–10.

McCloskey, M., and Glucksberg, S. 1978. Natural categories: well-defined or fuzzy sets? *Memory and Cognition, 6:* 462–472.

McCloskey, M., and Glucksberg, S. 1979. Decision processes in verifying category membership statements: implications for models of semantic memory. *Cognitive Psychology, 11:* 1–37.

McCormack, P. D., and Swenson, A. L. 1972. Recognition memory for common and rare words. *Journal of Experimental Psychology, 95:* 72–77.

McGeoch, J. A. 1932. Forgetting and the law of disuse. *Psychological Review, 39:* 352–370.

McGeoch, J. A. 1942. *The psychology of human learning.* New York: McKay.

McKoon, G., and Ratcliff, R. 1980. Priming in item recognition: The organization of propositions in memory for text. *Journal of Verbal Learning and Verbal Behavior, 19:* 369–386.

McMahon, L. E. 1963. Grammatical analysis as part of understanding a sentence. Unpublished doctoral dissertation, Harvard University.

Mehler, J. 1963. Some effects of grammatical transformations on the recall of English sentences. *Journal of Verbal Learning and Verbal Behavior, 2:* 250–262.

Mehler, J.; Segui, J.; and Carey, P. 1978. Tails of words: Monitoring ambiguity. *Journal of Verbal Learning and Verbal Behavior, 17:* 29–35.

Melton, A. W., and Irwin, J. M. 1940. The influence of degree of interpolated learning on retroactive inhibition and the overt transfer of specific responses. *American Journal of Psychology, 53:* 173–203.

Merikle, P. M. 1980. Selection from visual persistence by perceptual groups and category membership. *Journal of Experimental Psychology: General, 109:* 279–295.

Mervis, C. B., and Pani, J. R. 1980. Acquisition of basic object categories. *Cognitive Psychology, 12:* 496–522.

Meyer, D. E., and Schaneveldt, R. W. 1971. Facilitation in recognizing pairs of words: Evidence of a dependence between retrieval operations. *Journal of Experimental Psychology, 90:* 227–234.

Meyer, D. E.; Schaneveldt, R. W.; and Ruddy, M. G. 1975. Loci of contextual effects on visual word-recognition. In P. M. A. Rabbitt and S. Dornic (Eds.), *Attention and performance V.* New York: Academic Press. Pp. 98–118.

Miller, G. A. 1956. The magical number seven, plus or minus two: Some limits on our capacity for processing information. *Psychological Review, 63:* 81–97.

Miller, G. A. 1962. Some psychological studies of grammar. *American Psychologist, 17:* 748–762.

Miller, G. A.; Heise, G. A.; and Lichten, W. 1951. The intelligibility of speech as a function of the context of the test materials. *Journal of Experimental Psychology, 41:* 329–335.

Miller, J. D.; Wier, C. C.; Pastore, R.; Kelly, W. J.; and Dooling, R. J. 1976. Discrimination and labeling of noise-buzz sequences with varying noise-lead times: an example of categorical perception. *Journal of the Acoustical Society of America, 60:* 410–417.

Miller, P. H. 1973. Attention to stimulus dimensions in the conservation of liquid quantity. *Child Development, 44:* 129–136.

Milner, B. 1966. Amnesia following operation on the temporal lobes. In C. W. M. Whitty and O. L. Zangwill (Eds.), *Amnesia.* London: Butterworths, Pp. 109–133.

Milner, B.; Corkin, S.; and Teuber, H. L. 1968. Further analysis of the hippocampal-amnesic syndrome: 14 year follow-up study of H.M. *Neuropsychologia, 6:* 215–234.

Minsky, M. A. 1975. A framework for representing knowledge. In P. H. Winston (Ed.), *The psychology of computer vision.* New York: McGraw-Hill.

Mistler-Lachman, J. L. 1972. Levels of comprehension in processing of normal and ambiguous sentences. *Journal of Verbal Learning and Verbal Behavior, 11:* 614–623.

Miyawaki, K.; Strange, W.; Verbugge, R. R.; Liberman, A. M.; Jenkins, J. J.; and Fujimura, O. 1975. An effect of linguistic experience: The discrimination of [r] and [l] by native speakers of Japanese and English. *Perception and Psychophysics, 18:* 331–340.

Moray, N. 1959. Attention in dichotic listening: Affective cues and the influence of instructions. *Quarterly Journal of Experimental Psychology, 11:* 56–60.

Moray, N.; Bates, A.; and Barnett, T. 1965. Experiments on the four-eared man. *Journal of the Acoustical Society of America, 38:* 196–201.

Morris, C. C.; Bransford, J. D.; and Franks, J. J. 1977. Levels of processing versus transfer appropriate processing. *Journal of Verbal Learning and Verbal Behavior, 16:* 519–533.

Morse, P. A. 1978. Infant speech perception: origins, processes, and *Alpha Centauri.* In F. Minifie and L. Lloyd (Eds.), *Communicative and cognitive abilities: early behavioral assessment.* Baltimore: University Park Press.

Morse, P. A., and Snowdon, C. T. 1975. An investigation of categorical speech discrimination by rhesus monkeys. *Perception and Psychophysics, 17:* 9–16.

Moscovitch, M., and Craik, F. I. M. 1976. Depth of processing, retrieval cues and uniqueness of encoding as factors in recall. *Journal of Verbal Learning and Verbal Behavior, 15:* 447–458.

Moynahan, E. D. 1973. The development of knowledge concerning the effects of categorization upon free recall. *Child Development, 44:* 238–246.

Muensterburg, H. 1908. *On the witness stand.* New York: McClure.

Müller, G. E. 1913. Zur Analyse der Gedächtnistatiglieit und des Vorstellungsverlaufe, III. Teil. *Zeitschrift für Psychologie, Ergänzungsband* 8.

Myers, M., and Paris, S. G. 1978. Children's metacognitive knowledge about reading. *Journal of Educational Psychology, 70:* 680–690.

Mynatt, B. T., and Smith, H. K. 1977. Constructive processes in linear order problems revealed by sentence study times. *Journal of Experimental Psychology: Human Learning and Memory, 3:* 357–374.

Navon, D. 1977. Forest before trees: The precedence of global features in visual perception. *Cognitive Psychology, 9:* 353–383.

Nebes, R. D. 1974. Hemisphere specialization in commissurotomized man. *Psychological Bulletin, 81:* 1–14.

Neisser, U. 1964. Visual search. *Scientific American, 210:* 94–102.

Neisser, U. 1967. *Cognitive psychology.* Englewood Cliffs, N.J.: Prentice-Hall.

Neisser, U. 1976. *Cognition and reality.* San Francisco: Freeman.

Neisser, U., and Becklen, R. 1975. Selective looking: Attending to visually specified events. *Cognitive Psychology, 7:* 480–494.

Neisser, U.; Novick, R.; and Lazar, R. 1963. Searching for ten targets simultaneously. *Perceptual and Motor Skills, 17:* 955–961.

Neisser, U., and Weene, P. 1962. Hierarchies in concept formation. *Journal of Experimental Psychology, 64:* 644–645.

Nelson, D. L. 1979. Remembering pictures and words: Appearance, significance and name. In L. S. Cermak and F. I. M. Craik (Eds.), *Levels of processing in human memory.* Hillsdale, N.J.: Erlbaum. Pp. 45–76.

Nelson, T. O. 1977. Repetition and depth of processing. *Journal of Verbal Learning and Verbal Behavior, 16:* 151–171.

Nemiah, J. C. 1969. Hysterical amnesia. In G. A. Talland and N. C. Waugh (Eds.), *The pathology of memory.* New York: Academic Press. Pp. 107–113.

Neumann, P. G. 1974. An attribute frequency model for the abstraction of prototypes. *Memory and Cognition, 2:* 241–248.

Neumann, P. G. 1977. Visual prototype formation with discontinuous representation of dimensions of variability. *Memory and cognition, 5:* 187–197.

Newell, A. 1973. Production systems: Models of control structures. In W. G. Chase (Ed.), *Visual information processing.* New York: Academic Press.

Newell, A.; Shaw, J. C.; and Simon, H. A. 1958. Elements of a theory of human problem solving. *Psychological Review, 65:* 151–166.

Newell, A., and Simon, H. 1972. *Human problem solving.* Englewood-Cliffs, N.J.; Prentice-Hall.

Nisbett, R. E., and Wilson, T. D. 1977. Telling more than we know: Verbal reports on mental processes. *Psychological Review, 84:* 231–259.

Noble, C. E. 1952. An analysis of meaning. *Psychological Review, 59:* 421–430.

Norman, D. A. 1968. Toward a theory of memory and attention. *Psychological Review, 75:* 522–536.

Norman, D. A. 1976. *Memory and attention* (second edition). New York: Wiley.

Norman, D. A. 1979. Perception, memory and mental processes. In Lars-Goran Nilsson (Ed.), *Perspectives on memory research: Essays in honor of Uppsala University's 500th anniversary.* Hillsdale, N.J.: Erlbaum. Pp. 121–144.

Norman, D. A., and Bobrow, D. G. 1975. On data-limited and resource-limited processes. *Cognitive Psychology, 7:* 44–64.

Norman, D. A., and Bobrow, D. G. 1979. Descriptions: An intermediate stage in memory retrieval. *Cognitive Psychology, 11:* 107–123.

Norman, D. A., and Rumelhart, D. E. 1975. *Explorations in cognition.* San Francisco: Freeman.

Ornstein, P. A., and Naus, M. J. 1978. Rehearsal processes in children's memory. In P. A. Ornstein (Ed.), *Memory development in children.* Hillsdale, N.J.: Erlbaum. Pp. 1–20.

Ornstein, P. A.; Naus, M. J.; and Liberty, C. 1975. Rehearsal and organizational processes in children's memory. *Child Development, 46:* 818–830.

Ornstein, P. A.; Naus, M. J.; and Stone, B. P. 1977. Rehearsal training and developmental differences in memory. *Developmental Psychology, 13:* 15–24.

Osherson, D. N., and Smith, E. E. 1981. On the inadequacy of prototype theory as a theory of concepts. *Cognition, 9:* 35–58.

Overton, D. A. 1972. State-dependent learning produced by alcohol and its relevance to alcoholism. In B. Kissen and H. Begleiter (Eds.), *The biology of alcoholism. Vol. II: Physiology and Behavior.* New York: Plenum.

Paivio, A. 1971. *Imagery and verbal processes.* New York: Holt, Rinehart and Winston.

Paivio, A. 1978. The relationship between verbal and perceptual codes. In E. C. Carterette and M. P. Friedman (Eds.), *Handbook of perception* Vol. VIII. New York: Academic Press. Pp. 375–397.

Paivio, A., and Csapo, K. 1973. Picture superiority in free recall: Imagery or dual coding? *Cognitive psychology, 5:* 176–206.

Palmer, S. E. 1975. Visual perception and world knowledge: Notes on a model of sensory-cognitive interaction. In D. A. Norman and D. E. Rumelhart (Eds.), *Explorations in cognition.* San Francisco: Freeman.

Palmer, S. E. 1980. What makes triangles point: Local and global effects in configurations of ambiguous triangles. *Cognitive Psychology, 12:* 285–305.

Peterson, L. R., and Peterson, M. J. 1959. Short-term retention of individual verbal items. *Journal of Experimental Psychology, 58:* 193–198.

Pezdek, K. 1977. Cross-modality semantic integration of sentence and picture memory. *Journal of Experimental Psychology: Human Learning and Memory, 3:* 515–524.

Piaget, J. 1952. *The child's conception of number.* New York: Humanities Press.

Piaget, J., and Inhelder, B. 1956. *The child's conception of space.* London: Routledge & Kegan Paul.

Pinker, S. 1980. Mental imagery and the third dimension. *Journal of Experimental Psychology: General, 109:* 354–371.

Pinker, S., and Finke, R. A. 1980. Emergent two-dimensional patterns in images rotated in depth. *Journal of Experimental Psychology: Human Perception and Performance, 6:* 244–264.

Pisoni, D. B. 1978. Speech perception. In W. K. Estes (Ed.), *Handbook of learning and cognitive processes* Vol. 6. Hillsdale, N.J.: Erlbaum. Pp. 167–234.

Pisoni, D. B., and Tash, J. B. 1974. Reaction times to comparisons within and across phonetic categories. *Perception and Psychophysics, 15:* 285–290.

Platt, J. R. 1964. Strong inference. *Science, 146:* 347–353.

Pomerantz, J. R.; Sager, L. C.; and Stoever, R. J. 1977. Perception of wholes and their component parts: some configural superiority effects. *Journal of Experimental Psychology: Human Perception and Performance, 3:* 422–435.

Popper, K. 1972. *Objective Knowledge.* Oxford: Oxford University Press.

Posner, M. I. 1969. Abstraction and the process of recognition. In J. T. Spence and G. H. Bower (Eds.), *Advances in learning and motivation* Vol. 3. New York: Academic Press. Pp. 43–100.

Posner, M. I. 1970. Retention of abstract ideas. *Journal of Experimental Psychology, 83:* 304–308.

Posner, M. I. 1978. *Chronometric explorations of mind.* Hillsdale, N.J.: Erlbaum.

Posner, M. I., and Boies, S. J. 1971. Components of attention. *Psychological Review, 78:* 391–408.

Posner, M. I., and Keele, S. W. 1968. On the genesis of abstract ideas. *Journal of Experimental Psychology, 77:* 353–363.

Posner, M. I., and Klein, R. M. 1973. On the functions of consciousness. In S. Kornblum (Ed.), *Attention and performance IV*. New York: Academic Press.

Posner, M. I., and Rossman, E. 1965. Effect of size and location of information transforms upon short-term retention. *Journal of Experimental Psychology, 70:* 496–505.

Postman, L. 1961. The present status of interference theory. In C. N. Cofer (Ed.), *Verbal learning and verbal behavior*. New York: McGraw-Hill. Pp. 152–178.

Postman, L. 1963. One-trial learning. In C. N. Cofer and B. S. Musgrave (Eds.), *Verbal behavior and learning*. New York: McGraw-Hill.

Postman, L. 1971. Transfer, interference and forgetting. In J. W. Kling and L. A. Riggs (Eds.), *Woodworth and Schlosberg's experimental psychology* (third edition). New York: Holt, Rinehart and Winston. Pp. 1019–1132.

Postman, L. 1976a. Interference theory revisited. In J. Brown (Ed.), *Recall and recognition*. New York: Wiley. Pp. 157–182.

Postman, L. 1976b. Methodology of human learning. In W. K. Estes (Ed.), *Handbook of learning and cognitive processes* Vol. 3. Hillsdale, N.J.: Erlbaum. Pp. 11–70.

Postman, L., and Gray, W. 1977. Maintenance of prior associations and proactive inhibition. *Journal of Experimental Psychology: Human Learning and Memory, 3:* 255–263.

Postman, L., and Stark, K. 1969. The role of response availability in transfer and interference. *Journal of Experimental Psychology, 79:* 168–177.

Postman, L.; Thompkins, B. A.; and Gray, W. D. 1978. The interpretation of encoding effects in retention. *Journal of Verbal Learning and Verbal Behavior, 17:* 681–705.

Postman, L., and Underwood, B. J. 1973. Critical issues in interference theory. *Memory and Cognition, 1:* 19–40.

Potts, G. R. 1972. Information processing strategies used in the encoding of linear orderings. *Journal of Verbal Learning and Verbal Behavior, 11:* 727–740.

Potts, G. R. 1974. Storing and retrieving information about ordered relationships. *Journal of Experimental Psychology, 103:* 431–439.

Prentice, W. C. H. 1954. Visual recognition of verbally labelled figures. *American Journal of Psychology, 67:* 315–320.

Presley, M.; Levin, J. R.; Hall, J. W.; Miller, G. E.; and Berry, J. K. 1980. The keyword method and foreign word acquisition. *Journal of Experimental Psychology: Human Learning and Memory, 6:* 163–173.

Pylyshyn, Z. W. 1973. What the mind's eye tells the mind's brain: A critique of mental imagery. *Psychological Bulletin, 80:* 1–24.

Pylyshyn, Z. W. 1978. Imagery and artificial intelligence. In W. Savage (Ed.), *Perception and cognition: Issues in the foundation of psychology. Volume IX of the Minnesota studies in the philosophy of science*. Minneapolis: University of Minnesota Press. Pp. 19–55.

Pylyshyn, Z. W. 1980. Computation and cognition: Issues in the foundations of cognitive science. *The Behavioral and Brain Sciences, 3:* 111–132.

Rabbitt, P. 1978. Sorting, categorization, and visual search. In E. C. Carterette and M. P. Friedman (Eds.), *Handbook of perception* Vol. IX. New York: Academic Press. Pp. 85–134.

Rabinowitz, J. C.; Mandler, G.; and Barsalou, L. W. 1977. Recognition failure: Another case of retrieval failure. *Journal of Verbal Learning and Verbal Behavior, 16:* 639–663.

Rabinowitz, J. C; Mandler, G.; and Barsalou, L. W. 1979. Generation-recognition as an auxiliary retrieval strategy. *Journal of Verbal Learning and Verbal Behavior, 18:* 57–72.

Raeburn, V. P. 1974. Priorities in item recognition. *Memory and Cognition, 2:* 663–669.

Raphael, B. 1976. *The thinking computer.* San Francisco: Freeman.

Ratcliff, R., and McKoon, G. 1981. Automatic and strategic priming in recognition. *Journal of Verbal Learning and Verbal Behavior, 20:* 204–215.

Reber, A. S. 1973. Locating clicks in sentences: Left, center and right. *Perception and Psychophysics, 13:* 133–138.

Reber, A. S., and Allen, R. 1978. Analogic and abstraction strategies in synthetic grammar learning: A functionalist interpretation. *Cognition, 6:* 189–221.

Reber, A. S.; Kassin, S. M.; Lewis, S.; and Cantor, B. 1980. On the relationship between implicit and explicit modes in the learning of a complex rule structure. *Journal of Experimental Psychology: Human Learning and Memory, 6:* 492–502.

Reddy, R., and Newell, A. 1975. Knowledge and its representation in a speech understanding system. In L. W. Gregg (Ed.), *Knowledge and cognition.* Potomac, Md.: Erlbaum. Pp. 253–285.

Reed, S. K. 1972. Pattern recognition and categorization. *Cognitive Psychology, 3:* 382–467.

Reed, S. K. 1978. Schemes and theories of pattern recognition. In E. C. Carterette and M. P. Friedman (Eds.), *Handbook of perception* Vol. IX. New York: Academic Press. Pp. 137–162.

Reicher, G. M. 1969. Perceptual recognition as a function of meaningfulness of stimulus material. *Journal of Experimental Psychology, 81:* 275–280.

Reitman, J. S. 1971. Mechanisms of forgetting in short-term memory. *Cognitive Psychology, 2:* 185–195.

Reitman, J. S. 1974. Without surreptitious rehearsal information in short-term memory decays. *Journal of Verbal Learning and Verbal Behavior, 13:* 365–377.

Rep, B. H.; Healy, A. F.; and Crowder, R. G. 1979. Categories and context in the perception of isolated steady-state vowels. *Journal of Experimental Psychology: Human Perception and Performance, 5:* 129–145.

Restle, F. 1962. The selection of strategies in cue learning. *Psychological Review, 69:* 329–343.

Revlis, R. 1975. Syllogistic reasoning: Logical decisions from a complex data base. In R. J. Falmagne (Ed.), *Reasoning: Representation and process in children and adults.* Hillsdale, N.J.: Erlbaum.

Rips, L. J.; Shoben, E. J.; and Smith, E. E. 1973. Semantic distance and the verification of semantic relations. *Journal of Verbal Learning and Verbal Behavior, 12:* 1–20.

Rosch, E. 1973. On the internal structure of perceptual and semantic categories. In T. E. Moore (Ed.), *Cognitive development and the acquisition of
language.* New York: Academic Press.

Rosch, E. 1975. Cognitive representations of semantic categories. *Journal of
Experimental Psychology: General, 104:* 192–253.

Rosch, E. 1977. Human categorization. In N. Warren (Ed.), *Advances in cross-
cultural psychology* Vol. 1. London: Academic Press.

Rosch, E. 1978. Principles of categorization. In E. Rosch and B. Lloyd (Eds.),
Cognition and categorization. Hillsdale, N.J.: Erlbaum. Pp. 27–48.

Rosch, E., and Mervis, C. B. 1975. Family resemblances: Studies in the internal
structure of categories. *Cognitive Psychology, 7:* 573–605.

Rosch, E.; Mervis, C. B.; Gray, W.; Johnson, D.; and Boyes-Braem, P. 1976.
Basic objects in natural categories. *Cognitive Psychology, 8:* 382–439.

Rosch, E.; Simpson C.; and Miller, R. S. 1976. Structural bases of typicality effects. *Journal of Experimental Psychology: Human Perception and Performance, 2:* 491–502.

Rubin, D. C. 1977. Very long-term memory for prose and verse. *Journal of
Verbal Learning and Verbal Behavior, 16:* 611–621.

Rumelhart, D. 1977a. *Introduction to human information processing.* New
York: Wiley.

Rumelhart, D. E. 1977b. Understanding and summarizing brief stories. In D.
LaBerge and S. Jay Samuels (Eds.), *Basic processes in reading: perception
and comprehension.* Hillsdale, N.J.: Erlbaum. Pp. 265–304.

Rumelhart, D. E., and Ortony, A. 1977. The representation of knowledge in
memory. In R. C. Anderson, R. T. Spiro, and W. E. Montague (Eds.),
Schooling and the acquisition of knowledge. Hillsdale, N.J.: Erlbaum. Pp.
99–136.

Rumelhart, D. E., and Siple, P. 1974. Process of recognizing tachistoscopically
presented words. *Psychological Review, 81:* 99–118.

Rundus, D. 1977. Maintenance rehearsal and single-level processing. *Journal
of Verbal Learning and Verbal Behavior, 16:* 665–681.

Rundus, D. 1980. Maintenance rehearsal and long-term recency. *Memory and
Cognition, 8:* 226–230.

Rundus, D., and Atkinson, R. C. 1970. Rehearsal processes in free recall: A
procedure for direct observation. *Journal of Verbal Learning and Verbal
Behavior, 9:* 99–105.

Russell, W. R. 1971. *The traumatic amnesias.* London: Oxford University Press.

Russell, W. R., and Nathan, P. 1946. Traumatic amnesia. *Brain, 69:* 280–300.

Sachs, J. S. 1967. Recognition memory for syntactic and semantic aspects of
connected discourse. *Perception and Psychophysics, 2:* 437–442.

Sakitt, B. 1975. Locus of short-term visual storage. *Science, 190:* 1318–1319.

Sakitt, B. 1976. Iconic memory. *Psychological Review, 83:* 257–276.

Sakitt, B., and Long, G. M. 1978. Relative rod and cone contributions in iconic
storage. *Perception and Psychophysics, 23:* 527–536.

Sakitt, B., and Long, G. M. 1979. Spare the rod and spoil the icon. *Journal of
Experimental Psychology: Human Perception and Performance, 5:* 19–30.

Salzberg, P. M. 1976. On the generality of encoding specificity. *Journal of Experimental Psychology: Human Learning and Memory, 2:* 586–596.

Sapir, E. 1958. Language and environment. In D. G. Mandelbaum (Ed.), *Selected writings of Edward Sapir in language, culture and personality.* Berkeley: University of California Press. Pp. 89–103.

Scarborough, D. L. 1972. Memory for brief visual displays of symbols. *Cognitive Psychology, 3:* 408–429.

Schank, R. C., and Abelson, R. P. 1977. *Scripts, plans, goals and understanding.* Hillsdale, N.J.: Erlbaum.

Schneider, W., and Shiffrin, R. M. 1977. Controlled and automatic human information processing: I. Detection, search and attention. *Psychological Review, 84:* 1–66.

Scholz, K., and Potts, G. R. 1974. Cognitive processing of linear orderings. *Journal of Experimental Psychology, 102:* 323–326.

Schustack, M. W., and Sternber, R. J. 1981. Evaluation of evidence in causal inference. *Journal of Experimental Psychology: General, 110:* 101–120.

Seamon, J. G., and Virostek, S. 1978. Memory performance and subject-defined depth of processing. *Memory and Cognition, 6:* 283–287.

Searleman, A. 1977. A review of right hemisphere linguistic capabilities. *Psychological Bulletin, 84:* 503–528.

Selfridge, O. G., and Neisser, U. 1960. Pattern recognition by machine. *Scientific American, 203:* 60–68.

Shannon, C. E. 1948. A mathematical theory of communication. *Bell System Technical Journal, 27:* 379–423.

Shannon, C. E., and Weaver, W. 1949. *The mathematical theory of communication.* Urbana: University of Illinois Press.

Shepard, R. N. 1967. Recognition memory for words, sentences and pictures. *Journal of Verbal Learning and Verbal Behavior, 6:* 156–163.

Shepard, R. N., and Chipman, S. 1970. Second-order isomorphism of internal representations: shapes of states. *Cognitive Psychology, 1:* 1–17.

Shepard, R. N., and Metzler, J. 1971. Mental rotation of three-dimensional objects. *Science, 171:* 701–703.

Shiffrin, R. M. 1976. Capacity limitations in information processing, attention and memory. In W. K. Estes (Ed.), *Handbook of learning and cognitive processes* Vol. 4. Hillsdale, N.J.: Erlbaum. Pp. 177–236.

Shiffrin, R. M., and Cook, J. R. 1978. Short-term forgetting of item and order information. *Journal of Verbal Learning and Verbal Behavior, 17:* 189–218.

Shiffrin, R. M.; Craig, J. C.; and Cohen, E. 1976. On the degree of attention and capacity limitation in tactile processing. *Perception and Psychophysics, 13:* 328–336.

Shiffrin, R. M., and Gardner, G. T. 1972. Visual processing capacity and attentional control. *Journal of Experimental Psychology, 93:* 72–82.

Shiffrin, R. M., and Schneider, W. 1977. Controlled and automatic human information processing: II. Perceptual learning, automatic attending and a general theory. *Psychological Review, 84:* 127–190.

Shoben, E. J.; Wescourt, K. T.; and Smith, E. E. 1978. Sentence verification, sentence recognition and the semantic-episodic distinction. *Journal of Experimental Psychology: Human Learning and Memory, 4:* 304–317.

Shulman, H. G. 1972. Semantic confusion errors in short-term memory. *Journal of Verbal Learning and Verbal Behavior, 11:* 221–227.

Simon, H. A. 1975. The functional equivalence of problem solving skills. *Cognitive Psychology, 7:* 268–288.

Simon, H. A. 1978. Information processing theory of human problem solving. In W. K. Estes (Ed.), *Handbook of learning and cognitive processes* Vol. 5. Hillsdale, N.J.: Erlbaum. Pp. 271–295.

Simon H. A. 1979. Information processing models of cognition. *Annual Review of Psychology, 30:* 363–396.

Simon, H. A., and Feigenbaum, E. A. 1964. An information-processing theory of some effects of similarity, familiarization, and meaningfulness in verbal learning. *Journal of Verbal Learning and Verbal Behavior, 3:* 385–396.

Simon, H. A., and Reed, S. K. 1976. Modeling strategy shifts in a problem-solving task. *Cognitive Psychology, 8:* 86–97.

Simpson, P. J. 1972. High-speed memory scanning: Stability and generality. *Journal of Experimental Psychology, 96:* 239–246.

Slobin, D. I. 1966. Grammatical transformations and sentence comprehension in childhood and adulthood. *Journal of Verbal Learning and Verbal Behavior, 5:* 219–227.

Slobin, D. I. (Ed.), 1971. *The ontogenesis of grammar.* New York: Academic Press.

Smith, E. E. 1978. Theories of semantic memory. In W. K. Estes (Ed.), *Handbook of learning and cognitive processes,* Vol. 5. Hillsdale, N.J.: Erlbaum. Pp. 1–56.

Smith, E. E.; Shoben, E. J.; and Rips, L. J. 1974. Structure and process in semantic memory. A feature model for semantic decisions. *Psychological Review:* 214–241.

Smith, E. E., and Spoehr, K. T. 1974. The perception of printed English: A theoretical perspective. In B. H. Kantowitz (Ed.), *Human information processing: Tutorials in performance and cognition.* Hillsdale, N.J.: Erlbaum. Pp. 231–275.

Smith, S. M. 1979. Remembering in and out of context. *Journal of Experimental Psychology: Human Learning and Memory, 5:* 460–471.

Smoke, K. L. 1933. Negative instances in concept learning. *Journal of Experimental Psychology, 16:* 583–588.

Sperling, G. 1960. The information available in brief visual presentations. *Psychological Monographs, 74:* No. 498.

Sperry, R. W. 1968. Hemisphere deconnection and unity in conscious awareness. *American Psychologist, 23:* 723–783.

Spiro, R. J. 1977. Remembering information from text: The "state of schema" approach. In R. Anderson, R. Spiro and W. Montague (Eds.), *Schooling and the acquisition of knowledge.* Hillsdale, N.J.: Erlbaum. Pp. 137–165.

Spiro, R. J. 1980. Accommodative reconstruction in prose recall. *Journal of Verbal Learning and Verbal Behavior, 19:* 84–95.

Springer, S. P. 1977. Tachistoscopic and dichotic listening investigations of laterality in normal human subjects. In S. Harnard, R. W. Doty, J. Jaynes,

L. Goldstein, and G. Krauthamer (Eds.), *Lateralization in the nervous system.* New York: Academic Press.

Squire, L. R.; Slater, P. C.; and Chase, P. M. 1975. Retrograde amnesia: Temporal gradient in very long-term memory following electroconvulsive therapy. *Science, 187:* 77–79.

Standing, L. 1973. Learning 10,000 pictures. *Quarterly Journal of Experimental Psychology, 25:* 207–222.

Stein, B. S. 1978. Depth of processing reexamined: the effects of the precision of encoding and test appropriateness. *Journal of Verbal Learning and Verbal Behavior, 17:* 165–174.

Sternberg, R. J. 1977. *Intelligence, information processing and analogical reasoning: Componential analysis of human abilities.* Hillsdale, N.J.: Erlbaum.

Sternberg, S. 1966. High-speed scanning in human memory. *Science, 153:* 652–654.

Sternberg, S. 1969. The discovery of processing stages: Extensions of Donder's method. *Acta Psychologica, 30:* 276–315.

Sternberg, S. 1975. Memory scanning: New findings and current controversies. *Quarterly Journal of Experimental Psychology, 27:* 1–32.

Strange, W., and Jenkins, J. J. 1978. Role of experience in the perception of speech. In R. D. Walk and H. L. Pick (Eds.), *Perception and experience.* New York: Plenum. Pp. 125–1669.

Streeter, L. A., and Landauer, J. K. 1976. Effects of learning English as a second language on the acquisition of a new phonetic contrast. *Journal of the Acoustical Society of America, 59:* 448–451.

Stroop, J. R. 1935. Studies of interference in serial verbal reactions. *Journal of Experimental Psychology, 18:* 643–662.

Studdert-Kennedy, M. 1974. The perception of speech. In T. A. Sebeok (Ed.), *Current trends in linguistics* Vol XII. The Hague: Mouton. Pp. 2349–2385.

Swanson, J. M., and Kinsbourne, M. 1979. State-dependent learning and retrieval: Methodological cautions against theoretical considerations. In J. F. Kihlstrom and F. J. Evans (Eds.), *Functional disorders of memory.* Hillsdale, N.J.: Erlbaum. Pp. 275–299.

Swinney, D. A. 1979. Lexical access during sentence comprehension: (Re) Consideration of context effects. *Journal of Verbal Learning and Verbal Behavior, 18:* 645–659.

Tanenhaus, M. K.; Leiman, J. M.; and Seidenberg, M. S. 1979. Evidence for multiple stages in the processing of ambiguous words in syntactic contexts. *Journal of Verbal Learning and Verbal Behavior, 18:* 427–440

Thomas, J. C. 1974. An analysis of behavior in the Hobbits-Orcs problem. *Cognitive Psychology, 6:* 257–290.

Thomson, D. M., and Tulving, E. 1970. Associative encoding and retrieval: Weak and strong cues. *Journal of Experimental Psychology, 86:* 255–262.

Thorndike, E. L. 1914. *The psychology of learning.* New York: Teachers College.

Thorndyke, P. W. 1977. Cognitive structures in comprehension and memory of narrative discourse. *Cognitive Psychology, 9:* 77–110.

Townsend, J. T. 1971. A note on the identifiability of parallel and serial processes. *Perception and Psychophysics, 10:* 161–163.

Townsend, J. T. 1974. Issues and models concerning the processing of a finite number of inputs. In B. H. Kantowitz (Ed.), *Human information processing; Tutorials in performance and cognition.* Hillsdale, N.J.: Erlbaum. Pp. 133–185.

Treisman, A. M. 1964. Selective attention in man. *British Medical Bulletin, 20:* 12–16.

Treisman, A. M., and Davies, A. 1973. Divided attention to ear and eye. In S. Kornblum (Ed.), *Attention and performance* IV. New York: Academic Press. Pp. 101–117.

Treisman, A. M., and Geffen, G. 1967. Selective attention: Perception or response? *Quarterly Journal of Experimental Psychology, 19:* 1–17.

Treisman, A. M., and Gelade, G. 1980. A feature-integration theory of attention. *Cognitive Psychology, 12:* 97–136.

Treisman, A. M.; Russell, R.; and Green, J. 1975. Brief visual storage of shape and movement. In P. M. A. Rabbitt and S. Dornic (Eds.), *Attention and performance* Vol. V. New York: Academic Press.

Tulving, E. 1962. Subjective organization in free recall of unrelated words. *Psychological Review, 69:* 344–354.

Tulving, E. 1972. Episodic and semantic memory. In E. Tulving and W. Donaldson (Eds.), *Organization of memory.* New York: Academic Press. Pp. 381–403.

Tulving, E. 1974. Cue-dependent forgetting. *American Scientist, 62:* 74–82.

Tulving, E. 1976. Ecphoric processes in recall and recognition. In J. Brown (Ed.), *Recall and recognition.* New York: Wiley. Pp. 37–74.

Tulving, E. 1979a. Memory research: what kind of progress? In Lars-Goran Nilsson (Ed.), *Perspectives on memory research: Essays in honor of Uppsala University's 500th anniversary.* Hillsdale, N.J.: Erlbaum. Pp. 19–34.

Tulving, E. 1979b. Relation between encoding specificity and levels of processing. In L. S. Cermak and F. I. M. Craik (Eds.), *Levels of processing in human memory.* Hillsdale, N.J.: Erlbaum.

Tulving, E., and Gold, C. 1963. Stimulus information and contextual information as determinants of tachistoscopic recognition of words. *Journal of Experimental Psychology, 66:* 319–327.

Tulving, E., and Madigan, S. A. 1970. Memory and verbal learning. *Annual Review of Psychology, 21:* 437–484.

Tulving, E., and Pearlstone, Z. 1966. Availability versus accessibility of information in memory for words. *Journal of Verbal Learning and Verbal Behavior, 5:* 381–391.

Tulving, E., and Psotka, J. 1971. Retroactive inhibition in free recall: Inaccessibility of information available in the memory store. *Journal of Experimental Psychology, 87:* 1–8.

Tulving, E., and Thomspon, D. M. 1973. Encoding specificity and retrieval processes in episodic memory. *Psychological Review, 80:* 352–373.

Turvey, M. T. 1978. Visual processing and short-term memory. In W. K. Estes (Ed.), *Handbook of learning and cognitive processes* Vol. 5. Hillsdale, N.J.: Erlbaum. Pp. 91–142.

Turvey, M. T., and Kravetz, S. 1970. Retrieval from iconic memory with shape as the selection criterion. *Perception and psychophysics, 8:* 171-172.

Tversky, A., and Kahneman, A. 1973. Availability: a heuristic for judging frequency and probability. *Cognitive Psychology, 5:* 207-232.

Tyler L. K., and Marslen-Wilson, W. D. 1977. The on-line effects of semantic context on syntactic processing. *Journal of Verbal Learning and Verbal Behavior, 16:* 683-692.

Tyler, S. W.; Hertel, P. T.; McCallum, M. C.; and Ellis, H. C. 1979. Cognitive effort and memory. *Journal of Experimental Psychology: Human Learning and Memory, 5:* 607-617.

Underwood, B. J. 1948. Retroactive and proactive inhibition after five and forty-eight hours. *Journal of Experimental Psychology, 38:* 29-38.

Underwood, B. J. 1957. Interference and forgetting. *Psychological Review, 64:* 48-60.

Underwood, B. J. 1969. Attributes of memory. *Psychological Review, 76:* 559-573.

Underwood, B. J. 1972. Are we overloading memory? In A. Melton and E. Martin (Eds.), *Coding processes in human memory.* New York: Wiley.

Underwood, B. J., and Ekstrand, B. R. 1967. Studies of distributed practice: xxix. Differentiation and proactive inhibition. *Journal of Experimental Psychology, 74:* 574-580.

Underwood, B. J., and Freund, J. S. 1968. Effect of temporal separation of two tasks on proactive inhibition. *Journal of Experimental Psychology, 78:* 50-54.

von Wright, J. M. 1968. Selection in immediate memory. *Quarterly Journal of Experimental Psychology, 20:* 62-68.

von Wright, J. M. 1970. On selection in visual immediate memory. *Acta Psychologia, 33:* 280-292.

von Wright, J. M.; Anderson, K.; and Stenman, U. 1975. Generalization of conditioned GSRs in dichotic listening. In P. M. A. Rabbitt and S. Dornic (Eds.), *Attention and performance* V. London: Academic Press.

Wallace, W. P. 1978. Recognition failure of recallable words and recognizable words. *Journal of Experimental Psychology: Human Learning and Memory, 4:* 441-452.

Walsh, D. A., and Jenkins, J. J. 1973. Effects of orienting tasks on free recall in incidental learning: "Difficulty," "effort," and "process" explanations. *Journal of Verbal Learning and Verbal Behavior, 12:* 481-488.

Warren, R. M. 1970. Perceptual restoration of missing speech sounds. *Science, 167:* 392-393.

Wason, P. C. 1960. On the failure to eliminate hypotheses in a conceptual task. *Quarterly Journal of Experimental Psychology, 12:* 19-40.

Wason, P. C., and Johnson-Laird, P. N. 1972. *Psychology of reasoning.* Cambridge, Mass.: Harvard University Press.

Waters, R. S., and Wilson, W. A., Jr. 1976. Speech perception by rhesus monkeys: The voicing distinction in synthesized labial and velar stop consonants. *Perception and Psychophysics, 19:* 285-289.

Watkins, M. J.; Watkins, O. C.; Craik, F. I. M.; and Mazuryk, K. G. 1973. Effect of verbal distraction on short-term storage. *Journal of Experimental Psychology, 101:* 296–300.

Waugh, N. C., and Norman, D. A. 1965. Primary memory. *Psychological Review, 72:* 89–104.

Weimer, W. B. 1977. Scientific inquiry, assessment, and logic: Comments on Bowers and Mahoney-DeMonbreun. *Cognitive Therapy and Research, 1:* 247–255.

Weizenbaum, J. 1976. *Computer power and human reason.* San Francisco: Freeman.

Wheeler, D. D. 1970. Processes in word recognition. *Cognitive Psychology, 1:* 59–85.

White, C. W. 1976. Visual masking during pursuit eye movements. *Journal of Experimental Psychology: Human Perception and Performance, 2:* 469–478.

Whorf, B. L. 1956. Science and linguistics. In J. B. Carroll (Ed.), *Language, thought and reality: Selected writings of Benjamin Lee Whorf.* New York: Wiley. Pp. 207–219.

Wickelgren, W. A. 1965. Acoustic similarity and retroactive interference in short-term memory. *Journal of Verbal Learning and Verbal Behavior, 4:* 53–61.

Wickens, D. D. 1972. Characteristics of word encoding. In A. Melton and E. Martin (Eds.), *Coding processes in human memory.* New York: Holt, Rinehart and Winston.

Wickens, D. D.; Born, D. G.; and Allen, C. K. 1963. Proactive inhibition and item similarity in short-term memory. *Journal of Verbal Learning and Verbal Behavior, 2:* 440–445.

Wilkins, A. 1971. Conjoint frequency, category size, and categorization time. *Journal of Verbal Learning and Verbal Behavior, 10:* 382–385.

Williams, A., and Weisstein, N. 1978. Line segments are perceived better in a coherent context than alone: An object-line effect in visual perception. *Memory and Cognition, 6:* 85–90.

Wingfield, A. 1979. *Human learning and memory.* New York: Harper & Row.

Wingfield, A., and Byrnes, D. L. 1972. Decay of information in short-term memory. *Science, 176:* 490–492.

Wiseman, S., and Tulving, E. 1975. A test of confusion theory of encoding specificity. *Journal of Verbal Learning and Verbal Behavior, 14:* 370–381.

Wiseman, S., and Tulving, E. 1976. Encoding specificity: Relation between recall superiority and recognition failure. *Journal of Experimental Psychology: Human Learning and Memory, 2:* 349–361.

Wittgenstein, L. 1953. *Philosophical investigations.* New York: Macmillan.

Woodword, A. E.; Bjork, R. A.; and Jongeward, R. H. 1973. Recall and recognition as a function of primary rehearsal. *Journal of Verbal Learning and Verbal Behavior, 12:* 608–614.

Woodworth, R. S. 1938. *Experimental psychology.* New York: Holt, Rinehart and Winston.

Woodworth, R. S., and Sells, S. B. 1935. An atmosphere effect in formal syllogistic reasoning. *Journal of Experimental Psychology, 18:* 451–460.

Yarmey, A. D. 1979. *The psychology of eyewitness testimony.* New York: Free Press.

Yates, F. A. 1966. *The art of memory.* London: Routledge & Kegan Paul.

Yonge, G. D. 1966. Structure of experience and functional fixedness. *Journal of Educational Psychology, 57:* 115–120.

Yussen, S. R., and Levy, V. M., Jr. 1975. Developmental changes in predicting one's own span of short-term memory. *Journal of Experimental Child Psychology, 19:* 502–508.

Zadeh, L. A.; Fu, K. S.; Tanaka, K.; and Shimura, M. (Eds.), 1975. *Fuzzy sets and their applications to cognitive and decision processes.* New York: Academic Press.

Zaidel, D., and Sperry, R. W. 1973. Performance on the Raven's Colored Progressive Matrices Test by subjects with cerebral commissurotomy. *Cortex, IX:* 34–39.

Zajonc, R. B. 1980. Feeling and thinking. Preferences need no inferences. *American Psychologist, 35:* 151–175.

Zangwill, O. L. 1946. Some qualitative observations on verbal memory in cases of cerebral lesion. *British Journal of Psychology, 37:* 8–19.

Zurif, E. B. 1980. Language mechanisms: A neuropsycholinguistic perspective. *American Scientist, 68:* 305–311.

Index

81 82 83 84 9 8 7 6 5 4 3 2 1

GHOTI

FISH